D0075507

GUIDE TO
THE CINEMA OF
SWEDEN AND FINLAND

Reference Guides to the World's Cinema

Guide to the Cinema of Spain
Marvin D'Lugo

Guide to American Cinema, 1965–1995
Daniel Curran

Guide to African Cinema
Sharon A. Russell

Guide to American Cinema, 1930–1965
Thomas R. Whissen

Guide to the Silent Years of American Cinema
Donald W. McCaffrey and Christopher P. Jacobs

GUIDE TO THE CINEMA OF SWEDEN AND FINLAND

PER OLOV QVIST AND PETER VON BAGH

Reference Guides to the World's Cinema
Pierre L. Horn, Series Adviser

GREENWOOD PRESS
Westport, Connecticut • London

Library of Congress Cataloging-in-Publication Data

Qvist, Per Olov.
 Guide to the cinema of Sweden and Finland / Per Olov Qvist and
Peter von Bagh.
  p. cm. — (Reference guides to the world's cinema, ISSN
1090–8234)
 Includes bibliographical references and index.
 ISBN 0–313–30377–0 (alk. paper)
 1. Motion pictures—Sweden—History. 2. Motion pictures—Finland—
History. I. Bagh, Peter von, 1943– . II. Title. III. Series.
PN1993.5.S8Q86   2000
791.43'09485—dc21   99–10110

British Library Cataloguing in Publication Data is available.

Copyright © 2000 by Per Olov Qvist and Peter von Bagh

All rights reserved. No portion of this book may be
reproduced, by any process or technique, without the
express written consent of the publisher.

Library of Congress Catalog Card Number: 99–10110
ISBN: 0–313–30377–0
ISSN: 1090–8234

First published in 2000

Greenwood Press, 88 Post Road West, Westport, CT 06881
An imprint of Greenwood Publishing Group, Inc.
www.greenwood.com

Printed in the United States of America

The paper used in this book complies with the
Permanent Paper Standard issued by the National
Information Standards Organization (Z39.48–1984).

10 9 8 7 6 5 4 3 2 1

CONTENTS

SERIES FOREWORD

For the first time, on 28 December 1895, at the Grand Café in Paris, France, the inventors of the *Cinématographe*, Auguste and Louis Lumière, showed a series of eleven two-minute silent shorts to a public of thirty-five people, each paying the high entry fee of one gold franc. From that moment, a new era had begun, for the Lumière brothers not only were successful in their commercial venture, but they also unknowingly created a new visual medium quickly to become, throughout the world, a half popular entertainment, half sophisticated art of the cinema. Eventually, the contribution of each member of the profession, especially that of the director and the performers, took on enormous importance. A century later, the situation remains very much the same.

The purpose of Greenwood's *Reference Guides to the World's Cinema* is to give a representative idea of what each country or region has to offer to the evolution, development, and richness of film. At the same time, because each volume seeks to present a balance between the interests of the general public and those of students and scholars of the medium, the choices are by necessity selective (although as comprehensive as possible) and often reflect the author's own idiosyncracies.

André Malraux, the French novelist and essayist, wrote about the cinema and filmmakers: "The desire to build up a world apart and self-contained, existing in its own right . . . represents humanization in the deepest, certainly the most enigmatic, sense of the word." On the one hand, then, every *Guide* explores this observation by offering discussions, written in a jargon-free style, of the motion-picture art and its practitioners and, on the other, provides much-needed information, seldom available in English, including filmographies, awards and honors, and ad hoc bibliographies.

Pierre L. Horn
Wright State University

SWEDISH CINEMA

PREFACE

Swedish cinema is both well known and unknown to a foreign audience and scholars from other countries. Most people interested in film and film history are probably acquainted with names such as Ingmar Bergman, Victor Sjöström, Alf Sjöberg, and perhaps a few others. Most of what has been written in English concerns these internationally established directors and their works. Bergman is, of course, famous in the United States, not least in academia, where dozens of dissertations have been written about him.

But there are certainly gaps as well in the common knowledge of Swedish cinema abroad. Whole periods, such as film of the 1930s, are generally dismissed by most writers—even in Sweden—and many names worth wider attention are simply overlooked or forgotten. No doubt there are practical reasons for this neglect. A scholar who cannot speak or understand Swedish is dependent on the existence of subtitled prints, the dearth of which becomes a great obstacle to overcome.

Another reason for the current state of affairs is the fact that most writers on Swedish cinema have chosen to consider the subject matter from a quite narrow perspective. They select the names and films they regard as "high art" and ignore the rest. But the primary aim of film historians should not be to hand out gold stars to the best pupils in the classroom, although some comment on artistic achievements of various kinds in the long process of establishing a national cinema is both desirable and inevitable.

I have had a long-standing personal interest in film genres and in examining film and film history from a historical and sociological point of view. After all, historically, most films have been aimed at a wide audience and have reflected its dreams, hopes, fears, and so on. Film in general also gives voice to cultural patterns that construct society as a whole. Every person connected with filmmaking has roots in a specific national culture and provides an interpretation of it. This view can sometimes be incomprehensible to a foreigner, and it may be that an American audience cannot fully appreciate the more subtle references and ironies in an Ingmar Bergman film, to take one example. He is, after all, very deeply rooted in Swedish culture and in a broad tradition of filmmaking that scholars have partially overlooked. However, the opposite may also apply: A foreigner may more easily detect matters that to someone native to a given culture may seem too commonplace to arouse notice or commentary. One example is the perspective offered by the English-born film director Colin Nutley, now active within the Swedish film industry.

I have chosen names and titles from both perspectives. What is considered worth mentioning from an artistic point of view is of course highly personal. Some of the selections are well known and obvious, but many are certainly new. Other directors have been included for different reasons; although they also are or were quite competent in their art, they may, for example, have preferred to work within more folksy genres like the rural drama or comedy, which are virtually the backbone of Swedish cinema as a whole. I have excluded a very familiar name like Greta Garbo, since her entire career, one film excepted, falls within American film.

It is not an easy task to pick out a few dozen films from the thousands that have been made since 1910. In many cases, I have chosen those that can be regarded as "milestones" from one point of view or another, films that either have been big moneymakers or have reflected important social changes in a significant or profound way. Sometimes these factors coincide, as in *One Summer of Happiness*. Some films are certainly well known to a foreign audience; others are definitively unknown territory, but I hope that fact will spur the reader's further interest in learning more about Swedish film history.

I owe special thanks to Rochelle Wright at the University of Indiana for all her help. I am also grateful to Arne Lindahl, Rolf Lindfors, and Bertil Wredlund at The Swedish Film Institute. I also want to thank the Holger and Thyra Lauritzen Foundation for their financial support.

INTRODUCTION

The story of Swedish film production begins not in Stockholm but in the southern province of Skåne at the beginning of the century, when the first regular cinema theaters were established. The first public showing of moving pictures took place in Malmö in June 1896. The company Svenska Biografteatern (Svenska Bio for short) was founded in 1907 by some businessmen in Kristianstad, the second-largest city in the province. Initially they were satisfied merely to screen films through a chain of cinema theaters in various cities in southern Sweden, but they soon recognized the importance of producing their own films and hired a cinematographer, Robert Olsson, who traveled around making short documentaries. Later the company managed to hire a second skilled cinematographer from Göteborg, Charles Magnusson, who successfully organized their entire production for the following two decades. In Malmö another cinema owner, Frans Lundberg, began film production activities around 1910.

Svenska Bio's productions were intended primarily for a Swedish audience and had high cultural aspirations. The company soon engaged people from the established stages, most notably the Royal Dramatic Theater in Stockholm. Frans Lundberg's aim was more international and sensational, and many of his films were produced in Denmark with Danish actors. When the Swedish Board of Film Censors was established in 1911, many of Lundberg's films encountered difficulties or were banned outright, which eventually forced him to halt production. Production activities in Stockholm were rather modest in comparison at this stage, although some production had started there, most notably by established cinema owner N. P. Nilsson, who financed the works of the first female director in Sweden, Anna Hofman-Uddgren. She received the great Strindberg's carte blanche permission to film his plays, which resulted in the first two movie versions of *Fadren* [The father] and *Fröken Julie* [Miss Julie] in 1912.

After a few years Svenska Bio moved to Stockholm and in 1912 established a studio at Lidingö, a municipality just outside the city limits of Stockholm. One reason for this move was to facilitate distribution to the chain of cinemas owned by the company, by this time about ninety scattered throughout Sweden. Magnusson was able to hire two established directors, *Victor Sjöström and *Mauritz Stiller. Production manager *Georg af Klercker also played a significant role.

Svenska Bio was to dominate the Swedish production scene in the 1910s. N. P. Nilsson died in 1912, and Frans Lundberg ceased production the following year; so Svenska Bio was virtually alone on the market except for the Swedish branch of French Pathé. Svenska Bio established cooperation with the latter in their first years in Stockholm, although the companies later went separate ways. Much of Svenska Bio's success was also owed to the work of Sjöström and Stiller, who each directed a large number of films. Another key factor, of course, was the chain of theaters that expanded throughout the major cities of Sweden. This guaranteed a market for the films produced. Later Svenska Bio acquired distribution rights from the American Triangle Company, a move that was of further economic importance when American films began to dominate the market in the late 1910s.

Beginning in mid-decade, the camera company Hasselblad in Göteborg tried to compete with the big Stockholm production company, hiring Georg af Klercker and managing to produce more than two dozen features between 1915 and 1918. Hasselblad, too, was affiliated with a cinema theater company, Victoria, that owned a chain of theaters in the larger cities. In 1918 Hasselblad merged with Victoria and the Swedish branch of French Pathé to form the company Skandia in direct competition with Svenska Bio. Skandia did not, however, last long. In 1919 it was amalgamated with Svenska Bio—with some financial shares held by the "Match King," Ivar Kreuger—and a new, big company, Svensk Filmindustri, was born—still the dominant film company in Sweden. A new film studio was built in 1920 in Råsunda, just north of Stockholm. Some years later, another independent company, Skandinavisk Filmcentral, founded by a former employee at Svenska Bio, encountered difficulties and was swallowed by Svensk Filmindustri, which could now add another chain of cinema theaters to its own.

Filmmakers were deeply affected by this monopolizing process. Until then, directors like Sjöström and Stiller had a relatively large degree of artistic freedom in their work. Their creative efforts had gradually shifted from sensational melodrama—in the case of Sjöström, often with a social content—to more specifically Swedish topics, a reflection of the fact that film was gradually becoming more respectable. In reality, it had to be, as the demands from the Board of Censors, the general public, and critics called for this change in various ways. Sjöström's film of Selma Lagerlöf's *Tösen från Stormyrtorpet/The Girl from the Marsh Croft* (1917) was the starting point for a genre of great importance for Swedish film during the following decades—the rural melodrama. This film was followed by others with the same roots: the heritage from turn-of-the-century literary romanticism and its idealization of the countryside. Sjöström's version of Lagerlöf's *Jerusalem I*, called *Ingmarssönerna* [The sons of Ingmar] (1919), turned out to be the most successful production of the entire decade.

The period from 1917 to about 1924 has generally been characterized as the "Golden Age of Swedish Cinema," after which Swedish film is said to have declined. Both the term and the reasons given for the eventual disintegration of Swedish cinema in the late 1920s have nowadays been disputed. First, one can point to various remarkable achievements even in the early 1910s. Second, it is inaccurate to consider productions from around 1920 as constituting a homogeneous "Swedish film school," as many historians have claimed.

The Swedish film industry undoubtedly benefited from the war, which is said to have caused the shift in production toward fewer but better and more expensive films. But as suggested above, other, more important factors lay behind this change. It also turned out to be a risky policy when, after the war, the financial backers of Svensk Filmindustri aimed at the international market with larger-budget, more lavish films. Especially after the postwar depression hit society as a whole, it became harder to earn a profit on the huge investments made—Svensk Filmindustri, in fact, had two film studios to keep operational, since Skandia also had built one during its short life span. At the same time, directors became economically involved in production in a more direct way, which was not a satisfactory arrangement for them because it hampered their artistic freedom. This contributed to the decision of both Sjöström and Stiller to accept offers from the U.S. film industry, and both left for Hollywood in the mid-1920s, Stiller accompanied by a female star he had introduced in his last Swedish film, *Gösta Berlings saga/The Legend of Gösta Berling* (1924), Greta Garbo.

At that time there were already disputes among the critics as to whether the international direction of production had brought about the apparent overall decline of Swedish film or if the cause was the opposite: Clinging to a national orientation had made Swedish films less marketable. Further developments at least proved the latter to be untrue if one examines the Swedish market itself.

Swedish cinema of the late 1920s can roughly be divided into several distinct categories. One was the lavish, internationally aimed films produced by Svensk Filmindustri and its affiliated companies (many were joint ventures with companies in Germany and England). Although the films, many directed by *Gustaf Molander, who had become the leading director at Svensk Filmindustri, were not particularly bad, they could not compete successfully with the tide of films from Hollywood that simultaneously swept the European market. A second category consisted of films with obvious provincial themes, including many rural melodramas, mostly produced by small companies, some of them located in provinces such as Värmland and Skåne. In general, this aspect of film production did a much better business. The filming of the play *Värmlänningarna* [The people of Värmland] (1921), a celebration of the Swedish peasantry, turned out to be the smash hit of the decade, and it was followed by more films of the same kind. The rural motif was particularly dominant in the middle of the decade.

Another group of films belongs to a nationalistic vein that evolved in response to the much-debated reduction of the defense forces in the mid-1920s. A direct result was one of the biggest production ventures in Swedish film history, the two-part film *Carl XII/Charles XII* (1925), starring *Gösta Ekman [Sr.], financed by wealthy industrialist Herman Rasch. The film attracted a very large audience but nevertheless did not recover costs. Despite this, more films with historical motifs were produced, such as *Fänrik Ståls sägner* [The tales of Second Lieutenant Stål] (1926), about the 1808–1809 war against Russia, and *Gustaf Wasa* (1928), about the sixteenth-century king who may be regarded as the founder of the centralized state of Sweden.

The provincial segment of the production, however, spawned the more commercially successful efforts of the 1930s. Some of the leading actors and directors of the 1930s emerged from the provincial branches of the industry. *Edvard Persson, the most successful Swedish actor of all time, started as an actor and director in his home province of Skåne before being engaged by Europa Film and moving to Stockholm in the early 1930s. From Värmland came director *Gustaf Edgren, together with his discovery, *Fridolf Rhudin, who became the most popular film actor in the first half of the 1930s.

THE ADVENT OF TALKING FILM

The 1930s started at point zero for Swedish film. The failure of the "international" productions from Svensk Filmindustri in the late 1920s nearly caused the company to halt production completely. One can say that the introduction of sound saved the Swedish cinema. Svensk Filmindustri achieved a real success in the nick of time with the modest little comedy *Säg det i toner/The Dream Waltz*, which premiered in the final days of 1929. It had no talking parts, just a soundtrack with music and sound effects on discs, but its immediate success convinced the directorial board to continue.

The initially high cost of sound recording was prohibitive for smaller companies. In the first year, only Svensk Filmindustri could afford to make sound films (with the German recording system they acquired from Tobis-Klang). Parallel with this, Swedish-language films were a part of Paramount's attempt to dominate the European market with the production of multilingual films in Paris (Joinville). All together, a dozen Swedish-language films were produced by Paramount in 1930–1931. After a relatively large initial success with *När rosorna slå ut* [When the roses bloom], directed by *Edvin Adolphson, who had made *Säg det i toner*, succeeding films were generally total failures. The films were too "un-Swedish" to meet with audience approval.

Soon, however, it became less expensive to record sound, as the patent rights could be evaded by inventive firms. One result was the founding of new important production companies. Europa Film was established in 1930 but started production in 1931 with Finnish-designed sound recording equipment. Irefilm began in 1931 with an apparatus constructed by two Swedish engineers. Svensk Filmindustri soon followed with one made by Swedish Aga-Baltic, which helped reduce costs.

Soon the film market began to flourish, and after the initial depression years, one can speak of an actual "boom." Cinema attendance rose from about 30 million a year in the mid-1930s to almost 60 million by the end of the decade. New movie theaters were built, especially after 1935, and in 1939 an infrastructure had been established that would remain until the 1980s, with three major companies, Svensk Filmindustri, Europa Film, and Sandrews. The latter was the last to be founded. Its origins was an important theater chain owned by grocery store magnate Anders Sandrew, who began producing films in 1939 in order to secure them for his own establishments. All three companies owned their own studios, distribution outlets, and most important, their own chains of movie theaters.

In addition to the major companies, there were a number of smaller ones, often living at the mercy of the large ones and their distribution and production apparatus. In many cases the small companies tried to finance their films with the help of independent cinema owners who gave financial guarantees in advance. This was a risky business, however, and the production scene in the 1930s (and also later) is characterized by a string of financial failures; many of the small companies went bankrupt after one or two productions.

The advent of talking films nevertheless was very beneficial overall for domestic Swedish film production, since audiences preferred films in their own language. Some attempts were made to dub films from the United States, but this was generally unsuccessful; consequently, virtually all foreign films shown in Sweden since then have been subtitled. The effect, naturally, was that Swedish films in general were provincial and national with regard to both content and style.

Films of the 1930s coincide with an important phase in contemporary Swedish history—the forming of the welfare state—which left a distinctive mark on film production. The period has generally been overlooked by critics and film historians, regarded a void or parenthesis, but this is an unjustified assessment. Besides the fascinating sociological aspects of films of the period, one can point to many distinguished creative efforts by directors like Gustaf Molander, *Per-Axel Branner, *Schamyl Bauman, or director/producer *Lorens Marmstedt. Neither should one dismiss more ordinary craftsmen such as Gustaf Edgren or *Sigurd Wallén.

The 1932 election victory of the Social Democratic Party and the "historical compromise" with the Farmer's League Party in 1933 shaped the necessary conditions for the founding of a new welfare policy to begin a practical realization of the "people's home" that had been part of the social democratic ideological vision since the 1920s. This was initially, in fact, a socially conservative concept founded on the norms of traditional, agrarian Swedish society. This is evident even in the radical political visions expressed by Alva and Gunnar Myrdal, who most clearly formulated the aims of the new order in their 1934 book *Kris i befolkningsfrågan* [The nativity crisis].

This compromise between old and new, between traditional values and utopian vision—the very essence of the "Swedish model"—was perhaps an attempt at presenting a solution to the problems caused by industrialization and the rapid modernization of society as a whole. Such a mixture is also a cornerstone of most Swedish films of the period, no matter what genre an individual film belonged to. A classic example is *Karl-Fredrik regerar/Karl Fredrik Reigns* (1934), which emphasizes the growth of political unity and formulation of utopian goals for the future while placing the foundation of these policies in the belief that everyone, regardless of class, is bound to the Swedish soil, home region, and native country.

Another important motif in films of the 1930s is the expression of the myths and commonplaces of a shared Swedish culture, identity, and tradition. Examples are an interest in the landscape and Swedish nature or in history and historical dramas. This orientation was very prominent even in the silent days and has continued to play an important role since then. Great emphasis is placed on the common will to defend this heritage, as demonstrated in films about the military, especially after the middle of the decade when the Nazi threat against all of Europe became increasingly evident.

A didactic element is present in the attempt to describe which deeds and attitudes are most valuable for preserving and building the new "people's home." Many films contributed to the lively debate elicited by the declining birthrate—the topic of the Myrdal book mentioned above—by expressing a pro-natalist stance while simultaneously stressing that all children, regardless of the circumstances of their birth, should be cared for (the percentage of children born out of wedlock in Sweden was then among the highest in the world). Obvious examples are Edgren's *Valborgsmässoafton/Walpurgis Night* (1935) and Bauman's *Vi två* [The two of us] (1939). Another prominent theme was the importance, especially for young people, of diligence and striving to better themselves, to climb the social ladder, but the pursuit of this goal was not only for the sake of individual happiness but also for the collective good. Both motivations provided a strong incentive for young men to succeed in the world of commerce and technology. This was a common theme, especially in the many films belonging to the folksy genre, often based on outdoor theater plays, that became very popular with the advent of sound. The excessive drinking habits depicted elicited debate among critics, and a somewhat derogatory label, "pilsnerfilm" (literally "light beer film"), was applied to this part of the production.

Not surprisingly, the focus on unity and progress revealed another, less positive side, that is, the sharp distinction between the ideal Swede and all others—the foreigner and the Jew. In fact, almost 10 percent of Swedish films of the 1930s contain elements that, to a greater or lesser degree, are openly anti-Semitic. In summary, Swedish film of the prewar decade establishes a highly ethnocentric and nationalistic tone. It stresses the overriding principle of the leveling of class distinctions in order to make all members of the audience feel they belong to the same society, progressing toward the same bright, utopian future: a society that would be a home for all Swedes.

THE WAR YEARS

World War II caused drastic changes in Sweden's social life. Although Sweden managed to avoid direct involvement in the conflict—to a large degree by making various concessions to Nazi Germany in the early 1940s—war conditions affected Sweden in a decisive way. A substantial segment of Sweden's adult male population was drafted to defend the long borders of the country. Both domestic and foreign consumer goods had to be rationed. As long as Nazi Germany seemed invincible, Swedish society as a whole lived under a constant threat.

This period in Swedish contemporary history, generally referred to as the "time of preparedness," was very beneficial to the film industry since the market to a high degree became isolated. Although American films were still available, many were not shown; sometimes they were forbidden by the Board of Film Censors if they reflected too strong an anti-Nazi standpoint. Furthermore, the climate of the times created a greater demand for entertainment and escapism, so cinema attendance figures continued to rise. So did domestic film production. In the late 1930s, production had reached about thirty features a year. Now more than forty films were produced annually, and the market share for Swedish films was as high as 50 percent.

Film production reflected this "preparedness" in various ways. Relatively few films dealt directly with the military—in fact, no more than in the previous decade. Military films tended to fall into two categories: simple farces or more serious melodramas like *Hasse Ekman's *Första divisionen* [First squadron] (1941), a film about bomber pilots with a virtually obligatory sacrificial theme.

Many films were pure escapism, but even so, there were hints about actual circumstances. Restrictions, rationing, and related conditions as part of everyday life were natural ingredients even in the simplest comedies or farces. Reflections of the dark times were of course more evident in melodramas, which became a greater segment of the whole repertoire than before. A substantial number were adaptations of works of established authors, a pattern that also became more common. Many films had an allegorical dimension, a consequence of the need to avoid conflict with the Board of Censors and other state authorities keeping a stern eye on film production and the content of individual films.

Some of these allegorical films set their action in the past, in traditional agrarian society. Such was the case with two of the most interesting films, *Alf Sjöberg's *Himlaspelet/The Heavenly Play* (1942) and Gustaf Molander's film version of Vilhelm Moberg's antifascist novel *Rid i natt!* [Ride this night!] (1942). The action of that film takes place in the seventeenth century and concerns free peasants who have been subjugated by a foreign nobleman, a German. One man alone actively resists and, of course, eventually sacrifices his life for the sake of freedom. Only toward the end of the war did producers dare to consider more contemporary war themes. A handful of films from 1943–1944 dealt more explicitly with conditions in occupied countries such as Norway. Such was the case with Gustaf Molander's *Det brinner en eld* [There's a fire burning] (1943), which was attacked by Norwegian critics after the war. Even at that late stage, German representatives in Sweden made official complaints about films such as Hasse Ekman's *Excellensen* [His excellency] (1944), set in Austria at the time of the Anschluss.

AFTER THE WAR

After the war, representatives of the Swedish film industry feared, not without reason, that competition from the U.S. film industry would be much stronger than before and that the market would be flooded with American films. At first these fears were proven wrong. For a few years, Swedish film held its strong market position, and movie attendance continued to rise. There were other kinds of threats, however. In early 1948 the government decided to double the tax rate on movie tickets overnight, from an average of about 20 percent to 37.5 percent. This was truly a harsh blow, and representatives of the film industry tried vainly to persuade the authorities that it was unjust. The latter were convinced that the film industry was still prospering but finally at least agreed to undertake another official investigation, which took place in 1951. That same year, film producers staged a voluntary strike, and production was halted for a few months. One production was exempted, *Arne Mattsson's *Hon dansade en sommar/One Summer of Happiness*, a film that proved to be one of the most successful in Swedish film history.

This film was produced by Nordisk Tonefilm, for a while another important company on the production scene. This company was closely linked with the labor movement and had its origin in an affiliated theater chain, which bought the Swedish branch of a Danish distribution company in the mid-1940s and became a producer in the later years of the decade. They had great initial success with two rural melodramas set in a contemporary milieu, *På dessa skuldror* [On these shoulders] (1948) and *Människors rike* [Realm of man] (1949), which led to more films of the same type in the 1950s.

The final outcome of the 1951 investigation was a subvention system that refunded part of the tax money collected by the state to the producers. This was paid in direct proportion to the revenues of the individual film; so the larger the audience, the more money was refunded. The system was widely criticized but lasted until 1963, when a totally new film subvention system was introduced. Attendance still climbed in the 1950s until the peak year 1957, with about 80 million spectators, but by that time the market share of Swedish films had shrunk to not more than 25 percent. There was perhaps some comfort in the fact that certain Swedish films and filmmakers now did much better internationally. Awards such as the Cannes Grand Prix given to Alf Sjöberg's *Fröken Julie/Miss Julie* (1951) helped draw the world's attention to Swedish films once again. *One Summer of Happiness* swept the world film market, and after the mid-1950s *Ingmar Bergman gradually became an international celebrity.

As indicated earlier, producers encountered stiffer competition in the postwar years and had to respond more sensitively to public demand. Folksy comedies and simple farces formed a substantial segment of the production, as before. Society as a whole also underwent radical changes that were reflected in film. The migration from the countryside to the cities accelerated. Industry, undamaged from the war, could meet the demand for consumer goods from a continent that had been devastated. The Swedish economy prospered, and industry desperately needed more manpower. As wages were raised, the welfare state became a reality for more and more people. Many social reforms could now be implemented.

The transformation from a conservative, agrarian society was not, however, without problems, especially on a mental or a psychological level, when traditional values underwent drastic change. This can help to explain the major trends in postwar Swedish film. One, and the most important, is the increased output of films set in agrarian milieus, ranging from historical rural melodramas such as *Driver dagg, faller regn/Sunshine Follows Rain* (1946), which set the pace, to more contemporary ones such as *One Summer of Happiness,* to simple-minded farces such as those with highly popular "hillbilly" character Åsa-Nisse (*Åsa-Nisse films), about whom twenty films were made between 1949 and 1969.

Most films dealing with rural themes were very popular with audiences. For many, attendance reached the 1 million mark (in a population of not more than about 6 million); some were seen by 2 or even 3 million spectators. Films set in a rural milieu reached their peak in 1947–1948, when every third film belonged to the genre, most of them among the most commercially successful. After a short downswing around 1950, the genre was revived toward the middle of the decade, when all the big companies produced new, lavish color versions of some of the classics. Veteran Gustaf Molander directed the third Swedish version of *Sången om den eldröda blomman* [The song of the scarlet flower] (1956); *Gunnar Hellström made his highly personal *Synnöve Solbakken* (1957); and opera director Göran Gentele undertook another film version of the number-one classic of the Swedish stage, *Värmlänningarna* (1957). The two first films, at least, attracted a large audience, but since they had been costly to produce, all went into the red.

Even some of Ingmar Bergman's films dealing with the theme of escaping into nature belong to the periphery of the genre. The willingness to break out of an ordinary, dull life and flee to some far-off place is in fact a very common motif in postwar Swedish cinema, for instance, in *Hon kom som en vind* [She came like the wind] (1951), by another important director of the time, *Erik "Hampe" Faustman. Another relevant example is Gunnar Skoglund's *Vägen till*

Klockrike [The road to Klockrike] (1953), from the novel by Harry Martinson, who subsequently won the Nobel Prize.

One common theme in all the various types of film with rural settings is skepticism about contemporary society, a stance that can actually be traced back to the late 1930s to pastoral films such as **Kalle på Spången/Kalle paa Spaangen*, a.k.a. *Charlie, the Inn-keeper* (1939). This negative view is also shared by certain more "intellectual" filmmakers when they depict alienation and a sense of discomfort with a materially prosperous but spiritually bankrupt society.

In some cases the theme of alienation in modern society is coupled with the assertion that God is dead or the belief that human beings have lost their spiritual guideposts. There is also a sense of guilt because Sweden had merely been a spectator to all the violence the war had unleashed. When French existentialist philosophy spread throughout Europe, it found fertile ground in Swedish intellectual circles, aided by an established Kierkegaardian tradition in Swedish and Nordic spiritual life.

Bergman is an obvious example of this orientation, although he opposed the pessimistic view of existentialism. Related themes can be found in films like **Fängelse/The Devil's Wanton*, a.k.a. *Prison* (1949), *Det sjunde inseglet/The Seventh Seal* (1956), and many others. The whole range of philosophical ideas can also be found in the works of other directors. One who may be compared to Bergman is Rune Lindström, author of the script of *The Heavenly Play*, in which he also played the lead. A former student of theology, he became a very productive screenwriter in the postwar years and is characterized by the ability to put a very personal stamp even on literary adaptations. Although Lindström never reached the same artistic level as Bergman, in many respects his work expresses the same themes in a simpler manner. *The Heavenly Play*, in essence, dealt with questions about the existence of God in an evil and destructive world. An obvious later example is Lindström's script to Gustaf Molander's *Nu börjar livet* [Now life begins] (1948), about a minister who falls in love with a young girl, loses his faith when he is abandoned, and dies. Incidentally, Bergman cast Lindström as a doubting preacher in *The Devil's Wanton*, a role that was cut, however, before the premiere. Hasse Ekman, another big name in postwar cinema, contributed to this thematic concentration on loneliness and alienation in modern society, though in a less heavy-handed way, in films such as *Flickan från tredje raden* [The girl from the gallery] (1949) and **Flicka och hyacinter* [Girl with hyacinths] (1950).

The "people's home" theme is common and complex in postwar Swedish cinema. If its conception had been optimistic in prewar cinema, subsequent developments in Swedish society made things appear in a different light. As already mentioned, forced urbanization and industrialization had set the stage for agrarian and pastoral themes. There were nevertheless other aspects of urban growth. Concern about juvenile delinquency is as old as modern society, and the topic had generated heated debate even at the turn of the century, but the question became acute toward the end of the 1930s, when many problems were blamed on urbanization and the growth of the modern entertainment industry.

The problems and the alienation of young people, a focus as early as 1942 in *Anders Henrikson's *Ungdom i bojor* [Youth in chains] (1942), became another prominent theme in postwar cinema. One can distinguish two types of films about juvenile delinquents, those that expressed an optimistic view about the possibility of reform and those that presented the opposite view, claiming that an evolving welfare state was unable to cope with the problem, partly because the notion of "people's home" concealed the fact that Sweden was still a class society; young people from the dregs never had a chance. This particular view was expressed in various films by Egil Holmsen, Gunnar Hellström, and Arne Ragneborn. In several instances, the nihilistic vision of the films caused problems with the Board of Censors. Such was the case with Holmsen's *Fartfeber* [Speed fever] (1953), one of the best Swedish films about delinquency, and Ragneborn's *Farlig frihet/The Vicious Breed* (1954).

THE 1960s

At the beginning of the 1960s the crisis of the entire film industry had become acute. As in most other countries, the film industry and movie theaters encountered strong competition from television. In Sweden, TV had been cautiously introduced toward the end of 1954. The official premiere of public television broadcasting was in the autumn of 1956; by 1958, the number of television sets and licenses required for them began to rise dramatically. The effect was that cinema attendance fell precipitously in only a few years: From 80 million annually in 1957 it dropped to 55 million in 1960, and to a mere 40 million by 1963. Many small movie theaters were closed during these years.

This called for action. There had been another official investigation of the film industry toward the end of the 1950s, but the new subvention system that was introduced in 1963 was the work of one man, Harry Schein. His ideas were not new—they had been proposed from time to time since the 1930s—but he managed to persuade the government to adapt them. The basic idea was an abolishment of the government tax on tickets. Instead, a 10 percent fee was introduced, where all income generated was destined for film-related purposes. One portion or fund (30 percent) was still redistributed according to the revenues of the individual film, but another 20 percent went to "quality" productions as determined by a jury of film critics. A third fund (15 percent) was designated to adjust for losses to films regarded as quality pictures. The Swedish Film Institute was founded to administer the various funds and to serve as a central clearinghouse for film matters. The proportions were adjusted in 1968 when the first and third funds were reduced and the Film Institute received a separate fund to provide guarantees and loans to certain productions. In 1972 the agreement was rewritten, so the general distribution fund and the one for adjusting losses were abolished. Instead, there was a general fund to give guarantees in advance to selected film projects. The fund was split into two parts, where each board had the same share. One board was dominated by people from the film industry, the other by representatives of film workers. The Film Institute had a fund for its own productions. In 1975 another fund was introduced, to which the Swedish Broadcasting Company contributed money.

The reformed film subvention system coincided with the introduction of a whole new generation of filmmakers who were aided by the new policies because they enabled production companies to take more chances. With regard to some directors, the influence of the so-called French New Wave is apparent. Even American independent cinema represented by Cassavetes and British "kitchen sink" realism left their mark. It became more common to shoot outside the heavy-handed and costly film studios, a change facilitated by better and lighter equipment. Sandrews closed its studio in 1962, whereas Svensk Filmindustri and Europa Film kept theirs operational for many years.

One should not, however, overestimate the effects of the 1963 reform, although there did evolve an entire group of filmmakers representing something new, for example, *Bo Widerberg, *Vilgot Sjöman, and *Jan Troell. From the film school founded at the same time as the Film Institute came filmmakers such as *Roy Andersson, Jonas Cornell, and others. Still, many films were made in the old, traditional manner and style, and comedies and farces generally attracted a large portion of the remaining audience. Other reliable moneymakers were the numerous children's films directed by Olle Hellbom from the stories of Astrid Lindgren (such as all the films about Saltkråkan in the 1960s, or in the 1970s, Pippi Longstocking and Emil of Lönneberga), and they did not exactly break new ground, either.

The now-established Bergman and Sjöman had several box office hits, too, when they challenged the norms set by the Board of Censors. The 1960s promoted a more open-minded view in general on certain topics like sex and women's issues. When such material also invaded the cinema scene, it sometimes caused controversy and conflict. The heated sex scenes in Bergman's *Tystnaden/The Silence* (1963) and Sjöman's *491* (1964) are good examples. Less talented filmmakers followed in the same path. When censorship gradually retreated from the old barricades, this made room for what has generally been referred to as "Schwedenfilm." At the end of the 1960s and during the 1970s these soft-core films became virtually a cliché but generally did good business in the export market. A few so-called educational films about the "language of love," as the titles usually read, did very well in both domestic and foreign markets. The soft-core genre gradually developed into plain hard-core but also had to meet stronger competition from U.S. films, and the Swedish sex film has virtually disappeared since the 1980s. New distribution channels such as the video market also contributed to the demise of overly explicit sex for its own sake in feature films.

FROM THE 1970s TO THE PRESENT

The many changes in the subvention system in the 1970s reflect to a high degree the fact that the Film Institute had acquired a growing responsibility for film production itself. The effect was that more people were given the chance to make their dreams come true: The number of first-time directors increased, and some of their efforts were remarkable. But in general the positive effects of the first reform waned, and too many films were merely a waste of the money and talent involved. Many films were simply cranked out, a circumstance that may have inspired film critic Peter Cowie's often-cited words from the end of the 1970s that Swedish film was passing through the "shadow of the valley of death."

One can, of course, question this as a general assessment. There were note-worthy films in the 1970s, such as those of Jan Troell, who directed the 1970s box office hit *Utvandrarna/The Emigrants* (1971). There were also talented newcomers like Roy Andersson and *Lars Lennart Forsberg, but they often encountered obstacles and ceased making feature films.

On a more popular level the duo *Tage Danielsson and *Hans Alfredson, who had appeared in the mid-1960s, continued to be successful during the following two decades. The cinematic quality of their films was often uneven, but they revealed a talent for social relevance as well as for comedy. Both audiences and critics were pleased, and all the films were big moneymakers. The same can be said of the Astrid Lindgren films—all were commercially successful. Pippi Longstocking was later replaced in the 1970s by the rascal Emil of Lönneberga. The director of all these films, Olle Hellbom, made a more serious effort based on a novel by the same author with *Bröderna Lejonhjäärta* [The Brothers Lionheart] (1977).

In 1982 the subvention system was adjusted once again. The funds handled by the Film Institute and the one financed with television money were merged with the guarantee funds, and two new funds were created. One was administered by the Film Institute itself; the other, and somewhat larger, was split between two different boards with the same representation as before. In order to increase production, in the second half of the 1980s the Film Institute manager tried different ways of raising money by attracting big business to invest in certain film productions. This effort was based on a complicated tax deduction scheme (not unlike that of certain countries), but this practice was called into question, not least by the tax authorities, and disappeared after a couple of years.

The film industry also underwent some changes, although the structure remained basically as before. Europa Film, one of the main companies, experienced serious difficulties in the early 1980s owing to several ill-fated and costly productions and was swallowed up by Svensk Filmindustri, which became even more dominant with regard to both production and distribution, now challenged only by Sandrews. The new subvention system had nevertheless been beneficial for a string of small companies, which could survive thanks to the advance guarantees from Film Institute funds. If they could manage to keep real costs below the official budget, the whole system was foolproof. A very common production scheme in the 1980s consisted of a joint venture, with a small company handling the technical production and one of the large ones, such as Svensk Filmindustri, taking care of distribution, while in reality being financed entirely by the Film Institute.

In 1993 the subvention system was changed again, with a partial return to the oldest system of them all: A big share of the money was once again distributed afterward in accordance with revenues from ticket sales. If a film does enough business, it receives the maximum aid. This has caused heated debate among filmmakers and critics who are less than thrilled about the increased dominance of the commercial film industry. Still, a large segment of the money is handled in the old way, although the boards have been replaced by individual consultants responsible for promoting new, and hopefully worthwhile, film projects. In 1990 a fund for Nordic cooperation was established to stimulate co-productions.

At the end of 1998, author Per Olov Enquist presented another official governmental investigation where he proposed a radical change in the state film policy on many points. Just recently an agreement has been reached between the government, film industry, and television (state television and commercial TV 4). Following the year 2000 there will be an increase in aid from the state toward production and distribution. Scriptwriters will receive developmental aid to allow them more time to write better scripts; young filmmakers will be given a chance to test their ideas on smaller projects before entering into bigger productions. The special destined aid to cinema distribution of Swedish films has already caused opposition from representatives of the U.S. film industry, as noted by correspondence from the U.S. embassy in Stockholm to the Swedish minister of culture on their behalf.

It is difficult to give a general assessment of film production in the 1970s, 1980s, and onward, in large part because the entire system has encouraged the personal vision of individual directors, thus decreasing the importance of traditional genres. Film comedy has remained strong, however, and perhaps even more dominant than before, thanks to two individuals, *Lasse Åberg and *Gösta Ekman [Jr.]. Åberg started 1979 with a modest comedy about military life that proved to be a sleeper hit and continued with a series of films about Swedish tourists taking chartered trips to various places. Each of his films has reached about 1.5 million spectators. The small independent company Nordisk Tonefilm (no relation to the older one of the same name) struck a gold mine in 1981 with a Swedish remake of the Danish detective film spoof *Olsenbanden* [The Olsen gang]. The Swedish version with Gösta Ekman as the gang leader Jönsson proved to be very popular with audiences; so far six sequels have been produced, although Ekman has been replaced by other actors in later films. Sweden has also witnessed the birth of new popular genres as well. One is the modern police film, to which Bo Widerberg contributed a couple of widely acclaimed efforts, *Mannen på taket/Man on the Roof* (1976), based on a novel by Sjöwall and Wahlöö, and *Mannen från Mallorca* [The man from Majorca] (1981). Both films contained criticism of authoritarian tendencies in modern Swedish society. The secret agent film is a brand-new Swedish genre—if one excepts a film like Ingmar Bergman's early parody effort, *Sånt händer inte här* [This doesn't happen here] (1950). Jan Guillou's best-selling novels about Carl Gustaf Hamilton, a Swedish military officer with a license to kill, have so far led to five films and TV serials. The popularity of these films may be linked to the breakdown of the old myth of Swedish neutrality with the acknowledgment that Sweden, too, has been involved in the shady business of international espionage.

The documentary film has an important place in the contemporary scene, at least on an artistic level. Documentaries seldom attract large audiences, but because they also receive television distribution, they can contribute to the general social debate. One can point to a skilled director like *Stefan Jarl, who works primarily in the same vein as *Arne Sucksdorff.

Another aspect of contemporary film is the appearance of a whole generation of female film directors. With the exception of pioneers like Anna Hofman-Uddgren, *Karin Swanström, or *Mai Zetterling, women were virtually absent before the 1970s. Now we have names such as *Gunnel Lindblom, *Marianne Ahrne, Suzanne Osten, Marie-Louise Ekman, and *Agneta Fagerström-Olsson, not to mention skilled documentary filmmakers such as Ingela Romare, Nina Hedenius, Ylva Floreman, and Christina Olofson.

The legacy from Bergman was perhaps more prominent in the 1960s, when he could be viewed both as a source of inspiration and as a spiritual burden. Another trend has grown in importance for the past ten or fifteen years—the search for a lost national identity. The fact that Sweden at present is a country of immigration, where almost 20 percent of the population has a foreign origin or ancestry, combined with the European integration process, has made this issue highly topical. One result of the focus on national identity has been the revival of the old rural tradition in film, most successfully in *Änglagård/House of Angels*, parts 1 and 2, both directed by *Colin Nutley, an Englishman who himself is an immigrant.

Another representation of ongoing change in modern society is, as several film critics have pointed out, the theme of the missing father. The paternity issue in Swedish film is actually quite old—Swedish film history is filled with lone mothers and absent fathers—but new films about the search for a father may have a new dimension nevertheless. Films like *Söndagsbarn/Sunday's Children* (1991), from a script by Bergman and directed by his son Daniel, *Min store tjocke far* [My big fat dad] (1992), and others contain an element of nostalgia that was previously absent. This focus incorporates a melancholy tone, perhaps reflecting a society that is virtually fatherless now that the whole concept of the "people's home" has been called into question and its cornerstone, the cradle-to-grave welfare policy, has been undermined by the current economic crisis.

Although the more explicit criticism of society of the late 1960s and early 1970s has vanished, many contemporary filmmakers have continued to offer critical or negative views. This criticism, however, tends to be represented on a psychological or spiritual level through the depiction of alienation among ordinary people or various kinds of mental breakdown.

Another crucial trend is the redefinition of the traditional concept of masculinity in modern society. This was expressed in an interesting way in Troell's film *Ingeniör Andrées luftfärd/The Flight of the Eagle* (1983). When the protagonist Andrée realizes that he and his men are about to die in the Arctic ice, he confesses that he was driven to lead his expedition by the masculine ideals promoted by a nationalistic society.

THE TELEVISION SCENE

It is impossible to talk about Swedish film production in recent decades without mentioning the role of Swedish television. State television has, in fact, become one of the most important producers nowadays. It has also been a training ground for many new directors. Currently, established names such as *Lasse Hallström and *Richard Hobert all began by directing for the small screen. Television has also accommodated many of the talents that did not succeed within the commercial film industry.

As mentioned before, the beginnings of Swedish television were in the late 1950s. Initially it was a monopoly partly owned by the state and under parliamentary control. Viewers were served by a single channel. During the 1960s the output of fiction was mainly limited to staged dramas, occasionally complemented by individual films or series produced outside television. Conditions changed in 1969 when a second channel began broadcasting, drawing mainly from local or regional branches. The production of staged or filmed fiction increased drastically after the channel split. Much of the new production took place in the regional studios, in particular the one in Göteborg, which virtually specialized in long-running series dealing with contemporary social issues. Such was the case with the most popular and longest-lasting series *Hem till byn* [Home to the village], produced in six different parts from 1971 to 1999, which once again returned to traditional rural themes by following the development of a small village and showing how changes in contemporary Sweden affected the lives of the villagers. The Göteborg studio had another smash hit with another series set in traditional agrarian society, *Raskens*, based on a novel by Vilhelm Moberg.

Since the 1980s, television's own production of ordinary feature films has almost outnumbered those produced by the privately owned film industry, and now television has become directly involved in many film ventures produced there. Swedish television, together with the state, contributes money to the projects organized by the Film Institute. Television also appears frequently as co-producer of many films made for theatrical release. It is not uncommon for films or other productions to be shown first on television and then in movie theaters, or vice versa. Such was the case with the famous film/film series *Fanny och Alexander/Fanny and Alexander*, where the shorter film version was released theatrically in 1982 and the longer, five-hour series shown on television in 1984 (this version also had a limited distribution in movie theaters). *Den goda viljan/The Best Intentions*, another Ingmar Bergman project, was first shown as a television series in 1991 and then in an edited version in movie theaters in 1992.

The new commercial Swedish television channels also contribute to film production. TV 4 has been involved in many productions, such as *Vendetta* (1995), a film in the series about agent Hamilton, and the much-debated *Jägarna* [The hunters] (1996). The even more commercial TV 3 contributed to such projects as *Kjell Grede's acclaimed film about Raoul Wallenberg.

NOTES TO THE FILMOGRAPHIES

SHORT

For films before 1920, *short* is defined as a film of three reels or less (approximately 3,000 feet or 900 meters).

TVD/TVDS/TVM/TVMS

I have tried to distinguish between TV-Drama (TVD), TV-Drama/Series (TVDS), TV-Movie (TVM), and TV-Movie/Series (TVMS). TVDs are normally studio productions of plays or original scripts shot on videotape. Before the introduction of videotape recording (VTR) (in Sweden, autumn 1959), these productions were staged live. Some of the plays, however, were preserved by filming off the television screen with a 16mm camera (such as Alf Sjöberg's staging of *Hamlet* in 1955). TVMs are defined as more conventional film productions produced for direct broadcasting purposes. Sometimes they have also received normal commercial cinema release, usually in edited versions. TVM and TVMS are usually produced on film stock, but in later years, video technique has been more common. It is, however, no longer easy to make any technical distinction, owing to the refinement of modern video equipment.

NCF

Noncommercial features (NCFs) have been produced for different purposes in Sweden. In the early decades of film, it was not uncommon to find films of almost feature length produced by various commercial industries for advertising purposes. These films were shown free of change in rented cinemas. Political parties—mainly the Social Democratic Party—have also used the film medium for propaganda purposes, principally for election campaigns. These films resembled ordinary feature film productions, with established actors and directors involved. The productions were normally handled by commercial film production companies such as Svensk Filmindustri and Europa Film.

ORDER OF FILMS

The date of a film is normally the release year according to the international filmography standard. If there is a considerable time lapse between production year and release year, I make note of it. I have also tried to order the films according to actual release date. For Swedish productions, these are the dates given by *Svensk filmografi* (in a few cases, I have altered the order or year where the filmography has not noted different dates). For the television productions, I have followed the order of first broadcast date.

ENGLISH TITLES

Italicized titles given are U.S. distribution titles. When the same title appears after a slash, this means that the film has been distributed in the United States under its original Swedish title. Translations of films not shown commercially in the United States appear in brackets. When the U.S. distribution title (as was the case with many of Ingmar Bergman's films) differs significantly from the original, I have in a few cases given a more faithful translation in brackets. Sometimes the films have been shown under these titles in festival or retrospective/rerun showings.

I have tried to make the filmographies as complete as possible but have excluded compilation films and (generally) TV documentaries. It is sometimes very hard to find the titles of some actor's foreign films. One must be very cautious about the filmographies found in various film databases (like IMDb). Many titles are for projects planned but never realized.

AWARDS

I have restricted myself to Academy Awards (AAs), Academy Award Nominations (AANs), Emmy, major prizes at the three major European festivals (Cannes, Berlin, Venezia), and finally the Swedish annual prize Guldbaggen [The Golden Bug] (GB), given by a jury appointed by the Swedish Film Institute.

BIBLIOGRAPHIES

In a few cases, I have used abbreviated sources—for example, Forslund, 1995—where a particular work contains several articles about single persons or films. The full bibliographic information is given in the "General Bibliography" at the end of this part.

LIST BY CAREER

DIRECTORS

Lars "Lasse" Åberg
Edvin Adolphson
Börje Ahlstedt
Marianne Ahrne
Hans Alfredson
Roy Andersson
Schamyl Bauman
Johan Bergenstråhle
Ingmar Bergman
Per-Axel Branner
Tage Danielsson
Gustaf Edgren
Allan Edwall
Hasse Ekman
Agneta Fagerström-Olsson
Erik "Hampe" Faustman
Lars Lennart Forsberg
Ewa Fröling
Kjell Grede
Lasse Hallström

Gunnar Hellström
Anders Henrikson
Keve Hjelm
Richard Hobert
Stefan Jarl
Ivar Johansson
Erland Josephson
Alf Kjellin
Georg af Klercker
Jarl Kulle
Per Lindberg
Gunnel Lindblom
Lorens Marmstedt
Arne Mattsson
Gustaf Molander
Lars Molin
Colin Nutley
Stellan Olsson
Per Oscarsson
Edvard Persson
Nils Poppe
Alf Sjöberg

Vilgot Sjöman
Victor Sjöström
Mauritz Stiller
Peter Stormare
Arne Sucksdorff
Karin Swanström
Ingrid Thulin
Jan Troell
Sigurd Wallén
Bo Widerberg
Mai Zetterling

ACTORS/ACTRESSES

Lars "Lasse" Åberg
Edvin Adolphson
Börje Ahlstedt
Hans Alfredson
Bibi [Berith Elisabeth] Andersson
Harriet Andersson
Pernilla August
Thommy Berggren
Ingrid Bergman
Helena Bergström
Anita Björk
Gunnar Björnstrand
Hilda Borgström
Eva Dahlbeck
Tage Danielsson
Allan Edwall
Gösta Ekman [Jr.]
Gösta Ekman [Sr.]
Hasse Ekman
Lena Endre
Agneta Fagerström-Olsson

Erik "Hampe" Faustman
Samuel Fröler
Ewa Fröling
Lars Hanson
Signe Hasso
Gunnar Hellström
Anders Henrikson
Keve Hjelm
Erland Josephson
Alf Kjellin
Georg af Klencker
Jarl Kulle
Gunnel Lindblom
Viveca Lindfors
Jan Malmsjö
Birger Malmsten
Gustaf Molander
Lena Olin
Per Oscarsson
Edvard Persson
Nils Poppe
Fridolf Rhudin
Tutta Rolf
Christina Schollin
Viveka Seldahl
Victor Sjöström
Stellan Skarsgård
Peter Stormare
Karin Swanström
Max von Sydow
Birgit Tengroth
Ingrid Thulin
Sigurd Wallén
Sven Wollter
Mai Zetterling

ACTORS, ACTRESSES, DIRECTORS

LARS "LASSE" ÅBERG (Hofors, 5 May 1940–), actor, director. Åberg is versatile throughout Swedish cultural life. A trained artist and painter, he entered the film world via children's television programs. He made a series of acclaimed shows for children, acting the role of Trazan, a parody of the Tarzan character. He also made a series of programs for older viewers entitled *Hur bär du dig åt människa?* [How do you behave?]. These contained small sketches reflecting everyday behavior to prompt viewers to reflect upon their own behaviors. While working at the Swedish television company, Åberg cooperated with, among others, *Lasse Hallström of the entertainment department. Their cooperation resulted in the sitcom *Fredag med Familjen Kruse*, which was about an eccentric family and their seemingly abnormal behavior in an otherwise apparently normal daily routine.

This background information helps one understand Åberg's later feature films, which with their special comic nature have been tremendously popular with audiences and even, of late, with the film critics. Åberg has directed and acted in five of the eight top-grossing Swedish films of the 1980s and 1990s. His first film, *Repmånad* [The call up], about some middle-aged men doing their reserve duty in the army, was scorned by many critics who thought it too simple and vulgar. Åberg also had defenders, and his next films on package tour adventures in various milieus were better accepted.

As a film comedian, he often resembles Jacques Tati, and he has certainly been influenced by the French comedian. Sweden is one of the few countries (outside of France) where Tati is appreciated. Like Tati, much of Åberg's humor lies in his discrete observation of how people act and react in strange milieus and confrontations with foreign cultures. He often deals with middle-aged people, the old-fashioned "products" of the "people's home" who meet the modern world and some of its peculiar activities like alpine skiing or golf. The hero, always played by Åberg himself, looks at first like a very awkward nerd, but in the end, he triumphs over his modern opponents at their own game. In these portrayals, Åberg reminds one of another comedian, *Fridolf Rhudin, who represented another time of transition in Swedish society.

FILMOGRAPHY

Actor

1966: *Ojojoj eller berättelsen om den eldröda hummern* [Whoops! or, The song of the flaming red lobster] (also art direction). 1968: *Lejonsommar/Vibration; Het snö* [Hot snow] (art director only); *Klart spår till Tomteboda* [Clear track to Tomteboda] (TVMS). 1969: *Kameleonterna* [The chameleons] (art director only). 1971: *Fredag med Familjen Kruse* [Friday with the Kruse family] (TVDS; script only). 1972: *Violen från Flen* [The violet from Flen] (TVDS); *47: an Löken blåser på* [No. 47: The onion hurries on]. 1977: *Semlons gröna dalar* [Semlon's green valleys] (TVMS); *Söndagsseglaren* [The Sunday Sailor] (TVM, short). 1980: *Räkan från Maxim* [The shrimp from Maxim's] (TVD). 1981: *Montenegro eller Pärlor och svin/Montenegro or Pigs and Pearls.* 1983: *Kalabaliken i Bender* [The uproar in Bender]. 1988: *Folk och rövare i Kamomillastad* [People and robbers in Kamomilla village].

Director, Scriptwriter, Actor

1979: *Repmånad* [The call up]. 1980: *Sällskapsresan* [The package tour]. 1985: *Sällskapsresan II—Snowroller* [The package tour II—Snowroller]. 1988: *S.O.S.—en segelsällskapsresa* [S.O.S.—a guided sailing trip]. 1991: *Den ofrivillige golfaren* [The involuntary golf player].

BIBLIOGRAPHY

Sjögren, Olle. "Från kronvrak till mystönt." *Filmhäftet*, nos. 32–33 (Sept. 1981):37–80. Gives an overview of the Swedish films about the army and a detailed analysis of Åberg's first film, *Repmånad.*
Sjögren, Olle. "Svenskarna och deras sällskapsresor." *Filmhäftet*, nos. 38–40 (Dec. 1982): 129–143. An analysis of Åberg's second film, *Sällskapsresan*, and its place in Swedish film tradition.

EDVIN ADOLPHSON (Furingstad, 25 Feb. 1893–31 Oct. 1979), actor, director. He was born outside the industrial town of Norrköping, where at first he was active in workers' theater groups. His interest in social issues remained in old age when he became a champion for retired actors and their rights. During his long career, he was a much-appreciated film actor, slowly shifting from legendary romantic roles in the 1930s and 1940s to more mature and fatherlike figures, often in rural milieus, in later decades. Because he was dark, he was also, early in his career, periodically cast in various ethnic outsider roles, for instance, as Latin lovers or gypsies. An example of this development is that he acted in both sound versions of the rural classic *Sången om den eldröda blomman* [The song of the scarlet flower]. In the first, from 1934, he played the young male lead, Olof, who seduces every girl he encounters. In the second, from 1956, he plays the father of the female lead, who in the end becomes Olof's wife. Another memorable screen appearance was as the uncle of the young male protagonist in *Hon dansade en sommar/One Summer of Happiness*. He probably experienced one of his greatest triumphs at the end of his career when he portrayed the Hjalmar Bergman character Markurell in the television film *Markurells i Wadköping* [The Markurells of Wadköping].

His acting career was somewhat uneven. In the hands of less-talented directors he sometimes becomes affected in his acting style, but top directors such as *Hasse Ekman or *Anders Henrikson could achieve electrifying results in such films as *En dag skall gry* [A day will dawn] or *Ett brott* [A crime].

Adolphson also directed a handful of feature films. *Säg det i toner/The Dream Waltz*, the breakthrough for sound in Swedish films, gave him the opportunity to direct the first Swedish Paramount multilingual talkie in Paris, *När rosorna slå ut* [When the roses bloom]. His ability as a director may be characterized as uneven, if competent. He nevertheless directed at least one more notable film, the modernist comedy *Atlantäventyret* [The Atlantic adventure], made in collaboration with producer *Lorens Marmstedt.

FILMOGRAPHY

1918: *Thomas Graals bästa barn/Marriage a la mode* [Thomas Graal's best child]. 1920: *Gyurkovicsarna* [The Gyurkovics family]; *Mästerman* [Masterman]. 1921: *Körkarlen/The Stroke of Midnight*, a.k.a. *The Phantom Chariot*; *En vildfågel* [A wild bird]; *De landsflyktige/In Self Defence*. 1922: *Vem dömer/Mortal Clay; Kärlekens ögon* [The eyes of love]; *Thomas Graals myndling* [Thomas Graal's ward]; *Det omringade huset* [The house surrounded]. 1923: *Anderssonskans Kalle på nya äventyr* [New pranks of Mrs. Andersson's Kalle]; *Andersson, Pettersson och Lundström; Friaren från landsvägen* [The suitor from the highway]. 1924: *Sten Stensson Stéen från Eslöv* [Sten Stensson Stéen from Eslöv]; *Där fyren blinkar* [Where the lighthouse flashes]. 1925: *Carl XII/Charles XII; Polis Paulus påskasmäll* [Constable Paulus's Easter firecracker]; *Flygande holländaren* [The flying Dutchman]. 1926: *Till Österland* [To the Orient]; *Fänrik Ståls sägner* [Stories of Second Lieutenant Stål]; *Hon, den enda* [She is the only one]; *Bröllopet i Bränna* [The wedding at Bränna]. 1927: *Förseglade läppar/Sealed Lips*. 1928: *Gustaf Wasa; Janssons frestelse* [Jansson's temptation]. 1929: *Hjärtats triumf* [The triumph of the heart]; *Säg det i toner/The Dream Waltz* [Say it with music] (also director). 1930: *När rosorna slå ut/Nar Rosorna Sla ut* [When the roses bloom] (director only); *Vi två* [We two]. 1931: *Brokiga Blad/Brokiga Blad* [Colorful pages] (also director); *Generalen* [The general]; *I bönhuset* [In the chapel] (also director, short); *Faderwäll* [Farewell] (also director, short); *Längtan till havet/Marius* [Longing for the sea]; *Skepp ohoj!* [Ship ahoy!]; *Halvvägs till himlen* [Halfway to heaven]. 1932: *Skråköpings rundradio invigs* [The inauguration of Skråköping broadcasting] (also director, short); *Kärlek och kassabrist* [Love and deficit]; *Modärna fruar* [Modern wives]; *Tango* (short). 1933: *Kära släkten/Kaera slaekten* [Dear family]. 1934: *Atlantäventyret* [The Atlantic adventure] (also director, with Lorens Marmstedt); *Sången om den eldröda blomman* [The song of the scarlet flower]. 1935: *Munkbrogreven/The Count of Monk's Bridge* (also director, with *Sigurd Wallén). 1936: *Bröllopsresan* [The wedding trip]; *På Solsidan/On the Sunnyside; Johan Ulfstjerna*. 1937: *Ryska snuvan* [The Russian flu]; *Klart till drabbning/ Klart till Drabbning* [Clear for action] (director only); *John Ericsson—segraren vid Hampton Roads/John Ericsson—Victor at Hampton Roads*. 1938: *Dollar/Dollar*. 1939:

Gubben kommer [The old man's coming]; *Efterlyst* [Wanted]; *En enda natt/Only One Night*. 1940: *Ett brott* [A crime]; *Med dej i mina armar* [With you in my arms]. 1941: *Livet går vidare* [Life goes on]; *Fröken Kyrkråtta* [Miss churchmouse]; *En kvinna ombord* [Woman on board]. 1942: *Lågor i dunklet* [Flames in the gloom]; *General von Döbeln*; *Man glömmer ingenting* [Nothing is forgotten]. 1943: *Hon trodde det var han* [She thought it was he]; *Sjätte skottet* [The sixth shot]. 1944: *En dag skall gry* [A day will dawn]. 1945: *Maria på Kvarngården* [Maria of Kvarngården]; *Kungliga patrasket* [Royal rabble]; *Mans kvinna* [Man's woman]; *Galgmannen* [The gallows man]. 1946: *Åsa-Hanna; Begär* [Desire] (also director). 1947: *Supé för två* [Dinner for two]; *Ingen väg tillbaka* [No way back] (also director); *Folket i Simlångsdalen* [The people of Simlång Valley]. 1948: *En svensk Tiger* [A Swede keeps his mouth shut]; *De valde friheten* [They chose liberty] (NCF); *Flottans kavaljerer* [The navy's cavaliers]. 1949: *Skolka skolan* [Playing hookey]; *Singoalla/Gypsy Fury*. 1950: *Frökens första barn* [Teacher's first child]; *När kärleken kom till byn* [When love came to the village]; *Kastrullresan* [The saucepan voyage]; *Kvartetten som sprängdes* [The quartet that split up]. 1951: *Bärande hav* [In the arms of the sea]; *Hon dansade en sommar/One Summer of Happiness*. 1952: *En fästman i taget* [One fiancé at a time]; *Hård Klang* [The clang of the pick]; *Bättre 50-tal* [A better 50s] (NCF). 1953: *Vägen till Klockrike* [The road to Klockrike]; *Vingslag i natten* [Beat of wings in the night]; *Göingehövdingen* [The chieftain of Göinge]. 1954: *Förtrollad vandring* [Enchanted journey]; *Vad bygden behöver* [What the countryside needs] (NCF); *Ung sommar* [Young summer]. 1955: *Männen i mörker* [Men in the dark]; *Ute blåser sommarvind* [Outside the summer breezes blow]; *Älskling på vågen* [Darling of mine]; *Giftas/Of Love and Lust* [Getting married]; *Enhörningen* [The unicorn]; *Paradiset* [The paradise]; *Hamlet* (TVD). 1956: *Litet bo* [A little nest]; *Pettersson i Annorlunda* [Pettersson in different country] (NCF); *Sceningång* [Stage entrance]; *Sången om den eldröda blomman* [The song of the scarlet flower]. 1957: *Synnöve Solbakken*. 1958: *Bock i Örtagård* [Goat in the herb garden]; *Körkarlen* [The phantom chariot]; *Laila/Make Way for Lila*. 1959: *Får jag låna din fru?* [May I borrow your wife?]; *Paw*. 1960: *Av hjärtans lust* [Heart's desire]; *Bröllopsdagen* [The wedding day]; *Goda vänner trogna grannar* [Good friends, faithful neighbors]. 1961: *Swedenhielms* (TVD); *Den gamle skådespelaren* [The old actor] (TVD, also director, short); *Änglar, finns dom?/Love Mates*; *Pärlemor* [Mother of pearl]. 1962: *Dödsdansen* [The dance of death] (TVD); *Kvartetten som sprängdes* [The quartet that split up] (TVD). 1963: *Prins Hatt under jorden* [The singing leaves]; *Sällskapslek* [Parlor game]. 1964: *Bröllopsbesvär/Swedish Wedding Night*. 1966: *Hemsöborna* [The people of Hemsö] (TVMS). 1968: *Leleus testamente* [Leleu's will] (TVD); *Markurells i Wadköping* [The Markurells of Wadköping] (TVMS).

BIBLIOGRAPHY

Adolphson, Edvin. *Edvin Adolphson berättar om sitt liv med fru Thalia fru Filmia och andra fruar*. Stockholm: Bonnier, 1972. Autobiography. Not very reliable concerning facts.

Bjärlund, Eva. "Det är åt helvete att kapitalet ska styra konstnärerna." *Aftonbladet*, 12 Jan. 1975. Interview.

Holm, 1947.

BÖRJE AHLSTEDT (Stockholm, 21 Feb. 1939–), actor, director. Born in a working-class home, which has influenced his acting, Ahlstedt likes to see himself as a humble, ambitious, and hardworking craftsman. Like many others, he was educated at the Royal Dramatic Theater School in the early 1960s. Before that, he had practiced acting at the state touring theater company. After theater school he was engaged by the Royal Stage and had one insignificant film part before his breakthrough as the curious Lena's boyfriend in *Sjöman's *Jag är nyfiken/I Am Curious. For a long time he appeared mostly as a rather uncomplicated comedian or as an everyday character. He starred in Swedish television's first soap opera, Lösa förbindelser [Loose connections], as a rather lighthearted artist and gourmet. He has also embodied the "new man" of the 1980s, one allowed to reveal fragility and weakness, as Ronja's father in *Ronja Rövardotter [Ronja, the robber's daughter]. He has gradually turned toward more meaningful roles, of a sometimes very tragicomic nature. He says that the role of Peer Gynt is his favorite on the stage, and cinemagoers know him as the very pitiful Uncle Carl in *Fanny och Alexander/Fanny and Alexander, a role he has duplicated on three other occasions: in Söndagsbarn/Sunday's Children; in Den goda viljan/The Best Intentions; and finally, in *Bergman's television movie Larmar och gör sig till [Fussing and fuming], where the uncle is at the center of the action.

FILMOGRAPHY

Actor

1965: Flygplan saknas [Aircraft missing]. 1967: Jag är nyfiken-gul/I Am Curious (Yellow). 1968: Jag är nyfiken-blå/I Am Curious (Blue); Exercis [Drill] (TVM). 1969: Biprodukten [The by-product] (TVD); Made in Sweden; Bröllopsdag [Wedding day] (TVD); Blanco Posnets hängning [The hanging of Blanco Posnet] (TVD); Helkväll [All night] (TVD); Håll polisen utanför [Keep the police outside] (TVMS); Den girige [The miser] (TVD); Ni ljuger/You're Lying; Kuppen i Stockholm [The coup in Stockholm] (TVD). 1970: Röda rummet [The red room] (TVMS); Reservatet [The sanctuary] (TVD). 1971: Den byxlöse äventyraren [The adventurer without pants] (TVMS); Tolstoj (TVD); Troll (also script). 1972–1973: Bröderna Malm [The brothers Malm] (TVMS). 1973: Håll alla dörrar öppna [Keep all doors open]; Mumindalen [The Moomin valley] (TVDS). 1974: Två sätt att skrämma en flicka [Two ways to scare a girl] (TVM); Marktjänst [Home service] (TVD). 1975: Ägget är löst/Egg, Egg, A Hard-boiled Story; Robert och Jessica [Robert and Jessica] (TVMS); Justine och Juliette [Justine and Juliette] (voice); En kille och tjej [A guy and a gal]. 1976: Bestigningen av Fujijama [Climbing Fujijama] (TVD). 1977: Conny och Tojan (TVMS); Nationalmonumentet [The national monument] (TVD); Soldat med brutet gevär [Soldier with a broken rifle] (TVMS). 1978: Kvinnoborgen [The women's castle] (TVM); Dante, akta're för hajen! [Dante, beware of the shark!]; Hedebyborna [The people of Hedeby] (TVMS). 1979: Bänken [The bench] (TVM); Kristoffers hus [Kristoffer's house]; Misantropen [The Misanthrope] (TVD); En handelsresandes död [Death of a salesman] (TVD). 1980: Marmeladupproret [The marmalade rebellion]; Swedenhielms (TVD); Ett drömspel [A dream play] (TVD); Barnens ö [Children's island]. 1981: Höjdhoppar'n [The high jumper]; Fru Carrars gevär [Mrs. Carrar's rifles] (TVD); Victor eller När barnen tar makten [Victor-Or when the children seize power] (TVD); Linje lusta [A streetcar named desire] (TVD). 1982: Sova räv [Deceptive sleep] (TVM); Fanny och Alexander/Fanny and Alexander.[1] 1983: En gal-

nings dagbok [A madman's diary] (TVD); *Limpan* [Loafie]; *Mäster Olof* [Master Olof] (TVD); *Savannen* [The savanna] (TVD). 1984: *Hur ska det gå för Pettersson?* [What will become of Pettersson?] (TVDS); *Björnen* [The bear] (TVD); *Ronja Rövardotter* [Ronja, the robber's daughter]. 1985: *Lösa förbindelser* [Loose connections] (TVDS). 1986: *Amorosa.* 1987: *Dåså* [Well then] (TVM). 1988: *Skyggen af Emma* [The shadow of Emma]; *En far* [A father] (TVM); *Begriper du inte att jag älskar dig?* [Don't you realize that I love you?] (TVD). 1989: *Fallgropen* [The pitfall]; *Nallar och människor* [Teddy bears and men] (docu.). 1990: *Raoul Wallenberg—fånge i sovjet* [Raoul Wallenberg—prisoner in Soviet Union] (TVD); *Kvartssamtal* [Quarter conversation] (TVM, short); *Kaninmannen* [The rabbit man]. 1991: *Fiskafänget* [The fishing trip] (TVM, short); *Majmördaren* [Murder of May] (TVM, short); *Den goda viljan/The Best Intentions* (TVM).[2] 1992: *Söndagsbarn/Sunday's Children.* 1993: *Chefen fru Ingeborg* [Mrs. Ingeborg, the head of the firm] (TVMS); *Morsarvet* [Mother's inheritance] (TVMS). 1994: *"Vänta mörker, vänta ljus"* ["Wait for darkness, wait for light"] (TVD, short). 1995: *Höst i paradiset* [Autumn in paradise]. 1996: *Belma.* 1997: *Den siste yankeen* [The last Yankee] (TVD); *Larmar och gör sig till* [Fussing and fuming] (TVM). *Pippi Långstrump/Pippi Longstocking* (voice). 1998–1999: *Tre Kronor* [Three crowns] (TVDS). 1999: *Magnetisörens femte vinter* [The magnetizer's fifth winter].

Director

1976: *Redogörelse framlagd för en akademi* [Statement proposed for an academy] (TVD). 1977: *Möss och människor* [Of mice and men] (TVD, also actor). 1981: *Liten Karin* [Little Karin] (TVDS, also actor). 1982: *Vår stad* [Our town] (TVD, also actor).

BIBLIOGRAPHY

"Arbetare Ahlstedt." *Nöjesguiden*, no. 9 (1990):6–8.
Liljedahl, Ola. "Man begår ett misstag om man tror att man är märkvärdig för att folk känner igen en på stan." *Expressen*, 29 Oct. 1995.
Vogel, Viveka."En självklar Peer Gynt." *Göteborgs-Posten*, 14 Apr. 1991.

AWARD

GB 1990

NOTES

1. Longer version for television 1984 with limited cinema release 1983.
2. Theatrically released in 1992 in an edited version.

MARIANNE AHRNE (Lund, 25 May 1940–), director. After grammar school she studied literature and drama in the United States and then drama at Lund University, where she was active in student theater activities as both an actor and a director. She graduated from the Film School of the Swedish Film Institute in the late 1960s and is now regarded as one of the most interesting of the many female directors who emerged in the 1970s. She worked with Simone de Beauvoir on an acclaimed documentary about the elderly and on a planned feature that was never realized. Despite this she claims that she does not regard herself a "feminist" director. She specializes in depicting individuals living on the borders of society, as, for example, internees of mental institutions. In her debut *Långt borta och nära/Near and Far Away* she gave a vivid and sensitive portrayal of a complicated relationship between a female attendant and a mute male. In *Frihetens murar* [The walls of freedom] she described the difficulties of Latin American refugees in Sweden who, despite, or perhaps because of, the best intentions of Swedes, face an invisible cultural wall. The film was criticized for being too clichéd, but this is a matter of opinion. In later years she has had difficulties finding production facilities for her film projects, and most of her efforts have been devoted to the small screen. She has directed a couple of well-made sensitive television serials about young girls growing up and their adolescent problems. *Den tredje lyckan* [The third happiness] is about three girls interested in horseback riding discovering their first love. The somewhat autobiographical *Maskrosbarn* [Dandelion children] depicts a young girl who, despite growing up in very poor and miserable conditions, remains a free and independent soul. Ahrne has also written several novels in which she has further developed her interest in the irrational nature of passion.

FILMOGRAPHY

Actor

1968: *Fanny Hill*. 1972: *Du gamla, dunfria* [Thou old, thou free]. 1990: *Jag skall bli Svenriges Rembrandt eller dö!* [I will become Sweden's Rembrandt or die!]; *Utan återvändo . . . ?* [No return . . . ?] (short). 1997: *Safari* (short).

Director, Scriptwriter

Documentaries (Not Complete)

1968: *Från ett avlägset land* [From a distant country] (short). 1970: *Få mig att skratta* [Make me laugh]; *Ferai*. 1971: *Abortproblem i Frankrike* [Problems of abortion in France]; *Skilsmässoproblem i Italien* [Problems of divorce in Italy]; *Camargue—det förlorade landet* [Camargue—the lost country]. 1974: *Drakar, drömmar och en flicka från verkligheten* [Dragons, dreams, and a girl from the reality]; *En promenad i de gamlas land*, a.k.a. *Une promenade dans les pays de veillesse*. 1986: *Wien—skuggan av det förflutna* [Vienna—the shadow of the past]. 1989: *Anand—en pojke med två ansikten* [Anand—a boy with two faces]; *Kamelresan* [The camel trip]; *Santosh—ökenflickan* [Santosh—the desert girl]. 1991: *Viaggio nella mente della spettatore*. 1995: *Gott om pojkar—ont om män* [Plenty of boys—shortage of men]. 1997: *Flickor, kvinnor—och en och annan drake* [Girls, women—and a dragon or two].

Fiction

1972: *Den siste riddarvampyren* [The last knight vampire] (short); *Storstadsvampyrer* [Vampires of the big city] (short). 1975: *Fem dagar i Falköping* [Five days in Falköping]. 1976: *Långt borta och nära/Near and Far Away*. 1978: *Frihetens murar* [The walls of freedom]. 1981: *Svenska färger* [Swedish colors] (short). 1983: *Den tredje lyckan* [The third happiness] (TVMS). 1986: *På liv och död* [A life or death matter]. 1989: *Maskrosbarn* [Dandelion children] (TVMS); *Flickan vid stenbänken* [The girl by the stone bench] (TVMS). 1991: *Rosenholm* (TVMS).

BIBLIOGRAPHY

Ahrne, Marianne. *Hur jag blev författare*. Stockholm: Norstedts, 1996.

HANS ALFREDSON (Malmö, 28 June 1931–) and **Tage Danielsson** (Linköping, 5 Feb. 1928–13 Oct. 1985), actors, directors. They cannot be separated, although each occasionally made films on his own. More often, they worked as a team through their own company, AB Svenska Ord (Swedish Words, Inc.). Although their films belong to mainstream cinema, they established themselves as important figures in the overall history of Swedish entertainment. They also had similar backgrounds in the somewhat peculiar humor tradition of the university world. Hans Alfredson studied at Lund University, where he participated in a parody feature produced by the student union. Tage Danielsson studied at the University of Uppsala, where he was involved in student-produced farces. In the late 1950s he was employed as head of the entertainment department of the Swedish Broadcasting Company. There he met Hans Alfredson, and they began to collaborate, creating various entertainment programs for radio and television, including several very popular revues that were broadcast.

In 1964 they made their first feature film, *Svenska Bilder* [Swedish pictures], the title taken from a well-known collection of lyrics from the nineteenth century. The film was rather loosely constructed as a series of parody sketches reflecting the oddities of contemporary Sweden. It was followed by a black farce with a more distinct plot, *Att angöra en brygga* [Docking the boat], about a failed attempt to do precisely that. All their subsequent films, whether joint or separate ventures, proved very popular with audiences. Tage Danielsson's last effort, made without Alfredson's involvement, was the filming of Astrid Lindgren's mythic tale **Ronja Rövardotter* [Ronja, the robber's daughter].

The first films of Hasse & Tage—their joint signature—clearly evolved from their background in academic humor. In large measure they travesty and parody the cultural heritage, whether of so-called high or low origin. Gradually their films became more socially oriented. "Politically correct" may be a derogatory expression, but with considerable accuracy, they can be characterized in that fashion. **Äppelkriget* [The apple war] became a crusading vehicle for environmental causes. The film *Släpp fångarne loss . . .* [Release the prisoners . . .]—the title taken from a well-known poem—was a satiric attack on the prison welfare system and advocated a more humane treatment of criminals. Alfredson and Danielsson usually managed to avoid the pitfall of overexplicitness, but occasionally this flaw is apparent, most obviously in the feature Alfredson made on his own after the death of his partner, *Vargens tid* [Time of the wolf]. It was meant to be a counterattack on the growing xenophobia of Swedish society, but the result was a disaster. Critics lambasted the film, and the audience stayed home for once.

To speak of a personal style in the films of Alfredson and Danielsson is a misnomer. Whether made together or single-handedly, the films may be characterized as composites. As *Ronja* exemplifies, they tend to be heavily dependent on Swedish film tradition with regard to both content and style.

FILMOGRAPHY

Tage D. and Hans A. Together (TD as director, scriptwriter, and actor; HA as scriptwriter and actor)

1963: *Svenska öden* [Swedish destinies] (TVD). 1964: *Svenska Bilder* [Swedish pictures] 1965: *Att angöra en brygga* [Docking the boat]. 1967: *Odygdens belöning* [The virtue's reward] (episode in *Stimulantia*, TD not actor). 1968: *Lådan* [The box]; *I huvet på en gammal gubbe* [Inside an old man's head]. 1970: *Spader Madame!* [Spades madame!] (TVM). 1978: *Picassos äventyr/The Adventures of Picasso* (HA not actor). 1984: *Fröken Fleggmans mustasch* [Miss Fleggman's mustache] (TVD, HA codirector).

Hans Alfredson

Actor

1958: *Ett svårskött pastorat* [A difficult parish]. 1967: *Skrållan, Ruskprick och Knorr-hane* [Skrållan, Nasty, and Grumble]. 1968: *Skammen/The Shame*. 1970: *Grisjakten* [The hunt for pigs]; *På rymmen med Pippi Långstrump* [On the lam with Pippi Longstocking]; *Du sparbanken* [You savings bank] (short). 1971: *Utvandrarna/The Emigrants*; *Broster Broster* (TVMS). 1972: *Nybyggarna/The New Land*. 1973: *Elsa får piano* [Elsa gets a piano] (TVM, short). 1974: *Dunderklumpen* [Thundering Fatty] (voice); *Gangsterfilmen, a.k.a. En främling steg av tåget* [The gangster movie, a.k.a. A stranger got off the train]. 1975: *Långtradarchaufförens berättelser* [Tales of a lorry driver] (TVMS); *Släpp fångarne loss–det är vår!* [Release the prisoners, it is spring!]. 1977: *Den allvarsamma leken* [The serious game]. 1978: *Fusket* [The cheat] (TVM, short). 1979: *Sommarön* [The summer island] (TVM). 1981: *Sista budet* [The last commandment]; *Sopor* [Garbage]. 1989: *Resan till Melonia* [The voyage to Melonia] (voice). 1990: *Macken* [The gas station]. 1991: *Tre terminer* [Three termins] (TVM); *Den store badedag* [The big bathing day]; *Den goda viljan/The Best Intentions* (TVM).[1] 1992: *Kvällspressen* [The evening newspaper] (TVM). 1993: *Drömkåken* [The dream house]. 1996: *Jerusalem; Enskilda samtal/Private Confessions* (TVM). 1997: *Solskenspojkarna* [The sunshine boys] (TVD). 1998: *Längtans blåa blomma* [The blue flower of longing] (TVM).

Scriptwriter

1959: *Det svänger på slottet* [A high old time at the castle] (song lyrics); *Bara en kypare* [Only a waiter] (song lyrics). 1960: *Bröderna Karlsson* [The Karlsson brothers] (TVM); *16 år* [Sixteen years] (TVDS). 1964: *Nils Poppe Show* (TVD). 1981: *Tuppen* [The cock] (idea). 1996: *Cluedo. En mordgåta* [Cluedo. A murder mystery] (TVMS). 1998: *När kanusellerna sover* [When the carousels sleep] (TVMS) (also actor).

Director, Scriptwriter, Actor

1973: *Kvartetten som sprängdes* [The quartet that split up] (TVMS). 1975: *Ägget är löst/Egg, Egg, A Hard-boiled Story*. 1980: *Räkan från Maxim* [The shrimp from Maxim's] (TVD); *H.M.S. Pinafore* (TVD). 1982: *Den enfaldige mördaren* [The simple-minded murderer]. 1983: *P & B*. 1985: *Falsk som vatten* [False like water]. 1987: *Jim och piraterna Blom* [Jim and the Blom pirates]. 1988: *Vargens tid* [Time of the wolf]; *Familjen Schedblad* [The Schedblad family] (TVDS). 1996: *Älvakungen dyker upp* [The king of the elfs] (short).

Tage Danielsson

Actor

1967: *Skrållan, Ruskprick och Knorrhane* [Skrållan, Nasty, and Grumble]. 1975: *Ägget är löst/Egg, Egg, A Hard-boiled Story*. 1980: *Sista varningen* [The last warning] (docu.). 1983: *P & B*. 1985: *Falsk som vatten* [False like water].

Scriptwriter

1955: *Så tuktas kärleken* [The taming of love] (song lyrics). 1959: *Det svänger på slottet* [A high old time at the castle] (song lyrics); *Bara en kypare* [Only a waiter] (song lyrics). 1964: *Nils Poppe Show* (TVD). 1971: *En skön tanke* [A nice thought] (TVD).

Director, Scriptwriter

1969: *Herkules Jonssons storverk* [The great works of Herkules Jonsson] (TVMS, also actor). 1971: *Typer* [Characters] (TVM short, also actor). 1972: *Mannen som slutade röka/The Man Who Gave Up Smoking*. 1975: *Släpp fångarne loss–det är vår!* [Release the prisoners, it is spring!] (also actor); *Sagan om Karl Bertil Jonssons julafton* [The tale of Karl Bertil Jonsson's Christmas Eve] (short, also voice). 1981: *Sopor* [Garbage]; *Konsumentpropaganda* [Consumer's propaganda] (short). 1984: *Ronja Rövardotter* [Ronja, the robber's daughter].

BIBLIOGRAPHY

Anderson, Pat. "Tage Danielsson." *Films in Review* (Nov. 1980): 545–547.
Moberg, Karin. *Hans Alfredsons rörliga bilder*. Skanör: Discantus, 1998.
Roth-Lindberg, Örjan. "Den enfaldige mördaren: en närläsning" in Hedling (1998).
Tonström, Göran. *Hasse & Tage och deras Svenska ord: en krönika*. Västerås: ICA, 1994.

AWARDS

Hans Alfredson

GB 1975

GB 1982

GB 1985

Tage Danielsson

GB 1972

NOTE

1. Theatrically released in 1992 in an edited version.

BIBI [BERITH ELISABETH] ANDERSSON (Stockholm, 11 Nov. 1935–), actress. BA was educated at the Royal Dramatic Theater School and was discovered by *Ingmar Bergman as early as 1953, when she acted in the soap commercials he made during the producers' strike. Her first major part was in *Nils Poppe's *Dumbom* [Dummy]. While affiliated with the Malmö Municipal

Theater, she became part of Bergman's stock company, which led to a string of successful roles in his most famous films of the 1950s, such as *Smultronstället/Wild Strawberries* and *Det sjunde inseglet/The Seventh Seal*. Her part in *Nära livet/Brink of Life* earned her the best actress prize at the Cannes film festival, which eventually led to an international career as well. She continued her cooperation with Bergman in further films like *Persona, The Touch* and *En passion/The Passion of Anna*. In recent years, in addition to acting, she has been involved in politics, for instance, as a candidate for the independent "Sarajevo List" in the European Community, election in 1995.

Bibi Andersson represents the type of actor who depends on radiating sheer purity or innocence. This is especially true early in her career, when her most successful roles depend on this quality. One need only watch the aforementioned films by Bergman or her part in *Dumbom*, an antibureaucratic satire, where she was used as an effective contrast to the rigid civil servant played by Nils Poppe himself. As Andersson has grown older, she naturally has played more mature roles, often as a strong mother and wife, yet in many cases still with a streak of unconscious innocence.

FILMOGRAPHY[1]

1951: *Fröken Julie/Miss Julie*. 1952: *Ubåt 39* [Submarine 39]. 1953: *Vingslag i natten* [The beat of wings in the night]; *Dumbom* [Dummy]; *Bris* (short commercials). 1954: *Herr Arnes penningar* [Sir Arne's money]; *En natt på Glimmingehus* [A night at Glimmingehus]; *Din dagliga dryck* [Your daily drink] (short). 1955: *Flickan i regnet* [The girl in the rain]; *Sommarnattens leende/Smiles of a Summer Night*. 1956: *Egen ingång* [Private entry]; *Sista paret ut* [Last pair out]. 1957: *Det sjunde inseglet/The Seventh Seal*; *Herr Sleeman kommer* [Mr. Sleeman is coming] (TVD); *Sommarnöje sökes* [Wanted; summer residence]; *Smultronstället/Wild Strawberries*. 1958: *Nära livet/Brink of Life*; *Du är mitt äventyr* [You are my adventure]; *Rabies* (TVD); *Ansiktet/The Magician* [The face]. 1959: *Lilith* (TVD); *Den kära leken* [The beloved game]. 1960: *Bröllopsdagen* [The wedding day]; *Djävulens öga/The Devil's Eye*. 1961: *Karneval* [Carnival]; *Nasilje na trgu/Square of Violence*; *Det låter som ett hjärta* [It sounds like a heart] (TVD); *Lustgården* [The pleasure garden]; *Ljuva ungdomstid* [Ah, wilderness] (TVD). 1962: *Älskarinnan/The Swedish Mistress*; *Kort är sommaren/Short Is the Summer*. 1964: *För att inte tala om alla dessa kvinnor/All These Women*. 1965: *Juninatt* [June night]. 1966: *Ön* [The island]; *Syskonbädd/My Sister, My Love*; *Duel at Diablo*; *Persona/Persona*; *Scusi, lei è favorevole o contrario?* 1967: *Trettondagsafton* [The twelfth night] (TVD); *Le viol/Le viol*, a.k.a. *The Rape*. 1968: *Flickorna/The Girls*; *Svarta palmkronor* [Black palm trees]. 1969: *Tänk på et tal* [Think of a number]; *Storia di una donna/Story of a Woman*; *L'isola*; *En passion/The Passion of Anna*; *Fröken Julie* [Miss Julie] (TVM). 1970: *The Kremlin Letter*; *Beröringen/The Touch*. 1972: *Mannen från andra sidan*, a.k.a. *Tjelovek s drugo storoni* [The man from the other side]. 1973: *Makt på spel* [Power game] (TVD); *Scener ur ett äktenskap/Scenes from a Marriage* (TVM);[2] *Afskedens time* [The leaving hour]. 1974: *La rivale*. 1975: *Il pleut sur Santiago*. 1976: *Blondy*; *En dåres försvarstal* [A madman's defense] (TVM). 1977: *Vårbrytning* [Break-up in spring] (TVM); *I Never Promised You a Rose Garden*; *An Enemy of the People*; *A Look at Liv* (docu.). 1978: *L'amour en question*. 1979: *Quintet; Twee Vrouven/Two Women*; *The*

Concorde—Airport '79; Barnförbjudet [Prohibited for children]. 1980: *Marmeladuppro-ret* [The marmalade rebellion]. 1981: *Skapelsens krona* [The crown of creation] (TVD); *Antigone* (TVD); *Jag rodnar* [I blush]; *Linje Lusta* [A streetcar named desire] (TVD). 1982: *Fångarna i Altona* [The prisoners in Altona] (TVD). 1983: *Gråtvalsen* [The crying waltz] (TVM); *Berget på månens baksida* [The mountain on the back of the moon]; *Exposed; Savannen* [The savanna] (TVD); *Svarte fugler* [Black birds]. 1984: *Sista leken* [The last game]. 1985: *Wallenberg: A Hero's Story* (TVM); *Fridas flykt* [Frida's escape] (TVM). 1986: *Huomenna; Pobre mariposa*. 1987: *Svart gryning*, a.k.a. *Los dueños del silencio* [Black dawn]; *Babettes gæstebud/Babette's feast*. 1988: *Måsen* [The sea gull] (TVD); *Fordringsägare* [Creditors]. 1991: *Till Julia* [To Julia] (TVD). 1992: *Una esta-ción de Pasio*. 1993: *Blank päls och starka tassar* [Shiny fur and strong paws] (TVM). 1994: *Drømspel* [A dream play]; *Il Sogno della farfalla*; *Musikbussen* [The music bus] (short, voice). 1995: *Memento* (short, voice); *Lilly* (short). 1996: *I rollerna tre* [In three roles] (docu.). 1998: *Längtans blåa blomma* [The blue flower of longing] (TVM).

BIBLIOGRAPHY

Andersson, Bibi. *Ett ögonblick*. Stockholm: Norstedts, 1996. Autobiography.
"Bibi Andersson. Dialogue on Film." *American Film* (Mar. 1977):33–48.
Forslund, 1995.
Parra, D. "Eviter la nostalgie . . ." *La revue du cinéma*, no. 461 (June 1990):36–40.

AWARDS

Cannes 1958: Best Actress (*Brink of Life*)

Berlin 1963: Best Actress (*The Swedish Mistress*)

GB 1967

NOTES

1. Beware of confusion with a Spanish drag artist sometimes appearing in films as "Bibi Anderson."

2. Theatrically released in 1974 in an edited version.

HARRIET ANDERSSON (Stockholm, 14 Feb. 1932–), actress. With no formal training, she made her debut on the revue stage and continued acting at various theaters in Stockholm. She had a few small film parts before her breakthrough, also internationally, in *Bergman's Sommaren med Monika/Monica*, a.k.a. *Summer with Monica* (though she had actually appeared as an extra in one of his early films, as a screaming girl in *Hamnstad/Port of Call*). In the 1950s she became one of several actresses in the "Bergman company."

Monika is no doubt the role that has left the most indelible impression. The mixture of innocence and proletarian vulgarity embodied in one young girl established her as an icon of so-called Swedish sin. She clearly made a great impression on certain French New Wave directors like Jean Luc Godard, who wrote an enthusiastic piece on the film in *Arts*, and François Truffaut, whose young hero in *Les quatre cent coups/The 400 Blows* steals a still of her from a shop window. Harriet Andersson played similar young women in several other films in the 1950s, such as the servant girl in Bergman's *Sommarnattens leende/Smiles of a Summer Night*. As she has aged, of course, her roles have changed; for instance, she portrayed the sinister maid at the bishop's house in *Fanny and Alexander*. In recent years, she has worked mainly in television.

FILMOGRAPHY

1948: *Hamnstad/Port of Call*. 1949: *Skolka skolan* [Playing hookey]. 1950: *Motorkavaljerer* [The motor cavaliers]; *Frökens första barn* [Teacher's first child]; *Stjärnsmäll i frukostklubben* [Knockout at the breakfast club]; *Medan staden sover* [While the city sleeps]; *Två trappor över gården* [Across the yard and two flights up]; *Kyssen på kryssen* [The kiss on the cruise]; *Anderssonskans Kalle* [Mrs. Andersson's Kalle]. 1951: *Biffen och Bananen* [Beef and the banana]; *Puck heter jag* [My name is Puck]; *Dårskapens hus* [The nuthouse]; *Frånskild* [Divorced]; *Talande träden* [Talking trees] (short). 1952: *Sabotage* (NCF); *Ubåt 39* [Submarine 39]; *Trots* [Contempt]. 1953: *Sommaren med Monika/Monica: The Story of a Bad Girl*, a.k.a. *Summer with Monica*; *Gycklarnas afton/The Naked Night*, a.k.a. *Sawdust and Tinsel* [Eve of the jesters]. 1954: *En lektion i kärlek/A Lesson in Love*. 1955: *Kvinnodröm/Dreams* [Women's dreams]; *Hoppsan!* [Whoops!]; *Sommarnattens leende/Smiles of a Summer Night*. 1956: *Nattbarn* [Night child]; *Sista paret ut* [The last couple out]. 1957: *Synnöve Solbakken*. 1958: *Flottans överman* [More than a match for the navy]; *Kvinna i leopard* [The woman in the leopard-skin coat]. 1959: *Noc poslubna*, a.k.a. *Hääyö*, a.k.a. *En bröllopsnatt* [A wedding night]; *Brott i Paradiset* [Crime in paradise]. 1961: *Barbara; Såsom i en spegel/Through a Glass Darkly*. 1962: *Siska*. 1963: *Lyckodrömmen* [Dream of happiness]; *En söndag i september* [A Sunday in September]. 1964: *För att inte tala om alla dessa kvinnor/All These Women*; *Att älska/To Love*; *Älskande par/Loving Couples*. 1965: *För vänskaps skull* [For friendship's sake]; *Lianbron* [Bridge of vines]; *Här börjar äventyret* [The adventure starts here]. 1966: *Ormen* [The snake]. 1967: *The Deadly Affair; Han-hon* [She-her] (episode in *Stimulantia*); *Tvärbalk* [Crossbeam]; *Mennesker mødes og søm musik opstår i hjertet/People Meet and Sweet Music Fills the Heart*. 1968: *Jag älskar Du älskar* [I love you/love]; *Flickorna/The Girls*; *Pygmalion* (TVD); *Beslut i morgondagen* [Decision tomorrow] (TVD). 1969: *Hissen som gick ner i helvetet* [The elevator that went down to hell] (TVD); *Tigerlek* [Tiger game] (TVD); *Kampf um Rom*, a.k.a. *Batalia pentru Roma*. 1970: *Anna*. 1971: *I havsbandet* [By the open sea] (TVM). 1972: *Viskningar och rop/Cries and Whispers* (also coproducer). 1973: *Barnet* [The child] (TVM). 1975: *Den vita väggen/The White Wall; Monismanien 1995* [Monismania 1995]. 1977: *Hempas bar* [Hempa's bar]; *Semlons gröna dalar* [Semlon's green valleys] (TVM); *Min son, min son!* [My son, my son!] (TVD). 1979: *Linus eller Tegelhusets hemlighet* [Linus, or The secret of the brick house]. 1980: *Mary Lou* (TVD); *Mördare . . . mördare . . .* [Murderer . . . murderer . . .] (TVM). 1981: *La Sabina*. 1982: *Pappa är död* [Father is dead] (TVM); *Fanny och Alexander/Fanny and Alexander*.[1] 1983: *Raskenstam; Herr Sleeman kommer* [Mr. Sleeman is coming] (TVD); *Vid din sida* [By your side] (TVMS); *Satellit 84* (TVD). 1984: *AB Lif och Död eller Änkans skärf . . .* [Life and death, inc., or the widow's penny . . .] (TVM). 1985: *Änglaverket* [The angel office] (TVM). 1986: *De två saliga/The Blessed Ones* (TVM); *Gösta Berlings saga* [The legend of Gösta Berling] (TVMS). 1987: *Sommarkvällar på jorden* [Summer evenings on earth]; *Damorkestern* [The woman's orchestra] (TVD). 1989: *Kajsa Kavat* (short); *Himmel og Helvede* [Heaven and hell]. 1990: *Destination Nordsjön*

[Destination North Sea] (TVMS); *Blankt vapen* [Honorable weapon]. 1991: *Ålder okänd* [Age unknown] (TVM). 1993: *Høyere enn himmelen* [Higher than heaven]. 1995: *Majken* (TVM); *Öppna dörrar* [Open doors] (episode in *Love + Hate*). 1996: *A Woman Interrupted* (short); *I rollerna tre* [In three roles] (docu.). 1997: *Emma—åklagare* [Emma—district attorney] (TVMS); *Selma & Johanna—en roadmovie*. 1998: *Det sjunde skottet* [The seventh shot]; *Längtans blåa blomma* [The blue flower of longing] (TVM); *Pip-Larssons* [The Whistle-Larsson family] (TVMS). 1999: *Happy End*.

BIBLIOGRAPHY

Björkman, Stig. "Harriet Andersson—une creature de cinema." *Chaplin* 248, no. 5 (1993):50–57. Interview.
Forslund, 1995.

AWARDS

Venezia 1964: Best Actress (*To Love*)

GB 1973

NOTE

1. Longer version for television in 1984, with limited cinema release in 1983.

ROY ANDERSSON (Göteborg, 31 March 1943–), director. After university study he was educated at the Film School of the Swedish Film Institute in the late 1960s. He served as assistant to *Bo Widerberg at the same time. His examination film brought general attention to this gifted filmmaker, and his first feature, *En kärlekshistoria* [A love story], was unanimously hailed as a true masterpiece; it also did well at the box office. But when Andersson began work on his second venture, he encountered difficulties. Not only did his perfectionism cause the project to run well over budget, but postproduction dragged on for a long time. When the film *Giliap* was finally premiered, critics were cool, although not everyone shared their negative attitude, and there was a heated newspaper debate. This did not alter the fact that the overly expensive film never stood a chance of recovering costs, and Andersson was virtually frozen out of the film industry. Instead, he has occupied himself primarily as a producer and director of short commercials. He made an educational short about AIDS, *Någonting har hänt* [Something has happened], for the Swedish Board of Health that was withdrawn because it was perceived as too controversial.

Roy Andersson is unusual in contemporary Swedish film because his fame rests only on two features and a handful of shorts, although all Swedish moviegoers have seen his charming commercials for chocolate, insurance policies, and other goods. (Such shorts routinely precede the feature presentation in Swedish movie theaters.) As film critic Maaret Koskinen has pointed out: "Andersson's contributions to this genre can be defined as miniature art films in their own right: absurdist contemplations on modern life in a brave new world that at times bears an uncanny resemblance to contemporary Sweden." One key word when describing him is *integrity*. His films are totally uncompromising. They generally give a dark view of contemporary Swedish society, where human beings suffer from alienation. One can construe his films as alluding to the downfall of the whole concept of the "people's home," as implying that this goal remained a myth that was never fulfilled. Andersson expresses this stance in a very distinctive, personal manner; the gloominess is everywhere, in the settings and the acting style. He nevertheless defends core values against the threat of an impersonal, technorational society that robs individuals of their essential humanity.

FILMOGRAPHY

Director, Scriptwriter

1967: *Besöka sin son* [A visit to a son] (short). 1968: *Hämta sin cykel* [To fetch one's bike] (short); *Lördagen den 5.10* [Saturday 5.10] (short); *Den vita sporten* [The white game] (docu., as member of collective "Groupe 13"). 1970: *En kärlekshistoria* [A love story]. 1975: *Giliap*. 1980: *Så fruktansvärt onödigt* [How terribly needless] (short). 1985: *Varför skall vi bry oss om varandra?* [Why should we care about each other?] (short). 1987: *Någonting har hänt* [Something has happened] (short). 1988: *Kan vi bry oss om varandra* [Can we care about each other] (short). 1991: *Härlig är jorden* [Lovely is the earth] (short). 1999: *Sånger från andra våningen* [Songs from the second floor] (under production).

BIBLIOGRAPHY

Andersson, Roy. "Vår tids rädsla för allvar." *Filmkonst*, no. 33 (1995). Special issue. Björkman, 1977.
Dahlén, Peter, Michael Forsman, and Klas Viklund. "Folkhemsdrömmen som sprack." *Filmhäftet*, nos. 69–70 (1990):33–44.

PERNILLA AUGUST (Stockholm, 13 Feb. 1958–), actress. Pernilla August has appeared as an actress under three different names: her maiden name, Pernilla Wallgren; Pernilla Östergren, when she was married to author Klas Östergren; and from 1992, Pernilla August, when she married Danish film director Bille August. She began acting in the children's theater group Vår Teater when she was only eight years old. In grammar school she was often absent without permission, preferring to practice acting instead. At fifteen she had her first film role as a young, innocent girl in *Roy Andersson's *Giliap*. After grammar school she worked for a while as an attendant at a home for retarded children before deciding to try her luck at the state school of stage art. She was accepted after her second trial and studied there from 1979 until 1982. While a student she was offered a part as the limping maid in *Bergman's *Fanny och Alexander/Fanny and Alexander*, which became her breakthrough. She has acted the role of Bergman's mother on three occasions, in *Den goda viljan/The Best Intentions*, *Enskilda samtal/Private Confessions*, and *Larmar och gör sig till* [Fussing and fuming].

It is not difficult to see why she has been described as a Bergman favorite. She personifies Bergman's ideal of the perfect woman. She has a strong screen presence as a down-to-earth woman, rather more sensual than sexy. She embodies the virtues of motherhood, life, and fertility. She is the type of woman who expresses more through feelings and sensitivity than through being intellectual.

FILMOGRAPHY

1975: *Giliap*. 1979: *Linus eller Tegelhusets hemlighet* [Linus, or The secret of the brick house]. 1981: *Tuppen* [The cock]. 1982: *Fanny och Alexander/Fanny and Alexander*.[1] 1983: *Herr Sleeman kommer* [Mr. Sleeman is coming] (TVD); *Hej du himlen!* [Hello heaven!] (TVD). 1984: *Hur ska det gå för Pettersson?* [What will become of Pettersson?] (TVDS); *Blomsterbudet* [The flower messenger] (short). 1985: *Den tragiska historien om Hamlet—prins av Danmark* [The tragic story of Hamlet-prince of Denmark] (TVM). 1986: *Ormens väg på hälleberget/The Serpent's Way*. 1987: *Ägget* [The egg] (short). 1989: *Den döende dandyn* [The dying dandy] (TVM); *Vildanden* [The wild duck] (TVD); *7 maj 1945* (short). 1990: *Saras ande* [Sara's spirit] (short). 1991: *Den goda viljan/The Best Intentions* (TVMS).[2] 1992: *Young Indiana Jones Chronicles* (one episode) (TVM). 1995: *En nämndemans död* [Death of a juror] (TVMS). 1996: *Jerusalem; Enskilda samtal/Private Confessions* (TVM). 1997: *Persons parfymeri* [Person's perfumerie] (TVDS); *Larmar och gör sig till* [Fussing and fuming] (TVM); *Den siste yankeen* [The last Yankee] (TVD). 1998: *Kök* [Kitchen] (short); *Glasblåsarns barn* [The glassblower's children]; *Sista kontraktet* [The last contract]; 1999: *Konsulten och sveket* [The advisor and the treason] (TVM); *Star Wars: First Episode—The Phantom Menace*; *Där regnbågen slutar* [Where the rainbow ends].

BIBLIOGRAPHY

Forslund, 1995.

AWARDS

Cannes 1992: Best Actress (*The Best Intentions*)
GB 1992

NOTES

1. Longer version for television in 1984, with limited cinema release in 1983.
2. Theatrically released in 1992 in an edited version.

SCHAMYL BAUMAN (Vimmerby, 4 Dec. 1893–28 Feb. 1966), director, producer. Schamyl Bauman began his directing career by pure accident. He was one of the founders of the company Europa Film (1930), whose first film venture, a simple military farce called *Kärlek och landstorm* [Love and the militia], ran into trouble, partly for technical reasons. The original director was fired, and Bauman had to take over. He acquired a taste for the work and continued to direct films for Europa Film until the end of the 1930s, when he broke with the company and eventually became his own producer. In 1938 he teamed with Anders Sandrew, then owner of an important chains of cinemas, and formed the distribution company AB Sandrew Bauman Film, which was to be of great importance for Swedish film production in the following decades.

It has been claimed that of Bauman's total production, only one film lost money. He worked mainly in the genre of comedy, with seemingly light and unsophisticated films. This impression, however, is somewhat deceptive. His first films in the 1930s may have been simple in terms of plot, but even then he had developed a feeling for atmosphere and style. A film like *Flickorna från Gamla Sta'n/Flickorna Fran Gamla Stan* [The girls from Old Town], which was a huge success, reminds one of contemporary films by René Clair. Bauman's best films came toward the end of that decade when he persuaded *Signe Hasso to begin making films again after her debut in 1933 in the disastrous *Tystnadens hus* [House of silence]. His first film with Hasso, *Häxnatten* [Witches' night] got rather mixed reviews, but when he teamed her with Sture Lagerwall in *Karriär* [Career], one of the most interesting films of the entire decade, the success was stunning. He continued with several more films using the same leading couple, most notably *Vi två/Vi Tvaa* [The two of us], where the subject matter alludes to the much-debated "nativity crisis." After Hasso's departure for Hollywood, Bauman continued his successful career for another two decades, but he never regained the cinematic touch he achieved in his films with Hasso, although the later films are usually interesting enough. In the 1940s he turned primarily to the very popular rural genre with films set in the past, including one about his native region based on the short stories of Albert Engström, *I mörkaste Småland* [In darkest Småland]. In the 1950s he made another string of popular comedies with female comedy star Sickan Carlsson.

Film historian and former producer Rune Waldekranz has related that the young *Ingmar Bergman actually was a great admirer of Schamyl Bauman. This is not so odd as it may seem. Bauman's habit of using the same small team of coworkers and actors is strongly reminiscent of Bergman's own working method. But there are other similarities between the two, both stylistically and thematically. Bauman's light-handed direction of his actors and his very frequent use of close-up establishes an intimate style that may resemble that of a "typical" Bergman film. A film like *Vi två* also anticipates early Bergman films in that it deals with existential questions (and can also be regarded as a 1930s version of *Scener ur ett äktenskap/Scenes from a Marriage*).

FILMOGRAPHY

Scriptwriter

1932: *Söderkåkar/Soederkaakar* [Southsiders]. 1933: *Fridolf i lejonkulan* [Fridolf in the lion's den]. 1938: *Vi som går scenvägen* [We who use the stage door].

Director (From 1939, Also Producer)

1931: *Kärlek och landstorm* [Love and the militia] (also script, codir. John Lindlöf). 1933: *Lördagskvällar/Loerdagskvaellar* [Saturday evenings]; *Hemliga Svensson* [Secret

Svensson] (also script). 1934: *Flickorna från Gamla Sta'n/Flickorna Fran Gamla Stan* [The girls from Old Town] (also script); *Kvinnorna kring Larsson/Kvinnorna Kring Larsson* [The women around Larsson]. 1935: *Larsson i andra giftet/Larsson I Andra Giftet* [Second-marriage Larsson]. 1936: *Raggen—det är jag det/Raggen Det Aer Jag Det* [Raggen—that's me]; *Familjen som var en karusell/Familjen Som Var En Karusel* [The family that was a carousel] (also script). 1937: *Än leva de gamla gudar/Old Gods Still Live* (also script, codir. Gideon Wahlberg); *Häxnatten* [Witches' night]; *Skicka hem nr. 7/Skicka Hem Nr. 7* [Send home no. 7] (also script, codir. Gideon Wahlberg). 1938: *Kamrater i vapenrocken* [Comrades in uniform] (also script); *Karriär* [Career]. 1939: *Efterlyst* [Wanted] (also dialogue); *Vi två/Vi Tvaa* [The two of us]; *I dag börjar livet* [Life begins today] (also script); *Hennes lilla majestät/Hennes Lilla Majestat* [Her little majesty]. 1940: *Hjältar i gult och blått* [Heroes in yellow and blue] (also script); *Än en gång Gösta Ekman* [Gösta Ekman once again];[1] *Karl för sin hatt* [A real man]; *Vi tre* [The three of us]; *Swing it, magistern!* [Swing it, teacher!] (also script). 1941: *Fröken Kyrkråtta* [Miss churchmouse]; *Spökreportern* [The ghost reporter]; *Magistrarna på sommarlov* [The teachers on vacation]; *Vi hemslavinnor* [We house slaves] (also script). 1942: *Rospiggar* [Roslagers]. 1943: *I mörkaste Småland* [In darkest Småland]. 1944: *Prins Gustaf* [Prince Gustaf]. 1945: *I Roslagens famn* [In Roslag's embrace]; *Flickorna i Småland* [The girls in Småland] (also script). 1946: *Saltstänk och krutgubbar* [Salt spray and old salts]; *Hotell Kåkbrinken* [Kåkbrinken hotel] (also script). 1947: *Maj på Malö* [Maj of Malö]. 1948: *Robinson i Roslagen* [Robinson in Roslagen] (also script). 1949: *Skolka skolan* [Playing hookey]. 1950: *Min syster och jag* [My sister and I]; *Frökens första barn* [Teacher's first child]. 1951: *Puck heter jag* [My name is Puck] (also script). 1952: *En fästman i taget* [One fiancé at a time]; *Klasskamrater* [Class comrades] (also script). 1954: *Dans på rosor* [Dance on roses] (also script). 1955: *Älskling på vågen* [Darling of mine] (also script). 1957: *Mamma tar semester* [Mother takes a vacation] (also script).

BIBLIOGRAPHY

Waldekranz, Rune. "En svensk filmstil." *Ergo*, no. 5 (1939):76–77.

NOTE

1. The shooting of the film (working title: *Far och son* [Father and son]) was interrupted by *Gösta Ekman's [Sr.] death in 1938. The unfinished film was released in 1940.

JOHAN BERGENSTRÅHLE (Stockholm, 15 July 1935–23 Aug. 1995), director. B was among the most famous stage directors in Sweden from the 1960s on. After studying psychology at the university, he first wanted to be an actor, but overwhelming stage fright made him turn to directing instead. After 1965 he was affiliated mainly with the Stockholm Municipal Theater. A specialist on modern drama, especially Bertolt Brecht, he drew on the Brechtian tradition (with "Verfremdung" effects and so on) in his films. He was not primarily an ideologue, however; his goal was to create atmosphere. Shakespeare served as an ideal when he tried to make art that appealed to the audience in a more immediate way. In *Made in Sweden* he depicted the imbalance of power between the rich, developed West, and the underdeveloped Third World. The film deals mainly with the unscrupulous nature of capitalism and big business, which will do anything that serves their purposes. Bergenstråhle told the story partly through symbols, thus confusing many spectators, and he was critized for not making the message explicit enough. His next film was *Baltutlämningen* [The extradition of the Balts], about a historic event that took place just after World War II when the Swedish government extradited a group of Baltic prisoners of war to the Soviet Union, a decision that caused much debate at the time. Bergenstråhle's film was based on a documentary novel by Per Olov Enquist. Bergenstråhle directed in a semidocumentary style designed to force the spectators to reflect on the content. *Jag heter Stelios/Foreigners*, about a group of Greek immigrants in Stockholm, is one of the rare contemporary Swedish films that depicts the lives of the "new Swedes" in a more profound way. It is a film about their dreams and hopes but also their frustrations in a foreign culture that is very unlike their own.

One of Bergenstråhle's greatest achievements was the television series about August Strindberg he made in cooperation with *Kjell Grede. Whereas Grede's episodes tended, in his customary manner, to be vague and symbolic, Bergenstråhle's were more straightforward and realistic, which was perhaps the happier solution. One of his last films for theatrical release, *Slumrande toner* [Dormant tones], was also among his finest and quite unlike previous efforts. It was a sensitive and poetic tale about a third-rate traveling theater company in the Swedish-speaking parts of the Finnish countryside, but many Fenno-Swedes were annoyed by the not-so-flattering view of their culture as insular and narrowminded. Much of Bergenstråhle's television work also deserves a place among the classics of Swedish TV drama. He was for a time married to actress Marie-Louise de Geer-Bergenstråhle (now Marie-Louise Ekman) and is the father of TV director Joachim Bergenstråhle.

FILMOGRAPHY

1965: *Nattcafé* [Night café] (TVD); *Herr Dardanell och hans upptåg på landet* [Mr. Dardanell and his pranks in the countryside] (TVD); *Villa med staket* [House with a fence] (TVD). 1966: *Hotet* [The threat] (TVD); *Skuggan av Mart* [Shadow of Mart] (TVD); *I afton bönemöte* [Prayer meeting tonight] (TVD). 1967: *Onkel Vanja* [Uncle Vanya] (TVD); *Katarina* (TVM, also script). 1969: *Made in Sweden* (also script). 1970: *Baltutlämningen* [The extradition of the Balts] (also script). 1972: *Spöksonaten* [Ghost sonata] (TVD); *Jag heter Stelios/Foreigners* [My name is Stelios] (also script). 1974: *Gustav III* (TVD). 1976: *Hallo Baby* (also script). 1978: *Slumrande toner* [Dormant tones] (also script). 1979: *Resan till San Michele* [The voyage to San Michele] (TVD). 1980: *Ett drömspel* [A dream play] (TVD). 1981: *Tamara—la donna d'oro* [Tamara—the woman of gold] (short, actor only); *Fru Carrars gevär* [Mrs. Carrar's rifles] (TVD). 1982: *Den goda människan i Sezuan* [The good woman of Sezuan] (TVM).[1] 1983: *Emma!—drömmen om friheten* [Emma!—the dream of freedom] (TVM, actor only).

1985: *August Strindberg ett live* [August Strindberg, a life] (TVMS, codirector Kjell Grede). 1991: *Mitt barn är mitt* [My child is mine] (TVD). 1994: *Bröllopsfotografen* [The wedding photographer] (also script).

BIBLIOGRAPHY

Björkman, 1977.
Sjögren, Olle. "Made in Sweden." *Svensk filmografi* 6 (1977):443–447.

AWARDS

Berlin 1969: Silver Bear (*Made in Sweden*)

Venezia 1972: Best Film (*Foreigners*)

GB 1973

NOTE

1. Filmed in 1972.

THOMMY BERGGREN (Mölndal, 12 Aug. 1937–), actor. As a teenager he was a sailor for a couple of years and then worked in a factory before being accepted as a student by the Göteborg Municipal Theater School. After graduation, he performed in his hometown until 1963, when he was engaged by the Royal Dramatic Theater in Stockholm. By then he had already begun his film career and soon became acquainted with director *Bo Widerberg, who made him his special star. His role in *Elvira Madigan* brought him international fame, though he has seldom accepted offers from abroad. Since then he has worked mainly on the stage and also as a teacher at the state school of stage art.

Berggren's film credits are not extensive, but on the other hand, they are quite impressive when one considers the significance of the roles. Bo Widerberg has characterized his magic as "screen presence"—that is, he can convey many layers of meaning just by appearing in front of the camera. Berggren has also stated that he favors a more immediate style of acting and that he is drawn toward portraying all kinds of social outcasts, a preference he attributes to his upbringing in a proletarian milieu and to his socialist convictions. In his most memorable roles he is a dreamer, like the young man from a working-class background in *Kvarteret Korpen/Raven's End* who wants to break away and become an author, the waiter in *Roy Andersson's *Giliap*, or Lieutenant Sparre in *Elvira Madigan* who elopes with a circus girl and then commits suicide with her. When Swedish television produced a remake of the old classic *Gösta Berlings saga* [The legend of Gösta Berling], Thommy Berggren was the obvious choice for the part of the outcast minister. Another extraordinary personality he portrayed was August Strindberg, in the big, lavish TV production directed by *Johan Bergenstråhle and *Kjell Grede. A striking contrast was the role of the weak father in *Ingrid Thulin's autobiographical *Brusten himmel/Broken Sky*. Berggren is the kind of actor who can turn down a $2.2 million offer just because he thinks the part is unworthy, and he has often publicly criticized the Swedish film industry for avoiding serious subject matter.

FILMOGRAPHY

1961: *Pärlemor* [Mother of pearl]. 1962: *Generalskan* [The general's wife] (TVD). 1963: *Barnvagnen* [The pram]; *En söndag i september* [A sunday in September]; *Kvarteret Korpen/Raven's End*. 1965: *Kärlek 65* [Love 65]. 1966: *Heja Roland* [Come on, Roland]. 1967: *Elvira Madigan/Elvira Madigan*. 1968: *Svarta palmkronor* [Black palm trees]. 1969: *The Adventurers*; *Fröken Julie* [Miss Julie] (TVM). 1971: *Joe Hill/Joe Hill*. 1972: *Fru Carrars gevär* [Mrs. Carrar's rifles] (TVD). 1975: *Giliap*. 1976: *Livet en dröm* [Life a dream] (TVD). 1979: *Kristoffers hus* [Kristoffer's house] (also script with *Vilgot Sjöman and *Lars Lennart Forsberg); Fruen tra havet [The women from the sea] (TVM). 1980: *Räkan från Maxim* [The shrimp from Maxim's] (TVD). 1982: *Brusten himmel/Broken Sky*. 1983: *Berget på månens baksida* [The mountain on the back of the moon]. 1985: *August Strindberg ett liv* [August Strindberg, a life]. 1986: *Gösta Berlings saga* [The legend of Gösta Berling] (TVMS); *La sposa americana/The American fiancée*. 1987: *Hjärtat* [The heart] (TVM). 1988: *En far* [A father] (TVD). 1992: *Söndagsbarn/Sunday's Child*; *Maskeraden* [The masquerade] (TVM). 1994: *Onkel Vanja* [Uncle Vanya] (TVD). 1995: *Stora och små män* [Big and small men]. 1998: *Liv till varje pris* [Life at every cost] (docu.); *Glasblåsarns barn* [The glassblower's children]. 1999: *Entreprenörer i kärlek* [Contractors in love] (TVM).

BIBLIOGRAPHY

Jordahl, Anneli, and Håkan Lagher. "Thommy Berggren. Den intellektuella tystnaden." *Chaplin* 241 (Sept.–Oct. 1992):49–57.

AWARDS

GB 1966

GB 1999

INGMAR BERGMAN (Uppsala, 14 July 1918–), director. Bergman began in his youth as a stage director for amateurs, which led to being hired as a scriptwriter by Svensk Filmindustri (SF) in 1943. His script to *Hets/Torment*, directed by *Alf Sjöberg in 1944, introduced him to a wide audience. Bergman was appointed manager of the Municipal Theatre of Helsingborg that same year, and SF allowed him to direct his first feature in 1945. That film, *Kris* [Crisis], received rather mixed reviews and was a flop with the audience. Bergman's film career might have ended there if he had not been given another chance by producer *Lorens Marmstedt, who let Bergman direct a couple of films for Sveriges Folkbiografer (a company associated with the Swedish workers' movement) and one for Marmstedt's own company, Terraproduktion. These films, at least the one for Terra, were better received by the Swedish audience, and in 1948, SF once again hired Bergman to direct (meanwhile, veteran SF director *Gustaf Molander had directed two Bergman scripts, *Kvinna utan ansikte* [Woman without a face] and *Eva*). This was the beginning of a singularly successful film career, and from the mid-1950s, Bergman gradually became an

international celebrity. His breakthrough in U.S. intellectual circles came later
in the decade. During his entire career he has alternated between theatrical and
film work. In 1976 he ran afoul of the Swedish Internal Revenue Service and
chose to leave Sweden for Germany, although he later was acquitted of charges
of tax evasion and eventually returned to his native country to make his last
theatrical feature, the partly autobiographical *Fanny och Alexander/Fanny and
Alexander*. Subsequently he has turned out several additional scripts about his
parents and family, directed by others, including his own son Daniel. In the last
decade he has continued directing for the stage and occasionally for television.

Bergman is occasionally hailed as the greatest film director of all time, and
it is not difficult to see why. There is something for everyone in his work. After
the first experimental years during which his personal themes evolved, he soon
achieved a technical mastery of the medium. From the very beginning he was
convinced that sophisticated technical knowledge was necessary to achieve full
artistic control. The custom of the Swedish film industry (determined by economic factors) to shoot with minimal film teams contributed to his development
and may be one reason he has turned down most offers from abroad. Early
Swedish critics were impressed by his technical mastery and his hand with
actors, whereas they were more divided about the content of his films. Many
were repelled by Bergman's obsession with the dark side of life and society,
with whores, pimps, suicide, and so on.

It is a mistake to regard Bergman as an "intellectual" director. On the contrary, his method is an intuitive one, which explains the rather eclectic nature
of his films, both formally and thematically. Bergman has always been an almost
obsessive film buff who has watched thousands of films, and influences from
other directors and styles are readily apparent, ranging from classical Swedish
films to French works of the period between the wars to American film noir,
all transformed into a distinctive, personal style. One might even mention similarities to the intimate, sensitive, actor-oriented style of a Swedish director of
the 1930s such as *Schamyl Bauman. Neither should the influence of his producer in the early years, Lorens Marmstedt, be overlooked nor the more folksy,
popular dramatic art of Sweden. Thematically one finds the same kind of mixing
and borrowing. In Bergman's first films there are strong influences from the
existentialist movement that dominated postwar Europe. Although he has denied
ever having read anything by writers like Sartre, from the very beginning Bergman's films have dealt with existential questions about the meaning of life in
an "Entzauberte Welt," to borrow a phrase from Max Weber, a universe that
apparently is lacking meaning, where God is absent. It is a world where human
beings, to quote Sartre, are "doomed to freedom." From these fundamental pre-
suppositions, Bergman has gradually developed a thematic universe to which he
constantly returns to refine these basic questions and answers. Human beings
must seek their own salvation, and Bergman finds it in art, in community with
others, in nature (a common theme in Scandinavian film), and in life itself. The
birth of a new life is the great moment in many of Bergman's films, from *Eva*

to *Fanny och Alexander*. Other important thematic clusters concern the role of the artist in contemporary society and reflections on the art of film itself (cf. *Persona*).

FILMOGRAPHY

Director, Scriptwriter[1]

1946: *Kris* [Crisis]; *Det regnar på vår kärlek* [It rains on our love]. 1947: *Skepp till India land/Frustration* [Ship to Indialand]. 1948: *Musik i mörker/Night Is My Future*, a.k.a. *Music in Darkness* (director only); *Hamnstad/Port of Call*. 1949: **Fängelse/The Devil's Wanton*, a.k.a. *Prison*; *Törst/Three Strange Loves* [Thirst]. 1950: *Till glädje/To Joy*; *Sånt händer inte här* [This doesn't happen here] (director only). 1951–1953: *Bris* (nine one-minute soap commercials); *Sommarlek/Illicit Interlude* [Summer play]. 1952: *Kvinnors väntan/Secrets of Women* [Women's waiting]. 1953: *Sommaren med Monika/Monica: The Story of a Bad Girl*, a.k.a. *Summer with Monica*; *Gycklarnas afton/The Naked Night*, a.k.a. *Sawdust and Tinsel* [Eve of the jesters]. 1954: *En lektion i kärlek/A Lesson in Love*. 1955: *Kvinnodröm/Dreams* [Women's dream]; *Sommarnattens leende/Smiles of a Summer Night*. 1957: *Det sjunde inseglet/The Seventh Seal*; *Herr Sleeman kommer* [Mr. Sleeman is coming] (TVD, director only); **Smultronstället/Wild Strawberries*; *Venetianskan* [The Venetian woman] (TVD, director only). 1958: *Nära livet/Brink of Life*; *Rabies* (TVD, director only); *Ansiktet/The Magician* [The face]. 1960: *Jungfrukällan/The Virgin Spring* (director only); *Oväder* [Storm] (TVD, director only); *Djävulens öga/The Devil's Eye*. 1961: *Såsom i en spegel/Through a Glass Darkly*. 1963: *Nattvardsgästerna/Winter Light* [The communicants]; *Ett drömspel* [A dream play] (TVD, director only); *Tystnaden/The Silence*. 1964: *För att inte tala om alla dessa kvinnor/All These Women*. 1966: *Persona/Persona*. 1967: *Daniel* (episode in *Stimulantia*, also photo). 1968: *Vargtimmen/Hour of the Wolf*; *Skammen/Shame*. 1969: *Riten/The Ritual* (TVM); *En passion/The Passion of Anna*. 1970: *Fårödokument* (docu.). 1971: *Beröringen/The Touch* (also producer). 1972: *Viskningar och rop/Cries and Whispers*. 1973: *Scener ur ett äktenskap/Scenes from a Marriage* (TVM).[2] 1975: *Trollflöjten/The Magic Flute* (TVM, director only).[3] 1976: *Ansikte mot ansikte/Face to Face* (TVM).[4] 1977: *Das Schlangenei/The Serpent's Egg*. 1978: *Herbstsonate*, a.k.a. *Höstsonaten/Autumn Sonata*. 1979: *Fårödokument 2/Fårö 79* (docu.). 1980: *Aus dem Leben der Marionetten/From the Life of the Marionettes*. 1982: *Fanny och Alexander/Fanny and Alexander*.[5] 1983: *Hustruskolan* [School for wives] (TVD, director only). 1984: *Efter repetitionen/After the Rehearsal* (TVM). 1985: *Karins ansikte* [Karin's face] (docu., short). 1986: *De två saliga/The Blessed Ones* (TVM, director only). 1992: *Markisinnan de Sade* [The Marquise de Sade] (TVD, director only). 1993: *Backanterna* [The Bacchantae] (TVD, director only). 1995: *Sista skriket* [The last scream] (TVD). 1996: *Harald & Harald* (TVD, short). 1997: *Larmar och gör sig till* [Fussing and fuming] (TVM).

Filmscripts

1944: *Hets/Torment*. 1947: *Kvinna utan ansikte* [Woman without a face]. 1948: *Eva*. 1950: *Medan staden sover* [While the city sleeps] (idea by IB). 1951: *Frånskild* [Divorced]. 1956: *Sista paret ut* [Last couple out]. 1961: *Lustgården* [The pleasure garden] (with *Erland Josephson as "Buntel Ericsson"). 1963: *Trämålning* [Wood painting] (TVD). 1970: *Reservatet* [The sanctuary] (TVD). 1970 and 1973: *The Lie* (TVM British resp. American versions of the latter). 1991: *Den goda viljan/The Best Intentions* (TVM).[6]

1994: *Söndagsbarn/Sunday's Children*. 1996: *Enskilda samtal/Private Confessions* (TVM). Finished script, *Trolösa* [Unfaithful], that will be directed by Liv Ullmann, is planned for release in 2000.

BIBLIOGRAPHY

Bergman, Ingmar. *Images. My Life in Film*. New York: Arcade Publishing, 1994.
Bergman, Ingmar. *The Magic Lantern*. New York: Viking, 1988.
Björkman, Stig, Torsten Manns, and Jonas Sima. *Bergman on Bergman*. New York: Simon and Schuster, 1973.
Donner, Jörn: *The Films of Ingmar Bergman*. New York: Dover, 1972.
Koskinen, Maaret. *Spel och speglingar*. Stockholm: Stockholms Universitet, 1995.
Livingston, Paisley. *Ingmar Bergman and the Rituals of Art*. Ithaca, NY: Cornell University Press, 1982.
Steene, Birgitta. *Ingmar Bergman. A Guide to References and Resources*. Boston: G. K. Hall, 1987. Gives an exhaustive overview of the very extensive literature about Bergman through the late 1980s (more than fifty books to date), awards and so on. Updated version, *Ingmar Bergman: A Reference Guide*, Amsterdam: Amsterdam University Press/Ann Arbor: University of Michigan Press (forthcoming).
Wood, Robin. *Ingmar Bergman*. New York: Praeger, 1969.

AWARDS

Cannes 1956: Special Prize of the Jury (*Smiles of a Summer Night*)

Cannes 1957: Special Prize of the Jury (*The Seventh Seal*)

Cannes 1958: Best Director (*Brink of Life*)

AA 1961: Best Foreign Film (*The Virgin Spring*)

AA 1962: Best Foreign Film (*Through a Glass Darkly*)

GB 1964

AAN 1974: Best Film, Director, Script (*Cries and Whispers*)

AAN 1977: Best Film (*Face to Face*)

AAN 1979: Best Script (*Autumn Sonata*)

GB 1983

GB 1992

Cannes 1997: Honor Golden Palm

NOTES

1. Bergman has often performed cameo performances in his own films—not noted here.
2. Theatrically released in 1974 in an edited version.
3. Later theatrically released.
4. Theatrically released abroad in an edited version.
5. Longer version for television in 1984, with limited cinema release in 1983.
6. Theatrically released in 1992 in an edited version.

INGRID BERGMAN (Stockholm, 29 Aug. 1916–30 Aug. 1982), actress. Orphaned young, she was determined to be an actress and was accepted by the Royal Dramatic Theater School in 1934, only to leave after one year when she was offered a contract by Svensk Filmindustri. In the following years, she made ten films for the company, six directed by *Gustaf Molander, who had discovered her when she was still a pupil at the theater school. Before that she had actually appeared as an extra in *Landskamp* [International match], where she can be seen standing in a line of girls looking for employment. Within short order, when she starred in *Valborgsmässoafton/Walpurgis Night*, she was noticed by the reviewer in *Variety*. Her performance in Molander's *Intermezzo* attracted the attention of David O. Selznick, who produced an American remake with her in 1939. She returned temporarily to Sweden the following year to star in *Per Lindberg's *Juninatten/A Night in June* before definitively deciding to aim for an international career. From the very beginning she was the reviewers' favorite.

Ingrid Bergman may be characterized as resolute, unafraid, and open-minded, to which may be added a striking, unusual screen presence and charisma. These qualities were not just superficial but were part of her nature, which may explain why she was always willing to reach out and try new things, regardless of the consequences. At the height of her career, she chose to work with the Italian director Roberto Rossellini, with whom she made several films quite different from her previous glamorous vehicles. She even dared leave her marriage and live openly with Rossellini, which caused much anger in the United States, where she was publicly condemned in various forums, including the Senate. But she managed to continue despite this and other setbacks. In her last roles she was already marked by cancer, but her professionalism gave her the strength to finish the assignments. Ingrid Bergman is the mother of actress Isabella Rossellini.

FILMOGRAPHY

1932: *Landskamp* [International match]. 1935: *Bränningar/The Surf*; *Munkbrogreven/The Count of Monk's Bridge*; *Swedenhielms/Swedenhielms*; *Valborgsmässoafton/Walpurgis Night*. 1936: *På Solsidan/On the Sunnyside*; *Intermezzo/Intermezzo*. 1938: *Dollar/Dollar*; *Die Vier Gesellen*; *En kvinnas ansikte/A Woman's Face*. 1939: *En enda natt/Only One Night*; *Intermezzo—A Love Story*. 1940: *Juninatten/A Night in June*. 1941: *Adam Had Four Sons*; *Rage in Heaven*; *Dr. Jekyll and Mr. Hyde*. 1942: *Casablanca*. 1943: *Swedes in America* (docu., short); *For Whom the Bell Tolls*. 1944: *Gaslight*. 1945: *The Bells of St. Mary's*; *Spellbound*. 1946: *Saratoga Trunk*; *Notorious*. 1948: *The Arch of Triumph*; *Joan of Arc*. 1949: *Under Capricorn*. 1950: *Terra di Dio/Stromboli*. 1951: *Europa '51/The Greatest Love*. 1952: *Siamo Donne*. 1953: *Viaggio in Italia/Strangers*, a.k.a. *Voyage in Italy*. 1954: *Giovanna d'Arco al rogo*; *Angst*, a.k.a. *La Paura*. 1956: *Élena et les hommes/Paris Does Strange Things*; *Anastasia*. 1958: *Indiscreet*; *The Inn of Sixth Happiness*. 1959: *The Turn of the Screw* (TVD). 1961: *24 Hours in a Woman's Life* (TVD); *Goodbye Again/Aimez-vous Brahms?* 1962: *Hedda Gabler* (TVD). 1964: *Der Besuch/La rancune/La vendetta della signora/The Visit*; *The Yellow Rolls Royce*. 1967:

Smycket [The necklace] (episode in *Stimulantia*); *The Human Voice* (TVD). 1969: *Cactus Flower*; *A Walk in the Spring Rain*. 1973: *From the Mixed-Up Files of Mrs. Basil E. Frankweiler*. 1974: *Murder on the Orient Express*. 1976: *Nina, a Matter of Time*. 1978: *Herbstsonate*, a.k.a. *Höstsonaten/Autumn Sonata*. 1982: *A Woman Called Golda* (TVM).

BIBLIOGRAPHY

Bergman, Ingrid, and Alan Burgess. *My Story*. New York: Delacorte Press, 1980. Forslund, 1995.
Spoto, Donald. *Notorious. The Life of Ingrid Bergman*. New York: HarperCollins, 1997.

AWARDS

AA 1944: Best Actress (*Gaslight*)

AA 1956: Best Actress (*Anastasia*)

AA 1974: Best Supporting Actress (*Murder on the Orient Express*)

HELENA BERGSTRÖM (Göteborg, 5 Feb. 1964–), actress. Bergström is one of the most promising younger actresses in Swedish film. She comes from a family with a long acting tradition. Her parents are both actors, and her grandfather was the distinguished veteran actor Olof Widgren. She debuted at the age of fourteen in a television family sitcom directed by her father. She continued with various roles in television, including acting the role of a basketball player in the youth series "*Time Out*" and working with a youth entertainment program, *Vidöppet* [Wide open], where, among other things, she performed in short, satirical sketches. She graduated from the state school of stage art in 1988 and has had engagements at both the Royal Dramatic Theater and Stockholm Municipal Theater. Her starring role in *Kvinnorna på taket* [The women on the roof], directed by Sven Nykvist's son Carl Gustaf, was applauaded by the film critics, but the film was not a box office success. Her public appeal, however, rose with her vivid portrayal of the tough city girl Berit in the epic **1939*, an otherwise unjustifiably underrated account of Sweden during World War II. At this time she also met director *Colin Nutley, who eventually became her husband.

She has had her best, most complex roles in Nutley's films, including **Änglagård/House of Angels* and *BlackJack*, where she portrayed an unwed mother living in the countryside. Nutley's free and improvising style seems to fit her sensitive and complex acting style perfectly.

FILMOGRAPHY

1978: *Hem, ljuva hem* [Home, sweet home] (TVDS). 1982: "*Time Out*" (TVMS). 1987: *Uppvaknandet* [The awakening] (TVM, short). 1988: *Det blir bättre i vår* [It will be better in the spring] (TVM); *Friends; V.D.* [Managing director] (TVD); *Råttornas vinter* [Winter of the rats]; *Bara Sara* [Only Sara] (TVM). 1989: *Ängel* [Angel]; *Kvinnorna på taket* [The women on the roof]; *Husbonden* [The master] (TVMS); *1939*. 1990: *BlackJack*. 1991: *Änglagård/House of Angels*. 1993: *Familjeband* [Family ties] (TVMS, episode in anthology *Snoken* [The sleuth]); *Pariserhjulet* [The Paris wheel]; *Sista dan-*

sen/The Last Dance. 1994: *Änglagård—andra sommaren* [House of angels—the second summer]. 1996: *Jägarna* [The hunters]; *Sånt är livet* [Such is life]. 1998: *Still Crazy*; *Under solen* [Under the sun].

BIBLIOGRAPHY

Forslund, 1995.
Mårtensson, Jan. "Livet snurrar fort för Helena." *Arbetet*, 7 Apr. 1991.

AWARD

GB 1993

ANITA BJÖRK (Tällberg, 25 Apr. 1923–), actress. Like so many others, she was trained at the Royal Dramatic Theater School, graduating the same year as *Mai Zetterling, who has described Björk as her diametric opposite. In her memoirs, Zetterling portrays herself as eager but rather unsure of herself, whereas Anita Björk seemed secure and self-possessed. This characterization is applicable to many of Björk's screen characters as well: They are often stern and serious, with overtones of melancholy. Her international breakthrough came in *Alf Sjöberg's film version of *Fröken Julie/Miss Julie*, one of Strindberg's most complex dramatic creations. Björk was able to embody the many sides of Julie's character, the mixture of determination, capriciousness, and tragedy. Before *Miss Julie*, Anita Björk portrayed another interesting, more down-to-earth woman, the nurse and wife of the peasant hero in two rural dramas set in the present, *På dessa skuldror* [On these shoulders] and *Människors rike* [Realm of man].

After the success of *Miss Julie*, Anita Björk received an offer from Hollywood and moved there with her common-law husband, writer Stig Dagerman. That they were not formally married aroused consternation; the contract was canceled, and Björk returned home. Since then she has been a regular member of the ensemble at the Royal Dramatic Theater, with only occasional work in film. She was the stern heroine Kyllikki in the rural classic *Sången om den eldröda blomman* [The song of the scarlet flower], and *Arne Mattsson used her sometimes "eerie" appearance effectively in many of his Hillman thrillers, such as *Damen i svart* [The lady in black], *Mannekäng i rött* [Mannequin in red], and *Vita frun* [The white lady].

FILMOGRAPHY

1942: *Det är min musik* [It is my music]; *Himlaspelet/The Heavenly Play*. 1944: *Räkna de lyckliga stunderna blott* [Count only the happy moments]. 1946: *Hundra dragspel och en flicka* [A hundred accordions and one girl]. 1947: *Ingen väg tillbaka* [No way back]; *Kvinna utan ansikte* [Woman without a face]; *Det kom en gäst . . .* [A guest arrived . . .]. 1948: *På dessa skuldror* [On these shoulders]. 1949: *Människors rike* [Realm of man]. 1950: *Kvartetten som sprängdes* [The quartet that split up]. 1951: *Fröken Julie/Miss Julie*. 1952: *Kvinnors väntan/Secrets of Women* [Women's waiting]; *Han glömde henne aldrig/Memory of Love*.[1] 1954: *Night People*; *Die Hexe*. 1955: *Giftas/Of Love and Lust* [Getting married]; *Der Cornet; Hamlet* (TVD). 1956: *Moln över Hellesta*

[Clouds over Hellesta]; *Sången om den eldröda blomman* [The song of the scarlet flower]. 1957: *Gäst i eget hus* [A guest in his own house]. 1958: *Damen i svart* [The lady in black]; *Körkarlen* [The Phantom Chariot]; *Mannekäng i rött* [Mannequin in red]. 1960: *Tärningen är kastad* [The die is cast]; *Goda vänner trogna grannar* [Good friends, faithful neighbors]. 1961: *Testunden* [The tea hour] (short); *Nasilje na trgu/Square of Violence*. 1962: *Vita frun* [The white lady]; *Bacchusfesten* [The Bacchus festival] (TVD); *Handen på hjärtat* [Cross my heart] (TVD). 1963: *Misantropen* [The misanthrope] (TVD); *Gertrud* (TVD); *Anna Sophia Hedvig* (TVD); *Hittebarnet* [The foundling] (TVD). 1964: *Bandet* [The bond] (TVD); *Älskande par/Loving Couples*. 1965: *Väntande vatten* [Waiting water] (short). 1966: *Utro* [Unfaithful]. 1967: *"Tofflan"—en lycklig komedi* [Henpecked]; *Katarina* (TVM); *Etienne* (TVD). 1968: *Komedi i Hägerskog* [Comedy in Hägerskog]. 1969: *Ådalen 31/Ådalen '31*. 1972: *Kommer hem och är snäll* [Comes home and is nice] (TVM, short). 1974: *Karl XII* (TVD). 1976: *Sjung vackert om kärlek* [Sing sweetly about love] (TVM); *Bestigningen av Fujijama* [Climbing Fujijama] (TVD). 1977: *Bröderna* [The brothers] (TVMS). 1978: *Tribadernas natt* [Night of the tribades] (TVD). 1979: *Arven* [The inheritance]. 1980: *Midsommardröm i fattighuset* [Midsummer night's dream in the poorhouse] (TVD). 1981: *Forfølgelsen*, a.k.a. *Förföljelsen* [The persecution]; *Zéb-un-nisá—prinsessa av Indien* [Zéb-un-nisá—princess of India] (TVD). 1986: *Amorosa*. 1987: *En afton på Gripsholm* [An evening at Gripsholm] (TVD); *Damorkestern* [The ladies' orchestra] (TVD). 1989: *Flickan vid stenbänken* [The girl by the stone bench] (TVMS); *I lodjurets timme* [Hour of the lynx] (TVD). 1991: *Den goda viljan/The Best Intentions* (TVM).[2] 1992: *Markisinnan de Sade* [The Marquise de Sade] (TVD). 1993: *Avskedsföreställningen* [Final performance] (TVM, part of anthology *Snoken* [The sleuth]). 1996: *Enskilda samtal/Private Confessions* (TVM). 1997: *Larmar och gör sig till* [Fussing and fuming] (TVM). 1998: *Sanna ögonblick* [True moments].

BIBLIOGRAPHY

Burke, P. E. "Fame Came Too Soon to 'Miss Julie.' " *Films and Filming* 3, no. 7 (July 1957):10.

Forslund, 1995.

Waldekranz, Rune. "Anita Björk." *OBS!*, no. 14 (1951):7–11. Written by producer of *Miss Julie*.

NOTES

1. Swedish-U.S. coproduction made in bilingual versions. In United States, released only on television.

2. Theatrically released in 1992 in an edited version.

GUNNAR BJÖRNSTRAND (Stockholm, 13 Nov. 1909–24 May 1986), actor. He was perhaps the most versatile actor to have appeared in Swedish films, as well as one of the most productive. His father, Oscar Johanson, was a talented but not particularly successful actor. Despite this, Gunnar was determined to be an actor, too, a kind of "inner compulsion," as he later described it. He earned his living at odd jobs until he dared approach a theater manager. After acquiring some experience with walk-on parts, he began studying at a private theater school, where he changed his name. *Gösta Ekman [Sr]. offered him small roles in his theaters, and finally Björnstrand was accepted by the Royal Dramatic Theater School. He graduated in 1935 and asked for engagement at Svensk Filmindustri, but since producer *Karin Swanström thought he looked too much like an Italian, they had no use for him. He and his actress wife Lillie struggled during the 1930s; according to Lillie's memoirs, they nearly starved during a stint on a Swedish-speaking stage in Finland. Back in Stockholm, Gunnar found some temporary engagements, during one of which he met *Ingmar Bergman, at that time an unknown director of amateurs. Gunnar also got bit parts in various movies. In the early 1940s he was engaged by *Per-Axel Branner's Nya Teatern, and his career finally took off. He began to be assigned more important film roles, too. He himself claims that the part of the poor and struggling young physician in *Gustaf Edgren's *Kristin kommenderar* [Kristin commands] was his real breakthrough in films.

Many spectators may identify him as the serious parson in Bergman's *Natt-vardsgästerna/Winter Light*, a tormented seeker who has lost his faith. But Björnstrand was mainly a comedian, and his particular forte was the ironic cynic. Bergman consequently used him on various occasions to portray characters he wanted his audience to dislike intensely, such as the cold and rational physician in *Ansiktet/The Magician*, to take just one example. In other Bergman films Björnstrand is more pitiful, for instance, in *Kvinnors väntan/Secrets of Women* or *Sommarnattens leende/Smiles of a Summer Night*, where he is emotionally humiliated by *Eva Dahlbeck. Early in his career Björnstrand occasionally assumed the role of the heavy, for instance, as a very sinister Nazi officer in a couple of films of the 1940s. Another memorable screen portrait was the sadistic subaltern in *Nils Poppe's satire *Soldat Bom* [Soldier Bom], played with a huge dose of irony.

FILMOGRAPHY

1931: *Mon coeur et ses millions; Skepp ohoj!* [Ship ahoy!]. 1932: *Hans livs match* [The game of his life]; *Landskamp* [International match]. 1937: *Bergslagsfolk/Bergslagsfolk* [The people of Bergslagen]. 1938: *Vi som går scenvägen* [We who use the stage door]. 1939: *Panik* [Panic]; *Vi två/Vi Tvaa* [The two of us]; *Mot nya tider* [Toward new times]. 1940: *Hjältar i gult och blått* [Heroes in yellow and blue]; *Juninatten/A Night in June*; *Karl för sin hatt* [A real man]; *Hennes melodi* [Her melody]; *Alle man på post* [Man your posts]. 1941: *Snapphanar* [Partisans]; *Spökreportern* [The ghost reporter]. 1942: *En äventyrare* [An adventurer]; *General von Döbeln*; *Trygghet och trivsel* [Safety and cosiness] (NCF). 1943: *Natt i hamn* [Night in harbor]; *Jag dräpte* [I slew]. 1944: *Apassionata*; *Lev farligt* [Live dangerously]; *Mitt folk är icke ditt* [My people are not yours]; *Hets/Torment*; *Nyordning på Sjögårda* [New order at Sjögårda]. 1945: *Sussie*; *I som här inträden* [All ye who enter here]. 1946: *Peggy på vift* [Peggy on the loose]; *Kristin kommenderar* [Kristin commands]; *Rötägg/Incorrigible*; *Det regnar på vår kärlek* [It rains on our love]; *Medan porten var stängd* [While the door was closed]; *Midvinterblot* [Midwinter sacrifice] (short). 1947: *Bruden kom genom taket* [The bride came through the roof]; *Pappa sökes* [Wanted: a daddy]; *Krigsmans erinran* [A soldier's oath]; *En fluga gör ingen sommar* [One swallow doesn't make a summer]; *Här kommer vi . . .*

[Here we come . . .]; *Två kvinnor* [Two women]. 1948: *Musik i mörker/Night Is My Future*, a.k.a. *Music in Darkness*; *Var sin väg* [Each his own way]; *En svensk Tiger* [A Swede keeps his mouth shut]; *Lilla Märta kommer tillbaka* [Little Märta returns]; *Soldat Bom* [Soldier Bom]. 1949: *Skolka skolan* [Playing hookey]; *Flickan från tredje raden* [The girl in the gallery]; *Pappa Bom* [Daddy Bom]. 1950: *Min syster och jag* [My sister and I]; *Fästmö uthyres* [Fiancée for hire]; *Kyssen på kryssen* [The kiss on the cruise]; *Den vita katten* [The white cat]; *Kvartetten som sprängdes* [The quartet that split up]. 1951: *Tull-Bom* [Bom at the customs barrier]. 1952: *Säg det med blommor* [Say it with flowers]; *En fästman i taget* [One fiancé at a time]; *Kvinnors väntan/Secrets of Women* [Women's waiting]; *Flyg-Bom* [Bom in the air]; *Oppåt med Gröna Hissen* [Going up with the green elevator]. 1953: *Dansa min docka* [Dance, my doll]; *Vi tre debutera* [We three make our début]; *Gycklarnas afton/The Naked Night*, a.k.a. *Sawdust and Tinsel* [Eve of the jesters]; *Glasberget* [The glass mountain]. 1954: *Flottans glada gossar* [The navy's happy lads]; *Seger i mörker* [Victory in darkness]; *En lektion i kärlek/A Lesson in Love*; *Gabrielle*. 1955: *Stampen* ["Uncle's"]; *Kvinnodröm/Dreams* [Women's dream]; *Sommarnattens leende/Smiles of a Summer Night*. 1956: *Det är aldrig för sent* [It's never too late]; *Sjunde himlen* [Seventh heaven]; *Skorpan* [The biscuit]. 1957: *Det sjunde inseglet/The Seventh Seal*; *Nattens ljus* [Lights in the night]; *Sommarnöje sökes* [Wanted: summer residence]; *Smultronstället/Wild Strawberries*. 1958: *Du är mitt äventyr* [You are my adventure]; *Jazzgossen* [The jazz kid];[1] *Fröken April* [Miss April]; *Ansiktet/The Magician* [The face]. 1959: *Det svänger på slottet* [A high old time at the castle]; *Brott i Paradiset* [Crime in paradise]; *Himmel och pannkaka* [Heaven and pancake]; *Mälarpirater* [Pirates of lake Mälaren]; *Låna mig en miljon* [Lend me a million] (short). 1960: *Djävulens öga/The Devil's Eye*; *Samlevnad* [Living together] (short). 1961: *Såsom i en spegel/Through a Glass Darkly*; *Lustgården* [The pleasure garden]. 1962: *Handen på hjärtat* [Cross my heart] (TVD). 1963: *Nattvardsgästerna/Winter Light* [The communicants]; *Lyckodrömmen* [Dream of happiness]; *Min kära är en ros* [My beloved is a rose]; *Hittebarnet* [The foundling] (TVD). 1964: *Klänningen/The Dress*; *Äktenskapsbrottaren* [Mixed doubles]: *Älskande par/Loving Couples*; *Kristianstad—filmstaden* [Kristianstad— the city of film] (short, narrator). 1965: *Sissan* (TVD); *Hans nåds testamente* [His grace's will] (TVD). 1966: *Frank Heller berättar* [Frank Heller tells] (TVM), *Syskonbädd 1782/My Sister, My Love*; *Träfracken* [The coffin]; *Persona/Persona*; *Här har du ditt liv/Here's Your Life*; *Pälsen* [The fur coat] (TVM, short). 1967: *Den røde kappe/Hagbard and Signe* [The red robe]; *Smycket* [The necklace] (episode in *Stimulantia*); *"Tofflan"— en lycklig komedi* [Henpecked]; *Candida* (TVD). 1968: *Flickorna/The Girls*; *Skammen/The Shame*; *Pappa varför är du arg—du gjorde likadant själv när du var ung* [Daddy, why are you angry? You did the same yourself when you were young]; *Nina* (TVD); *Pygmalion* (TVD). 1969: *Tunneln* [The tunnel] (TVD); *Hissen som gick ner i helvetet* [The elevator that went down to hell] (TVD); *Riten/The Ritual* (TVM); *L'isola*. 1971: *Lockfågeln* [The decoy]. *Mamsell Josabeth* (short). 1972: *Spöksonaten* [The ghost sonata] (TVD). 1973: *Pistolen/The Pistol*; *Näsan* [The nose] (TVD); *ITT:s hemliga dokument* [ITT:s secret documents] (TVD); *Någonstans i Sverige* [Somewhere in Sweden] (TVMS). 1974: *Gustav III* (TVD); *Engeln* [The angel] (TVMS); 1976: *Ansikte mot ansikte/Face to Face* (TVMS).[2] 1977: *Tabu* [Taboo]; *Kalkonen* [The turkey] (TVM); *Nationalmonumentet* [The national monument] (TVD); *Isgraven* [The icy grave] (TVM). 1978: *Forskaren* [The scientist] (TVMS); *Herbstsonate*, a.k.a. *Höstsonaten/Autumn Sonata*; *I väntrummet* [In the waiting room] (TVD). 1979: *Skeppsredaren* [The ship owner] (TVDS); *Charlotte Löwensköld*.[3] 1981: *Fortunios visa* [Fortunio's melody]

(TVD). 1982: *Jäähyväiset* a.k.a. *Avskedet* [The Farewell]; **Fanny och Alexander/Fanny and Alexander.*[4] 1983: *Farmor och vår herre* [Grandma and Our Lord] (TVDS).

BIBLIOGRAPHY

Björnstrand, Lillie: "*Inte bara applåder.*" Stockholm: Tiden, 1975.
Holm, 1947.

NOTES

1. Björnstrand's part was cut before the premiere.
2. Theatrically released abroad in edited version.
3. Longer version for television in 1981.
4. Longer version for television in 1984, with limited cinema release in 1983.

HILDA BORGSTRÖM (Stockholm, 13 Oct. 1871–2 Jan. 1953), actress. Borgström was a veteran actress who trained as a ballet dancer at the Royal Opera in the 1880s. She acted on various stages before finding steady engagement at the Royal Dramatic Theater at the turn of the century. It was considered sensational when she was engaged by Svenska Bio in 1912, and many thought film work would merely be a sideline, but her film career would last until the late 1940s.

Her first important film role, which brought her fame, was as the suffering Ingeborg Holm in *Victor Sjöström's important social epic. Sjöström also used her as the poor wife of the alcoholic lead David Holm in *Körkarlen/The Stroke of Midnight*. Later she virtually specialized in wise old women from various classes. Many times the parts were small but nevertheless significant. As a teacher at the Royal Dramatic Theater School, she played an important role in training new generations of actors. *Signe Hasso and *Gunnar Björnstrand, among many others, have paid warm tribute and expressed gratitude to Hilda Borgström as an inspiring mentor.

FILMOGRAPHY

1912: *En sommarsaga* [A summer tale] (short);[1] *Ett hemligt giftermål eller Bekännelsen på dödsbädden* [A secret marriage or the deathbed confession] (short). 1913: *Lady Marions sommarflirt* [Lady Marion's summer flirtation] (short); **Ingeborg Holm.* 1914: *Vägen till mannens hjärta* [The way to a man's heart] (short); *Dömen icke* [Do not condemn]. 1916: *Brandsoldaten* [The fireman] (short). 1917: *Fru Kristina* [Mrs. Kristina]; *Søster Karin* [Sister Karin]; *Moderens øjne* [Mother's eye]. 1920: *Carolina Rediviva.* 1921: *Körkarlen/The Stroke of Midnight*, a.k.a. *The Phantom Chariot.* 1923: *Anna-Clara och hennes bröder* [Anna-Clara and her brothers]. 1924: *Flickan från Paradiset* [The girl from Paradise]. 1925: *Damen med kameliorna* [The lady with camelias]. 1926: *Giftas* [Getting married]. 1928: *Ådalens poesi* [The poetry of Ådalen]. 1929: *Rågens rike* [The realm of the rye]. 1930: *Norrlänningar* [The people of Norrland]. 1932: *Värmlänningarna/Vaermlaeningarna* [The people of Värmland]. 1933: *Farmors revolution* [Grandma's revolution]; *Vad veta väl männen-* [What do men know-]. 1934: *Simon i Backabo* [Simon of Backabo]. 1935: *Flickornas Alfred* [Ladies' man Alfred]. 1937: *Fa-*

miljen Andersson/Familjen Andersson [The Andersson family]; *John Ericsson—Segraren vid Hampton Roads/John Ericsson—Victor at Hampton Roads.* 1938: *Med folket för fosterlandet/Med Folket Foer Fosterlandet* [With the people for the fatherland]; *Vingar kring fyren* [Wings around the lighthouse]; *En kvinnas ansikte/A Woman's Face*; *Du gamla du fria/Du Gamla Du Fria* [Thou ancient, thou free]. 1939: *Gläd dig i din ungdom* [Rejoice in thy youth]; *Folket på Högbogården/Folket paa Hogbogarden* [The people of Högbogården]. 1940: *Vildmarkens sång* [The song of the wilderness]; . . . *som en tjuv om natten* [. . . like a thief in the night]; *Ett brott* [A crime]; *Hennes melodi* [Her melody]. 1941: *Fransson den förskräcklige* [Fransson the terrible]; *Göranssons pojke* [Göransson's boy]; *Striden går vidare* [The battle goes on]; *Dunungen* [Downy]. 1942: *Farliga vägar* [Dangerous ways]; *Lågor i dunklet* [Flames in the gloom]; *Livet på en pinne* [Living in clover]; *Rid i natt!* [Ride this night!]; *Doktor Glas* [Doctor Glas]; *Tomten—en vintersaga* [The elf—a winter's tale] (short). 1943: *Kvinnor i fångenskap* [Women in captivity]; *Flickan är ett fynd* [The girl's a find]; *En flicka för mig* [A girl for me]; *Livet måste levas* [Life must be lived]; *Jag dräpte* [I slew]. 1944: *En dag skall gry* [A day will dawn]; *Appassionata*; *Släkten är bäst* [Family's family after all]; *Klockan på Rönneberga* [The clock at Rönneberga]; *Den osynliga muren* [The invisible wall]; *Jag är eld och luft* [I am fire and air]; **Hets/Torment*;[2] *Flickan och Djävulen* [The girl and the devil]; *Prins Gustaf* [Prince Gustaf]; *Kejsarn av Portugallien* [The emperor of Portugallia]. 1945: *Kungliga patrasket* [Royal rabble]; *Galgmannen* [The gallows man]; *Gomorron Bill!* [Good morning, Bill!]; *Trötte Teodor* [Tired Teodor]. 1946: *Försök inte med mej . . . !* [Don't try with me . . . !]; *Brita i grosshandlarhuset* [Brita in the merchant's house]; *Åsa-Hanna*; *Begär [Desire]; Bröder emellan* [Between brothers]; **Driver dagg, faller regn/Sunshine Follows Rain*; *Eviga länkar* [Eternal links]. 1947: *Dynamit* [Dynamite]; *Sången om Stockholm* [The song of Stockholm]; *Nyckeln och ringen* [The key and the ring]. 1948: *Musik i mörker/The Night Is My Future*, a.k.a. *Music in Darkness*; *Var sin väg* [Each his own way]; *Vart hjärta har sin saga/Each Heart Has Its Own Story*; *Synd* [Sin]; *Solkatten* [Sunshine]; *Banketten* [The banquet]; *Eva*. 1949: *Flickan från tredje raden* [The girl in the gallery].

BIBLIOGRAPHY

Holm, 1947.

NOTES

1. This attribution is somewhat uncertain. The film has wrongly been attributed to Victor Sjöström, and its existence has even been called into question. Though it seems to have existed, it is not certain that Hilda Borgström appeared in it.

2. Role (as Caligula's mother) cut before premiere.

PER-AXEL BRANNER (Linköping, 25 Jan. 1899–31 July 1977), director. Born Per-Axel Larsson, he is perhaps best remembered as a stage director and manager of Nya Teatern in the 1940s. Too little attention has been paid to his film work. His best-known effort happens to be the notorious *Pettersson & Bendel*, infamous for its overt anti-Semitic passages (the film was later a success in Nazi

Germany, where it was officially designated "Staatspolitisch wertvoll"). Branner nevertheless deserves a place in Swedish film history for his overall contribution; one must also keep in mind that anti-Semitism was a common attitude in general in prewar Sweden. Moreover, Branner staged anti-Nazi plays and satirical revues at his theater during World War II, a decision that was risky and controversial.

Branner began as a promising stage director. In the early 1930s he received a grant to visit the USSR, where he studied experimental revolutionary art and stage direction. His first film work was actually a propaganda film for the Social Democratic Party in the 1931 Stockholm local elections, but this reflects few influences from Soviet theater and filmmaking, nor do any of his subsequent films. Branner had an eye for visual poetics and a gentle touch with his actors, qualities that are most evident in his films about youth but may also be seen in the underrated melodrama *Konflikt* [Conflict].

As a filmmaker in the 1930s he was identified as a specialist on youth. Both *Unga hjärtan* [Young hearts] and *Ungdom av i dag* [Today's youth] are quite startling, even from today's point of view. The first film in particular is still very fresh with its rather modern treatment of the delicate emotional life of young people. Branner's first feature, *Hans livs match* [The game of his life], about the love between a young soccer player, the son of a building contractor, and the daughter of an ordinary worker, has this perspective. At the same time it is an homage to the ideals of "people's home" politics. Even his version of the rural classic *Sången om den eldröda blomman* [The song of the scarlet flower] can be viewed from this perspective. In comparison with *Mauritz Stiller's 1919 version, Branner's deals more with the emotional conflicts of youth and the necessity of resolving turmoil to achieve order and maturity.

In *Konflikt* he deals with another theme that is still timely, the conflict (as the title indicates) between male rationality and female focus on the emotional. On the surface, the film depicts the course of events at a shipyard where the workers feel exploited and begin a strike, a conflict that is resolved in due time after some compromise. The most interesting aspect of the film, however, concerns interpersonal discord. The young wife of the shipyard manager, unsatisfied in her marriage, is attracted to an engineer who seems to offer an alternative. But even he is trapped in a technically oriented male world, though at least he longs for a different kind of life. Eventually she must choose between the two men. In the meantime her husband has concluded that his busy existence lacks meaning, and in the end, husband and wife are reconciled. He has learned his lesson and acknowledged his inner and perhaps more "female" dimensions. This is a key film of the period because it depicts a fundamental principle in the concept of the "people's home": the necessity of fusing rationality and emotional expressiveness in both the social sphere and private life. At the same time the film also contains a partially disguised critique of the fundamental patriarchal values that support this same concept.

After the 1930s Branner practically ceased film work. It is a pity that this director who is so obviously modern in his orientation never got the chance to realize his ambitions in the following decade, when there were more opportunities for serious film.

FILMOGRAPHY

1926: *Giftas* [Getting married] (script only). 1930: *Tango—foxtrot* (short). 1931: *Fröken, Ni liknar Greta Garbo* [Miss, you look like Greta Garbo] (short); *Under röda fanor* [Under red banners] (NCF). 1932: *Hans livs match* [The game of his life] (also script). 1933: *Pettersson & Bendel/Pettersson & Bendel* (also script); *Farmors revolution* [Grandma's revolution]. 1934: *Unga hjärtan* [Young hearts] (also script); *Sången om den eldröda blomman* [The song of the scarlet flower]. 1935: *Ungdom av i dag/Ungdom Av I Dag* [Today's youth] (also script). 1936: *Äventyret* [The adventure]. 1937: *Konflikt* [Conflict] (also script). 1938: *På kryss med Albertina/Paa Kryss Med Albertina* [Cruising on the Albertina]. 1939: *Swedish Rhapsody* (docu.); *Adolf i eld och lågor* [Adolf all fired up]; *Rosor varje kväll* [Roses every evening] (also script). 1942: *Hon trodde det var han* [She thought it was he]. 1944: *På farliga vägar* [On dangerous ways] (also script). 1966: *Kvinnas man* [Woman's man] (TVD).

BIBLIOGRAPHY

Cyrano [Flodén, Torsten]. "Kanske en filmregissör." *Dagens Nyheter*, 3 Sept. 1933.
Filmqvist [Almqvist, Stig]. "En regissör som vågar välja." *Filmjournalen*, no. 42 (1933): 8–9.

EVA DAHLBECK (Saltsjö-Duvnäs, 8 Mar. 1920–), actress. Eva Dahlbeck first did clerical work but began studies at a private theater school. In 1944, after already playing a major film role, she became a pupil at the Royal Dramatic Theater School. Until the 1960s she worked continually in film, but in the early 1970s, she gave up acting completely and became a successful novelist.

Eva Dahlbeck was once nicknamed "the armoured ship Womanhood," and it is not difficult to see why. On the screen, she has portrayed a long line of strong, stern, and independent women, never ready to submit to the so-called stronger sex, which in fact becomes the weaker one in her presence. This is particularly evident in her more famous *Ingmar Bergman roles, for instance, in *Sommarnattens leende/Smiles of a Summer Night*, where she plays the ironic actress Desirée Armfeldt. Her blond appearance also made her useful in many of the rural dramas that have been such a staple of postwar Swedish film. She actually made her real screen debut in one of the more famous of these, *Rid i natt!* [Ride this night!], where she played the fiancée of the hero Svedje, the lone peasant who dares oppose the oppressing bailiff and pays for freedom with his life. Her most famous role in that genre is as Rya-Rya in *Alf Sjöberg's *Bara en mor* [Only a mother], where she was a strong, independent, proletarian earth mother, who despite numerous difficulties remains a free soul and manages to hold her family together.

FILMOGRAPHY

1941: *Bara en kvinna* [Only a woman]; *Det sägs på stan* [The talk of the town]. 1942: *Rid i natt!* [Ride this night!]. 1944: *Räkna de lyckliga stunderna blott* [Count only the happy moments]. 1945: Oss *tjuvar emellan eller En burk ananas* [Just among us thieves, or A can of pineapples]; *Svarta rosor* [Black roses]; *Den allvarsamma leken* [The serious game]. 1946: *Pengar—en tragikomisk saga* [Money—a tragicomic tale] (voice); *Brita i grosshandlarhuset* [Brita in the merchant's house]; *Kärlek och störtlopp* [Love and downhill skiing]; *Möte i natten* [Encounter at night]. 1947: *Nyckeln och ringen* [The key and the ring]; *Två kvinnor* [Two women]; *Folket i Simlångsdalen* [The people of Simlång Valley]. 1948: *Var sin väg* [Each his own way]; *Lars Hård*; *Eva*; *Flickan från fjällbyn* [The girl from the mountain village]. 1949: *Kvinna i vitt* [Woman in white]; *Bara en mor* [Only a mother]. 1950: *Fästmö uthyres* [Fiancée for hire]; *Hjärter Knekt* [Jack of hearts]; *Kastrullresan* [The saucepan journey]. 1951: *Bärande hav* [In the arms of the sea]; *Sköna Helena* [Beautiful Helena]. 1952: *Sabotage* (NCF); *Ubåt 39* [Submarine 39]; *Trots* [Contempt]; *Kvinnors väntan/Secrets of Women* [Women's waiting]; *The Linetski Forest Massacre* (TVM, episode in *Foreign Intrigue*). 1953: *Reunion in Berlin* (TVM, episode in *Foreign Intrigue*); *Das Pestaloizzidorf/The Village*; *Skuggan* [The shadow]; *Barabbas*; *Kvinnohuset* [House of women]; *Göingehövdingen* [The chieftain of Göinge]; *En lektion i kärlek/A Lesson in Love*. 1955: *The Model Lady* (TVM, episode in *Foreign Intrigue*); *Resa i natten* [Journey in the night]; *Nina* (TVM, episode in *Foreign Intrigue*); *Kvinnodröm/Dreams* [Women's dream]; *Paradiset* [Paradise]; *Sommarnattens leende/Smiles of a Summer Night*. 1956: *Sista paret ut* [Last couple out]; *Tarps Elin* [Tarp's Elin]. 1957: *Möten i skymningen* [Encounters in the twilight]; *Sommarnöje sökes* [Wanted: summer residence]. 1958: *Nära livet/Brink of Life*. 1960: *A Matter of Morals*; *Kärlekens decimaler* [Decimals of love]; *Tre önskningar* [Three wishes]; *Samlevnad* [Living together] (short). 1962: *Biljett till Paradiset* [Ticket to paradise]; *The Counterfeit Traitor*. 1964: *För att inte tala om alla dessa kvinnor/All These Women*; *Älskande par/Loving Couples*. 1965: *Kattorna/The Cats*; *Morianerna/Morianna*, a.k.a. *I, the Body*. 1966: *Les créatures*, a.k.a. *Varelserna*. 1967: *Den røde kappe/Hagbard and Signe* [The red robe]; *Mennesker mødes og sød musik opstår i hjertet/People Meet and Sweet Music Fills the Heart*. 1968: *Markurells i Wadköping* [The Markurells of Wadköping] (TVM). 1970: *Tintomara*.

Film Script

1967: *Yngsjömordet/Woman of Darkness*.

BIBLIOGRAPHY

Björnstrand, Gunnar. "En stor kvinna." *Allt*, no. 4 (1956):13–14.
Forslund, 1995.
Holm, 1947.

AWARD

GB 1965

GUSTAF EDGREN (Östra Fågelvik, 1 Apr. 1895–10 June 1954), director. Edgren began as a journalist in Kristinehamn in the western province of Värmland. He also worked in amateur theater and became interested in film when he staged folk dances for the first film version of the folk classic *Värmlänningarna* [The people of Värmland] (1921). He soon took up filmmaking himself and founded his own company, Värmlandsfilm. His first features were primarily folksy rural dramas, in which he introduced a new star, actor *Fridolf Rhudin, who rapidly became a very popular film actor. In the mid-1920s Edgren was engaged by Svensk Filmindustri and established himself as one of the company's most successful directors in the 1930s and 1940s, working with diverse subject matter and in various genres. His forte, however, and the core of his audience success, was the rural melodrama, such as his last film with Rhudin, *Simon i Backabo* [Simon of Backabo], *Karl-Fredrik regerar/Karl-Fredrik Reigns*, the great social democratic vision, or *Driver dagg, faller regn/Sunshine Follows Rain*, which became the smash hit of the 1940s. Edgren was also responsible for the much-discussed melodrama on the nativity question, *Valborgsmässoafton/Walpurgis Night*. He was also engaged as a director at the Royal Opera.

Edgren's directorial style can be described as competent if not original; he was fundamentally a craftsman. His strong sense for outdoor scenes is evident in his many films set in rural milieus. Sometimes, however, the influence of American film farce is apparent, for instance, in certain efforts with Fridolf Rhudin from the early 1930s like the still quite hilarious *Skepp ohoj!* [Ship ahoy!]. He also revealed a comic vein in his anticommunist satire *Ryska snuvan* [The Russian flu].

FILMOGRAPHY

Actor

1921: *Värmlänningarna* [The people of Värmland].

Director, Scriptwriter

1922: *Fröken på Björneborg* [The young lady of Björneborg]. 1923: *Närkingarna* [The people of Närke]. 1924: *Trollebokungen* [King of Trollebo]. 1925: *Skeppargatan 40* [No. 40 Skipper street]; *Styrman Karlssons flammor* [First-mate Karlsson's sweethearts]. 1926: *Hon, han och Andersson* [She, he and Andersson]. 1927: *Spökbaronen* [The ghost baron]. 1928: *Svarte Rudolf* [Black Rudolf]. 1929: *Konstgjorda Svensson* [Artificial Svensson]. 1930: *Kronans kavaljerer* [Cavaliers of the crown]. 1931: *Brokiga Blad/Brokiga Blad* [Colorful pages] (actor only); *Röda dagen/Roeda Dagen* [The red day] (director only); *Trötte Teodor/Troette Teodor* [Tired Teodor] (director only, also actor); *Skepp ohoj!* [Ship ahoy!]. 1932: *Värmlänningarna/Vœrmlœnningarna* [The people of Värmland]. 1934: *Karl-Fredrik regerar/Karl-Fredrik Reigns* (also actor); *Simon i Backabo* [Simon of Backabo] (director only). 1935: *Valborgsmässoafton/Walpurgis Night*. 1936: *Johan Ulfstjerna*. 1937: *Ryska snuvan* [The Russian flu]; *John Ericsson—segraren vid Hampton Roads/John Ericsson—Victor at Hampton Roads*. 1938: *Styrman Karlssons flammor* [First-mate Karlsson's sweethearts]. 1940: *Stora famnen* [With open arms]. 1943: *Lille Napoleon* [Little Napoleon]; *Katrina/Katrina*. 1944: *Dolly tar chansen* [Dolly takes a chance]. 1945: *Hans Majestät får vänta* [His majesty must wait]. 1946: *Kristin kommenderar* [Kristin commands]; *Driver dagg, faller regn/Sunshine Follows Rain*. 1947: *Tösen från Stormyrtorpet* [The girl from the Marsh Croft]. 1948: *En svensk Tiger* [A

Swede keeps his mouth shut]; *Flottans kavaljerer* [The navy's cavaliers]. 1949: *Svenske ryttaren* [The Swedish horseman]. 1951: *Sköna Helena* [Beautiful Helena].

BIBLIOGRAPHY

Soila, Tytti, "*Valborgsmässoafton:* Melodrama and Gender Politics in Swedish Cinema." In *Popular European Cinema*, ed. R. Dyer and G. Vincendeau. London and New York: Routledge, 1992.

Waldekranz, Rune. "Gustaf Edgren. En publikfilmens arkitekt." *Svensk filmografi 4* (1980):554–558. The only study of any length about Edgren.

ALLAN EDWALL (Rödön, 25 Aug. 1924–7 Feb. 1997), actor, director. Born in northern Sweden, Edwall came to Stockholm at the beginning of the 1940s and first earned his living as an author and an artist. He was accepted by the Royal Dramatic Theater School in 1949 and after graduating worked on various stages, including the Royal one. In his last years, he managed his own one-man theater in Stockholm.

Edwall was one of the best loved of contemporary actors, largely because of his ability to give vivid portrayals of ingenious older men, with traces of philosophical greatness behind their masks. He can be described as the "tramp of the Swedish soul," someone with real roots in the essence of being Swedish. One of his most popular creations was the shabby private eye in the television series *Engeln* [The Angel], which was produced twice. He was one of the Swedish actors who best mastered the art of monologue. He was also a great tragedy actor, as, for example, the dying actor in the lead of **Fanny och Alexander/Fanny and Alexander*. This was one of his many roles for **Bergman. In quite a different role he was the choleric father of Emil in the films based on Astrid Lindgren's popular stories. He also established himself as a competent director with "adult-children" film *Åke och hans värld/Åke and His World* as his best effort.

FILMOGRAPHY

Actor

1948: *En man gör sitt val* [A man makes his choice] (NCF). 1953: *Resan till dig* [The voyage to you]. 1954: *Gud Fader och tattaren*, a.k.a. *Tattarblod* [Our Father and the gypsy, a.k.a. Gypsy blood]; *Dans på rosor* [Dance on roses]. 1955: *Snaran* [The noose] (TVD); *Vildfåglar* [Wild birds]. 1956: *Flamman/Girls without Rooms* [The flame]. 1957: *Kabaret Maskrosen* [Cabaret dandelion] (TVD); *Ingen morgondag* [No tomorrow]. 1958: *Körkarlen* [The phantom chariot]; *Hughie* (TVD). 1959: *Lilith* (TVD). 1960: *Jungfrukällan/The Virgin Spring*; *Tärningen är kastad* [The die is cast]; *Av hjärtans lust* [Heart's desire]; *Bröllopsdagen* [The wedding day]; *Djävulens öga/The Devil's Eye*; *På en bänk i en park* [On a bench in a park]. 1961: *Ljuvlig är sommarnatten* [Lovely is the summer night]; *Mr Ernest* (TVD); *Briggen Tre Liljor* [HMS Three Lilies]. 1962: *Stolarna* [The chairs] (TVD); *Kvartetten som sprängdes* [The quartet that split up] (TVD); *Kort är sommaren/Short Is the Summer*. 1963: *Misantropen* [The misanthrope] (TVD); *Nattvardsgästerna/Winter Light* [The communicants]; *Topaze* (TVD); *Ett drömspel* [A dream play] (TVD). 1964: *För att inte tala om alla dessa kvinnor/All These Women*; *Henry IV*

(TVD). 1965: *Uppehåll i myrlandet* [Stopover in the marshland] (episode in *4x4*); *Mitt hem är Copacabana* [My home is Copacabana] (narrator); *Janus* (TVD); *Hängivelsen* [Devotion] (short); *Thérèse Raquin* (TVD); *Festivitetssalongen* [The banquet room]; *En florentinsk tragedi* [A Florentine tragedy] (TVD); *Gustav Vasa* (TVD); *Hans nåds testamente* [His grace's will] (TVD); *Ängelsmannen* [Angel man] (short). 1966: *Hemsöborna* [The people of Hemsö] (TVMS); *Träfracken* [The coffin]; **Här har du ditt liv/Here's Your Life*. 1967: *Mördaren—en helt vanlig person* [The murderer—a perfectly ordinary person]. 1968: *Slättemölla by* [Slättemölla village] (TVMS). 1969: *Bokhandlaren som slutade bada* [The bookseller who gave up bathing]; *Klabautermannen/We Are All Demons*. 1970: *Röda rummet* [The red room] (TVMS); *Ministern* [The minister]. 1971: **Utvandrarna/The Emigrants*; *Emil i Lönneberga* [Emil in Lönneberga]. 1972: *Nybyggarna/The New Land*; *Nya hyss av Emil i Lönneberga* [New pranks by Emil in Lönneberga]; *Hemma hos Karlssons* [At home with Karlssons] (TVDS); *Spöksonaten* [The ghost sonata] (TVD). 1973: *Vem älskar Yngve Frej?* [Who loves Yngve Frej?] (TVM); *Emil och griseknoen* [Emil and the little pig]. 1974/76: *Engeln* [The Angel] (TVMS, also script); *Nattens konung* [King of the night] (TVM). 1975: *Liv* [Life] (TVM); *Kulstötaren* [The shot-putter] (TVM, short); *Vad ska Joel göra?* [What shall Joel do?] (short). 1977: *Elvis! Elvis!*; *Den allvarsamma leken* [The serious game]; *Måndagarna med Fanny* [Mondays with Fanny]; *Bröderna Lejonhjärta* [The brothers Lionheart]; *Soldat med brutet gevär* [Soldier with a broken rifle] (TVMS). 1978: *Bröllopsfesten* [The wedding party] (TVD). 1979: *Du är inte klok Madicken* [You're crazy, Madicken]. 1980: *Mannen som blev miljonär* [The man who became a millionaire]; *Sverige åt svenskarna* [Sweden for the Swedes]; *Madicken på Junibacken* [Madicken at Junibacken]; *Midsommardröm i fattighuset* [Midsummer night's dream in the poorhouse] (TVD). 1981: *Sopor* [Garbage]; *Tuppen* [The cock]; *Rasmus på luffen* [Rasmus the tramp]. 1982: *Fanny och Alexander/Fanny and Alexander*.[1] 1983: *Limpan* [Loafie] (also script); *P & B*; *Hustruskolan* [School for wives] (TVD). 1984: **Ronja Rövardotter* [Ronja, the robber's daughter]. 1986: *Offret/The Sacrifice*. 1989: *Resan till Melonia* [The voyage to Melonia] (voice). 1990: *I morgon var en dröm* [Tomorrow was a dream] (TVD). 1991: *Duo jag* [You and me] (TVMS).

Director

1969: *Eriksson* (also script and actor). 1974: *Tjena Gary* [Hello Gary] (TVM, script only). 1984: *Svenska folkets sex och snusk* [The dirty sex life of the Swedes] (TVM); *Åke och hans värld/Åke and His World* (also script and actor). 1985: *Fröken Margarida* [Miss Margarida] (TVD); *Det är mänskligt att fela* [It is human to error] (TVM, script only). 1986: *Den nervöse mannen* [The nervous man] (TVM, also actor). 1987: *Mälarpirater* [Pirates of Lake Mälaren] (also script and actor). 1988: *Det blir bättre i vår* [It will be better in the spring] (TVM, also actor); *Tunneln* [The tunnel] (TVD). 1989: *Doktor Glas* (TVD, also actor). 1996: *Den milda* [The gentle one] (TVD, short, also actor); *Bättre utan hund* [Better without a dog] (TVD, short, also actor).

BIBLIOGRAPHY

Edwall, Allan. *Allan och hans värld: Allan Edwall berättar om sitt liv och sin konst*. Stockholm: Sveriges Radio, 1988.

AWARD

GB 1974

NOTE

1. Longer version for television in 1984, with limited cinema release in 1983.

GÖSTA EKMAN [Jr.] (Stockholm, 28 July 1939–), actor. Son of *Hasse Ekman. Like his father, he entered the film business at an early age, working as an assistant to both his father and *Ingmar Bergman. Early in his film acting career he generally played sensitive young men. His popular breakthrough, however, came on the stage when he appeared in the satirical revues of *Hans Alfredson and *Tage Danielsson, later followed by much-appreciated roles in their films. Gradually he developed into one of Sweden's leading film comedians. When he began starring in the "Jönsson gang" series, spoofs of the crime genre taken from a Danish source, he definitively secured that position, challenged only by the enormous popularity of *Lasse Åberg. Ekman has showed other sides, too, for instance, as the worn-down police lieutenant Martin Beck in a series of films based on the novels of Sjöwall and Wahlöö.

Ekman is a very physical comedian. His characters are often stumbling and awkward, both literally and figuratively. He honed this feeble, socially incapacitated persona into perfection in a series of shorts with the character Papphammar, originally made for television. Over the years a dark aspect to Ekman's humor has also evolved, especially in his most recent films, made in collaboration with his current wife, film director Marie-Louise Ekman.

FILMOGRAPHY

1956: *Swing it, fröken!* [Swing it, miss!]. 1962: *Chans/Just Once More*; *Nils Holgerssons underbara resa/The Wonderful Adventures of Nils*. 1964: *Markisinnan* [The marquise] (TVD); *Svenska bilder* [Swedish pictures]; *Äktenskapsbrottaren* [Mixed doubles]. 1965: *Nattcafé* [Night café] (TVD); *Alla mina söner* [All my sons] (TVD); *Festivitetssalongen* [The banquet room]; *Niklasons* (TVMS); *Herr Dardanell och hans upptåg på landet* [Mr. Dardanell and his pranks in the countryside] (TVD); *Villa med staket* [House with a fence] (TVD); *Att angöra en brygga* [Docking the boat]; *Nilsson* (short); *Hans nåds testamente* [His grace's will] (TVD). 1966: *Hotet* [The threat] (TVD); *Skuggan av Mart* [Shadow of Mart] (TVD); *Kvinnas man* [Woman's man] (TVD); *Farfar till häst* [Grandpa on horseback] (TVD); *Tartuffe* (TVD); *Yngsjömordet/Woman of Darkness*. 1967: *Trettondagsafton* [Twelfth night] (TVD); *OBS! Sammanträde pågår* [Attention! Meeting in session] (TVD); *Mördarligan* [Gang of murderers] (TVD); *ABC* (TVM). 1968: *Lådan* [The box]; *Jag älskar Du älskar* [I love, you love]; *I huvet på en gammal gubbe* [Inside an old man's head]. 1969: *Som natt och dag* [Like night and day]; *Duett för kannibaler/Duet for Cannibals*; *Mumintrollet* [Moomin troll] (TVDS). 1970: *Spader, Madame!* [Spades, madame!] (TVM). 1971: *Niklas och figuren* [Niklas and the figure]; *Äppelkriget* [The apple war]. 1972: *Hundarna* [The dogs] (TVD); *Trummor i natten* [Drums in the night] (TVD); *Mannen som slutade rökal/The Man Who Gave Up Smoking*. 1973: *Träben och emaljöga* [Wooden leg and glass eye] (TVM, short); *Kvartetten som sprängdes* [The quartet that split up] (TVM). 1974: *Gustav III* (TVM); *Dunderklumpen* [Thundering Fatty] (voice only). 1975: *Ägget är löst/Egg, Egg, a Hard-boiled Story*; *Släpp fångarne loss—det är vår!* [Let the prisoners free—it's spring!]. 1976: *Ansikte mot*

ansikte/Face to Face (TVM);[1] *En dåres försvarstal* [A madman's defense] (TVM). 1977:
Semlons gröna dalar [Semlon's green valleys] (TVM). 1978: *Picassos äventyr!/The Adventures of Picasso* (also idea); *En vandring i solen* [A walk in the sun]. 1979: *En kärleks sommar* [A summer of love]; *Lucie*. 1980: *Mannen som blev miljonär* [The man who became a millionaire]; *Sällskapsresan* [The charter trip]; *Från och med Herr Gunnar Papphammar* [By and with Mr. Gunnar Papphammar] (TVM also director).[2] 1981: *Sopor* [Garbage]; *Varn!ng för Jönssonligan* [Beware of the Jönsson gang!]. 1982: *Skulden* [Guilt] (TVM); *Den enfaldige mördaren* [The simple-minded murderer]; *En flicka på halsen* [Saddled with a girl]; *Jönssonligan & Dynamit Harry* [The Jönsson gang and Dynamite-Harry]; *Gräsänklingar* [Grass widowers]. 1983: *Kalabaliken i Bender* [The uproar in Bender]; *P & B*. 1984: *Slagskämpen/The Inside Man*; *Fröken Fleggmans mustasch* [Miss Fleggman's mustache] (TVD); *Jönssonligan får guldfeber* [The Jönsson gang gets gold fever]. 1985: *Dödspolare* [Buddies till death]. 1986: *Morrhår och ärtor* [Whiskers and peas] (also director and script); *Jönssonligan dyker upp igen* [The Jönsson gang shows up again]. 1988: *Vargens tid* [Time of the wolf]. 1989: *Kronvittnet* [Witness for the crown]; *Jönssonligan på Mallorca* [The Jönsson gang on Majorca]; *7 maj 1945* (short). 1990: *Den hemlige vännen* [The secret friend]. 1991: *Underjordens hemlighet* [Secret of the underworld]; *Duo jag* [You and me] (TVM, also script, co-director). 1992: *Vennerman & Winge* (TVM, also script, co-director). 1993: *Maklean* (TVM); *Brandbilen som försvann* [The firetruck that disappeared]; *Mannen på balkongen* [The man on the balcony]. 1994: *Roseanna* (TVM);[3] *Polismördaren* [Cop killer] (TVM); *Polis polis potatismos* [Police, police, potato-head] (TVM);[3] *Stockholm Marathon*. 1995: *En på miljonen* [One in a million]. 1996: *Nu är pappa trött igen* [Now daddy's tired again]. 1997: *Ogifta par—en film som skiljer sig* [Unmarried couples—a film that splits-up]. 1999: *Papphammar* (TVM).

BIBLIOGRAPHY

Forslund, Bengt: *Från Gösta Ekman till Gösta Ekman*. Stockholm: Askild & Kärnekull, 1977.

AWARD

GB 1973

NOTES

1. Theatrically released abroad in edited version.
2. Originally a series of shorts for television. Edited for cinemas in 1981.
3. These last three films are among the six with Ekman as Martin Beck. So far they have only been shown on Swedish television.

GÖSTA EKMAN [Sr.] (Stockholm, 28 Dec. 1890–12 Jan. 1938), actor. It is unusual for the death of an actor to trigger nationwide mourning, but that is what occurred when Gösta Ekman died prematurely in 1938. He made relatively few films, and it has also been claimed that the silver screen never did justice to his stage charisma, but he nevertheless deserves a place in Swedish film history. He also left a living legacy to Swedish film through his son *Hasse

Ekman, a leading director and actor. His grandchildren and great-grandchildren have also become prominent names in the Swedish film and theater world. *Max von Sydow has stated that Gösta Ekman served as an inspiration when he decided to become an actor himself.

Ekman was above all a stage actor, but he also functioned as a theater manager. He lived a hectic life, constantly battling to keep his enterprise afloat economically; during the mid-1920s, furthermore, while living in Berlin to play the lead in Murnau's *Faust*, he became addicted to cocaine. It is no cliché to say that Ekman burned his candle from both ends. In the evenings he appeared on stage; that same day, or even more frequently, at night, he acted for the camera. Still, he seems to have remained optimistic, always considering new projects. His son Hasse has depicted this in his film *Kungliga patrasket* [Royal rabble], a partly biographical account of the Ekman family in the 1930s.

It is perhaps no coincidence that so many of Gösta Ekman's film characters have specific traits in common: They are unrealistic dreamers. This important aspect of Ekman's persona has been considered a "typically Swedish" feature. Although the notion of a specific national character can be questioned, many critics used this label when they tried to characterize his film roles. A good example is *Swedenhielms*, where Ekman portrayed an inventive genius, rational and certainly a man of honor but at the same time an irresponsible dreamer, filled with unrealistic plans. Many observers of "Swedishness" pointed to the blend of desire and rationality, dreaming and icy clear mindedness, as representative. And who could embody this better than Gösta Ekman? He played this type of character in other films, for instance, *Intermezzo*, where the violin virtuoso—another of his most famous roles—is a Faustian character, willing to sacrifice his family for the sake of his art and the love of a young woman. Yet he learns in the end to be a responsible father to his family. A third example is *Häxnatten* [Witches' night], where for a moment the protagonist wants to leave his dull, everyday life as a teacher and begins to dream of running away with a former pupil (played by *Signe Hasso), with the same outcome.

The basis for this impression may be found in Ekman's acting technique, which always verges on theatricality and yet seems improvised. His particular style was used to great advantage by the directors of his best films, *Gustaf Molander (*Swedenhielms* and *Intermezzo*) and *Schamyl Bauman (*Häxnatten*), who apparently gave their actors relative freedom to improvise within the overall framework of the roles.

FILMOGRAPHY

1911: *Stockholmsfrestelser* [Temptations of Stockholm] (short); *Blott en dröm* [Just a dream] (short). 1912: *Systrarna* [The sisters] (short); *Trädgårdsmästaren/The Broken Spring Rose*.[1] 1913: *Den okända* [The unknown]. 1918: *Mästerkatten i stövlar* [Master cat in boots]. 1920: *Bomben* [The bomb]; *Thora van Deken*; *Gyurkovicsarna* [The Gyurkovics family]; *Familjens traditioner* [Family traditions]. 1921: *En lyckoriddare* [A fortune hunter]; *En hjulsaga* [A wheel tale] (short). 1922: *Vem dömer/Mortal Clay*;

Kärlekens ögon [The eyes of love]. 1924: *Carl XII:s kurir* [Karl XII:s courier]; *Unga greven tar flickan och priset* [The young count wins the girl and the prize]. 1925: *Carl XII/Charles XII*. 1926: *Faust*; *Klovnen/Heart of a Clown*. 1927: *Hans engelska fru/Discord*; *En perfekt gentleman/A Husband by Proxy* (also director). 1928: *Gustaf Wasa*; *Revolutionshochzeit/The Last Night*. 1930: *För hennes skull/For Her Sake*; *Mach'mir die Welt zum Paradies* (German version). 1931: *Brokiga Blad/Brokiga Blad* [Colorful pages]. 1932: *Journey's End* (Swedish speaker). 1933: *Kanske en diktare* [Perhaps a poet]; *Kära släkten/Kaera slaekten* [Dear family]; *Två man om en änka* [Two men after one widow]. 1934: *København, Kalundborg og-?* 1935: *Swedenhielms/Swedenhielms*. 1936: *Kungen kommer* [The king is coming]; *Johan Ulfstjerna*; *Intermezzo/Intermezzo*. 1937: *Häxnatten* [Witches' night]. 1940: *Än en gång Gösta Ekman* [Gösta Ekman once again] (the shooting of the film, working title "Far och son" [Father and son], was interrupted by Gösta Ekman's death, but the incomplete film was released in 1940).

BIBLIOGRAPHY

Ekman, Gösta. *Den tänkande August*. Stockholm: Bonniers, 1928.
Ekman, Hasse. *Gösta Ekman*. Stockholm: Bonniers, 1938.
Forslund, Bengt. *Från Gösta Ekman till Gösta Ekman*. Stockholm: Askild & Kärnekull, 1977.
Lindberg, Per. *Gösta Ekman. Skådespelaren och människan*. Stockholm: Natur & Kultur, 1942.

NOTE

1. Banned in Sweden.

HASSE EKMAN (Stockholm, 10 Sept. 1915–), actor, director. Son of actor *Gösta Ekman [Sr.] and father of yet another generation of actors and directors, *Gösta Ekman [Jr.] and Mikael Ekman (his grandchildren Sanna Ekman and Måns Ekman have also begun acting careers). Hasse Ekman can be described as the "boy wonder" of Swedish film. He made an early debut as a stage actor in the early 1930s, acted with his father in *Intermezzo*, and wrote his first screenplay, *Blixt och dunder* [Thunder and lightning], based on a story by P. G. Wodehouse, by age twenty. His career as a director began with a light comedy, *Med deg i dina armar* [With you in my arms], but eventually he was to mix light entertainment with heavier, more melodramatic material. His best films are the result of his cooperation with producer *Lorens Marmstedt at Terrafilm, who apparently both taught him the trade (just as in the case of *Ingmar Bergman) and gave him enough freedom to express himself.

Ekman has often been described as a very competent craftsman, whereas it is harder to distinguish a more personal vision like Bergman's. When Bergman's star began to rise, critics compared the two directors in a manner that was not beneficial to Ekman. He felt compelled to "play in the same garden," and despite the quality of films like *Flickan från tredje raden* [The girl from the gallery]—a kind of positive response to the negative worldview of Bergman's *Fängelse/The Devil's Wanton*, where Ekman actually plays the film director—or

Flicka och hyacinter [Girl with hyacinths], perhaps the best film Ekman made, he apparently suffered from an inferiority complex that he was not able to give satisfactory cinematic expression. While Bergman became a world-famous celebrity toward the end of the 1950s, Ekman found it more difficult to work in a domestic film industry that was hard hit by the general economic crisis. He felt compelled to make successful but in many cases rather lightweight comedies. Still, many of his later films were unjustly underrated by the contemporary critics. Ekman stopped directing films in the early 1960s and immigrated to Spain. His last directing task was a satirical family series for Swedish television in 1965. Subsequently he has worked only occasionally with stage direction.

It is possible to distinguish a thematic line in Ekman's rather mixed career that is not far removed from Bergman's "favorite" theme: the need for togetherness in a cold and hostile world. Ekman, however, never paints the world as black as Bergman sometimes does. Ekman's films have more poetic dimensions when he describes loneliness in *Ombyte av tåg* [Changing trains] and other films. He is also more subtle in his expression, which may be the reason it took so long for him to be rediscovered and revived by Swedish critics and film historians.

FILMOGRAPHY

Actor

1924: *Unga greven tar flickan och priset* [The young count wins the girl and the prize]. 1933: *Hemslavinnor* [We slaves at home]; *En natt på Smygeholm* [An evening at Smygeholm]. 1936: *Intermezzo/Intermezzo*. 1937: *John Ericsson—segraren vid Hampton Roads/John Ericsson—Victor at Hampton Roads*. 1938: *Med folket för fosterlandet/Med Folket For Fosterlandet* [With the people for the fatherland]. 1939: *Kadettkamrater* [Cadets together]. 1940: *Juninatten/A Night in June*. 1941: *Livet går vidare* [Life goes on]. 1944: *Jag är eld och luft* [I am fire and air]; *Stopp! Tänk på något annat* [Stop! Think of something else]. 1949: *Fängelse/The Devil's Wanton*, a.k.a. *Prison*; *Törst/Three Strange Loves* [Thirst]. 1953: *Robin Hood of Monteville* (TVM, episode in *Foreign Intrigue*); *The Corpse Goes West* (TVM, episode in *Foreign Intrigue*); *Gycklarnas afton/The Naked Night*, a.k.a. *Sawdust and Tinsel* [Eve of the jesters]; 1954: *I rök och dans* [Dance in the smoke]; *Gula divisionen* [Yellow squadron]; *Souvenir de Paris* (TVM, episode in *Foreign Intrigue*). 1955: *The Blush* (TVM, episode in *Foreign Intrigue*).

Scriptwriter

1938: *Blixt och dunder* [Thunder and lightning] (also actor). 1940: *Hjältar i gult och blått* [Heroes in yellow and blue]; *Karl för sin hatt* [A real man]; *Swing it, magistern!* [Swing it, teacher!]. 1941: *Fröken Kyrkråtta* [Miss churchmouse]; *Spökreportern* [The ghost reporter]; *Magistrarna på sommarlov* [The teachers on summer vacation]. 1943: *Örlogsmän* [Men of war]; *På liv och död* [A life or death matter] (also actor). 1946: *Kärlek och störtlopp* [Love and downhill skiing]. 1950: *Kyssen på kryssen* [The kiss on the cruise]. 1953: *Resan till dej* [The journey to you]; *Glasberget* [The glass mountain] (also actor). 1959: *Det svänger på slottet* [A high old time at the castle].

Director, Actor, Scriptwriter

1940: *Med dej i mina armar* [With you in my arms] (not actor). 1941: *Första divisionen* [First squadron]. 1942: *Lågor i dunklet* [Flames in the gloom]; *Lyckan kommer* [Happiness comes] (not actor). 1943: *Ombyte av tåg* [Changing trains]; *Sjätte skottet* [The sixth shot] (director only). 1944: *En dag skall gry* [A day will dawn]; *Excellensen* [His excellency] (director only); *Som folk är mest* [Like most people] (not actor). 1945: *Kungliga patrasket* [Royal rabble]; *Vandring med månen* [Wandering with the moon]; *Fram för lilla Märta* [Here's to little Märta] (not script). 1946: *I dödens väntrum/Interlude* [In death's waiting room]; *Möte i natten* [Encounter at night]; *Medan porten var stängd* [While the door was closed]. 1947: *En fluga gör ingen sommar* [One swallow doesn't make a summer]. 1948: *Var sin väg* [Each his own way]; *Lilla Märta kommer tillbaka* [Little Märta returns] (not script); *Banketten* [The banquet]. 1949: *Flickan från tredje raden* [The girl in the gallery]. 1950: *Flicka och hyacinter* [Girl with hyacinths] (not actor); *Hjärter Knekt* [Knave of hearts]; *Den vita katten* [The white cat] (not actor). 1951: *Dårskapens hus* [The nuthouse] (compilation film). 1952: *Eldfågeln* [The fire bird] (not actor). 1953: *Vi tre debutera* [We three make our debut] (director only). 1954: *Gabrielle*. 1956: *Egen ingång* [Private entry]; *Sjunde himlen* [Seventh heaven]; *Ratataa eller Staffan Stolle Story* (not actor). 1957: *Med glorian på sned* [The crooked halo]; *Sommarnöje sökes* [Wanted: summer residence] (not actor). 1958: *Den store amatören* [The great amateur]; *Jazzgossen* [The jazz kid]. 1959: *Fröken Chic* [Miss Chic]; *Himmel och pannkaka* [Heaven and pancake]. 1960: *Kärlekens decimaler* [Decimals of love]; *På en bänk i en park* [On a bench in a park]. 1961: *Stöten* [The heist] (director only). 1963: *Min kära är en ros* [My beloved is a rose] (director only). 1964: *Äktenskapsbrottaren* [Mixed doubles] (not actor). 1965: *Niklasons* (TVMS, not script).

BIBLIOGRAPHY

Axelsson, Cecilia. "Bergman vs. Ekman. En uppgörelse mellan saga och helvete." *Chaplin*, no. 259 (Sept.–Oct. 1995):16–21.

Ekman, Hasse. *Den vackra ankungen*. Stockholm: Wahlström & Widstrand, 1955. Autobiography.

Forslund, Bengt. *Från Gösta Ekman till Gösta Ekman*. Stockholm: Askild & Kärnekull, 1977.

Furhammar, Leif, and Jannike Åhlund. "En liten bok om Hasse." *Filmkonst*, no. 16 (1993). Special issue including an interesting commentary by Ingmar Bergman.

Holm, 1947.

AWARD

GB 1995

LENA ENDRE (Härnösand, 8 July 1955–), actress. While working as a shop clerk, she took part in an amateur actors' workshop, Teaterstudion, and then joined a so-called free group, Teater Sputnik, in 1979. Eventually she was accepted by the state school of stage art, where she studied from 1983 to 1986. In the meantime she made her film debut as the hero's girlfriend in *Slagskämpen/The Inside Man*, an utterly failed attempt at an "international" Swedish spy film. With inadequate direction, she gave no hint of a budding talent. Then she became a regular in the long-running and widely seen soap opera *Varuhuset* [The department store]. This brought her fame, but soap operas do not earn an actress prestige. At the same time, however, Lena Endre was employed by the

Royal Dramatic Theater, where she has managed to establish herself as a leading—or at least one of the most interesting—actresses in contemporary Sweden.
She is now a regular at the national stage and has received widespread recognition, not least from *Ingmar Bergman, who gave her several important stage
roles as well as a part in his latest television movie, *Larmar och gör sig till*
[Fussing and fuming]. Incidentally, Endre has been directed by two generations
of Bergmans, since she also had parts in Daniel Bergman's *Söndags-
barn/Sunday's Children* and Eva Bergman's television movie *Den ena kärleken
och den andra* [One love and another], a unique circumstance. She also played
the waitress who is abandoned by Bergman's father in the television production
Den goda viljan/The Best Intentions. In 1993 she was awarded the prestigious
O'Neil grant of the royal stage. Her film work is not yet extensive, but she has
appeared in a number of important roles, including a truly impressive *Hedda
Gabler* on television. She also revealed real talent in Liv Ullmann's film *Kristin
Lavransdatter*, where Endre was the only breath of life in an otherwise static
film.

FILMOGRAPHY

1984: *Slagskämpen/The Inside Man*. 1987: *Porttelefonen* [The buzzer] (TVM, short);
Varuhuset [The department store] (TVDS, also in 1988); *Mio min Mio* [Mio my Mio]
(dubbing only); *När lämnade vi varandra?* [When did we leave each other?] (short).
1988: *Vendetta i en etta* [Revenge in a studio apartment] (TVM, short); *Besökarna* [The
visitors]; *Kråsnålen* [The tie pin] (TVMS). 1989: *Istanbul*. 1990: *Orfeus* (TVM, short);
Pelle flyttar till Komfusenbo [Pelle moves to Komfusenbo] (TVM, short). 1991: *Den
goda viljan/The Best Intentions* (TVM);[1] *Trappen* [The staircase] (TVMS). 1992: *Sön-
dagsbarn/Sunday's Children*. 1993: *Den ena kärleken och den andra* [One love and
another] (TVM); *Hedda Gabler* (TVD). 1994: *Yrrol—en kolossalt genomtänkt film*
[Yrrol—a terribly well-thought-out film]. 1995: *Kristin Lavransdatter*. *"Brudkransen"*
[Kristin Lavransdatter: "The bridal wreath"]; *Slottet* [The castle] (short). 1996: *Jerusalem*;
Juloratoriet [The Christmas oratorio]; *The Return of Jésus, part II*. 1997: *Svenska hjältar*
[Swedish heroes]; *Spring för livet* [Run for your life]; *Ogifta par—en film som skiljer
sig* [Unmarried couples—a film that splits up]; *Larmar och gör sig till* [Fussing and
fuming] (TVM). 1998: *Från regnormarnas liv* [Rain snakes] (TVD); *Sanna ögonblick*
[True moments]; *Ögat* [The eye]; *Trädgård* [Garden] (short). 1999: *Fatimas tredje hemlighet* [Fatima's third secret] (short); *Jävla Kajsa* [Damn Kajsa] (TVMS).

BIBLIOGRAPHY

Björkvall, Lars. "Jag heter Lena, inte Ingrid." *Expressen*, 5 Nov. 1988. Interview.
Tollstoy, Camilla. "Lena Endre." *Clara*, no. 2 (1991):16–17, 120, 122. Interview.

AWARD

GB 1996

NOTE

1. Theatrically released in 1992 in an edited version.

AGNETA FAGERSTRÖM-OLSSON (Tullinge, 22 Oct. 1948–), actor, director. During her university studies she was active in student theater. She was involved with film before being accepted at the Dramatic Institute as a director trainee in 1978. After several shorts, she made the widely acclaimed television movie *Seppan*, set in a small industrial town outside of Stockholm during her growing-up years. The film was awarded a Prix Italia the same year. Her second feature, *Hjälten* [The Hero], about an adolescent girl and her problematic relationship with her father, had a mixed reception. The film's unevenness can perhaps be explained by a difficult production process during which she was forced to rework the script. Despite its problems, this poetic and visually rich film explores Fagerström-Olsson's main theme—young persons growing into maturity—and it deserves better than just to be ignored. Fagerström-Olsson further demonstrated her ability for visual fantasy in her third feature, *Kärlekens himmelska helvete* [The heavenly hell of love]. One might say that she is somewhat un-Swedish in letting her story be subordinated to the visual. She has also co-directed the remarkable documentary feature *Hårga* with her husband, cinematographer John O. Olsson. This is a visually rich depiction of sheep farmers, saturated with the nature mystique of older Swedish film tradition.

FILMOGRAPHY

Actress

1978: *Slumrande toner* [Dormant tones]. 1983: *G.*

Director, Scriptwriter

1973: *Ådalen 73* (docu., collective). 1982: *Jag går upp på morgonen med girafferna* [I get up in the morning with the giraffes] (short). 1984: *Suzanne* (short). 1986: *Seppan* (TVM); *Hårga* (docu., codir. John O. Olsson). 1989: *Här har ju inte ens Ernst Rolf spelat* [Not even Ernst Rolf performed here] (docu.). 1990: *Hjälten* [The hero]. 1991: *Sista vinden från Kap Horn* [Last wind from Cape Horn] (TVM). 1992: *Vi ses i Krakow* [We'll meet in Krakow] (short). 1993: *Kärlekens himmelska helvete* [The heavenly hell of love]. 1997: *Hammarkullen eller Vi ses i Kaliningrad* [Hammarkullen, or See you in Kaliningrad] (TVMS).[1]

BIBLIOGRAPHY

Jordahl, Anneli. "Agneta Fagerström-Olsson." *Arbetaren*, 24 Feb. 1989. Interview.
Mårtensson, Jan. "Hon vill väcka drömmar, längtan och passioner." *Arbetet*, 27 Aug. 1995.

NOTE

1. The director was awarded the 1998 *Ingmar Bergman personal film prize for this television movie.

ERIK "HAMPE" FAUSTMAN (Stockholm, 3 July 1919–26 Aug. 1961), actor, director. He started as an actor, attending the Royal Dramatic Theater School with a talented and ambitious group that included actor George Fant, brother of

"Kenne" Fant, who later headed Svensk Filmindustri. Faustman began directing films in 1943 with a story about saboteurs in a Swedish port during the war. A committed socialist, he was determined from the very beginning to depict the life of the working class. His political affiliation and thematic ambitions make Faustman stand out among Swedish film directors in the 1940s and 1950s, although he was rather traditional in his directing style.

Among his more remarkable films in the 1940s are two about the miserable conditions of the *statare*, or estate workers, the most oppressed of the rural proletariat who were paid partly in kind. *När ängarna blommar* [When the meadows blossom] was made just after the system had been abolished in 1945. The second film, *Lars Hård*, with his old comrade George Fant in the lead, was initially turned down by the production company Filmo, tied to the labor movement. Instead, Sandrews gave him the chance, and the film was quite successful with audiences. Reviews were generally favorable as well, though some leftist critics thought the class conflict had been toned down in this tale of a proletarian Don Juan. Then Sandrews and producer Rune Waldekranz let Faustman direct *Främmande hamn* [Foreign port], a tale about class solidarity among sailors. The crew of a Swedish ship mutinies in a foreign harbor when they discover that the ship is used for gun running to Franco during the Spanish civil war. Eventually they are victorious when the captain discovers his responsibility for freedom and democracy and gives his life for these ideals.

Faustman continued to depict the life of the working class in a series of films. *Restaurant Intim* is about restaurant workers. *Hon kom som en vind* [She came like the wind], perhaps one of his more remarkable films about the working man in modern society, concerns a middle-aged worker who is lured away by a seductive girl when he finds his ordinary life dull and meaningless. Although he finally gives in and returns home, the film is a sensitive account of alienation in the modern welfare state, where material goals have been achieved but in a spiritual void. This is typical for Faustman. Despite his political orientation, he periodically reveals an attraction to more existential themes.

Forming their own production company, F-Produktion, Faustman and George Fant made additional films with proletarian themes, such as the truck driver drama *Resa i natten* [Voyage in the night]. In later years, Faustman's growing addiction to alcohol—and the fact that his last film was a total disaster—resulted in his disappearance from the film industry and premature death.

FILMOGRAPHY

Actor

1940: *Med livet som insats* [Life at stake]. 1941: *Kvinna ombord* [Woman on board]. 1942: *Rid i natt!* [Ride this night!]. 1943: *En vår i vapen* [A spring at arms]; *Vi mötte stormen* [We met the storm] (narrator); *Kvinnor i fångenskap* [Women in captivity]; *Katrina/Katrina*; *Det brinner en eld* [There's a fire burning]; *Älskling jag ger mig!* [Darling, I surrender!]. 1944: *Excellensen* [His excellency]; *Mitt folk är icke ditt* [My people are not yours]; *Den osynliga muren* [The invisible wall]. 1946: *Medan porten var stängd*

[While the door was closed]. 1953: *The Ghost* (TVM, episode in *Foreign Intrigue*). 1954: *Souvenir de Paris* (TVM, episode in *Foreign Intrigue*); *Mr. Landstrasse—Haupsta* (TVM, episode in *Foreign Intrigue*). 1957: *Aldrig i livet* [Not in your life]. 1960: *A Matter of Morals*.

Director

1943: *Natt i hamn* [Night in port]; *Sonja* (also actor, script). 1944: *Vi behöver varann* [We need each other] (NCF, also actor); *Flickan och Djävulen* [The girl and the devil]. 1945: *Brott och straff/Crime and Punishment* (also actor). 1946: *När ängarna blommar* [When the meadows blossom] (also actor, script); *Harald Handfaste* [Harald the stalwart] (also actor). 1947: *Krigsmans erinran* [A soldier's oath] (also script). 1948: *Lars Hård* (also actor); *Främmande hamn* [Foreign port]. 1949: *Smeder på luffen* [Blacksmiths on the road] (also actor, script). 1950: *Restaurant Intim* (also script). 1951: *Kvinnan bakom allt* [The woman behind it all] (also script, episode). 1952: *Ubåt 39* [Submarine 39]; *Hon kom som en vind* [She came like the wind] (also actor). 1953: *Kvinnohuset* [The women's house] (also script). 1954: *Gud Fader och tattaren*, a.k.a. *Tattarblod* [Our Father and the gypsy, a.k.a. Gypsy blood]; *Café Lunchrasten* [The lunchbreak café]. 1955: *Resa i natten* [Voyage in the night]; *Kärlek på turné*, a.k.a. *Ingen så tokig som jag* [Love on tour, a.k.a. Nobody's as crazy as me] (also actor).

BIBLIOGRAPHY

Schmalensee, Oscar von. "Bergman og Hampe Faustman." *Kosmorama*, no. 137 (Spring 1978):137–139.
Strauss, Ulf von. "Hampe. En partisk och patetisk essay." *Film & TV*, nos. 1–3 (1975): 46–52.
Vesterlund, Per. *Den glömde mannen.* Stockholm: Stockholms universitet, 1999. Dissertation on HF.
Vesterlund, Per. "Legenden om en 'äkta' superhjälte." *Filmhäftet*, no. 96 (1996):39–49. Essay on HF and the Swedish film critics.

LARS LENNART FORSBERG (Göteborg, 31 July 1933–) director. Forsberg is not to be confused with the other Göteborg director Lars Forsberg (the latter Forsberg is mainly active in television). Many directors of Lars Lennart Forsberg's generation have shared the same experience in the last decades. Forsberg's career is typical. He made an impressive debut on the big screen with *Misshandlingen* [The assault], in many ways a typical example of the late 1960s and early 1970s films critical of society. It depicted society's injustices in a rather provocative way, which was deliberately out of sync with the lead actor who was an unpleasant sociopath. This divided the audience, with many feeling unsettled when they revealed themselves not as humanitarian as would have been expected of them in the face of social injustice, when they were confronted with this aggressive film character. His next work was a controversial television serial for children, *Broster Broster*, set in the countryside. Here he gives a critique of modern society so typical of his time; the film is ecologically aware and pleads for solidarity with the oppressed of the world.

Like his contemporaries, Forsberg's career shifted, with the explicit politics he demonstrated so clearly with his debut vanishing to be replaced by a psychological treatment of such societal ills as alienation. A typical example is *Kristoffers hus* [Kristoffer's house] with *Thommy Berggren as a photographer. During a professional assignment the photographer discovers the loneliness among people when he starts to investigate the fate of a man who has been found dead in his apartment, apparently not missed by anyone, including even his relatives.

A similar critique of modernity was developed in a lighter and more subtle fashion in three films based on the writings of Stig Claesson. The first two were only shown on television, but the third was shown in the cinemas. *Vem älskar Yngve Frej?* [Who loves Yngve Frej?], *På palmblad och rosor* [On palm leaves and roses], and *Henrietta* all dealt with almost forgotten individuals living in the countryside. He films what is left of a once lively and prosperous milieu, now almost deserted with the exception of a few rather odd human beings. They persist in living in their old-fashioned ways, seemingly unabsorbed by modern culture and lifestyle. The films did not depict this situation as backward; instead, it is an alternative or a new way of life. This was underlined by rather discrete and poetic language in the film, which most spectators experienced quite profoundly as typically "Swedish." Among his later works for television has been the serial *Kråsnålen* [The tie pin], a big and lavish depiction of the early worker's movement in Sweden. He has also, over the years, done some documentary work for Swedish television.

FILMOGRAPHY

Director, Scriptwriter

1963: *Samtal* [Conversations] (short). 1965: *Pappas dockor* [Daddy's dolls] (short). 1966: *Min stad* [My town] (short). 1969: *Misshandlingen* [The assault]. 1971: *Broster Broster* (TVMS). 1973: *Vem älskar Yngve Frej?* [Who loves Yngve Frej?] (TVM). 1974: *Engeln* [The angel] (TVMS, not script). 1976: *På palmblad och rosor* [On palm leaves and roses] (TVM). 1977: *Måndagarna med Fanny* [Mondays with Fanny]. 1979: *Kristoffers hus* [Kristoffer's house]. 1981: *Hans Christian och sällskapet* [Hans Christian and the society] (TVM). 1983: *Henrietta*. 1986: *Prästkappan* [Preacher's coat] (TVMS). 1988: *Kråsnålen* [The tie pin] (TVMS). 1993: *Nästa man till rakning* [Next man for shave] (TVMS).

BIBLIOGRAPHY

Björkman, 1977.
Tournez, André. "Lasse Forsberg." *Jeune cinéma*, no. 57 (Sept.–Oct. 1971):25–29.

AWARD

GB 1970

SAMUEL FRÖLER (Madesjö, 24 Mar. 1957–), actor. His list of acting credits is really not extensive but very important, and he has made himself quite a name in contemporary Swedish filmmaking, above all in television. He was educated at the state school of stage art in Göteborg from 1982 to 1985 and then employed at Stockholm Municipal Theater. His first role as the male lead in *Lars Molin's family chronicle *Tre kärlekar* [Three loves] made him famous overnight and also convinced *Ingmar Bergman to cast him in the role as Bergman's father in his own family tale, *Den goda viljan/The Best Intentions*, where Fröler played another important role. One reason why he was so perfectly cast in that role is that Fröler himself was born in a clerical family. In the series, he makes a very look-a-like portrait of the middle-aged Bergman himself. Fröler was to repeat this role in Bergman's tale of his mother's extramarital affairs in Liv Ullmann's filming of *Enskilda samtal/Private Confessions*. In 1997–98 Fröler was very successful in the role of a country doctor working in the Stockholm archipelago in the series *Skärgårdsdoktorn* [Doctor of the archipelago]. Fröler is definitely not an actor of the "big gesture's school." On the contrary, he makes good use of his obvious strong screen presence, and some writers have described that his real magic lies in his intense eyes.

FILMOGRAPHY

1987: *Bröderna* [The brothers] (short). 1989/91: *Tre kärlekar* [Three loves] (TVMS). 1991: *Snöriket* [The snow realm] (TVM); *Den goda viljan/The Best Intentions* (TVM).[1] 1992: *Blueprint* (TVM). 1994: *Fallet Paragon* [The Paragon case] (TVM). 1995: *Sommaren* [The summer]. 1996: *Enskilda samtal/Private Confessions* (TVM). 1997–1998: *Skärgårdsdoktorn* [Doctor of the archipelago] (TVMS). 1998: *Ögat* [The eye]. 1999: *En doft av Paradiset* [A scent of paradise]; *Svar med foto* [Answer with photo].

BIBLIOGRAPHY

Hagen, Cecilia. "Frölers succéblick." *Expressen*, 15 Mar. 1998, Sunday sec.

NOTE

1. Theatrically released in 1992 in an edited version.

EWA FRÖLING (Stockholm, 9 Aug. 1952–), actress, director. After some amateur theater practice she was accepted, at only seventeen years of age, by the state school of stage art at the end of the 1960s. After graduating she worked for a while at the Stockholm Municipal Theater and its experimental stage, Unga Klara, before she was employed by the Royal Dramatic Theater in 1977, where she remained until 1990. She quickly became famous when *Ingmar Bergman offered her the female lead in *Fanny och Alexander/Fanny and Alexander*. This role brought world fame, and she received acting offers from abroad; however, she regarded the Hollywood offer as a gilded cage, and she has preferred to remain independent. She has also tried to rid herself of the notoriety of being just another in a long list of "Bergman Women" that came with the success of *Fanny och Alexander*. She has shown bright, comic sides in various roles and can be regarded a comedienne in contemporary Swedish cinema and television. Her film work has not been extensive, as she turns down offers that she considers inappropriate, a problem she shares with many other middle-aged actresses. She has also done some stage directing.

FILMOGRAPHY

Actor

1975: *Orestes* (TVD). 1976: *Vi har många namn* [We have many names] (TVM); *Drömmen om Amerika* [The dream about America]. 1977: *Fia i folkhemmet* [Fia in people's home] (TVM); *Månen är en grön ost* [The moon is a green cheese] (TVM). 1978: *Dagar med Knubbe* [Days with Stubby] (TVMS); *Chez nous*. 1979: *Misantropen* [The misanthrope] (TVD); *Katitzi* (TVMS). 1980: *Välkommen hem* [Welcome home] (TVD). 1981: *Sally och friheten* [Sally and freedom]; *Pelle Svanslös* [Pelle no-tail] (voice). 1982: *Fanny och Alexander/Fanny and Alexander*.[1] 1983: *G*; *Två killar och en tjej* [Two guys and a gal]. 1984: *Adoptionen* [The adoption] (TVD); *Hur ska det gå för Pettersson?* [What will become of Pettersson?] (TVDS). 1985: *Hålet* [The hole] (TVM, short); *Examen* [Exam] (TVM, short); *Pelle Svanslös i Amerikatt* [Pelle no-tail in America] (voice). 1986: *Demoner* [Demons]; *På liv och död* [A life or death matter]. 1987: *Ein Tieffen mit Rimbaud*; *Jim och piraterna Blom* [Jim and the Blom pirates]; *Varuhuset* [The department store] (TVDS); *Träff i helfigur* [Hit in full figure] (TVM). 1988: *Clark Kent* (TVMS); *Uppfinnarrock* [Inventor's coat] (TVMS); *En far* [A father] (TVD); *SOS—en segelsällskapsresa* [SOS—a guided sailing trip]. 1989: *Maskrosbarn* [Dandelion children] (TVMS); *Fallgropen* [The pitfall]. 1991: *Oxen/The Ox*. 1992: *Maskeraden* [The masquerade] (TVD). 1993: *Älska, älskar inte* [Love, love not] (short); *Rosenbaum: Det sista vittnet* [Rosenbaum: the last witness] (TVM); *Sista dansen* [The last dance]. 1995: *När alla vet* [When everybody knows]; *Bert—den siste oskulden* [Bert—the last virgin]. 1996: *Letters from the East*; *Ellinors bröllop* [Ellinor's wedding]. 1997: *Snoken* [The sleuth] (TVMS); *OP:7* (TVMS). 1998: *Glasblåsarns barn* [The glassblower's children] (voice); *OP:7* (TVMS). 1999: *Jakten på en mördare: Lögnen* [The search for a killer: The lie] (TVM); *OP:7* (TVMS).

Director

1991: *Finns vi?* [Do we exist?] (TVM).

BIBLIOGRAPHY

Mannberg-Zackari, Carin. "Jag tycker om stora utmaningar." *Hertha*, no. 1 (1987): 3–6.
Nilsson, Mats. "Jag vill slå hål på Emiliemyten." *Nöjesguiden*, no. 3 (1986): 4–6.

NOTE

1. In longer version for television in 1984, with limited cinema release in 1983.

KJELL GREDE (Stockholm, 12 Aug. 1936–), director. Grede studied at the University of Stockholm and later worked at a psychiatric ward for retarded children while writing film scripts and trying to interest various film companies. He approached *Ingmar Bergman, and when Bergman approved one of the scripts, Grede knew he had a future in the film business. One script, *Karneval* [Carnival], was accepted, and a few years later Grede made his directing debut with **Hugo och Josefin* [Hugo and Josefin], a film about two children. This was an instant sensation as critics and audiences were confronted with a fresh, new talent that seemed unusually mature in his mode of expression. The following two films also met with wide critical acclaim, but subsequent opinion on Grede's work has been rather divided. When *Min älskade* [My beloved] from 1979 was a critical flop and did poorly with audiences, Grede abandoned the business for many years and turned his attention to television. With *Johan Bergenstråhle, one of Sweden's best stage directors, he codirected a big, lavish series about August Strindberg. Grede returned to the silver screen with *Hip Hip Hurra!*— an account of the so-called Skagen painters. His latest film concerns the last days of Raoul Wallenberg in Budapest. Grede was once married to actress *Bibi Andersson and at present is head of the Dramatic Institute, responsible for training new film directors.

Grede is often characterized as a romantic who has both feet planted firmly on the ground. Most of his protagonists are rather odd individuals, standing outside so-called normal society. They are men who seem weak but in reality are strong: Don Quixote figures with strong Christian overtones. They are often confronted at some point with an existential crisis in which fear of death is intertwined with self-doubt, but this experience leads them to some kind of rebirth, a pattern that is evident in Grede's films, regardless of whether the characters are based on real persons, such as Wallenberg or painter Søren Krøyer (*Hip Hip Hurra!*), or are fictitious, like Harry Munter.

This may be seen as a general criticism of certain tendencies in modern society. Grede calls into question the traditional male role of dominance and power because this archetype in fact is a destructive one, and in his films such individuals are depicted as guilt ridden. They can only be redeemed if they acknowledge their hidden and repressed weak dimensions.

As a film director Grede is a pure poet with a strong feeling for the pictorial, symbolic narrative. This is a strength when he reveals the inner qualities of life and being but can also become a weakness when the story as such becomes blurred. This was the case, for instance, with his account of the turn-of-the-century Skagen painters; many critics objected that actions and individuals disappeared behind a veil of blotched symbolism.

FILMOGRAPHY

1961: *Karneval* [Carnival] (script only). 1966: *Sotaren* [The chimney sweep] (short). 1967: *Hugo och Josefin* [Hugo and Josefin] (also script). 1972: *Klara Lust* [Klara Desire] (also script). 1974: *En enkel melodi* [A simple melody] (also script). 1976: *En dåres försvarstal* [A madman's defense] (TVMS, also script). 1977: *Det låter som en saga* [It sounds like a fairy tale] (TVM, also script). 1979: *Min älskade* [My beloved] (also script). 1981: *Stängda dörrar* [No exit] (TVD). 1982: *Studenten* [The student] (TVM); *Fångarna i Altona* [Prisoners of Altona] (TVD). 1985: *August Strindberg, ett liv* [August Strindberg, a life] (TVMS, codir. Johan Bergenstråhle). 1987: *Hip Hip Hurra!* (also script). 1990: *God afton, herr Wallenberg/Good Evening, Mr. Wallenberg* (also script).

BIBLIOGRAPHY

Björkman, Stig. "Användbara drömmar." *Chaplin*, no. 95 (1969): 343–345. Interview.
Björkman, 1977.
Tournés, André. "Kjell Grede." *Jeune cinéma*, no. 57 (Sept.–Oct. 1971):37–41.

AWARDS

GB 1968

GB 1987

GB 1990

LASSE HALLSTRÖM (Stockholm, 2 June 1946–), director. Hallström is a child of Swedish television, which has served as a training ground for many directors of his generation. His father was also a skilled amateur documentary filmmaker. Hallström was a trained still photographer and had made several short documentaries about various Swedish pop groups when he entered the entertainment department of the state television company. Among his assignments was a series of short sketches for various entertainment shows, where he became part of the so-called OJ-gänget (the Oh! gang). One of his partners then was *Lasse Åberg, who was also to become a well-known film director. Hallström was discovered by the film industry when he made the hour-long television film *Skall vi hem till dig . . . ?* [Should we go to your place . . . ?]. Producer Bengt Forslund at Svensk Filmindustri let him direct a feature, *En kille och en tjej* [A guy and a gal], which became an immediate success both with the audience and with the critics and paved the way for a further career in Swedish film. After several additional light comedies about male-female relationships, he made the more serious *Mitt liv som hund/My Life as a Dog*, with its mix of nostalgia and tragicomedy. Since this film proved to be a minor hit on the U.S. market, he was offered work in the American film industry. A couple of projects never got off the ground—a remake of *Peter Pan* and a sequel to *Mitt liv som hund*—but he has subsequently made four English-language films, thus establishing himself as one of the few modern Swedish film directors to have an American career. He is married to actress *Lena Olin.

Hallström is a director who improvises, and consequently he is highly dependent on the skill and consistency of his actors, which may explain the uneven quality of his films. He is known to use endless quantities of film stock, filming the same scene over and over again. With the right actors, this method gives his films a free, open quality, but in other instances, the effect is only muddled. There is no obvious consistent theme in his films, at least none that can be labeled personal. One might say that he has frequently been attracted to the "buddy motif" and gives idealized or idyllic depictions of male companionship. But he can also criticize this stance, for instance, in *Jag är med barn* [I'm pregnant], about a young man who suddenly discovers he will be a father and is torn between the desire to continue his freewheeling bachelor lifestyle and the pressure to become mature and responsible. In the end, the latter wins.

FILMOGRAPHY

1971: *Kärlekssökaren* [The love seeker] (TVM); *Fredag med Familjen Kruse* [Friday with the Kruse family] (TVDS, also actor). 1973: *Ska vi hem till dig . . . eller hem till mig . . . eller var och en till sitt* [Shall we go to your place . . . or my place . . . or each go home alone] (TVM, also script, photo.); *Det är grisens fel* [It's the pig's fault] (TVM, short); *Pappas pojkar* [Daddy's boys] (TVM). 1975: *En kille och en tjej* [A guy and a gal]. 1977: *Flyttningen* [The move] (TVM, also script); *Semlons gröna dalar* [Semlon's green valleys] (TVM); *ABBA—The Movie* (semidocu.). 1979: *Jag är med barn* [I'm pregnant]. 1980: *Underbart är kort* [Short is wonderful] (short). 1981: *Kom igen nu'rå!* [Come on again] (TVM, short, also script); *Tuppen* [The cock]; *Gyllene Tider—parkliv* [Golden Times—life in the park] (docu.). 1983: *Två killar och en tjej* [Two guys and a gal]. 1985: *Mitt liv som hund/My Life as a Dog*. 1986: *Alla vi barn i Bullerbyn* [All of us kids from Bullerbyn]. 1987: *Mer om oss barn i Bullerbyn* [More about us kids from Bullerbyn]. 1991: *Once Around*. 1993: *What's Eating Gilbert Grape*. 1995: *Something to Talk About*. 1999: *The Cider House Rules*.

BIBLIOGRAPHY

Jordahl, Anneli, and Håkan Lagher. "Lasse Hallström—nu vågar han söka." *Chaplin*, no. 233 (April–May 1991): 47–53. Interview.
Olofsson, Marie. "Lasse Hallström." *Nöjesguiden* (Dec. 1985): 6, 8, 10. Interview.

LARS HANSON (Göteborg, 26 July 1886–8 Apr. 1965), actor. Hanson started as an engraver employed by a goldsmith, but he was interested in acting and in 1906 was accepted by the Royal Dramatic Theater School. In 1913 he was engaged by Intima Teatern, where he became acquainted with *Gustaf Molander and his wife Karin (who later would become Lars Hanson's wife). This led him to the motion-picture industry, and although Hanson filmed sparingly, he contributed to the success of Swedish silent film in the late 1910s and early 1920s with leading roles in major works such as *Sången om den eldröda blomman* [The song of the scarlet flower], *Erotikon/Just Like a Man*, and last but not least, as the defrocked minister in *Gösta Berlings saga/The Legend of Gösta Berling*. This film brought a temporary engagement in Hollywood, where he was paired several times with Greta Garbo. When he returned to Sweden he devoted himself primarily to the stage but made a film comeback in the mid-1930s.

Lars Hanson was one of the leading actors at the Royal Dramatic Theater for many years, deeply appreciated, even adored not least by the female audience. In their memoirs, many actresses also reveal their devotion to this tall and handsome man who seemingly could spellbind the audience with his art. But an actor like *Max von Sydow has also expressed his admiration, or as he stated in an interview: "For his sharp intellect: I imitated him shamelessly." From today's perspective Hanson's acting style may seem theatrical and pompous, at least in his films, but in its time it was enormously effective. In the early 1930s Hanson was much asked for in letters to film journals, and his comeback in film was greeted with applause. His screen presence was now adapted to encompass roles as patriarchal older men, for instance, the manager Borg, who seduces the much younger *Ingrid Bergman in *Valborgsmassoafton/Walpurgis Night*. This plot was virtually duplicated in their following film, *På Solsidan/On the Sunnyside*, and in his remaining film career Hanson continued to play patriarchs and venerable old men like the air force colonel in *Hasse Ekman's wartime drama *Första divisionen* [First squadron] and the poet von Blankenau, who suffers martyrdom in the same director's *Excellensen* [His excellency]. After the 1940s Hanson's career faded, and his last years were quite pitiful, at least according to *Ingmar Bergman, who gives an anonymous and unflattering portrait of him in *The Magic Lantern* as a lost soul, a shadow of his former self, who wanders about the corridors of the Royal Dramatic Theater.

FILMOGRAPHY

1915: *Dolken* [The dagger].[1] 1916: *Vingarne/The Wings*; *Thèrese/Therese*; *Guldspindeln* [The golden spider];[2] *Balettprimadonnan/Wolo Czawienko* [The ballet primadonna]. 1917: *Tösen från Stormyrtorpet/The Girl from the Marsh Croft*. 1919: *Sången om den eldröda blomman/The Song of the Scarlet Flower*; *Synnöve Solbakken*; *Ett farligt frieri* [A dangerous courtship]. 1920: *Fiskebyn* [The fishing village]; *Erotikon/Just Like a Man*. 1921: *De landsflyktige/In Self Defense*. 1924: *Gösta Berlings saga/The Legend of Gösta Berling*. 1925: *Ingmarsarvet* [Ingmar's inheritance]. 1926: *Till Österland* [To the Orient]; *The Scarlet Letter*. 1927: *The Flesh and the Devil*; *Captain Salvation*; *Buttons*. 1928: *The Divine Woman*; *Heimkehr*; *Synd* [Sin]; *The Wind*. 1930: *The Informer*. 1935: *Valborgsmässoafton/Walpurgis Night*. 1936: *På Solsidan/On the Sunnyside*. 1937: *Konflikt* [Conflict]. 1938: *Vingar kring fyren* [Wings by the lighthouse]. 1941: *Första divisionen* [First squadron]. 1942: *Rid i natt!* [Ride this night!]. 1943: *Det brinner en eld* [There's a fire burning]. 1944: *Excellensen* [His excellency]. 1948: *Intill helvetets portar* [By the gates of hell].

BIBLIOGRAPHY

Siwertz, Margit. *Lars Hanson*. Stockholm: Norstedts, 1947.

NOTES

1. Banned in Sweden.
2. Banned in Sweden.

SIGNE HASSO (Stockholm, 15 Aug. 1915–), actress. Born Signe Larsson. She made an early debut at age twelve as Louison in Moliere's *The Imaginary Invalid*, directed by Olof Molander at the Royal Dramatic Theater. Her talent was recognized, and she played a few more small parts before being accepted at age sixteen as a pupil, the youngest ever, at the school. According to her memoirs, she made her screen debut in 1928 in an advertisement for margarine.

Her movie debut was *Tystnadens hus* [The house of silence], an attempt at a
Swedish detective film that proved to be a total failure, although on location
she met her first husband, the German cinematographer Harry Hasso. The fiasco
made her vow never again to work in film. Instead, she focused on theater work,
making a smash debut in 1934 in *Mädchen in Uniform*. Three years later, however, *Schamyl Bauman persuaded her to star in the film *Häxnatten* [Witches'
night] by first signing *Gösta Ekman [Sr.] as the male lead. Although there was
no critical concensus concerning the film itself, reviewers agreed on one thing:
A new film star had been born. Bauman also cast her in other memorable roles,
for instance, in *Karriär* [Career] and *Vi två/Vi Tvaa* [The two of us]. In 1939
Hasso signed a contract with R.K.O. and the following summer traveled to Los
Angeles via Siberia and Japan. Disappointed at receiving no film roles, she went
to New York, where she stepped into a stage role when the regular actress
became ill. Now she was noticed by MGM. Under contract with that company,
she made a dozen films while continuing to give occasional theater performances.

Because her American film roles have been relatively insignificant, Signe
Hasso is perhaps best known in the United States for her theater work. Her
contribution to Swedish film is more central, since she helped give film in her
native land a new face, both literally and figuratively, during those important
years of transition.

Her greatness may be attributed to her quite complex screen presence, a quality that was apparent in her stage performances as well. As one reviewer wrote
about her breakthrough role in *Mädchen in Uniform*: "When a young naked soul
suddenly enters the stage and brightens the darkness of the auditorium, we, the
audience, are transformed. A miracle has happened, the liberating birth of art.
Everything is brought to life by this girl, the gaiety, the sorrow, the ecstasy, the
rage, the sorrow. She trembled all the way down to her toes from all this." The
reviews of her first Swedish films merely confirmed this reaction.

FILMOGRAPHY

1933: *Tystnadens hus* [The house of silence]. 1937: *Häxnatten* [Witches' night]. 1938:
Karriär [Career]; *Geld fällt vom Himmel*; *Pengar från skyn* [Money from the sky] (Swedish version of the latter). 1939: *Vi två/Vi Tvaa* [The two of us]; *Filmen om Emelie
Högqvist* [The film about Emelie Högqvist]. 1940: *Vildmarkens sång* [The song of the
wilderness]; *Stål* [Steel]; *Än en gång Gösta Ekman* [Gösta Ekman once again],[1] *Stora
famnen* [With open arms]; *Vi tre* [The three of us]. 1941: *Den ljusnande framtid* [Bright
future before us]. 1942: *Journey for Margaret*.[2] 1943: *Assignment in Brittany*; *Heaven
Can Wait*. 1944: *The Story of Dr. Wassel*; *The Seventh Cross*. 1945: *Dangerous Partners*;
Johnny Angel; *The House on 92nd Street*. 1946: *Strange Triangle*; *A Scandal in Paris*.
1947: *Where There's Life*. 1948: *Opium*; *To the End of the Earth*; *A Double Life*. 1950:
Outside the Wall; *Crisis*; *Sånt händer inte här* [This doesn't happen here]. 1951: *End of
Flight* (TVD); *Ticket to Oblivion* (TVD). 1952: *Reunion in Vienna* (TVD); *Cries the
String* (TVD); *The Two Mrs. Carrolls* (TVD); *Something to Celebrate* (TVD); *Two Wise
Women* (TVD); *Unclouded Summer* (TVD). 1953: *Lombardo* (TVM, episode in *Foreign*

Intrigue); *The Doctors* (TVM episode in *Foreign Intrigue*). 1954: *Taxi 13*; *Camille* (TVD); *Den underbara lögnen/The True and the False* (also producer); *Die Sonne von St. Moritz*. 1955: *The Diamond as Big as the Ritz* (TVD). 1956: *Till the End of Time* (TVD). 1960: *Mary Stuart* (TVD); *Duet for Two Hands* (TVD). 1961: *I sista minuten* [At the last minute] (TVD). 1962: *Dead on Nine* (TVD); *The Contenders* (TVD). 1964: *Productions and Decay of Strange Particles* (TVD). 1966: *Picture Mommy Dead*. 1967: *Codename: Heraclitus* (TVM). 1973: *Reflections of Fear*; *The Magician* (TVM). 1974: *QB VII* (TVM). 1975: *The Black Bird*; *Shell Game* (TVM). 1976: *Sherlock Holmes in New York* (TVM). 1977: *I Never Promised You a Rose Garden*; *Winner Take All* (TVM). 1981: *Evita Peron* (TVM). 1982: *Pappa är död* [Father is dead] (TVM). 1985: *Mirrors* (TVM). 1998: *One Hell of a Guy*.

Episodes in

Checkmate (1962), *Route 66* (1962), *Bonanza* (1963), *Run, Buddy Run* (1966), *Green Hornet* (1966), *T.H.E. Cat* (1966), *Road West* (1967), *The Girl from U.N.C.L.E.* (1967), *Coronet Blue* (1967), *Interns* (1971), *Cannon* (1971), *Ghost Story* (1972), *Streets of San Francisco* (1974), *Hawkins* (1974), *This Is the Life* (1974), *Ellery Queen* (1974), *City of Angels* (1977), *Starsky & Hutch* (1978), *Magnum* (1981), *Darkroom* (1981), *Quincy* (1982), *Fame* (1982), *Hart to Hart* (1983), *The Fall Guy* (1984), *Trapper John, MD* (1985).

BIBLIOGRAPHY[3]

Hasso, Signe. *Inte än*. Stockholm: Trevi, 1988.
Hasso, Signe. *Om igen*. Stockholm: Trevi, 1989.
Hasso, Signe. *Tidens vän*. Stockholm: Trevi, 1990.

NOTES

1. The shooting of the film began in 1937 but was interrupted by Gösta Ekman's death. The incomplete film was theatrically released in 1940.
2. According to Hasso's memoirs, she had a part in the film, but it was completely cut out before the premiere.
3. Memoirs in three parts.

GUNNAR HELLSTRÖM (Alnö, 6 Dec. 1928–), actor, director. Hellström's acting career followed the usual Swedish pattern: training at the Royal Dramatic Theater School (1950–1952), then quick recognition and a film career (he had actually appeared earlier in advertising films). It was not long, however, before he tried his luck in Hollywood, where he has been an efficient and competent director of various television series. He has occasionally returned to Sweden to make films. *Raskenstam*, based on real events of the 1940s and with himself in the lead as a gigolo, was a qualified success. His latest production, however, based on the life of the famous painter Anders Zorn, again with himself as the protagonist, was both a commercial and critical failure.

His main contributions, however, fall within an earlier period of Swedish film history. Above all, in the 1950s he became a spokesman for the restless younger generation. Although the youth question was hardly new, it drew increased attention in the postwar period. Together with actor-directors like Egil Holmsen and Arne Ragneborn, Hellström depicted troubled and troublesome young men who felt uneasy in the securely established "people's home." To a large degree they were inspired by American films about juvenile delinquents and young rebels opposing the moribund world of their parents and their consumer culture while at the same time being beneficiaries of that same world. This focus is particularly evident in *Nattbarn* [Night child] and the underrated *Chans/Just Once More*, but Hellström also managed to bring this dimension to the rural classic *Synnöve Solbakken*, where he cast himself as Aslak, the farmhand with gypsy blood who is torn between good and evil impulses, and made himself virtually the focus of the story. When playing social outcasts, Hellström could take advantage of his dark coloring and air of melancholy, most notably in his directoral debut *Simon syndaren* [Simon the sinner]. Here he was a gypsy figure whose apparent ability as a faith healer is commercially exploited by a religious movement.

FILMOGRAPHY

Actor

1950: *Medan staden sover* [While the city sleeps]. 1952: *Ubåt 39* [Submarine 39]; *Hon kom som en vind* [She came like the wind]. 1953: *Barabbas*; *Marianne*; *Göingehövdingen* [The chieftain of Göinge]. 1954: *Karin Månsdotter*. 1956: *Rough Sketch*. 1960: *Domaren* [The judge]. 1961: *Karneval* [Carnival]; *Stöten* [The heist]; *Return to Peyton Place*. 1965: *Nattmara* [Nightmare]. 1971: *Sea Burial* (TVM). 1976: *Djungeläventyret Campa Campa* [The jungle adventure Campa Campa]. 1977: *Ärliga blå ögon* [Honest blue eyes] (TVMS); *Skeppsredaren* [The shipowner] (TVMS). 1981: *Jag rodnar* [I blush]. 1997: *Solskenspojkarna* [The sunshine boys] (TVD).

Director, Scriptwriter, Actor

1954: *Simon syndaren* [Simon the sinner]. 1956: *Nattbarn* [Night child]. 1957: *Synnöve Solbakken*. 1962: *Chans/Just Once More* (director only). 1969: *The Name of the Game Is Kill* (director only). 1980: *Mark, I Love You* (TVM). 1983: *Raskenstam*. 1994: *Zorn*.[1]

Director in Television Series

Has directed episodes in the following TV series: *Gunsmoke*; *Bonanza*; *The Wild Wild West*; *Petrocelli*; *Dallas*; *The Powers of Matthew Star*.

Actor in Television Series

Has appeared in the following TV series—1962: *Combat* and *Codename Christopher*.

BIBLIOGRAPHY

Grundelius, Björn. "Är han hårdkokt?" *Bildjournalen*, no. 49 (1954):4–5, 30. Interview.
Hellström, Gunnar. "Hela mitt syndiga liv." *Vecko-Revyn* (1965): no. 9:16–19, 39; no. 10:32–33, 40.

NOTE

1. Longer version for television in 1995.

ANDERS HENRIKSON (Stockholm, 13 June 1896–17 Oct. 1965), actor, director. Educated at the Royal Dramatic Theater School, Henrikson was a character
actor in the truest sense of the word and for a long time a regular at the Royal
Dramatic Theater. But he was also a skilled film director. In the 1930s he was
regarded as one of the few who could master the then-popular genre of film
farce in a quite "un-Swedish" way, that is, by keeping up the requisite tempo.
He had great success with both critics and the audience with his adaptation of
the old stage play *It Pays to Advertise* in the film *Annonsera!* [Advertise!]. He
also made a rather personal P. G. Wodehouse adaptation with *Blixt och dunder*
[Thunder and lightning], scripted by young *Hasse Ekman. The film was criticized for not being faithful to the spirit of the Wodehouse original, but the film
still holds up reasonably well today. In the 1940s Henrikson turned to more
serious and dramatic material. One of his first efforts in this vein, *Ett brott* [A
crime], based on an actual murder case, was long regarded as a turning point
in Swedish cinema between the more "frivolous" 1930s and serious 1940s. This
opinion is nowadays called into question, but the film retains its interest. Other
similar examples are the Salvation Army melodrama *Blod och eld/Blood and
Fire* and *Farliga vägar* [Dangerous ways], one of the few films to address the
burning question of whether Sweden should grant help to refugees from foreign
countries. Henrikson's directoral efforts of the 1940s also include an adaptation
of Elin Wägner's rural novel *Åsa-Hanna*, a compelling account of a strong and
independent woman set in nineteenth-century peasant society.

As an actor, Henrikson virtually specialized in noble and tragic characters,
which was underscored by his melancholy but magnificently dignified appearance and style of acting. He was the surgeon who restores *Ingrid Bergman's
face in *En kvinnas ansikte/A Woman's Face* and then immigrates to China to
escape his ravaged domestic life. In *Alle man på post* [Man your posts], one of
the few serious films about military defense made during World War II, which
he himself directed, he was a lieutenant who sacrifices his own life in order to
prevent his brother from selling secrets to foreign agents.

FILMOGRAPHY

Actor

1913: *Gränsfolken/Brother against Brother*. 1919: *Synnöve Solbakken*. 1925: *Damen med
kameliorna* [The lady with the camelias]. 1929: *Den starkaste* [The strongest]. 1934:
Sången om den eldröda blomman [The song of the scarlet flower]. 1935: *Flickornas
Alfred* [Ladies' man Alfred]; *Valborgsmässoafton/Walpurgis Night*. 1936: *33.333*; *Intermezzo*. 1937: *Konflikt* [Conflict]; *Ryska snuvan* [The Russian flu]; *John Ericsson—
segraren vid Hampton Roads/John Ericsson—Victor at Hampton Roads*. 1938: *Fram för
framgång/Fram For Framgang* [Here's to success]; *Med folket för fosterlandet/Med

Folket Foer Fosterlandet [With the people for the fatherland]; *Styrman Karlssons flammor* [First-mate Karlsson's sweethearts]; *En kvinnas ansikte/A Woman's Face.* 1939: *Gläd dig i din ungdom* [Rejoice in thy youth]; *Frun tillhanda/Frun Tillhanda* [Domestic help]; *Hennes lilla Majestät/Hennes Lilla Majestat* [Her little majesty]. 1940: *Med livet som insats* [Life at stake]. 1941: *Hem från Babylon* [Home from Babylon]. 1942: **Himlaspelet/The Heavenly Play.* 1943: *Jag dräpte* [I slew]. 1949: **Fängelse/The Devil's Wanton,* a.k.a. *Prison.* 1951: *Fröken Julie/Miss Julie.* 1952: *Trots* [Contempt]; *Kärlek* [Love]. 1953: *Barabbas*; *Vägen till Klockrike* [The road to Klockrike]; *Resan till dej* [The voyage to you]. 1954: *Herr Arnes penningar* [Sir Arne's money]. 1955: *Nina* (TVM, episode in *Foreign Intrigue*). 1956: *Flickan i frack* [The girl in tails]. 1957: *Prästen i Uddarbo* [The vicar of Uddarbo]. 1959: *Åke och hans värld* [Åke and his world] (TVM, as narrator). 1961: *Pojken i trädet* [The boy in the tree]. 1965: *Morianerna/Morianna,* a.k.a. *I the Body.*

Director, Actor

1933: *Flickan från varuhuset* [The girl from the department store]. 1936: *Släkten är värst* [Unfriendly relations] (director only); *Annonsera!* [Advertise!]; *Han, hon och pengarna* [He, she and the money] (director only); *65, 66 och jag* [65, 66 and I] (director only). 1937: *O, en så'n natt!* [Oh, what a night!]. 1938: *Den stora kärleken* [The great love] (also script); *Blixt och dunder* [Thunder and lightning] (director only); *Bara en trumpetare* [Just a bugler]. 1939: *Valfångare/The Whalers* (director only, with Tancred Ibsen). 1940: *Familjen Björck* [The Björck family] (director only); *Ett brott* [A crime] (also script); *Alle man på post* [Man your posts] (also script). 1941: *Livet går vidare* [Life goes on] (also script); *Bara en kvinna* [Only a woman] (also script). 1942: *Farliga vägar* [Dangerous ways]; *Fallet Ingegerd Bremssen* [The Ingegerd Bremssen case]; *Ungdom i bojor* [Youth in chains]. 1943: *Herr Collins äventyr* [Mr. Collin's adventures] (also script); *Tåg 56* [Train 56]. 1944: *Jag är eld och luft* [I am fire and air]. 1945: *Idel ädel adel* [Nothing but noble nobility] (also script); *Blod och eld/Blood and Fire*; *Trötte Teodor* [Tired Teodor]. 1946: *Åsa-Hanna.* 1947: *Det vackraste på jorden* [The loveliest thing on earth]; *Nyckeln och ringen* [The key and the ring]. 1948: *Flickan från fjällbyn* [The girl from the mountain village] (director only). 1955: *Giftas* [Getting married]. 1956: *Ett dockhem* [A doll's house] (director only). Last two films distributed together in United States in edited version as *Of Love and Lust* (1959).

BIBLIOGRAPHY

Holm, 1947.
Malm, Ulfva W. "Artistisk yrkesman." *Teatern*, no. 6 (1937):12–13. Interview.
Waldekranz, Rune. "Kvalitetsfilmaren Anders Henrikson." *OBS!* no. 7 (1944):36–37.

KEVE HJELM (Gnesta, 23 June 1922–), actor, director. Hjelm studied direction at the Royal Dramatic Theater in 1949–1950, then was an actor and director at various municipal stages throughout Sweden. Later he returned to the royal stage and did considerable work for television. He has also been active as a teacher and actors' pedagogue.

Keve Hjelm is above all a character actor with a penchant for villainous—or at least cold and unpleasant—characters who really get under the spectator's skin. This is the case, for example, with the haute bourgeois manager in the recent epic *1939, who incarnates all the evils of the 1940s upper class such as arrogance and a thinly disguised enthusiasm for Nazi ideology. But Hjelm has also given memorable performances in utterly different roles such as that of the alcoholic father, pitifully self-deluded, living in a world of dreams, in *Bo Widerberg's *Kvarteret Korpen/Raven's End. As a director he has made at least one major contribution that deserves a special place in Swedish film history, his 1979 epic Godnatt, jord [Good night, earth], an eight-hour television film based on the novel by Ivar Lo-Johansson (whose Bara en mor had been filmed by *Alf Sjöberg).[1] This story about estate workers (Swedish: statare) was narrated in an extremely realistic manner, with long, static shots that appeared actionless but were nevertheless filled with meaning, like huge paintings. The film divided the critics and the audience. Some found it unbearably dull, but many others held the opposite view and regarded it as a remarkable milestone.

FILMOGRAPHY

Actor

1943: Det spökar—det spökar . . . [Ghosts! ghosts!]; Natt i hamn [Night in port]. 1946: När ängarna blommar [When the meadows blossom]. 1947: Krigsmans erinran [A soldier's oath]; Tösen från Stormyrtorpet [The girl from the Marsh Croft]; Får jag lov, magistern? [Teacher, may I have this dance?]; Rallare [Railroad workers]. 1948: På dessa skuldror [On these shoulders]. 1949: Gatan [The street]; Kvinnan som försvann [The woman who vanished]. 1950: *Flicka och hyacinter [Girl with hyacinths]. 1951: Sköna Helena [Beautiful Helena]. 1953: Double Exposure (TVM, episode in Foreign Intrigue). 1954: The Benefactor (TVM, episode in Foreign Intrigue); The Prophet (TVM, episode in Foreign Intrigue); Flottans glada gossar [The navy's happy lads]; The Mills of God (TVM, episode in Foreign Intrigue); Waterfront (TVM, episode in Foreign Intrigue); Off Beat (TVM, episode in Foreign Intrigue). 1955: Kurt Hallen Story (TVM, episode in Foreign Intrigue); Run Around (TVM, episode in Foreign Intrigue). 1956: Nattbarn [Night child]. 1957: Aldrig i livet [Not in your life]; En drömmares vandring [A dreamer's journey]. 1958: Vi på Väddö [We at Väddö]. 1959: Brevet [The letter] (short). 1962: Paria [Pariah] (TVD). 1963: Misantropen [The misanthrope] (TVD); Kurragömma [Hide and seek]; Smutsiga händer [Dirty hands] (TVD); Mordvapen till salu [Murder weapon for sale]; Kvarteret Korpen/Raven's End. 1964: Bandet [The bond] (TVD). 1965: Kärlek 65 [Love 65]. 1966: Nattlek/Night Games; I afton bönemöte [Prayer meeting tonight] (TVD). 1967: Livet är stenkul [Life is just great]; Onkel Vanja [Uncle Vanya] (TVD); Roseanna; Bränt barn [Burned child]. 1968: Vindingevals [Vindinge waltz]; Fordringsägare [Creditors] (TVD); Fanny Hill. 1969: Bära narrkåpa [Wearing a dunce cap] (TVD); Som natt och dag [Like night and day]; Solens barn [Children of the sun] (TVD); Res till Mallorca [Go to Majorca] (TVM). 1970: Grisjakten [The pig hunt]; Röda rummet [The red room] (TVMS); Nana. 1971: Den tunna hinnan som sprakar av färg [The thin colorful sparkling membrane] (TVD); Brother Carl; Vad säger du, Thomas? [What do you say, Thomas?] (TVM). 1972: Hemma hos Karlssons [At home with the Karlssons] (TVDS). 1973: Kvartetten som sprängdes [The quarter that split up] (TVMS). 1975: Fru Inger till Østraat [Mrs. Inger of Østraat]; Ungkarlshotellet [Bachelor's lodging]; Nisse och Greta (TVDS). 1976: Hallo Baby. 1977: Bluff Stop. 1979: Min älskade [My beloved]. 1980: Blomstrande tider [Prosperous times]; Döds-

dansen [The dance of death] (TVD). 1981: *Babels hus* [House of Babel] (TVMS); *Protest* (TVD). 1983: *Limpan* [Loafie]; *Svarte fugler* [Black birds]. 1984: *Rainfox*. 1985: *Wallenberg: A Hero's Story* (TVM). 1986: *Den frusna leoparden* [The frozen leopard]; *Prästkappan* [Preacher's coat] (TVDS); *Hud* [Skin]; *Resan hem* [The voyage home] (TVD). 1987: *Undanflykten* [The evasion] (TVM). 1989: *1939*. 1991: *Måker/Måsar* [Seaguls]; *Den goda viljan/The Best Intentions* (TVM).[2] 1994: *Betraktelse* [Meditation] (short). 1995: *Happy Days* (short). 1996: *Hører du ikke hva jeg sier!* [Don't you hear what I say!]; *Nu är pappa trött igen* [Now daddy's tired again]; *Istider* [Ice times] (short). 1997: *Kung Lear* [King Lear] (TVD); *Svenska hjältar* [Swedish heroes]. 1999: *Dödsklockan* [Death watch] (TVM).

Director

1961: *Utan fast bostad* [Without fixed abode] (TVD); *Soldaten och kvinnan* [The soldier and the woman] (TVD, also actor). 1962: *Dödsdansen* [The dance of death] (TVD). 1963: *Medea* (TVD); *Isak Juntti hade många söner* [Isak Juntti had many sons] (TVD). 1964: *Henry IV* (TVD). 1965: *Sissan* (TVD). 1967: *Fadren* [The father] (TVD). 1968: *Lärda fruntimmer* [Learned women] (TVD). 1969: *Fröken Julie* [Miss Julie] (TVM). 1970: *Tretton dagar* [Thirteen days] (TVM, also actor). 1971: *Paria* [Pariah] (TVD, also actor). 1972: *Askatasuna* (TVD). 1973: *Kommer hem och är snäll* [Comes home and is nice] (TVM, short, also actor). 1974: *Ett frieri* [A marriage proposal] (TVD, also actor); *Karl XII* (TVM, also script). 1979: *Godnatt, jord* [Good night, earth] (TVM, also script). 1988: *Fordringsägare* [Creditors] (codirectors Stefan Böhm, John O. Olsson).

BIBLIOGRAPHY

Hjelm, Keve. "Människokrossarteatern." *Aftonbladet*, 8–10, 19–20 Aug. 1989. KH on the theater with criticism of the Bergman tradition in Swedish theater.
Ståhlberg, Carin. "Huggtänderna har slipats av en smula." *Dagens Nyheter*, 29 Oct. 1994. Interview.

AWARDS

GB 1964

GB 1979

NOTES

1. The two Lo-Johansson novels have been translated into English as *Breaking Free* and *Only a Mother*.
2. Theatrically released in 1992 in an edited version.

RICHARD HOBERT (Kalmar, 1 Dec. 1951–), director. When Hobert was awarded *Ingmar Bergman's personal film prize in 1995 and thus recognized as an up-and-coming talent, the tribute in fact acknowledged a director who had been working in relative obscurity for almost two decades. This is the fate that meets any director working in television. Despite remarkable films like the two he made in 1986 based on actual crimes of the past in southern Sweden, *Yngsjömordet* [The Yngsjö murder] (previously filmed by *Arne Mattsson) and *Esarparen*, a feature with an almost Simenonian atmosphere, the newspapers and their reviewers paid little attention. His later television series *Den femtonde hövdingen* [The fifteenth chieftain], a remarkable action drama set in Lapland, elicited some debate, but the writer/director Hobert was still largely ignored. Bergman's corroboration of Hobert as a talent worth watching may have come a little late, but Hobert is still at his most productive, so the future may have much to offer. At present Hobert is occupied with a whole series of films that draw thematically on the seven deadly sins. So far this has resulted in six theatrical features, including the very moving and poetic *Glädjekällan/Spring of Joy* about an old widower's last journey with the ashes of his deceased wife, a trip that also serves to bring about a reconciliation with his estranged son and his girlfriend.

There is often an emotional heat and intensity in Hobert's films that seems rather "un-Swedish." One good example is the aforementioned *Den femtonde hövdingen*. The story opens in seventeenth-century Lapland when a delegation of Sami chieftains is slaughtered by Swedish soldiers at a so-called peace council. Only one of the chieftains manages to survive, badly wounded. Then the action shifts to present-day Lapland and the situation of the Sami population today. They are still threatened, now by the demands of exploiters who want to build a huge dam that would flood the grazing land of their reindeer. One of the Lapps begins to feel an inner power he at first can't understand. Eventually he realizes that he is the incarnation of the spirit of the surviving chieftain of the historic past. The action gradually escalates into a violent conflict and clash between the Lapps and the Swedish authorities and leads to a tragic end where the protagonist more or less sacrifices his own son. The story is told with an energy and a furor that are quite rare in Swedish film.

FILMOGRAPHY

Writer, Director

1977: *Olle Blom—reporter* [Olle Blom—reporter] (TVMS, actor only). 1978: *Gänget* [The Gang] (TVD). 1979: *Dick Ramberg* (TVM short, director only); *Kejsaren* [The emperor] (actor only). 1981: *Två slår den tredje* [Two beat the third] (TVD). 1982: *Kättaren* [The heretic] (TVD). 1983: *Polskan och puckelryggen* [The Polish woman and the hunchback] (TVD, director only). 1984: *Martin Frosts imperium* [Martin Frost's empire] (TVD). 1986: *Esarparen* (TVM, director only); *Yngsjömordet* [The Yngsjö murder] (TVM, director only). 1988: *Sommarens 12 månader* [The twelve months of summer] (TVMS). 1991: *Ålder okänd* [Age unknown] (TVMS). 1992: *Den femtonde hövdingen* [The fifteenth chieftain] (TVM). 1993: *Glädjekällan/Spring of Joy*. 1994: *Händerna* [The hands]. 1995: *Höst i paradiset—glädjekällan 2* [Autumn in paradise—spring of joy 2]. 1997: *Spring för livet* [Run for your life]. 1998: *Ögat* [The eye]. 1999: *Där regnbågen slutar* [Where the rainbow ends].

BIBLIOGRAPHY

Davidson, Kristina. "På resa i vårt inre." *Arbetet*, 8 Oct. 1995.
Hansson, Anders. "Dödssyndernas regissör." *Göteborgs-Posten*, 13 Feb. 1994. Interview.

Tapper, Michael. "Bakom Glädjekällan. Intervjunmed Richard Hobert." *Filmhäftet*, no.
    103 (1998):4–17.

STEFAN JARL (Skara, 18 Mar. 1941–), director. Jarl is the best known of the
new generation of documentary filmmakers who have become dominant, at least
from an artistic point of view, in contemporary Swedish cinema. He is internationally famous. In the 1960s he studied at the Film Institute Film School.
Among his first efforts were some shorts for Swedish television, made together
with fellow student Jan Lindqvist, about contemporary youth and their problems.
One dealing with youth confronting the police was so controversial that it was
never broadcast. Jarl continued his cooperation with Lindqvist with the long,
controversial documentary *Dom kallar oss Mods/They Call Us Misfits*, a depiction of social outcasts in the youth generation. Among other things the film
included a short, authentic depiction of sexual intercourse, and despite the Board
of Censorship's threat to ban the film, it was released without cuts and widely
recognized by the critics. Working on his own, Jarl later returned to the persons
depicted in *Dom kallar oss Mods*, in the film *Ett anständigt liv* [A decent life].

    Jarl belongs to a group of filmmakers who have stretched the boundaries of
the genre so far that it is difficult to distinguish the "documentary" from pure
fiction. Jarl (and his contemporaries) arrange and rearrange real events and characters to shape a new reality, which makes a point or statement about society
or existence itself. This is particularly true of his documentaries dealing with
man versus nature, such as *Naturens hämnd* [Nature's revenge] and *Hotet* [The
threat]. It is also evident in what has been called his social trilogy: *Dom kallar
oss Mods, Ett anständigt liv*, and *Det sociala arvet* [The social inheritance].

    His social trilogy, spanning a long period of time, follows several characters
on the edges of society. In the first film the two young male leads oppose the
"square" life of the middle class. They smoke joints, and their sense of freedom
seems unlimited. In the second film conditions are worse. They have grown up
and are hooked on stronger drugs. One of them actually dies in real life from
an overdose during the production of the film. In the third film we follow the
survivor who has managed to get out of the vicious circle and has now become
a member of the middle class he and his friends mocked in their youth. Although
the persons are real, it is very clear that much of what is happening in front of
the camera is arranged. The viewer is confronted with the director's view of
society. Jarl can be characterized, in part, as a romantic critic of modern society
and the big city. Stockholm, the setting of this film, is depicted in dark black
tones as a truly depressing place.

    The notion of Jarl as a romantic critic of modern civilization is consolidated
with his threatened nature and wilderness documentaries. These include people
living close to the wilderness in northern Sweden. In *Hotet* Jarl attacks what
the industrial society has done to original, pristine nature. He depicts the effects
of the Chernobyl nuclear plant disaster in 1986, when radiation spread in particular over northern areas. The reindeer that were the base of the indigenous

population's existence were contaminated by radioactive cesium. *Hotet* is in some ways a follow-up to his earlier feature *Naturens hämnd* that dealt with nature's revenge, the damage to humankind caused by their damage of nature. The use of chemical fertilizers and the like cause nature to strike back, making people and animals sick with cancer and other diseases.

In many senses Jarl is a true inheritor to the older documentarist *Arne Sucksdorff, and Jarl did, in his youth, begin his career as his assistant. They belong ideologically to the same romantic tradition, and Jarl has on various occasions paid homage to his older colleague.

FILMOGRAPHY[1]

1966: *Stänk* [Touch] (TV, 4 shorts)[2]; *Snutarna* [The cops] (TV short never broadcast).[3] 1968: *Dom kallar oss mods/They Call Us Misfits.*[4] 1969: *Bekämpa byråkratin* [Fight bureaucracy] (short, collective). 1973: *Gisslan berättar* [Hostages tell] (TV, short). 1974: *Förvandla Sverige* [Transform Sweden] (short).[5] 1975: *Bojkott* [Boycott] (short, collective). 1976: *Vi har vår egen sång* [We have our own song] (collective). 1979: *Ett anständigt liv* [A decent life]. 1981: *Memento mori* (short). 1983: *Naturens hämnd* [Nature's revenge]. 1984: *En av oss* [One of us] (short). 1985: *Själen är större än världen* [The soul is bigger than the world]. 1987: *Hotet*, a.k.a. *Uhkkádus* [The threat]. 1989: *Tiden har inget namn* [Time has no name]. 1990: *Goda människor* [Good people]. 1991: *Jåvna. Renskötare år 2000* [Jåvna. Reindeer keeper year 2000] (short). 1994: *Sameland*, a.k.a. *Sameätnam* [Same country] (short). 1997: *Jag är din krigare* [I am your warrior]. 1998: *Liv till varje pris* [Life at every cost].

BIBLIOGRAPHY

Hagman, Ingrid. "Välfärdsblues i tre ackord." *Chaplin* 244, no. 1 (1993):14–19. Interview on the "Social Trilogy."
Jarl, Stefan, and Jan Lindqvist. *Dom kallar oss Mods*. Stockholm: Aldus/Bonniers, 1968.
Nilsson, Mats. "Rebell i verkligheten. Stefan Jarl och hans filmer." *Filmkonst* 7 (1991). Special issue.
Qvist, Per Olov. "Naturens undergång." *Filmhäftet* no. 58–59 (1987 no. 2–3): 72–77. Mainly about the film *Hotet*.
Sørenssen, Bjørn. "Från fluga på väggen till fluga i soppan: om Stefan Jarls "Modstrilogi." In Hedling, 1998.

AWARDS

GB 1979

GB 1989

NOTES

1. All films except *Goda människor* and *Jag är din krigare* are documentaries.
2. Made in collaboration with Jan Lindqvist.
3. Ibid.
4. Ibid.
5. Ibid.

IVAR JOHANSSON (Stråtjära, 20 Nov. 1889–7 Dec. 1963), director. Johansson can perhaps be regarded as the outdoors expert among Swedish directors, establishing rural melodrama as the number-one genre in Swedish film from the 1930s until the middle of the 1950s. While psychological fine-tuning was perhaps not his forte, he compensated by expressing the more subtle feelings of his actors with strong visual cues. This was often enough to give a strong overall impression, as, for example, in *Bränningar/The Surf*, where *Ingrid Bergman had her first dramatic role. In this melodrama about a young fisherman's daughter who becomes pregnant by a young priest who then loses his memory, Johansson makes heavy use of the stormy sea to portray the turbulent inner feelings of the characters. He contrasts this with more pastoral segments that bring out his idealistic vision of life and the world.

Johansson began as a film editor and scriptwriter during the period of silent film in the 1920s and made his real directoral debut in 1929 with one of the last great silent Swedish films, *Rågens rike* [The realm of the rye], based on a poem by Jarl Hemmer. Although this film was long forgotten, it has recently been revived by Swedish film historians and is now regarded a minor masterpiece. Its visual qualities remind one of such contemporary Soviet filmmakers as Dovzhenko, and it is likely that Johansson was influenced by the Russians. Some of his later films also reflect this influence. In the mid-1930s he made the interesting film *Grabbarna i 57: an* [The boys of no. 57], which was one of the very first Swedish films to depict a young delinquent. This film reminds one of the German "Zillefilme" as well as later Italian neorealist movies.

Had he been able to produce scripts on the same high level as his visual imagination, he certainly would be regarded as a much more important name in the Swedish film history. While preferring to work within the rural genre, he also made important contributions to the social melodrama typical of the war years. One of these contributions is *Tänk, om jag gifter mig med prästen* [Imagine if I marry the vicar], where *Viveca Lindfors had her breakthrough.

FILMOGRAPHY

Scriptwriter

1925: *Carl XII/Charles XII.* 1926: *Flickan i frack.* [The girl in tails]; *Fänrik Ståls sägner* [Stories of Second Lieutenant Stål]. 1928: *Gustaf Wasa*; *A.-B. Gifta bort Baron Olsson* [Getting Baron Olsson married, inc.]. 1930: *Trollbruden* [The troll bride] (NCF). 1932: *Svärmor kommer* [Mother-in-law's coming]. 1940: *Vi masthuggspojkar* [We Masthugget boys].

Director, Scriptwriter

1921: *Filmrevyn 1922* [Film revue 1922] (short). 1929: *Rågens rike* [The realm of the rye]. 1931: *Skepparkärlek* [Skipper's love]. 1932: *Lyckans gullgossar* [Lucky devils] (director only, with *Sigurd Wallén). 1933: *Bomans pojke* [Boman's boy]; *Hälsingar/Hæelsingar* [The people of Hälsingland]. 1934: *Uppsagd* [Fired] (director only); *Sången till henne/The Song to Her.* 1935: *Bränningar/The Surf*; *Grabbarna i 57: an* [The boys of no. 57]. 1936: *Fröken blir piga/Froeken blir piga* [The lady becomes a housemaid]. 1937: *Mamma gifter sig* [Mama gets married]. 1938: *Storm över skären* [Storm over the skerries]; *I nöd och lust* [For better, for worse]. 1939: *Åh en så'n grabb* [Oh, what a boy!] (director only); *Oss baroner emellan* [Between us barons]. 1940: *Snurriga familjen* [The crazy family] (director only). 1941: *Springpojkar är vi allihopa* [We're all errand boys] (director only); *Tåget går klockan 9* [The train leaves at 9] (director only); *Gatans serenad* [Serenade of the street] (short, director only); *Tänk, om jag gifter mig med prästen* [Imagine if I marry the vicar]. 1942: *Gula kliniken* [The yellow clinic]; *Ta hand om Ulla* [Take care of Ulla]. 1943: *Fångad av en röst* [Captured by a voice]; *Ungt blod* [Young blood]. 1944: *Skogen är vår arvedel* [The forest is our heritage]; *Örnungar* [Eaglets] (director only). 1945: *Moderskapets kval och lycka* [The grief and joy of motherhood]; *Bröderna Östermans huskors* [The Österman Brothers' battle-ax]. 1946: *Bröllopet på Solö* [The wedding on Solö]. 1947: *Livet i Finnskogarna* [Life in the Finn forests]; *Ådalens poesi* [The poetry of Ådalen]. 1948: *Marknadsafton* [After the fair]. 1949: *Hin och smålänningen* [Old Nick and the Smålander]; *Lång-Lasse i Delsbo* [Lång-Lasse of Delsbo]. 1950: *Rågens rike* [The realm of the rye]. 1952: *När syrenerna blomma* [In lilac time] (director only); *Kalle Karlsson från Jularbo* [Kalle Karlsson of Jularbo]. 1953: *Ursula-flickan från Finnskogarna* [Ursula—the girl from the Finn forests]. 1954: *De röda hästarna* [The red horses] (director only). 1955: *Finnskogens folk* [The people of the Finn forests].

ERLAND JOSEPHSON (Stockholm, 15 June 1923–) actor, director. Josephson had no formal education as an actor. He began as an amateur actor at Stockholm University and eventually found his way to Helsingborg Municipal Theater in the late 1940s when *Ingmar Bergman was a manager there. In 1956 Josephson was engaged by the Royal Dramatic Theater in Stockholm and has been a regular there ever since. He served as the manager of the theater between 1966 and 1975. Josephson is one of Sweden's leading character actors and was for a long time associated with the films of Ingmar Bergman, with whom he has collaborated as a screenwriter. Josephson is even more versatile: He has a few directorial credits, he has written novels and radio plays, and he has been chairman of the Swedish Actors Equity Association. For the past two decades he has also had a respectable international acting career with parts in films by Tarkovsky, Szábo, and Angelopolous.

Josephson's style, both as an actor and as a screenwriter/director, is cultivated, witty, and ironic. In foreign films, he has often played different types of characters than when he acts in Sweden. His international roles are usually as rather odd and mysterious personalities, sometimes on the verge of insanity. As a member of a Jewish family, with many respectable artists in its ranks, he has occasionally focused on Jewish culture with a special kind of ironic humor (similar to that of Woody Allen). He has discussed this in his book *Föreställningar*. In his early, largely unnoticed, and now-forgotten television play *Benjamin* in 1960, he portrayed the latent, almost unnoticed anti-Semitism in contemporary Swedish society. Since then, there has been a tendency among artists in the Swedish Jewish community to express their own voice and culture more clearly, and some of Josephson's later parts have followed this trend. In

Fanny och Alexander/Fanny and Alexander he was the wise, old Jewish antique dealer saving Fanny and Alexander from the grips of the evil bishop. In
another role, he is the dignified defense lawyer Rosenbaum in a trilogy of films
made for television.

FILMOGRAPHY

Actor[1]

1946: *Det regnar på vår kärlek* [It rains on our love]. 1948: *Eva*. 1950: *Till glädje/To
Joy*. 1957: *Som man bäddar . . .* [You have made your bed . . .]; *Svarta handsken* [The
black glove] (TVD). 1958: *Nära livet/Brink of Life; Ansiktet/The Magician* [The face].
1961: *Kan du läxan?* [Do you know your homework?] (short). 1962: *Förändringens vind*
[Wind of change] (NCF, narrator). 1965: *Ett liv* [A life] (short). 1967: *Skollärare John
Chronschoughs memoarer* [Teacher John Chronschoughs's memoirs] (TVM); *En städad
flykt* [A neat escape] (short). 1968: *Vargtimmen/Hour of the Wolf; Flickorna/The Girls;
Beslut i morgon* [Decision tomorrow] (TVD). 1969: *En passion/The Passion of Anna;
Kuppen i Stockholm* [The coup in Stockholm] (TVD). 1970: *Röda rummet* [The red room]
(TVM); *Vem var jag?* [Who was I?] (TVD); *Reservatet* [The sanctuary] (TVD). 1972:
Sverige 1917–1918 [Sweden 1917–1918] (TVD); *Viskningar och rop/Cries and Whispers*. 1973: *Scener ur ett äktenskap/Scenes from a Marriage* (TVM).[2] 1974: *Brända
tomten* [The burnt site] (TVD); *Pane e cioccolata/Bread and Chocolate*. 1975: *Monismanien 1995*. 1976: *Ansikte mot ansikte/Face to Face* (TVM).[3] 1977: *Al di là bene e del
male/Beyond Good and Evil; Io ho paura/Timers*, a.k.a. *The Body Guard; Den allvarsamma leken* [The serious game]; *A Look at Liv* (docu.). 1978: *Herbstsonate*, a.k.a.
Höstsonaten/Autumn Sonata. 1979: *Die erste Polka; Dimenticare Venezia/Forget Venice*.
1980: *Kärleken* [The passion]; *Ett drömspel* [A dream play] (TVD). 1981: *Samo jednom
se ljubi var* [The melody haunts my reverie]; *Montenegro eller Pärlor och
svin/Montenegro or Pigs and Pearls; Zéb-un-nisá—prinsessa av Indien* [Zéb-un-nisá—
princess of India] (TVD); *Victor Sjöström* (docu.). 1982: *Dubbelsvindlarna* [The double
cheaters] (TVM); *Variola Vera; Fanny och Alexander/Fanny and Alexander*.[4] 1983: *Nos-
thalgia; Bella Donna; La casa del tappetto gallo; Savannen* [The savanna] (TVD). 1984:
Il giocatore invisible (TVM); *Efter repetitionen/After the Rehearsal* (TVM); *Der
Schimmelreiter* (TVM); *Un caso d'incoscienza* (TVM); *Angelan sota* [Angela's war];
Bakom jalusin [Behind the shutters]; *Dirty Story*. 1985: *De flygande djävlarna* [The flying
devils]. 1986: *Amorosa; Offret/The Sacrifice; Saving Grace; L'ultima Mazurka; Il ge-
nerale/Garibaldi—The General* (TVM); *La coda del diavolo*, a.k.a. *Le mal d'aimer* 1987:
Il giorno prima, a.k.a. *Côntrole; Le testament d'un poet juif assasiné*. 1988: *The
Unbearable Lightness of Being; Hanussen; La donna spezzata; Regi Andrej Tarkovskij*
[Direction Andrej Tarkovskij] (docu.); *La guerre la plus glorieuse: Migrations*, a.k.a.
Seobe/The Most Glorious War: Migrations.[5] 1989: *Il giudice istruttore* (TVM). 1990: *Il
sole buio/The Black Sun; God afton, herr Wallenberg/Good Evening, Mr. Wallenberg*.
1991: *Prospero's Books; Cattiva/Wicked; Meeting Venus; Oxen/The Ox; Den ofrivillige
golfaren* [The involuntary golf player]. 1992: *Holozän; Sofie*. 1993: *Rosenbaum: Bländ-
verk* [Rosenbaum: Blinding imagination] (TVM); *Rosenbaum: Målbrott* [Rosenbaum:
voice breaking] (TVM); *Rosenbaum: Det sista vittnet* [Rosenbaum: the last witness]
(TVM). 1994: *Drømspel* [A dream play]; *Skuggan* [The shadow] (TVM); *Dansaren* [The
dancer] (docu.); *Zabraneniyat plod*. 1995: *Vendetta; Som löven i Vallombrosa* [Like the
leaves in Vallombrosa] (TVD); *Pakten*, a.k.a. *The Sunset Boys; To vlemma tou Odys-*

sea/The Gaze of Odysseus; *Magisk cirkel* [Magic circle] (TVD); *Kristin Lavransdatter.
"Brudkransen"* [Kristin Lavransdatter. "The bridal wreath"]. 1997: *Larmar och gör sig
till* [Fussing and fuming] (TVM). 1998: *Från regnormarnas liv* [Rainsnakes] (TVD);
Den tatuerade änkan [The tattooed widow] (TVM); *Ivar Kreuger* (TVM). 1999: *Magnetisörens femte vinter* [The magnetist's fifth winter]; *På sista versen—en liten film om
döden* [Being on your last leg—a little film about death] (TVM).

Screenwriter

1956: *Sceningång* [Stage entrance] (also actor). 1960: *Benjamin* (TVD). 1961: *Lustgården* [The pleasure garden] (with Ingmar Bergman as "Buntel Ericsson"). 1962: *Generalskan* [The general's wife] (TVD). 1963: *Sällskapslek* [Parlor game]. 1964: *För att inte
tala om dessa kvinnor/All These Women* (with Ingmar Bergman). 1965: *Fröknarna i
parken* [The spinsters in the park] (TVD). 1967: *Smycket* [The necklace] (episode in
Stimulantia, with *Gustaf Molander). 1977: *Bröderna* [The brothers] (TVM).

Director, Screenwriter

1971: *I själva verket är det alltid någonting annat som händer* [In reality something else
always happens] (TVD). 1977: *Vårbrytning* [Break-up in spring] (TVM, also actor).
1978: *En och en/One and One* (also actor and producer, direction with Sven Nykvist and
*Ingrid Thulin); *Rätt ut i luften* [Straight into the air] (TVD). 1980: *Marmeladupproret*
[The marmelade rebellion] (also actor).

BIBLIOGRAPHY[6]

Josephson, Erland. *Föreställningar*. Stockholm: Brombergs, 1991.
Josephson, Erland. *Rollen*. Stockholm: Brombergs, 1989.
Josephson, Erland. *Sanningslekar*. Stockholm: Brombergs, 1990.
Josephson, Erland. *Svarslös*. Stockholm: Brombergs, 1996.
Josephson, Erland. *Vita sanningar*. Stockholm: Brombergs, 1995.

AWARD

GB 1986

NOTES

1. One film made in former Yugoslavia at the beginning of the 1990s still unidentified.
EJ doesn't remember the title.
2. Theatrically released in 1974 in an edited version.
3. Theatrically released abroad in edited version.
4. Longer version for television in 1984, with limited cinema release in 1983.
5. It is uncertain if it has been released in cinemas. However, it seems to have been
shown as a TV series.
6. Books containing autobiographical notices and reflections upon his art.

ALF KJELLIN (Lund, 28 Feb. 1920–5 Apr. 1988), actor, director. At the early
age of only seventeen, Kjellin ran away from his home in Karlstad to go to
Stockholm to try his luck at becoming an actor. He failed to be accepted by the
Royal Dramatic Theater School, partly because they thought him too young.

Not daunted, he approached others in the film business. *Karin Swanström at Svensk Filmindustri approved of this handsome young man, and Kjellin landed a contract as an apprentice. The company gave him a small part in the John Ericsson epic the same year. This was followed by a series of bit parts and extra appearances, and Kjellin gradually received bigger and bigger roles. His break-through came as the tormented grammar school pupil in *Sjöberg's *Hets/Torment. It has been said that screenwriter *Ingmar Bergman wished Kjellin to be cast in the part. In any case, he perfectly fit the role of the restless and very sensitive young "rebel with a cause" caught in a haute bourgeois, oppressive school system. This part was followed by somewhat similar roles. He portrayed the fiddler and half gypsy in *Gustaf Edgren's smash hit *Driver dagg, faller regn/Sunshine Follows Rain, with *Mai Zetterling, once again in the opposite lead. Although this film is set in the middle of the nineteenth century, it deals in part with modern youth problems.

Toward the end of the 1940s, Kjellin was approached by the British film industry, which had already engaged Zetterling, and by American David O. Selznick. Kjellin accepted Selznick's offer, and he made his American debut in *Madame Bovary* under the pseudonym Christopher Kent. He was not, however, particularly successful in America and returned to Sweden, where he directed a few features. None of these films were particularly remarkable. Eventually, through some contacts within the American film industry, he began directing in the expanding television market. He debuted with a few episodes of *Alfred Hitchcock Presents* in 1961, with which he apparently won the old master's approval. After that, Kjellin directed about three dozen different television series on the basis of his reputation as an efficient and competent director. In addition, he directed a few full-length features and television films and made occasional acting appearances. In 1981, he was contracted to direct the film *Slagskämpen/The Inside Man* in his native Sweden. This project failed, only being completed several years later with another director. Kjellin sued the producer and eventually won in the higher courts. Kjellin's last efforts in Sweden were a couple of stage productions.

FILMOGRAPHY

Actor

1937: *John Ericsson—segraren vid Hampton Roads/John Ericsson—Victor at Hampton Roads*. 1938: *Knut löser knuten* [Knut solves the problem](NCF); *Med folket för fosterlandet/Med Folket For Fosterlandet* [With the people for the fatherland]; *Goda vänner trogna grannar* [Good friends and good neighbors]. 1939: *Gläd dig i din ungdom* [Rejoice in thy youth]; *Valfångare/The Whalers*; *Kadettkamrater* [Cadets together]; *Filmen om Emelie Högqvist* [The film about Emelie Högqvist]. 1940: *Stål* [Steel]; *Juninatten/A Night in June*; *Hans Nåds testamente* [His grace's will]. 1941: *Den ljusnande framtid* [Bright future before us]; *Striden går vidare* [The battle goes on]. 1943: *Natt i hamn* [Night in port] (also script); *Jag dräpte* [I slew]; *Herre med portfölj* [Gentleman with a briefcase]. 1944: *Appassionata*; *Den osynliga muren* [The invisible wall]; *Hets/Torment*; *Prins Gustaf* [Prince Gustaf]. 1945: *Vandring med månen* [Wandering with the moon].

1946: *Det är min modell/Affairs of a Model*; *Iris och löjtnantshjärta* [Iris and the lieutenant]; *Driver dagg, faller regn/Sunshine Follows Rain*. 1947: *Tösen från Stormyrtorpet* [The girl from the Marsh Croft]; *Kvinna utan ansikte* [Woman without a face]. 1949: *Madame Bovary*; *Singoalla/Gypsy Fury*. 1950: *The Wind Is My Lover* (French version of the latter); *Sånt händer inte här* [This doesn't happen here]; *Den vita katten* [The white cat]. 1951: *Sommarlek/Illicit Interlude* [Summer play]; *Bärande hav* [In the arms of the sea]; *Frånskild* [Divorced]. 1952: *My Six Convicts*; *The Iron Mistress*; *The Indian* (TVD); *The Old Talbot* (TVD). 1953: *The Juggler*; *Ingen mans kvinna* [No man's woman]; *Göingehövdingen* [The chieftain of Göinge]. 1954: *The Fix* (TVM, episode in *Foreign Intrigue*); *Mona* (TVM, episode in *Foreign Intrigue*); *Waterfront Story* (TVM, episode in *Foreign Intrigue*); *The Brotherhood* (TVM, episode in *Foreign Intrigue*); *Insurance for Death* (episode in *Foreign Intrigue*); *Alibi* (episode in *Foreign Intrigue*); *Flicka utan namn* [Girl without a name]; *The Avenger* (TVM, episode in *Foreign Intrigue*); *The Third Partner* (TVM, episode in *Foreign Intrigue*); *Schoolteacher Story* (TVM, episode in *Foreign Intrigue*); *Blind Man's Bluff* (TVM, episode in *Foreign Intrigue*). 1955: *Sweet Revenge* (TVM, episode in *Foreign Intrigue*); *Miss Fortune* (TVM, episode in *Foreign Intrigue*); *Blockerat spår* [Blocked track]; *Comrade Lindermann's conscience* (TVD); *The Nightingale* (TVD); *Cross on the Hill* (TVD). 1956: *Egen ingång* [Private entry]; *Främlingen från skyn* [The stranger from the sky]; *Het är min längtan* [My passionate longing]; *The Nightingale* (TVD). 1957: *Gäst i eget hus* [A guest in his own house]; *Sommarnöje sökes* [Wanted: summer residence]. 1958: *Lek på regnbågen* [Playing on the rainbow]. 1960 *Panik i paradis* [Panic in paradise]; *The Peter Harkos Story* (TVD). 1961: *Karneval* [Carnival]; *Två levande och en död/Two Living, One Dead*. 1962: *Hans Brinker: or The Silver Skates* (TVM). 1963: *The Victors*. 1965: *Ship of Fools*. 1966: *Assault on a Queen*. 1968: *Ice Station Zebra*. 1976: *Francis Gary Powers: The True Story of the U-2 Spy Incident* (TVM). 1977: *The Cabot Connection* (TVM). 1982: *Vid din sida* [By your side] (TVMS).

Episodes in Series

Combat (1963); *12 O'Clock High* (1965–66); *Tarzan* (1967); *The FBI* (1967/ 70); *The Runaways*.

Director

1955: *Flickan i regnet* [The girl in the rain] (also actor, script). 1957: *Möten i skymningen* [Encounters in the twilight]; *Sjutton år* [Seventeen years old]. 1959: *Det svänger på slottet* [A high old time at the castle]; *Bara en kypare* [Only a waiter]. 1961: *Lustgården* [The pleasure garden]. 1962: *Siska*. 1969: *Midas Run*. 1970: *The McMasters*. 1971: *The Deadly Dream* (TVM). 1973: *The Girls of the Huntington House* (TVM). 1975: *The Family Holvak* (TVM).

Episodes in Series

Alfred Hitchcock Presents (also actor); *Doctor Kildaire*; *I Spy* (also actor); *The Doctors*; *The Man from U.N.C.L.E.*; *Mission: Impossible* (also actor)); *The Sixth Sense* (also actor); *Mannix*; *Hawai 5–0*; *Cannon* (also actor); *Columbo*; *McMillan and Wife*; *The Waltons*; *The Six Million Dollar Man*; *Police Woman*; *Barnaby Jones*; *The Family Holvak*; *Gibbsville*; *The Little House on the Prairie*; *Joe Forrester*; *Planet of the Apes*; *Switch*; *Code R.*; *Family*; *How the West Was Won*; *Paris*; *David Cassidy—Man Undercover*; *Trapper John, M.D.*; *Young Pioneers*; *Walking Tall*; *Cassie and Company*; *Dynasty*; *Whiz Kids*; *Finder of Lost Loves*; *Hotel*; *Dallas*.

BIBLIOGRAPHY

Hanson, Bo. "Alf Kjellin i tre akter." *Allers* (1968): no. 15:32–33, 90, 92; no. 16:32–
    33, 66, 68, 72; no. 17:32–33, 72–74. Interview.
Holm, 1947.

GEORG AF KLERCKER (Kristianstad, 15 Dec. 1877–13 Nov. 1951), actor,
director. K was an officer and a gentleman, born of a noble family and guaranteed a respectable social life. Yet he became an actor and film director at a
time when film was not regarded as high art. Moreover, he married an actress
below his social rank.

Klercker was hired to organize production by the newly established Svenska
Bio when it moved to Stockholm and established the first studio in Lidingö in
1912. He also directed and acted in a few films during the early years. It seems,
however, that it was difficult for him to cooperate with the two new star directors
of the company, *Sjöström and *Stiller. He left the company and spent time at
Pathé in Paris, where he apparently learned more about the craft. When the
photographic company Hasselblad in Göteborg decided to compete in a more
serious way with Svenska Bio, they hired Klercker. From 1915 to 1917 he
directed almost their entire output of more than thirty films, ranging from short
comedies and farces to feature melodramas. In 1918, when Hasselblad merged
with several smaller companies (later to be swallowed up by Svenska Bio
to become the dominant Svensk Filmindustri), Klercker vanished from the
filmmaking scene. In part he left because the trend toward more literary and
respectable films did not correspond with Klercker's preference for the melodramatic and sensational. He directed one insignificant film in the late 1920s
and made a few other acting appearances. In general, after leaving Hasselblad,
his name was lost in Swedish film history.

History is written by the victors, and when Swedish silent film history was
to be chronicled, Klercker was for a long time overshadowed by his former
rivals. He was rarely mentioned until the last decade; he has now been revived
by film historians, and retrospective showings of his films have taken place at
various film festivals around the world. Among his latter-day admirers is *Ingmar Bergman, who personally financed the restoration of one of Klercker's
films. To the benefit of Klercker, history does sometimes have its ironies; while
the negatives of Sjöström's and Stiller's films were almost entirely destroyed in
a Stockholm fire in 1941, the forgotten Klercker's negatives lingered on in a
laboratory in Göteborg. While most of the films of the masters have disappeared
forever, or can only be seen in poor or mutilated form, much of Klercker's work
has survived and can be seen in its full visual greatness.

Klercker's own life could have been the subject for one of the many melodramas he himself made. Ingmar Bergman has written a play, *Sista skriket* [The
last scream] (also made into a television drama), about a fictitious meeting
around 1920 between the defeated Klercker and the victorious and mighty

Charles Magnusson of Svensk Filmindustri. The intrigue of the play, the humiliated artist, fits exactly into Bergman's thematic universe.

The literary content of Klercker's film is not different than other contemporary films, including the early films of Sjöström and Stiller. Many of Klercker's films contain the sensational and thrilling devices that were so popular in European filmmaking of the early twentieth century. A couple of his films were actually banned by the Swedish film censors. His films are remarkable for their mise-en-scène and their high visual quality (where, of course, he had the expertise of Hasselblad's photographic firm at his disposal). Like Sjöström, Klercker often used the depth of the room to create tension and a sense of vividness. The quality of his films was highly regarded by contemporary reviewers, who generally considered him as great as Sjöström and Stiller.

FILMOGRAPHY

Actor

1912: *I livets vår/The Springtime of Life*. 1913: *Vampyren* [The Vampire]; *När kärleken dödar* [When love kills]. 1922: *Vem dömer/Mortal Clay*. 1925: *Bröderna Östermans huskors* [The Österman brothers' battle-ax]. 1931: *Hotell Paradisets hemlighet* [The secret of Hotel Paradise]. 1936: *Söder om landsvägen* [South of the highway]. 1938: *Svensson ordnar allt!* [Svensson fixes everything!].

Director, Scriptwriter

1912: *Två bröder* [Two brothers] (director only, short);[1] *Jupiter på jorden* [Jupiter on earth] (short); *Dödsritten under cirkuskupolen* [The death ride under the circus tent] (director only and actor); *Musikens makt* [The power of music] (director only and actor, short). 1913: *Med vapen i hand* [With weapon in hand] (also actor, short); *Skandalen* [The scandal] (also actor, short); *Ringvall på äventyr* [Ringvall on adventures] (short). 1914: *För fäderneslandet* [For the fatherland] (director only and actor). 1915: *Grottöns hemlighet*, a.k.a. *Rosen på Tistelön* [The secret of cave island, a.k.a. The rose of Thistle Island] (director only, short); *I kronans kläder* [In the king's uniform] (director only, short). 1916: *I minnenas band* [In memory's trammels] (director only and actor, short); *De pigorna, de pigorna* [Those servant girls, those servant girls] (director only, short); *Högsta vinsten* [The first prize] (director only and actor, short); *Calles nya kläder* [Calle's new clothes] (short); *Ministerpresidenten* [The minister president]; *Kärleken segrar* [Love conquers]; *Svärmor på vift* [Mother-in-law on a spree] (short); *Calle som miljonär* [Calle as millionaire]; *Trägen vinner eller Calle som skådespelare* [Perseverance does it or Calle as an actor] (short); *Nattens barn* [Children of the night]; *Fången på Karlstens fästning* [The prisoner of Karlsten's fortress]; *Ur en foxterriers dagbok* [From the diary of a fox terrier] (director only, short); *Aktiebolaget Hälsans gåva* [The gift of health, inc.] (director only); *Bengts nya kärlek eller var är barnet?* [Bengt's new love, or Where is the child?] (director only, short); *Vägen utför* [The downhill path] (short). 1917: *Mysteriet natten till den 25: e* [The mystery of the night before the 25th] (director only);[2] *Mellan liv och död* [Between life and death]; *I mörkrets bojor* [In the fetters of darkness] (director only, short); *Förstadsprästen* [The suburban vicar] (director only); *Löjtnant Galenpanna* [Lieutenant Galenpanna] (director only, short); *För hem och härd* [For hearth and home] (also actor, short); *Brottmålsdomaren* [The judge] (director only); *Ett konstnärsöde*, a.k.a. *Det finns inga gudar på jorden* [Fate of an artist, a.k.a. There are no gods on earth] (director only); *Revelj* [Reveille] (director only). 1918: *Nattliga toner* [Night music]; *Nobelpristagaren* [The Nobel prize winner] (director only); *Fyrvaktarens dotter* [The lighthouse keeper's daughter] (director only). 1926: *Flickorna på Solvik* [The girls on Solvik].

BIBLIOGRAPHY

Åhlund, Jannike: "Bergman vid källsprånget." *Chaplin*, no. 239 (1992):29–35. Bergman on af Klercker.

Björkman, Stig. "Une decouverte d'Ingmar Bergman." *Cahiers du cinéma*, nos. 467–468 (May 1993):90–92.

Ewald, Per. "George af Klercker—åren i Göteborg." *Filmkonst*, no. 25 (1994). Special issue.

Furhammar, Leif. "Filmpionjären i skuggan av Sjöström och Stiller." *Chaplin*, no. 208 (1987):26–29.

Söderbergh-Widding, Astrid. *Stumfilm i brytningstid. Stil och berättande i Georg af Klerckers filmer*. Stockholm: Filmvetenskapliga institutionen, 1998.

Wärring, Åke. "Georg af Klercker, en stor filmregissör." *Chaplin*, no. 186 (1983):109–112.

NOTES

1. Banned in Sweden.
2. Ibid.

JARL KULLE (Ekeby, 27 Feb. 1927–3 Oct. 1997), actor, director. Kulle made his debut on the Royal Dramatic Stage in 1947. In his first film roles he was just another youthful actor, but he gradually developed into a real superstar of the stage and screen in the 1950s and 1960s. He was mainly cast as a demonic first lover and seducer, and in that capacity, he contributed to several of the most profitable films of the 1960s: *Käre John/Dear John* and *Änglar, finns dom?/Love Mates*. The latter was, in fact, one of the all-time biggest money-makers in Swedish film history. *Bergman was also quick to use his talent and cast him as the jealous count and erotic he-man in *Sommarnattens leende/Smiles of a Summer Night*. In *Djävulens öga/The Devil's Eye* Kulle was, of course, the man for the role of Don Juan. It was not without a great deal of irony that Kulle later played the role of a music critic who is deeply humiliated by the women in *För att inte tala om alla dessa kvinnor/All These Women*. In one of Kulle's most important and last roles for Bergman, he was the self-indulgent Gustaf Adolf Ekdahl in *Fanny och Alexander/Fanny and Alexander*. This role was something of a tribute to Kulle's own image of himself as a popular comedian in film and on the stage, playing almost anything from musicals to Hamlet. He has also directed a few of his own films. His first, *Bokhandlaren som slutade bada* [The bookseller who gave up bathing], was well received by both the audience and the reviewers, but his last, *Vita nejlikan* [The white carnation], about a professional seducer, was a real disaster in every respect.

FILMOGRAPHY

Actor

1946: *Det är min modell/Affairs of a Model*; *Ungdom i fara* [Youth in danger]. 1950: *Kvartetten som sprängdes* [The quartet that split up]. 1951: *Leva på "Hoppet"* [Living on "Hope"]. 1952: *Trots* [Contempt]; *Kvinnors väntan/Secrets of Women* [Women's waiting]; *Kärlek* [Love]; *69: an, sergeanten och jag* [Private No. 69, the sergeant and I]. 1953: *Barabbas*. 1954: *Karin Månsdotter*. 1955: *Sommarnattens leende/Smiles of a Summer Night*. 1956: *Sista paret ut* [Last pair out]; **Sången om den eldröda blomman* [The song of the scarlet flower]. 1957: *En drömmares vandring* [A dreamer's journey]; *Ingen morgondag* [No tomorrow]. 1958: *Fröken April* [Miss April]. 1959: *Sängkammartjuven* [The bedroom thief]. 1960: *Av hjärtans lust* [Heart's desire]; *Djävulens öga/The Devil's Eye*. 1961: *Änglar, finns dom?/Love Mates*; *Lita på mej, älskling!* [Trust me, darling!]. 1962: *Nils Holgerssons underbara resa/The Wonderful Adventures of Nils* (voice); *Den kära familjen* [The dear family]; *Kort är sommaren/Short Is the Summer*. 1963: *Pigen og pressefotografen* [The girl and the press photographer]. 1964: *För att inte tala om alla dessa kvinnor/All These Women*; *Är du inte riktigt klok?* [Are you crazy?]; *Bröllopsbesvär/Swedish Wedding Night*; *Käre John/Dear John*. 1966: *Syskonbädd 1782/My Sister, My Love*. 1969: *Miss and Mrs. Sweden*. 1972: *Ture Sventon—privatdetektiv* [Ture Sventon—private eye]. 1974: *Kungen och haren* [The king and the hare] (TVD); *Karl XII* (TVM). 1975: *Jorden runt på 80 dagar* [Around the world in 80 days] (TVDS). 1980: *Swedenhielms* (TVD). 1981: *Rasmus på luffen* [Rasmus the tramp]. 1982: *Fanny och Alexander/Fanny and Alexander*.[1] 1987: *Babettes gæstebud/Babette's feast*; *En afton på Gripsholm* [An evening at Gripsholm] (TVD). 1990: *Herman*. 1993: *Telegrafisten* [The telegraph operator]; *Hemresa* [Journey home] (TVM). 1994: *Zorn*. 1995: *Alfred*. 1998: *HC Andersen og den skaeve skygge* [HC Andersen and the crooked shadow] (voice).

Director, Scriptwriter, Actor

1969: *Bokhandlaren som slutade bada* [The bookseller who gave up bathing]. 1970: *Ministern* [The minister]. 1973: *Per Omme* (TVM, short, director only). 1974: *Vita nejlikan* [The white carnation].

BIBLIOGRAPHY

Kulle, Jarl, and Eric Wennerholm. *Jag Kulle*. Stockholm: Bonniers, 1979.

AWARDS

GB 1965

GB 1983

NOTE

1. Longer version for television in 1983, with limited cinema release.

PER LINDBERG (Stockholm, 5 Mar. 1890–7 Feb. 1944), director. Lindberg can be compared with the better-known *Alf Sjöberg. For both, their reference point was stage work, and their film work was heavily influenced by this fact.

While Sjöberg has received much acclaim, Lindberg has, in comparison, been underrated. Besides the rich visual expression of Lindberg's films, Lindberg was better at bringing out the psychological dimension in his films.

Lindberg championed bringing the art of theater to everyone and felt that the screen was a suitable medium for this. Lindberg had already made a couple of films in the 1920s. One of these, Elin Wägner's *Norrtullsligan* [The Norrtull gang], appeared in the wake of the so-called Golden Age of silent film, which may explain why it has been somewhat unjustly forgotten. Lindberg returned to filmmaking in the late 1930s when he undertook two literary adaptations. The first one, *Gubben kommer* [The old man's coming], is an interesting fable shot just after the depression in which the catastrophe still hangs in the background like a dark cloud. This was brought to screen with Lindberg's typical flair for visual expression. The second, a filming of Vilhelm Moberg's semiautobiographical novel *Gläd dig i din ungdom* [Rejoice in thy youth], caused some controversy when the censors cut some of the love scenes. This was a lyrically made film about a young man's transition through puberty. It also depicts an "uneasiness with culture," a longing for a more genuine life close to nature. As such, this is another example of the trend toward the pastoral, typical of Swedish cinema in the late 1930s. Lindberg's next film, *Stål* [Steel], was set around a steel mill and reflects the break between tradition and modernity. While his interpretation of this theme is interesting, it is done in a conventional way. His next film, *Juninatten/A Night in June*, starred *Ingrid Bergman.

He made one of the most interesting contributions to the cinema of the early 1940s with the highly experimental *Det sägs på stan* [The talk of the town]. The story relates how gossip destroys an entire community, and it can be regarded as a symbolic representation of its time. It is told in a very expressionist style that was very unusual for Swedish cinema at the time. The style also explains why the film was both a critical and a financial disaster. This "film maudit" has, however, been revived and is now regarded as an interesting forerunner to later films of the same genre. When *Ingmar Bergman's first film, *Kris* [Crisis], premiered (having met almost the same fate as Lindberg's film), some critics noted the similarity of the two films. *Arne Mattsson was Lindberg's young assistant director on *Det sägs på stan*, and he later became one of Sweden's most interesting, if somewhat uneven, directors. It is likely that he was strongly influenced by Lindberg.

On the same day as *Det sägs på stan* was released, Lindberg experienced another fiasco with the film *I paradis* . . . [In paradise . . .], starring a young *Viveca Lindfors in her first main role. This was too much for Lindberg, and he disappeared forever from Swedish cinema, dying just a few years later. This was a great loss for both the Swedish stage and Swedish film.

FILMOGRAPHY

1923: *Anna-Clara och hennes bröder* [Anna-Clara and her brothers]; *Norrtullsligan* [The Norrtull gang]. 1939: *Gubben kommer* [The old man's coming] (also script); *Gläd dig i din ungdom* [Rejoice in thy youth] (also script). 1940: *Stål* [Steel]; *Juninatten/A Night in June* (also script); *Hans nåds testamente* [His grace's will]. 1941: *Det sägs på stan* [The talk of the town] (also script); *I paradis . . .* [In paradise . . .].

BIBLIOGRAPHY

Furhammar, Leif. "Per Lindberg och filmen." *Filmrutan*, no. 3 (1965):183–202.

GUNNEL LINDBLOM (Göteborg, 18 Dec. 1931–), actress, director. Lindblom began as an office clerk interested in amateur theater acting. She was accepted by the Göteborg Municipal Theater School in 1950 and was discovered by *Gustaf Molander's son Harald Molander, the production manager at Svensk Filmindustri. Gustaf Molander gave her a role in his 1952 *Kärlek* [Love], and in 1954 she was employed at the Malmö Municipal Theater, managed by *Ingmar Bergman. She became one of the "Bergman girls," with roles in some of his most important films. She also appeared in some of his early television stagings and served as his assistant stage director in the 1960s, during which time she developed an interest in doing her own directing. In the early 1970s she began stage directing and then progressed to television and film. Her screen work differs from the master, Bergman. Having played the roles of both sensitive and strong women in many films, Lindblom is interested in women's liberation issues. Her best contribution in this field has been *Sally och friheten* [Sally and freedom], starring *Ewa Fröling, in which the freedom-seeking Sally meets all kinds of obstacles, not least those within herself.

FILMOGRAPHY

Actor

1952: *Kärlek* [Love]. 1953: *Vi var några man* [We were a few men] (NCF). 1955: *Flickan i regnet* [The girl in the rain]. 1956: *Krut och kärlek* [Gunpowder and love]; *Sången om den eldröda blomman* [The song of the scarlet flower]. 1957: *Det sjunde inseglet/The Seventh Seal*; *Smultronstället/Wild Strawberries*. 1958: *Venetianskan* [The Venetian woman] (TVD); *Rabies* (TVD). 1959: *Skuggornas klubb* [The club of shadows] (TVD); *Oväder på Sycamore Street* [Thunder on Sycamore Street] (TVD); *Måsen* [The seagull] (TVD). 1960: *Jungfrukällan/The Virgin Spring*; *Den respektfulla skökan* [The respectful whore] (TVD); *Ett glas vatten* [A glass of water] (TVD); *Benjamin* (TVD); *Goda vänner trogna grannar* [Good friends, faithful neighbors]. 1961: *Bröllopet på Seine* [The wedding at Seine] (TVD); *Drottningar av Frankrike* [Queens of France] (TVD). 1963: *Nattvardsgästerna/Winter Light* [The communicants]; *Smutsiga händer* [Dirty hands] (TVD); *Och har du en ros . . .* [And do you have a rose . . .] (TVD); *Tystnaden/The Silence*; *Min kära är en ros* [My beloved is a rose]. 1964: *Är du inte riktigt klok?* [Are you crazy?]; *Älskande par/Loving Couples*. 1965: *Rapture*. 1966: *De dans van de Rieger*; *Sult/Hunger*; *Yngsjömordet/Woman of Darkness*. 1967: *Onkel Vanja* [Uncle Vanja] (TVD); *Den onda cirkeln* [The vicious circle]. 1968: *Flickorna/The Girls*. 1969: *Fadern* [The father]; *Lilla mahagonny* [Little mahagonny] (TVD). 1970: *Reservatet* [The sanctuary] (TVD). 1971: *Brother Carl*. 1973: *Scener ur ett äktenskap/Scenes from a Marriage* (TVM).[1] 1974: *Offret* [The victim] (TVM). 1978: *Bomsalva* [Misfire]. 1984: *Träpatronerna* [The lumber barons] (TVMS); *Bakom jalusin* [Behind shutters]. 1989:

Det var då . . . [It was then . . .] (TVMS). 1991: *Capitan Escalaborns*; *Guldburen* [The golden cage] (TVMS); *Sent i mars* [Late in March] (short). 1993: *Hedda Gabler* (TVD). 1995: *Nadja* (short). 1996: *I rollerna tre* [In three roles] (docu.). 1997: *Svenska hjältar* [Swedish heroes].

Director

1976: *Sjung vackert om kärlek* [Sing sweetly about love] (TVM). 1977: *Paradistorg/Summer Paradise* (also script). 1981: *Sally och friheten* [Sally and freedom] (also actor); *Zéb-un-nisá—prinsessa av Indien* [Zéb-un-nisá—princess of India] (TVD). 1991: *Sanna kvinnor* [True women] (TVM). 1994: *Betraktelse* [Meditation] (short, narrator).

BIBLIOGRAPHY

Forslund, 1995.
Jordan, I., and F. Andé. "Un paradis hanté." *Positif*, no. 199 (Nov. 1977):34–40. Interview.
Oukrete, F. "Brève rencontre avec Gunnel Lindblom." *Ecran*, no. 63 (Nov. 1977):8–10.

NOTE

1. Theatrically released in 1974 in an edited version.

VIVECA LINDFORS (Uppsala, 29 Dec. 1920–25 Oct. 1995), actress. The daughter of an officer, she was determined to become an actress and was accepted by the Royal Dramatic Theater School. She was discovered at the school while doing a bit part in a film comedy. Her first main role was in the disastrous *I paradis . . .* [In paradise . . .], directed by *Per Lindberg, but this proved to be an exception to her Swedish film career. She starred in some of the most successful melodramas produced during the war years and was then discovered by Hollywood. She moved there just after the war. The roles in Hollywood were less significant in comparison to her earlier period in Sweden, although she did continue to act for a very long time. She was married to director Don Siegel and playwright Georg Tabori, among others. In her later years she gradually became more interested in stage acting and direction, and she died in her hometown just after a well-received stage performance.

"Full-blooded" was a common cliché among film Swedish reviewers in the 1940s when they described Viveca Lindfors's appearance. She was also given roles that brought out her colorful radiance. In her breakthrough, *Ivar Johansson's *Tänk, om jag gifter mig med prästen* [Imagine if I marry the vicar], she played a village teacher who falls in love with the vicar and becomes pregnant. Unwilling to accept her pregnancy, the vicar disappears. She is a strong woman, though, who dares to stand up against the mores of the gossipy villagers by deciding to keep the child and continue her work as a teacher. This story caused scandal, although the unwed mother was rather common stock in the Swedish cinema of the time. The film proved to be successful and paved the way for more strong female roles in various social melodramas. This followed the trend of the Swedish cinema of the war years to deal more freely with certain social problems that hitherto had been more or less taboo (and restricted by the Board of Censorship). *Gula kliniken* [The yellow clinic] (dealing with abortions) and *Anna Lans* (streetwalkers) were examples of such films. One might classify Lindfors as a genre of her own. She became one of a very few female stars in Sweden with a box office appeal based solely on her acting merits. In her later stage work, such as her own play *I a Woman*, she gave expression to women's liberation ideals that were no less scandalous than her appearances in the Swedish films of the 1940s.

FILMOGRAPHY

1940: *Snurriga familjen* [Crazy family]. 1941: *I paradis . . .* [In paradise . . .]; *Tänk, om jag gifter mig med prästen* [Imagine if I marry the vicar]. 1942: *Morgondagens melodi* [Tomorrow's melody]; *La donna del peccato; Nebbie sul mare; Gula kliniken* [The yellow clinic]. 1943: *Anna Lans/The Sin of Anna Lans; Brödernas kvinna* [The brother's woman]. 1944: *Appassionata; Jag är eld och luft* [I am fire and air]. 1945: *Maria på Kvarngården* [Maria of Kvarngården]; *Svarta rosor* [Black roses]; *Den allvarsamma leken* [The serious game]. 1946: *I dödens väntrum/Interlude* [In death's waiting room]. 1948: *To the Victor; Adventures of Don Juan.* 1949: *Night unto Night; Singoalla/Gypsy Fury* (also made in French and English versions). 1950: *Backfire; No Sad Songs for Me; This Side of the Law; Dark City; The Flying Missile.* 1951: *Die Vier im Jeep; Journey into Light.* 1952: *The Raiders; No Time for Flowers; No Sad Songs for Me* (TVM). 1953: *Autumn Nocturne* (TVM); *The Bet* (TVM); *The Riddle of Mayerling* (TVM); *The Vanishing Point* (TVM). 1954: *The Court-Martial of Mata Hari* (TVM). 1955: *The Fateful Pilgrimage* (TVM); *Run for Cover; Moonfleet; The Passport* (TVM). 1956: *Kyral Katina* (TVM); *Adventure in Diamonds* (TVM). 1957: *They Never Forget* (TVM); *The Long Count* (TVM); *The Last Tycoon* (TVM); *The Halliday Brand.* 1958: *The Bridge of San Luis Rey* (TVM); *The Spell of the Tigress* (TVM); *I Accuse!; La tempesta,* a.k.a. *La tempete,* a.k.a. *Oluja/Tempest.* 1959: *Dangerous Episode* (TVM). 1960: *The Emperor's Clothes* (TVM); *The Story of Ruth; Weddings and Babies.* 1961: *King of Kings; Letemps du ghetto* (voice). 1962: *The Paradine Case* (TVM); *No Exit.* 1963: *The Damned/These Are the Damned; An Affair of the Skin.* 1964: *Sylvia.* 1965: *Brainstorm; Brecht om Brecht* [Brecht on Brecht] (TVD). 1967: *The Diary of Anne Frank* (TVM); *El coleccionista de cadaveres/Blind Man's Bluff.* 1968: *Oscuros sueños de agosto.* 1969: *Coming Apart.* 1970: *Puzzle of a Downfall Child.* 1971: *La casa sin fronteras.* 1973: *The Way We Were; La campana del infierno,* a.k.a. *Les cloches de l'enfer/Bell of Hell,* a.k.a. *Bell from Hell; The Stranger, The Jewish Wife, An Actor Works* (films collected as "Three Small Films"). 1976: *De lyckligt lottade* [The well situated] (TVM); *The 10th Level* (TVM); *Welcome to L.A.* 1977: *Tabu* [Taboo]. 1978: *Girlfriends; A Question of Guilt* (TVM); *A Wedding.* 1979: *Voices; Linus eller Tegelhusets hemlighet* [Linus, or The secret of the brick house]; *Natural Enemies.* 1980: *Marilyn: The Untold Story* (TVM); *Playing for Time* (TVM); *The Mom Wolfman and Me* (TVM); *Innan vintern kommer* [Before winter comes] (TVM). 1981: *The Hand; The Best Little Girl in the World* (TVM); *For Ladies Only* (TVM). 1982: *Divorce Wars: A Love Story; Inside the Third Reich* (TVM); *Creepshow; A Love Story* (TVM). 1983: *Dies rigorose Leben.* 1984: *A Doctor's Story* (TVM); *Silent Madness; Passions* (TVM); *The Three Wishes of Billy Grier* (TVM). 1985: *The Sure Thing; Secret Weapons* (TVM). 1986: *Frankensteins Tante* (TVM). 1987: *Unfinished Business* (also director, script); *Rachel River*; *Lady Beware*. 1988: *The Ann Jillian Story*; *Going Undercover*, a.k.a. *Yellow Pages*. 1989: *Flickan vid stenbänken* [The girl by the stone bench] (TVM); *Misplaced*; *Forced March*. 1990: *Going to Chicago*; *Exorcist III*; *Luba*; *Exiled in America*. 1991: *Zandalee*; *The Linguine Incident*; *Child of Darkness, Child of Light* (TVM). 1992: *North of Pittsburgh*. 1993: *Zelda* (TVM). 1994: *Stargate*; *Backstreet Justice*. 1995: *Last Summer in the Hamptons*. 1996: *Looking for Richard*.

Episodes in Series

Loretta Young Show (1957); *Rawhide* (1959); *Adventures in Paradise* (1960); *Five Fingers* (1960); *Naked City* (1961); *The Untouchables* (1962); *Defenders* (1962, 1964); *The Nurses* (1962, 1963); *12 O'Clock High* (1964); *Voyage to the Bottom of the Sea* (1964); *Ben Casey* (1965, 1966); *Bonanza* (1965); *Coronet Blue* (1967); *FBI* (1967, 1969); *Medical Center* (1969); *The Interns* (1970); *Dynasty* (1982); *Glitter* (1984); *Trapper John, M.D.* (1984); *Hotel* (1985); *The Wizard* (1986); *Life Goes On* (1989); *Law & Order* (1993).

BIBLIOGRAPHY

Forslund, 1995.
Lindfors, Viveca. *Viveka . . . Viveca*. New York: Everest House, 1981. Autobiography.

AWARDS

Berlin 1962: Best Actress (*No Exit*)
Emmy Award 1990: "Save the Last Dance" (from *Life Goes On*)

JAN MALMSJÖ (Lund, 29 May 1932–), actor. One of the most popular actors and entertainers in contemporary Sweden, he was born in Lund, in southern Sweden. As the child of show people, both of his parents having been dancers and singers, he was practically born on the stage. Malmsjö debuted at nine years of age in a revue act and was determined to be accepted into nothing less than the Royal Dramatic Theater stage in Stockholm. This dream came true when he was accepted at their school in 1950. He has since been engaged there for various periods.

As actor, stage artist, singer, and entertainer, he has showed remarkable versatility, his work having ranged from classic musicals to acting in folksy television serials to portraying the bishop in *Bergman's *Fanny och Alexander/Fanny and Alexander*. His portrayal of the bishop was brilliantly frightening, perhaps because it stood in such sharp contrast to his otherwise gay image. Among Bergman's antiauthoritarian depictions Malmsjö's is the darkest; he is both powerful and psychopathic, compassionate and understanding. "Out of love," he mistreats the young Alexander with extreme cruelty. Another of the roles Malmsjö regards as one of his favorites is quite different; he played the sometime alcoholic, ex-soccer player "The Danish killer" in the folksy television serial about caretaker N. P. Möller.

FILMOGRAPHY

1947: *Ebberöds bank* [Ebberöd bank]. 1951: *Het på gröten* [Eager] (short). 1953: *Vi var några man* [We were a few men] (NCF); *Marianne*. 1954: *Gud Fader och tattaren*, a.k.a.

Tattarblod [Our father and the gypsy, a.k.a. Gypsy blood]; *Flicka med melodi* [A Girl with a melody]. 1958: *Min syster och jag* [My sister and I] (TVD); *Jeppson* (TVD); *Döden som läromästare* [Death as master] (TVD); *Skandalskolan* [The school for scandals] (TVD); *Maria Angelica* (TVM); *Hemma klockan sju* [Home at seven o'clock]; *Oh, mein Papa* (TVD). 1959: *Romeo och Julia i Östberlin* [Romeo and Julia in East Berlin] (TVD); *Det var en annan historia* [It was another story] (TVD); *Lilith* (TVD); *En skugga* [A shadow] (TVD); *Porträtt av jägare* [Portrait of a hunter] (TVD); *Tillbaka till Eden* [Back to Eden] (TVD); *Cinderella öppnar balen* [Cinderella opens the ball] (TVD); *Den inbillade sjuke* [The imaginary invalid] (TVD); *Pojken Winslow* [The Winslow boy] (TVD); *Mälarpirater* [Pirates of Lake Mälaren]; *Brevet* [The letter] (short). 1960: *Tärningen är kastad* [The die is cast]; *Diana går på jakt* [French without tears] (TVD). 1961: *Nina, Nora, Nalle* [Nina, Nora, Nalle] (TVMS); *Svenska Floyd* [Swedish Floyd]. 1962: *Vita frun* [White lady]; *Trasiga änglar* [We are no angels] (TVD); *Gisslan* [Hostage] (TVD). 1963: *Kurragömma* [Hide and seek]; *Prins hatt under jorden* [The singing leaves]. 1964: *Narr* [Fool] (TVD); *Älskande par/Loving Couples*. 1965: *Gustav Vasa* (TVD); *Calle P.* 1966: *Torn Curtain*. 1968: *Mysinge Motell* (TVDS). 1970: *Garderoben* [The closet] (TVD); *Kärleksgåvan* [The love gift] (TVD). 1971: *Gunghästen* [The rocking horse] (TVD). 1972–1976: *N. P. Möller* (TVMS, 4 parts). 1972–1973: *Bröderna Malm* [The Malm brothers] (TVMS). 1973: *Träben och emaljöga* [Wooden leg and glass eye] (TVM, short); *Scener ur ett äktenskap/Scenes from a Marriage* (TVM).[1] 1974: *Den Italienska halmhatten* [The Italian straw hat] (TVD). 1975: *Familjelagen* [Family law] (TVD); *Släpp fångarne loss—det är vår!* [Let the prisoners free—it's spring!]. 1977: *Conny och Tojan* [Conny and Tojan] (TVMS); *Fia i folkhemmet* [Fia in people's home] (TVM); *Min son, min son!* [My son, my son!] (TVD); *Väljarnas förtroende* [Voter's confidence] (TVM); *Bluff Stop*. 1978: *Rätt ut i luften* [Straight into the air] (TVD). 1979: *Skeppsredaren* [The ship owner] (TVDS). 1980: *Marmeladupproret* [The marmalade rebellion]. 1982: *Ringlek* [Ring game] (TVD); *Hedebyborna* [The people of Hedeby] (TVMS); *Fanny och Alexander/Fanny and Alexander*.[2] 1983: *Mot härliga tider* [Happy times]. 1986–1987: *Kulla-Gulla* (TVMS); *Peter the Great* (TVM). 1987: *Jim och piraterna Blom* [Jim and the Blom pirates]; *Trädet* [The tree] (TVM); *En afton på Gripsholm* [An evening at Gripsholm] (TVD). 1989: *Walter og Carlo i Amerika* [Walter and Carlo in America]. 1990: *Esaias Tegne'r* (TVM); *Äkta makar* [Married couples] (TVD). 1991: *Uppfinnaren* [The inventor] (TVDS); *Kopplingen* [The junction] (TVMS). 1993: *Den korsikanske biskopen* [The Corsican bishop] (TVM); *Drömkåken* [The dream house]. 1994: *Good Night Irene*. 1995: *Petri tårar* [Petri tears]. 1996: *Dödsdansen* [Dance of death] (TVD). 1997: *Jag är din krigare* [I am your warrior]. *Förmannen som försvann* [The foreman that disappeared] (TVM); 1998: *Den tatuerade änkan* [The tattooed widow]; *Jobbet och jag* [The job and me] (TVDS).

Actor in Television Series

1966: *Blue light*; *Combat*; *Twelve O'Clock High*.

NOTES

1. Theatrically released in 1974 in an edited version.
2. Longer version for television in 1984, with limited cinema release in 1983.

BIRGER MALMSTEN (Gräsö, 23 Dec. 1920–15 Feb. 1991), actor. His way to fame was not easy. Born on a remote island outside Stockholm, he moved to the capital in his early teens. He made a living at various jobs, supporting his interest in both amateur acting and going to the movies with his meager salary. He did not always make ends meet. His first appearance in a stage revue was a failure, and he was unemployed until finding another job as a waiter. He continued with his plans to become an actor, and after many obstacles, including trying in vain to be accepted by the Royal Dramatic Theater School, he began to get small parts in movies and on the stage. At the student theater he became acquainted with *Ingmar Bergman for the first time. Then with an engagement at Helsingborg Municipal Theater, he at last had a breakthrough. He became one of Ingmar Bergman's favorites in Bergman's first movies; Malmsten perfectly embodied the young, rebellious, and sometimes tragic heroes (e.g., *Sommarlek/Illicit Interlude*) that were the central characters of the films. Malmsten's dark looks and somewhat vibrant, sexy radiation were perfect for the role. One might even claim that Malmsten's depiction of the author in *Fängelse/The Devil's Wanton* was, at the time, a rather precise portrait of Bergman himself. Even when not acting in Bergman movies, he continued to embody rather strange figures. He portrayed a real social outcast as the gypsy in *Ingen mans kvinna* [No man's woman]. For Bergman he made several more movies in the earlier vein of the rebel, first as the promiscuous stranger in *Tystnaden/The Silence*, then as a rapist in *Ansikte mot ansikte/Face to Face*. In his last years Malmsten was cast more as distinguished old men. He starred in the soap opera *Goda grannar* [Good neighbors], where he was the nice, humane landlord who, as the title suggests, made his tenants feel like "good neighbors."

FILMOGRAPHY

1940: *Snurriga familjen* [Crazy family]. 1942: *General von Döbeln*. 1943: *Ombyte av tåg* [Changing trains]; *På liv och död* [A life or death matter]. 1944: *Räkna de lyckliga stunderna blott* [Count only the happy moments]; *Vi behöver varann* [We need each other] (NCF); *Hets/Torment*. 1945: *Den allvarsamma leken* [The serious game]. 1946: *Det regnar på vår kärlek* [It rains on our love]; *När ängarna blommar* [When the meadows blossom]. 1947: *Skepp till India land/Frustration* [Ship to Indialand]; *Brott i sol* [Crime in the sun]. 1948: *Musik i mörker/Night Is My Future*, a.k.a. *Music in Darkness*; *Banketten* [The banquet]; *Eva*. 1949: *Farlig vår* [Dangerous springtime]; *Fängelse/The Devil's Wanton*, a.k.a. *Prison*; *Törst/Three Strange Loves* [Thirst]. 1950: *Till glädje/To Joy*; *Restaurant Intim*; *Regementets ros* [The rose of the regiment]. 1951: *Sommarlek/Illicit Interlude* [Summer play]. 1952: *Kvinnors väntan/Secrets of Women* [Women's waiting]. 1953: *Ursula—flickan från Finnskogarna* [Ursula—the girl from the Finn forests]; *All jordens fröjd* [All world's delight]; *Ingen mans kvinna* [No man's woman]. 1954: *I rök och dans* [Dance in the smoke]; *The Prince and I* (TVM, episode in *Foreign Intrigue*); *Hästhandlarens flickor/Time of Desire* [The horse-dealer's girls]; *Gabrielle*. 1955: *The Model* (TVM, episode in *Foreign Intrigue*); *Little Romeo* (TVM, episode in *Foreign Intrigue*); *Miss Fortune* (episode in *Foreign Intrigue*); *Enhörningen* [The unicorn]; *Finnskogens folk* [The people of the Finn forests]. 1956: *Rough Sketch* (TVM); *Moln över Hellesta* [Clouds over Hellesta]. 1957: *Som man bäddar . . .* [You have made your bed . . .]; Möten i skymningen [Encounter in the twilight]; *Nattens ljus* [Light in the night]. 1958: *Lek på regnbågen* [Playing on the rainbow]; *Laila/Make Way for Lila; Alla barn i början* [All kids in the beginning] (short). 1959: *Guldgrävarna* [The gold diggers]; *Med fara för livet/48 Hours to Live*. 1960: *Våld* [Violence] (TVD); *Fröken Rosita* [Miss Rosita] (TVD). 1961: *Vildanden* [The wild duck] (TVD); *Eurydike* (TVD); *Katten och kanariefågeln* [The cat and the canary] (TVD); *Frisöndag* [Free Sunday] (TVD). 1962: *Dödens arlekin* [Arlequin of death] (TVD); *På jakt efter lyckan* [In search of happiness] (TVD); *Bacchusfesten* [The Bacchus festival] (TVD). 1963: *Ett drömspel* [A dream play] (TVD); *Tystnaden/The Silence*. 1966: *Masculin Féminin*. 1968: *... som havets nakna vind/One Swedish Summer; Carmilla*. 1970: *Ann och Eve—de erotiska/Ann and Eve*. 1971: *Det händer i Sålunda* [It happens in Sålunda] (TVDS). 1972: *Tebjudningen som inte ville ta slut* [The tea party that had no end] (TVD). 1973: *ITT:s hemliga dokument* [ITT:s secret documents] (TVD). 1974: *Engeln* [The angel] (TVMS); *Det sista äventyret* [The last adventure]. 1976: *Meningen med föreningen* [The meaning of the society] (TVD); *Ansikte mot ansikte/Face to Face* (TVM).[1] 1977: *Tabu* [Taboo]. 1980: *SOS Harrisburg* (TVD); *Sinkadus* [Toss-up] (TVMS). 1982: *Dubbelsvindlarna* [The double cheaters] (TVMS); *Pappa är död* [Father is dead] (TVM). 1983: *Den tredje lyckan* [The third happiness] (TVMS). 1984: *Jönssonligan får guldfeber* [The Jönsson gang gets gold fever]. 1985: *Krympningen* [The shrinking] (TVD); *Lösa förbindelser* [Loose connections] (TVDS); *Fridas flykt* [Frida's escape] (TVM); *Nya Dagbladet* [The new dailies] (TVDS). 1987: *Goda grannar* [Good neighbors] (TVDS); *Paganini från Saltängen* [Paganini from Saltängen] (TVMS); *I dag röd* [Today red] (TVM). 1989: *Varuhuset* [The department store] (TVDS); *Det var då ... * [It was then ...] (TVDS). 1991: *Kopplingen* [The junction] (TVM).

BIBLIOGRAPHY

Holm, 1947.

NOTE

1. Theatrically released abroad in edited version.

LORENS MARMSTEDT (Stockholm, 29 Oct. 1908–4 Apr. 1966), director, producer. Although M was a key name in Swedish film history for three decades, nearly nothing has been written about him. He is rarely mentioned in the existing film history books. Though *Ingmar Bergman clearly states in his book *The Magic Lantern* that "Lorens Marmstedt taught me how to make movies," not one of the innumerable writers on Bergman seems to have reflected more closely on these words. Marmstedt should be thanked for helping at least two important directors, *Hasse Ekman and Ingmar Bergman, start their careers and make some of their most important films. Marmstedt produced Ekman's most personal and artistic contributions to Swedish film history and helped Bergman get over the first obstacles on his road to world fame. Bergman's first directorial effort, *Kris* [Crisis], was a disaster, and his career as a film director might have ended there, were it not that Marmstedt helped him to get another chance with several films financed by another company and one produced by Marmstedt's own Terrafilm. Marmstedt also let Bergman direct his first real personal vision, *Fängelse/The Devil's Wanton*, despite knowing that it would be a box office failure.

Marmstedt began as a film critic but soon turned to production and direction in the hectic 1930s. His first years as a producer are best characterized by his establishment of a string of short-lived companies. The turnover reflected both the volatile production scene and his own gambling nature. To produce a film in the 1930s without a film studio or one's own cinema theaters was to walk a financial tightrope. Despite this, Marmstedt continued again and again in a most intrepid style. He finally managed to gain financial stability when he founded his famous Terrafilm in 1938. He secured Terrafilm with the help of Anders Sandrew, then owner of one of the most important cinema theater chains in Sweden. At the same time, Sandrew also bought his own film studio and began, on a small scale, to produce himself. He gave Marmstedt his financial support, allowed him to use his film studio, and distributed Marmstedt's films in his cinemas.

Marmstedt put his mark on whatever he was responsible for. As a director and a producer in the 1930s, he favored a more modern form of cinematic narrative than was usual in contemporary Swedish film. Self-reflexivity is not uncommon in Marmstedt's films. *Kungen kommer* [The king is coming] (produced with *Gösta Ekman [Sr.] in a double role as both the nineteenth-century King Carl XV and his double, an actor of more humble origin) is an anachronistic and ironic tale, a reflexive discourse on the art of acting—or, as one critic pointed out, on the art of Gösta Ekman himself. With *Kungen kommer* one cannot but help thinking of later Ingmar Bergman films. This is also true of the remarkable *Vingar kring fyren* [Wings by the lighthouse], produced in 1938, where the barren coastal landscape surrounding an isolated lighthouse is used to act out a heavy, symbolic drama of love, jealousy, and longing for far horizons.

FILMOGRAPHY

Director

1932: *Kärleksexpressen* [The love express]; *En stulen vals* [A stolen waltz]. 1933: *Kanske en diktare* [Perhaps a poet]. 1934: *Atlantäventyret* [The Atlantic adventure] (codir. Edvin Adolphson); *Eva går ombord* [Eva goes aboard]. 1936: *Flickorna på Uppåkra* [The girls of Uppåkra] (codir. Alice Eklund).

Producer

1932: *Kärleksexpressen* [The love express]. 1933: *Kanske en diktare* [Perhaps a poet]; *Hemslavinnor* [We slaves at home]. 1934: *Eva går ombord* [Eva goes aboard]; *Pettersson-Sverige*. 1935: *Äktenskapsleken* [Marriage game]. 1936: *Kungen kommer* [The king is coming]; *Skeppsbrutne Max* [Shipwrecked Max]; *Flickorna på Uppåkra* [The girls of Uppåkra]. 1938: *Vingar kring fyren* [Wings by the lighthouse]. 1939: *Vi två/Vi Tvaa* [The two of us]; *Hennes lilla Majestät* [Her little majesty]. 1940: *Familjen Björck* [The Björck family]; *Ett brott* [A crime]; *Med dej i mina armar* [With you in my arms]. 1941: *Livet går vidare* [Life goes on]; *Första divisionen* [First squadron]; *En kvinna ombord* [Woman on board]. 1942: *Lågor i dunklet* [Flames in the gloom]; *Lyckan kommer* [Happiness comes]; *General von Döbeln*. 1943: *Ombyte av tåg* [Changing trains]; *Kvinnor i fångenskap* [Women in captivity]; *Sjätte skottet* [Sixth shot]; *Sonja*. 1944: *Narkos* [Narcosis]; *Excellensen* [His excellency]; *Som folk är mest* [Like most people]; *Vi behöver varann* [We need each other]. 1944: *Flickan och Djävulen* [The girl and the devil]. 1945: *Kungliga patrasket* [Royal rabble]; *Fram för lilla Märta* [Here to little Märta]. 1946: *I dödens väntrum/Interlude* [In death's waiting room]. 1947: *Supé för två* [Dinner for two]; *Brott i sol* [Crime in the sun]. 1948: *Musik i mörker/Night is my Future* [Music in darkness]; *Lilla Märta kommer tillbaka* [Little Märta returns]; *Banketten* [The Banquet]. 1949: *Fängelse/The Devil's Wanton*, a.k.a. *Prison*; *Flickan från tredje raden* [The girl in the gallery]; *Singoalla/Gypsy Fury*. 1950: *Flicka och hyacinter* [Girl with hyacinths]. 1951: *Min vän Oscar* [My friend Oscar]. 1952: *Eldfågeln* [Firebird]. 1953: *I dur och skur* [In rain and song]; *Resan till dej* [The journey to you]. 1954: *Gula divisionen* [Yellow squadron]. 1955: *Mord, lilla vän* [Murder, my friend]; *Hoppsan!* [Whoops!]. 1956: *Gorilla*; *Sceningång* [Stage entrance]. 1957: *Räkna med bråk* [Look out for trouble]. 1959: *Llegaron dos hombres*, a.k.a. *Det kom två män* [Two men were coming]. 1960: *Sommar och syndare* [Summer and sinners]. 1962: *Vaxdockan/The Doll*. 1963: *Adam och Eva* [Adam and Eve]. 1964: *Bröllopsbevär/Wedding Swedish Style*. 1965: *Kattorna* [The cats]; *Nattmara* [Nightmare].

BIBLIOGRAPHY

Janzon, Bengt. "Lorens Marmstedt." *Vecko-Journalen*, no. 3 (1948):14, 29–30.
Marmstedt, Lorens. "Ruda eller Gamba?" *OBS!*, no. 18 (1950):11–15. LM on his co-operation with Bergman.
Sellermark, Arne. "Il magnifico på Skeppargatan 6." *Allt*, no. 9 (1953):18–23.
Waldekranz, Rune. "Epoken Lorens Marmstedt." *Biografägaren*, nos. 4–5 (1966):8–9. Obituary.

ARNE MATTSSON (Uppsala, 2 Dec. 1918–27 June 1995), director. Mattsson was one of the most productive of all Swedish film directors. He was also perhaps one of the most style-conscious. This sometimes resulted in memorable and visually rich films, and at other times it led into the blind alley of mannerisms. The latter is most evident in his later films, when his career declined sharply. The last decades of his life were embittered by a constant feud with Swedish film critics, many of whom he regarded almost as personal enemies. In later years there was no longer any room for him on the established production scene, and he was forced to work with obscure producers, mainly abroad. Although there were some traces of his former grandeur in his last films, his final years were generally unremarkable.

Mattsson began his career as assistant director to *Per Lindberg when Lindberg made his "film maudit" *Det sägs på stan* [The talk of the town] in 1941. The influence of the expressionist style of this film became evident when Mattsson more or less specialized in the thriller genre. However, Mattsson's own directorial career began with several light comedies before he could make better use of his visual storytelling ability with more substantial work. He reached the peak of his career in the late 1940s and the 1950s with such memorable films as *Hon dansade en sommar/One Summer of Happiness*, *Kärlekens bröd* [The bread of love], and others. The rural melodrama *Hon dansade en sommar* was one of the most profitable films in Swedish film history.

The success of *Hon dansade en sommar* allowed Mattsson to make a film of his own choice, *Kärlekens bröd*, an almost experimental, highly stylized, and strange film set during the Finnish Winter War. This film was a commercial disaster, and Mattsson returned to the main road of commercial film-making. In the late 1950s and the beginning of the 1960s he made a string of thrillers starring the private eye John Hillman (each with the color references black, red, blue, yellow, and white in the title), which were very successful with the audience. He continued in the same genre during the 1960s, and his films included several scripted by "mystery writer queen" Maria Lang (real name Dagmar Lange). With Lang's scripts, he found a free outlet for his highly stylized and expressionist style, which seen from today's point of view is often remarkable. A film like *Ljuvlig är sommarnatten* [Lovely is the summer night], with its eerie and mystic atmosphere, might even be regarded as a 1960s version of *Twin Peaks*.

The first two decades of Mattsson's filmmaking were, despite some setbacks, his most successful. The last three can only be described as a steady decline. During the last years of his career, he became involved in more or less obscure film projects, some of which remained unfinished, making it almost impossible to complete the filmography for his last years.

FILMOGRAPHY

1941: *Det sägs på stan* [The talk of the town] (actor and assistant director). 1943: *I brist på bevis* [For lack of evidence] (script only). 1944: *Räkna de lyckliga stunderna blott* [Count only the happy moments] (script only);[1] . . . *och alla dessa kvinnor* [. . . and all these women]. 1945: *Maria på Kvarngården* [Maria of Kvarngården]; *Sussie*; *I som här inträden . . .* [All ye who enter here . . .]. 1946: *Peggy på vift* [Peggy on the loose]; *Rötägg/Incorrigible*. 1947: *Pappa sökes* [Wanted: a daddy]; *Det kom en gäst . . .* [There came a guest . . .] (also script); *Rallare* [Railroad workers] (also script). 1949: *Farlig vår* [Dangerous springtime]; *Kvinna i vitt* [Woman in white]. 1950: *När kärleken kom till byn* [When love came to the village]; *Kastrullresan* [The saucepan journey]; *Kyssen på kryssen* [The kiss on the cruise] (also script). 1951: *Bärande hav* [In the arms of the sea]; *Hon dansade en sommar/One Summer of Happiness*. 1952: *Hård klang* [The clang of the pick]; *För min heta ungdoms skull* [For the sake of my intemperate youth]. 1953: *Kärlekens bröd* [The bread of love]. 1954: *Förtrollad vandring* [Enchanted journey]; *Storm över Tjurö* [Storm over Tjurö]; *Salka Valka*. 1955: *Männen i mörker* [Men in the dark]; *Hemsöborna* [The people of Hemsö]. 1956: *Litet bo* [A little nest]; *Flickan i frack* [The girl in tails]. 1957: *Livets vår*, a.k.a. *Primavera de la vida* [The spring of life]; *Ingen morgondag* [No tomorrow]. 1958: *Damen i svart* [The lady in black]; *Körkarlen* [The phantom chariot]; *Mannekäng i rött* [Mannequin in red]. 1959: *Det kom två män*, a.k.a. *Llegaron dos hombres* [There came two men] (as "supervisor"); *Får jag låna din fru?* [May I borrow your wife?]; *Ryttare i blått* [Rider in blue]. 1960: *Sommar och syndare* [Summer and sinners]; *När mörkret faller* [When darkness falls]. 1961: *Ljuvlig är sommarnatten* [Lovely is the summer night]. 1962: *Biljett till paradiset* [Ticket to paradise]; *Vita frun* [The white lady] (also script); *Vaxdockan/The Doll*. 1963: *Det är hos mig han har varit* [He was with me]; *Den gula bilen* [The yellow car]. 1964: *Blåjackor* [Bluejackets]. 1965: *Här kommer bärsärkarna* [The wild vikings]; *Morianerna/Morianna*, a.k.a. *I, the Body* (also script); *Nattmara* [Nightmare] (also script). 1966: *Yngsjömordet/Woman of Darkness*. 1967: *Mördaren—en helt vanlig person* [The murderer—a perfectly ordinary person] (also script); *Den onda cirkeln* [The vicious circle]; *Ensam i natten* [Alone in the night] (TVM, short). 1968: *Bamse/Bamse* (also script). 1970: *Ann och Eve—de erotiska/Ann and Eve*. 1973: *Smutsiga fingrar* [Dirty fingers]. 1978: *Mannen i skuggan/Man in the Shadow* (also script). 1985: *Mask of Murder*.[2] 1987: *Destroying Angel*, a.k.a. *Sleep Well, My Love*; *The Girl*; *Somewhere Sometime*.[3] 1989: *The Mad Bunch* (codir. Mats Helge).

BIBLIOGRAPHY

Bengtsson, Bengt. "Ett svenskt filmaröde. Fallet Arne Mattsson." *Filmhäftet*, nos. 65–66 (1989): 47–57.
Wortzelius, Hugo. "Arne Mattsson. En regissörsprofil." *Perspektiv*, no. 2 (1953): 67–71.

NOTES

1. Mattsson also directed a few scenes (uncredited).
2. Production year; release year uncertain.
3. The existence of this film is somewhat doubtful. One source claims it was produced in 1977, together with *Boy in the Fog* (probably an unfinished project). The same source mentions another production—1990: *Hired Gun*.

GUSTAF MOLANDER (Helsinki, 18 Nov. 1888–19 June 1973), actor, director. Molander was the son of the manager of the Swedish theater in Helsinki, Finland. He moved to Stockholm with his brother Olof. (Olof would eventually become a famous stage director at the Royal Dramatic Theater, an important source of inspiration for *Ingmar Bergman's stage work. Although Olof also directed a few films, they were never as important as the ones made by his brother.) Gustaf Molander entered the Swedish film scene in the late 1910s when he scripted some films for *Mauritz Stiller. One can claim that Molander continued the Stiller tradition in Swedish film after Stiller died. Molander made his own debut as a film director in 1920 with the rural drama *Bodakungen* [The king of Boda], and he returned to the rural drama genre on various occasions during a long career, lasting until the late 1960s. Molander has produced the greatest number of films of any Swedish film director. This is probably because he became the leading director at Svensk Filmindustri when *Sjöström and Stiller departed for Hollywood. Molander was an efficient and trained craftsman, in a sort of "Hollywood-inspired" style. In the 1930s when Swedish film began to prosper again, Molander directed 10 percent of all of Sweden's output. The traditional view is that Molander was little else but a "Hollywood-style" director and that his features, whether elegant comedies or melodramas, are competent but shallow pieces of work.

Recent research has shown that his films are much more complex than the traditional view would have it and that they are fertile ground for analysis. This is especially true of his 1930s films, which are perhaps the highlights of his career. One might point to his interesting contributions to "women's film"—his great melodramas, *Intermezzo, En kvinnas ansikte/A Woman's Face*, and *En enda natt/Only One Night* with *Ingrid Bergman. The first two served as a springboard for Ingrid Bergman's international career and are among the very few Swedish films that have been remade in Hollywood. As Tytti Soila has pointed out, these films are complex in their treatment of the female character and give voice to a "repressed" feminist view of the world. His versions of Hjalmar Bergman's plays *Swedenhielms* and *Dollar* are also of great interest, especially as the last one has constantly been underrated by film historians. It is a fine example of Molander as inheritor of Stiller's modernist legacy and a link to certain elements of postwar Swedish cinema. Its theme of "unhappiness in modern culture" and the longing for a more natural, genuine way of being resemble later Ingmar Bergman films. Molander also directed two screenplays by Ingmar Bergman in the late 1940s, where it becomes clear that he and Bergman belong to the same Swedish film tradition.

FILMOGRAPHY

Actor

1931: *Brokiga Blad/Brokiga Blad* [Colorful pages]. 1946: *Kris* [Crisis] (narrator). 1961: *När seklet var ungt* [When the century was young] (docu., narrator).

Director

1920: *Bodakungen* [The king of Boda] (also script). 1922: *Thomas Graals myndling* [Thomas Graal's ward] (also script); *Amatörfilmen*, a.k.a. *Pärlorna* [The amateur movie, a.k.a. The pearls]. 1923: *Mälarpirater* [Pirates of Lake Mälaren] (also script). 1924: *33.333* (also script). 1925: *Polis Paulus påskasmäll* [Constable Paulus' Easter cracker] (also script); *Ingmarsarvet* [Ingmar's inheritance]. 1926: *Till Österland* [To the Orient] (also script); *Hon, den enda* [She is the only one]. 1927: *Hans engelska fru/Discord* [His English wife]; *Förseglade läppar/Sealed Lips*. 1928: *Pariserskor/The Doctor's Women* [Women of Paris]; *Synd* [Sin]. 1929: *Hjärtats triumf* [The triumph of the heart]. 1930: *Fridas visor* [Frida's songs]; *Charlotte Löwensköld/Charlotte Loewenskoeld*. 1931: *En natt/En natt* [One night]. 1932: *Svarta rosor* [Black roses]; *Kärlek och kassabrist* [Love and deficit]; *Vi som går köksvägen/Vi Som Gar Koeksvaegen* [We who use the servant's entrance] (also script).[1] 1933: *Kära släkten/Kaera Slaekten* [Dear family] (also script). 1934: *En stilla flirt* [A quiet flirt]; *Fasters millioner* [Auntie's millions]. 1935: *Ungkarlspappan/Ungkarlspappan* [Bachelor father] (also script); *Swedenhielms/Swedenhielms* (also script); *Under falsk flagg/Under False Flag*. 1936: *På Solsidan/On the Sunnyside*; *Bröllopsresan* [The wedding trip]; *Intermezzo/Intermezzo* (also script); *Familjens hemlighet* [The family secret]. 1937: *Sara lär sig folkvett/Sara Laer Sig Folkvett* [Sara learns manners]. 1938: *Dollar/Dollar* (also script); *En kvinnas ansikte/A Woman's Face*. 1939: *En enda natt/Only One Night*; *Ombyte förnöjer* [A pleasant change]; *Filmen om Emelie Högqvist* [The film about Emelie Högqvist]. 1940: *En, men ett lejon* [One man too many] (also script). 1941: *Den ljusnande framtid* [Bright future before us] (also script); *I natt eller aldrig* [Tonight or never]; *Striden går vidare*

[The battle goes on] (also script). 1942: *Jacobs stege* [Jacob's ladder] (also script); *Rid i natt!* [Ride this night!] (also script). 1943: *Det brinner en eld* [There's a fire burning] (also script); *Älskling, jag ger mig* [Darling, I surrender] (also script); *Ordet* [The word]. 1944: *Den osynliga muren* [The invisible wall]; *Kejsarn av Portugallien* [The emperor of Portugallia]. 1945: *Galgmannen* [The gallows man]. 1946: *Det är min modell/Affaire of a Model*. 1947: *Kvinna utan ansikte* [Woman without a face] (also script). 1948: *Nu börjar livet* [Now life starts] (also script); *Eva* (also script). 1949: *Kärleken segrar* [Love wins out] (also script). 1950: *Kvartetten som sprängdes* [The quartet that split up] (also script); *Fästmö uthyres* [Fiancée for hire]. 1951: *Frånskild* [Divorced]. 1952: *Trots* [Defiance]; *Kärlek* [Love] (also script). 1953: *Glasberget* [The glass mountain]. 1954: *Herr Arnes penningar* [Sir Arne's money] (also script). 1955: *Enhörningen* [The unicorn]. 1956: **Sången om den eldröda blomman* [The song of the scarlet flower]. 1959: *Pojken Winslow* [The Winslow boy] (TVD). 1960: *Ett glas vatten* [A glass of water] (TVD). 1961: *Frisöndag* [Free Sunday] (TVD). 1962: *Kardinalernas middag* [The dinner of the cardinals] (TVD). 1963: *Hittebarnet* [The foundling] (TVD). 1964: *Markisinnan* [The marchioness] (TVD). 1967: *Smycket* [The necklace] (episode in *Stimulantia*)]; *Candida* (TVD); *Vår i september* [Spring in September] (TVD).

Scriptwriter

1916: *Millers dokument* [Miller's document]. 1917: *Terje Vigen/A Man There Was*; *Thomas Graals bästa film/Wanted—A Film Actress* [Thomas Graal's best film]. 1918: *Thomas Graals bästa barn/Marriage à la Mode* [Thomas Graal's best child]. 1919: **Sången om den eldröda blomman/The Song of the Scarlet Flower*; *Herr Arnes pengar/Sir Arne's Treasure*. 1968: *Tant Grön, tant Brun, tant Gredelin* [Aunt Green, Aunt Brown, Aunt Lilac] (TVM); *Markurells i Wadköping* [The Markurells in Wadköping] (TVM); *Petter och Lottas jul* [The Christmas of Petter and Lotta] (TVM); *Olles skidfärd* [Olle's skiing] (TVM). 1970: *Farbror Blås nya båt* [Uncle Blue's new boat].

BIBLIOGRAPHY

Jerslev, Anne. "En kvinnas ansikte: en melankolisk berättelse on kvinnligheten." In Hedling, 1998.
Molander, Gustaf. *Jag minns så gärna.* Stockholm: Bonniers, 1972. Autobiography that, however, contains little of value concerning his film work.
Soila, 1991. Extended analysis of *Intermezzo* and *A Woman's Face.*
Waldekranz, Rune. "Intermezzo"; "En kvinnas ansikte"; "En enda natt." *Svensk filmografi* 3 (1979): 297–299, 385–389, 413–415. Longer and insightful commentaries on three Molander melodramas.

NOTE

1. Molander codirected the Norwegian version with Tancred Ibsen.

LARS MOLIN (Undersåker, 6 May 1942–7 Feb. 1999), director. Originally a civil servant in road maintenance, Molin turned to writing and directing. He was a fine example of the importance of television for today's Swedish film. While he made several cinema films, his main contributions have been for the small screen. He began as a screenwriter. Among his first work was the television film *Badjävlar* [Damned bathers]. Impossible to translate directly into English, "Badjävlar" is an insulting expression for ruthless, big-city people invading the idyllic countryside and pushing out the original inhabitants. The film was very controversial, not least because of its realistic depiction of "typical" Swedish behavior on the national holiday of Midsummer Eve. This film set the mark for Molin's later film work.

His first two cinema films have in common their realistic depiction of contemporary Swedish society, where the ideals of the "people's home" are being lost, and corruption is growing. The films *Bomsalva* [Misfire], about a rock blaster and his father, and *Höjdhoppar'n* [The high jumper], about a retarded man in a small town, did poorly at the box office, and Molin returned to television. His main focus was on contemporary themes, criticizing certain aspects of society and institutions, sometimes satirically. One of his best in this genre, *Kunglig Toilette* [Royal toilet], is about a planned royal visit to a small community. He presents a revealing picture of fussy officials and industrialists preparing for an event that is eventually canceled. Molin also made moving comedies about loneliness and melancholy among ordinary people living in small communities. In addition, he also directed classics such as a remake of Lagerlöf's tale *Kejsarn av Portugallien* [The emperor of Portugallia], previously filmed by *Gustaf Molander and by *Sjöström, in Hollywood, as *Tower of Lies*.

His greatest achievement in Swedish television was the family serial *Tre kärlekar* [Three loves], of which eight episodes were shown in 1989 and another eight in 1991. This almost fourteen-hour-long epic, which can easily be compared with the German *Heimat*, depicts the life of a rural family from the 1940s until the present, as mirrored through "three loves." It is a fascinating story chronicling contemporary history through the eyes of several individuals. One might describe it as another variation on the theme of innocence lost—how Sweden was built and achieved material prosperity while neglecting more spiritual matters. The serial plays on one of the traditional old, rural themes in Swedish film—how the magic of nature has been sold out, to be lost forever. Molin symbolizes this with streaming water. The old man in the family tries very hard, but without success, to stop the exploitation of a waterfall in the village. When a water power station is finally built, this mythical green ground is replaced by a stony desert. Most contemporary films for the big screen seem, in comparison to *Tre kärlekar*, rather bleak.

FILMOGRAPHY

Director, Scriptwriter

1973: *Mona och Marie* [Mona and Marie] (TVMS). 1978: *Bomsalva* [Misfire]. 1979: *Vårt lilla bo* [Our little nest] (TVM); *"Hallå, det är från kronofogden"* ["Hello, it is the enforcement officer calling"] (TVM, director only). 1981: *Höjdhoppar'n* [The high jumper]. 1982: *Zoombie* (TVM). 1983: *Midvinterduell* [Duel in the midwinter] (TVM). 1984: *Pengarna gör mannen* [Money makes the man] (TVM). 1985: *Korset* [The cross] (TVM). 1986: *Fläskfarmen* [The pork farm] (TVM); *Kunglig Toilette* [Royal toilet]

(TVM). 1987: *Saxofonhallicken* [The saxophone pimp] (TVM). 1989/91: *Tre kärlekar* [Three loves] (TVMS). 1992: *Kejsarn av Portugallien* [The emperor of Portugallia] (TVM). 1994: *Sommarmord* [Summer murder]. 1996: *Potatishandlaren* [The potato merchant] (TVM). 1998: *Den tatuerade änkan* [The tattooed widow] (TVM); *Ivar Kreuger* (TVM).

Scriptwriter

1971: *Hon kallade mej jävla mördare* [She called me damned murderer] (TVM); *Väckning kl 06.00* [Awakening at 6 AM] (TVM); *Badjävlar* [Damned bathers] (TVM). 1972: *Nybyggarland* [Settler's country] (TVMS). 1975: *Tjocka släkten* [Close relatives] (TVMS). 1976: *Polare* [Buddies]. 1979: *Repmånad* [The call-up]. 1983: *Hem på besök* [Home on visit] (TVM). 1985: *Kams—tokerier från Ådalen av Pelle Molin* [Barley cakes—drolls from the Ådalen by Pelle Molin] (TVM). 1987: *Die Bombe* (TVM).

BIBLIOGRAPHY

Löthwall, Lars Olof. "Den oväntade Lars Molin." *Filmrutan*, no. 1 (1981):7–9. Interview.
Molin, Lars. *Duell i gryningen och andra skrönor.* Stockholm: Alba, 1985.

AWARD

Emmy Award 1998: *The tattooed widow*

COLIN NUTLEY (Gosport, United Kingdom, 28 Feb. 1944–), director. Nutley is one of the best-known names in modern Swedish cinema. In many articles, he is treated as a paradox, an Englishman regarded as a prominent advocate of "Swedishness" in the new Swedish cinema. To some degree, one might attribute this to a lack of historical awareness among Swedish film critics, especially when they begin claiming that he is a pioneer in the field. Many Swedish directors have worked hard to uphold "Swedishness" in Swedish cinema both now and in the past. It is clear, however, that the "outsider," Colin Nutley, has given some very insightful views into the Swedish way of living and thinking. He has been able to portray the myths of the society with fresh, new eyes. He is a sharp-eyed observer of oddities and particularities, which are perhaps "invisible" to original inhabitants. One main theme in all his films is the depiction of clashes between different cultures and socioeconomic groups within Swedish society. This plays well when the Swedish welfare society seems to be cracking and might explain his success with both the audience and critics.

Nutley first studied for several years as a graphic designer at an arts school in his native England before he began making documentaries for British television. This background may explain the particular nature of his fiction films. His directorial style is to a large degree based upon improvisation where he lets his actors appear as natural as possible and allows them to act in a way they find suitable. His first Swedish directorial assignment was the television film serial *Annika*, about a young Swedish girl who goes to Britain on a language training course and meets a young English boy. He follows her back to Sweden, where he experiences all kinds of cultural differences. A similar theme was later developed in the television movie *Vägen hem* [The way home].

Despite the fact that Nutley's television work in Sweden was both well made and appreciated, he remained for a long time rather anonymous. His first cinema feature, *Nionde kompaniet* [The ninth company], the title referring to a nonexistent "ninth company" of a military regiment in which officers and privates begin to cooperate in the moonshine business, was not well received by the critics. It is nonetheless a fascinating study of corruption and the so-called affairs of recent years with dishonest politicians and others. This film was somewhat before its time. One might see it as a record of the progressive decline of those morals that upheld the "people's home." In *BlackJack* Nutley continued with his sharp-eyed observations of Swedish everyday life by exploring the Swedish way of entertaining on Saturday nights. The film is centered around an orchestra. It examines some of the mutual relations of the people surrounding it. The film also gives an interesting view of a Swedish society cracking at its joints. With **Änglagård/House of Angels*, however, Nutley finally had his first real breakthrough and has now been established on the Swedish film scene.

FILMOGRAPHY

1977: *Collis Pierce* (docu.); *The Flacton Flyer* (TVM); *Rule Britania* (docu. in *About Britain* series). 1979: *The Brontë Connection* (docu.); *Noah's Castle* (TVMS). 1981: *Henry Moore: Recollections of a Yorkshire Childhood* (docu.). 1982: *First Week* (TV, *Going Out* series). 1983: *In Search of Father Christmas* (docu.). 1985: *Annika—en kärlekshistoria* [Annika—a love story] (TVMS); *Faces of Communism: Italy—"Lenin Is Sometimes Puzzled..."* (docu.). 1986: *Där rosor aldrig dör* [Where roses never die] (docu, short); *Femte generationen* [The fifth generation] (TVMS). 1987: *DaSilva DaSilva* (docu.). 1988: *Nionde kompaniet* [The ninth company]. 1989: *Vägen hem* [The way home] (TVM); *Words of Love* (docu.). 1990: *BlackJack*. 1991: *Änglagård/House of Angels*. 1993: *Sista dansen* [The last dance]. 1994: *Änglagård—andra sommaren* [House of angels—the second summer]. 1996: *Sånt är livet* [Such is life]. 1998: *Under solen* [Under the sun].

BIBLIOGRAPHY

Johnston, T. "British Steel." *Time Out* 7 July 1993. Interview.
Jordahl, Annelie, and Håkan Lagher. "Colin Nutley—hantverkare med intiution." *Chaplin*, no. 244 (1993): 49–57. Interview.
Kemp, Philip. "Facing the Sun." *Sight & Sound*, 3, no. 7 (July 1993): 20–21. Interview.
Swanberg, Lena Katarina. *Vägen till Änglagård: en resa med Colin Nutley*. Stockholm: Bonnier Alba, 1994. Account of the production of the second film about *House of Angels*, with some biographical information.

AWARD

GB 1992

LENA OLIN (Stockholm, 22 Mar. 1955–), actress. Lena Olin is the daughter of actor, director, and songwriter Stig Olin and actress Britta Holmberg. Her early determination to make a career in show business was rewarded with the runner-up spot in the 1974 Miss Sweden contest and later being elected Miss Scandinavia. In 1976, after several unsuccessful attempts, she entered the state school for stage actors, where she studied for three years. Upon graduation she was employed at the Royal Dramatic Theater, where her talent was recognized by *Ingmar Bergman, who regarded her as a most promising actress. He gave her important stage roles in such productions as *King Lear* and *Ett drömspel* [A dream play]. This brought her international attention, and she had her first international film role in Philip Kaufman's *The Unbearable Lightness of Being*. Since then she has had more international acting parts, and the American critics have hailed her as a new Swedish superstar. The New York film critics awarded her their prize for best supporting actress in *Enemies—A Love Story* in 1989. At present she lives with director *Lasse Hallström.

Describing Olin, the critics abroad have generally employed the usual clichés—the Swedish dream girl, the new Garbo—constantly stressing her sexiness and exotic looks. While she might look like a Mediterranean beauty, she is indeed a northern star. In fact, she resembles her mother, who starred as a Lapland girl in the 1948 melodrama *Lappblod* [Lapp blood]. Lena Olin has also been described as a cool and distanced actress when she plays the roles of strong and sometimes violent women. In addition to evidently being strong minded, she also brings sensitivity and integrity to her roles. One example is her starring role in the early comedy *Gräsänklingar* [Grass widowers], where she played a single mother who encounters a grass widower. The original script depicted her as a call girl, but she demanded the role be totally altered, and the film was made as she wished (as the scenery for her apartment was already built, this led to some confusion among the viewers).

FILMOGRAPHY

1976: *Ansikte mot ansikte/Face to Face* (TVM).[1] 1977: *Friaren som inte ville gifta sig* [The suitor who wouldn't be married] (TVD); *Tabu* [Taboo]. 1978: *Picassos äventyr/The Adventures of Picasso*. 1980: *Kärleken* [The passion]; *Från Boston till Pop* [From Boston to Pop] (TVD). 1982: *Som ni behagar* [As you like it] (TVD); *Pappa är död* [Father is dead] (TVM); *Gräsänklingar* [Grass widowers]; *Fanny och Alexander/Fanny and Alexander*.[2] 1984: *Efter repetitionen/After the Rehearsal* (TVM). 1985: *Wallenberg: A Hero's Story* (TVM). 1986: *Flucht in den Norden*; *Glasmästarna* [The glass masters] (TVM, short); *På liv och död* [A life or death matter]. 1987: *Komedianter* [Comedians] (TVD). 1988: *Friends*; *The Unbearable Lightness of Being*; *s/y Glädjen* [S/S Joy]. 1989: *Enemies—A Love Story*. 1990: *Hebriana* (TVD); *Havanna*. 1993: *Romeo Is Bleeding*; *Mr. Jones*. 1994: *The Night and the Moment*. 1997: *Night Falls on Manhattan*. 1998: *Polish Wedding*; *Hamilton/Commander Hamilton*. 1999: *Mystery Men*; *Ninth Gate*.

BIBLIOGRAPHY

Forslund, 1995.

AWARD

AAN 1990: Best Supporting Actress (*Enemies—A Love Story*)

NOTES

1. Theatrically released abroad in edited version.
2. Longer version for television in 1984, with limited cinema release in 1983.

STELLAN OLSSON (Kattarp, 7 July 1936–), director. After university studies he worked as a teacher and was an enthusiastic amateur filmmaker. Accepted by the Film Institute Film School, he quit in protest after only one year because he felt that the pupils were treated like ordinary schoolchildren. Despite this he made his way into the film industry, debuting with the very interesting *Oss emellan* [Between us], a poetic tale about individuals living on a collective founded on socialist convictions. The film was poorly distributed, which reflects some of the difficulties he has had from time to time having his projects realized. His second feature, *Deadline*, was a critical view of a military cover-up after a disaster in which a biochemical weapon contaminates a large area. With the film *Sven Klangs kvintett* [Sven Klang's combo] he succeeded in overcoming distribution and other problems. It is a tale about a small-town dance orchestra, and it is both a nostalgic tour back to the 1950s and a leftist critique of Swedish society. This film was successful with the audience and the critics. Olsson has also been active in Denmark.

Much of his more remarkable television work is in the same political vein and has in some cases caused much controversy. This peaked with his serial *Det finns inga smålänningar* [There are no Smålanders] in which he tried to portray the Israeli-Palestinian conflict by transferring it to Swedish territory and society. The action takes place in the province of Småland, where the inhabitants are forced out by a foreign minority that has settled down in the province. The title is an allusion to the statement, attributed to Golda Meir, that "there are no Palestinians." The serial caused a heated debate in the newspapers and on television. Israel's supporters in Sweden were furious, and there were a record number of notifications to the state television policy board claiming that it had given a too one-sided view of the conflict and was thus an offense under the broadcast regulations. Another controversial television serial concerned the young Swedish woman, Jane Horney, allegedly executed by the Danish resistance at the end of World War II as a result of being suspected to be a double agent. The serial opened many wounds in this very sensitive era in Danish contemporary history, and there were some demands that it be withdrawn.

FILMOGRAPHY

1969: *Oss emellan* [Between us] (also script). 1971: *Deadline* (also script); *Julia och nattpappan* [Julia and the night daddy] (TVMS); *Pappa Pellerins dotter* [Daddy Pellerin's daughter] (TVMS, also script, actor). 1976: *Sven Klangs kvintett* [Sven Klang's combo]. 1978: *Bevisbördan* [Burden of evidence] (TVMS, also script). 1979: *Söndagen som sådan* [Sunday as such] (TVM). 1980: *Den enes död* . . . [The death of another . . .] (also script). 1981: *Det finns inga smålänningar* [There are no Smålanders] (TVMS). 1983: *Morfar med kikare* [Grandfather with binoculars] (TVM, also script); *Mannen som inte vågade frysa* [The man who didn't dare freeze] (TVM, also script). 1984: *Jag ska aldrig mer dricka öl* [I'll never again drink beer] (TVM, also script). 1985: *Jane Horney* (TVM, also script). 1989: *Det är väl ingen konst* [It's no big deal] (TVM, also script). 1991: *Den store badedag* [The great bathing day] (also script). 1992: *Yasemin på flykt* [Yasemin on the run] (TVMS, also script). 1994: *Good Night Irene* (also script). 1996: *En loppe kan også gø* [Fleas bark too, don't they?].

BIBLIOGRAPHY

Björkman, Stig. "Oss mellan. Intervju med Stellan Olsson." *Chaplin*, no. 91 (1969):166.

PER OSCARSSON (Stockholm, 28 Jan. 1927–), actor, director. Oscarsson is one of the odd personalities of the Swedish art of entertainment, both on and off the screen and stage. He graduated from the Royal Dramatic Theater School in 1947 and has been employed by various stages since. He has been very productive as a screen actor, usually being cast in the role of the nervous and socially disabled oddball character who is often very naive. His own first directorial effort, *Ebon Lundin*, was of a similar genre. It was made with great financial difficulties, which explains the unevenness of this otherwise rather interesting film. His role as the starving author in *Sult/Hunger*, based on Knut Hamsun's autobiographical novel, was awarded a Cannes Grand Prix in 1966. In later years his roles have sometimes been more conventional, as, for example, the Police Captain Jörgensson in the very popular television serials, *Polisen som* . . . [The policeman who . . .]. He is still, from time to time, cast as an eccentric old man, as, for example, the grandfather in **Änglagård/House of Angels*.

FILMOGRAPHY

Actor

1944: *Kärlekslivets offer* [Victims of love life]; *Örnungar* [Eaglets]. 1945: *Flickor i hamn* [Girls in port]; *Den allvarsamna leken* [The serious game]. 1946: *Kristin kommenderar* [Kristin commands]; *Ungdom i fara* [Youth in danger]. 1947: *Det vackraste på jorden* [The loveliest thing on earth]. 1949: *Gatan* [The street]; *Havets son/Son of the Sea*; *Vi flyger på Rio* [We fly to Rio]. 1951: *Leva på "Hoppet"* [Living on "Hope"]. 1952: *Möte med livet* [Encounter with life]; *Trots* [Defiance]. 1953: *Barabbas*; *Vi tre debutera* [We three make our debut]. 1954: *Karin Månsdotter*. 1955: *Vildfåglar* [Wild birds]; *Kärlek på turné* [Love on tour]. 1958: *Fröken April* [Miss April]. 1961: *Ljuvlig är sommarnatten* [Lovely is the summer night]. 1962: *Biljett till paradiset* [Ticket to paradise]; *Vaxdockan/The Doll*. 1963: *Jojk* (TVD); *Det är hos mig han har varit* [He was with me]; *Adam och Eva* [Adam and Eve]; *Någon av er* [One of you] (TVD). 1964: *Är du inte riktigt klok?* [Are you crazy?]. 1965: *Bödeln* [The hangman] (TVD). 1966: *Asmodeus* (TVD); *Syskonbädd 1782/My Sister, My Love*; *Doktor Knock* (TVD); *Myten* [The myth]; *Sult/Hunger*, *Patrasket* [The rabble] (TVD); *Noon Wine* (TVM); **Här har du ditt liv/Here's Your Life*. 1967: *Trettondagsafton* [The twelfth night] (TVD); *Drottningens* *juvelsmycke* [Queen's diadem] (TVDS); *De löjliga precisöserna* [The affected young ladies] (TVD); *Gengångare* [Ghosts] (TVD); *Britannicus* (TVD). 1968: *Ole Dole Doff* [Eeeny, meeny, miny, moe]; *Doktor Glas/Doctor Glas*; *A Dandy in Aspic*; *Vindingevals* [Windinge waltz]. 1969: *An-Magritt*; *La Madriguera*; *Oss emellan* [Between us] (also script); *Miss and Mrs. Sweden*. 1970: *Love Is War*. 1971: *The Last Valley*; *The Night Visitor*; *Secrets*. 1972: *Nybyggarna/The New Land*; *Endless Night*. 1973: *The Block House*; *Inferno* (TVM); *Traumstadt*. 1974: *Det blå hotellet* [The blue hotel] (TVM); *Gangsterfilmen*, a.k.a. *En främling steg av tåget* [The gangster movie, a.k.a. A stranger got off the train]. 1976: *Dagny*; *Förvandlingen* [The metamorphosis]. 1977: *Victor Frankenstein*; *Uppdraget* [The assignment]; *Bröderna Lejonhjärta* [The brothers Lionheart]; *Soldat med brutet gevär* [Soldier with a broken rifle] (TVMS). 1978: *Harry H* (TVMS); *Picassos äventyr/The Adventures of Picasso*; *Chez nous*; *Julkalendern* [The Christmas calendar] (TVDS). 1979: *Kristoffers hus* [Kristoffer's house]; *Charlotte Löwensköld*;[1] *Heja Sverige!* [Come on Sweden!] (also idea). 1980: *Tvingad att leva* [Forced to live]; *Attentatet* [The attempt]. 1981: *Hans Christian och sällskapet* [Hans Christian and the society] (TVM); *Inget att bråka om, Johansson* [Nothing to quarrel about, Johansson] (TVM); *Montenegro eller Pärlor och svin/Montenegro or Pigs and Pearls*; *För en liten snuvas skull* [Because of a little cold] (TVMS); *Ondskans värdshus* [The inn of evil]; *Kallocain* (TVDS); *Göta kanal* [Göta canal]. 1982: *Polisen som vägrade svara* [The policeman who refused to answer] (TVMS); *Kättaren* [The heretic] (TVD); *Privatliv* [Private lives] (TVD). 1983: *Vid din sida* [By your side] (TVMS); *Mannen som inte vågade frysa* [The man who didn't dare freeze] (TVM); *Mäster Olof* [Master Olof] (TVD); *Henrietta*. 1984: *Vargen* [The wolf] (TVM); *Polisen som vägrade ge upp* [The policeman who refused to give up] (TVMS); **Ronja Rövardotter* [Ronja, the robber's daughter]. 1985: *Da Capo* (docu.). 1986: *Kulla-Gulla* (TVMS); *Hud* [Skin]; *Nattseilere* [Night sailors]; *Julpussar och stjärnsmällar* [Christmas kisses and knockouts] (TVMS); *Flykten* [The escape] (TVMS); *Bödeln och skökan* [The hangman and the whore] (TVM). 1987: *Ondskans år* [Years of evil] (TVMS). 1988: *Oväder* [Storm] (TVD); *Polisen som vägrade ta semester* [The policeman who refused to take a vacation] (TVMS); *Venus 90*; *Kråsnålen* [The tie pin] (TVMS). 1989: *Sparvöga* [Sparrow's eye] (TVMS); *Ingen rövare finns i skogen* [There is no robber in the forest] (short); **1939*. 1990: *Kurt Olsson. Filmen om mitt liv som mej själv* [Kurt Olsson—the film about my life]; *Bulan* [The bump]; *Makedonia* (TVMS); *Makrellen är kommen* [The mackerel has come] (short). 1991: *Fasadklättraren* [The cat burglar] (TVMS); *Missförstå mig rätt* [Misunderstand me right] (TVDS). 1992: *Änglagård/House of Angels*; *Kejsarn av Portugallien* [The emperor of Portugallia] (TVM). 1993: *Drömmen om Rita* [The dream about Rita]; *Polisen och domarmordet* [The policeman and the judge murder] (TVMS); *Alfhild och Ortrud* [Alfhild and Ortrud] (TVDS); *En nypa mull—vad är vi mer* [A pinch of dust—what else are we more?] (short). 1994: *Håll huvet kallt* [Keep your head calm] (TVMS); *Kan du vissla, Johanna?* [Can you whistle, Johanna?] (TVM). 1995: *Ti kniver i hjertet/Cross My Heart and Hope to Die*; *Första, andra tredje* [First, second, third] (episode in *Snoken* [The sleuth]) (TVMS); *Anmäld försvunnen* [Missing persons department] (TVMS); *Den sidste viking* [The last Viking]. 1996: *Harry och Sonja* [Harry and Sonja]; *Polisen och pyromanen* [The policeman and the pyromaniac] (TVMS); *Juloratoriet* [The Christmas oratorio]; *Niemcy/The Germans*. 1997: *Rika barn leka bäst* [Rich kids do play best]. 1998: *Forbudt for børn* [Prohibited for children]; *Vita lögner* [White lies] (TVDS); *Stormen* [Tempest] (TVM). 1999: *Lukas 8:18* (TVMS).

Director, Scriptwriter, Actor

1973: *Ebon Lundin*. 1980: *Sverige åt svenskarna* [Sweden for the Swedes] (not script).

BIBLIOGRAPHY

Jordahl, Annelie, and Håkan Lagher. "Per Oscarsson—man på gränsen till nervsammanbrott." *Chaplin*, no. 236 (1991):51–57.

AWARDS

Cannes 1966: Best Actor (*Hunger*)

GB 1967

NOTE

1. Longer version for television in 1981.

EDVARD PERSSON (Malmö, 18 Jan. 1888–19 Sept. 1957), actor, director. Persson was born in the southern province of Skåne. At the beginning of his career he was a popular local revue stage artist and director, touring the countryside and staging, among other things, his own plays. In the mid-1920s he began filmmaking, at first as both director and star. For many years just a local celebrity, he got a small role in one of Europa Film's first folksy comedies, *Söderkåkar/Soederkaakar* [Southsiders], which was an immense success. He was offered a contract, and his star rose rapidly. From the mid-1930s until at least the end of the 1940s he was undoubtedly Sweden's most popular actor and male film star. Many of his films broke Swedish attendance records. Films like *Söder om landsvägen* [South of the highway], **Kalle på Spången/Kalle Paa Spaangen* and *Livet på landet* [Life in the country] belong to the most popular in Swedish film history. Persson was also well known as a revue actor and gramophone artist.

Several authors have tried to find an answer to his popularity. His physical appearance was not handsome. Instead, he was an icon of security and authority in a time of change. It is perhaps no coincidence that he functioned as a sort of film equivalent to Prime Minister Per Albin Hansson, one of the founders of Swedish welfare policy. They were both born in the same region and spoke the same dialect. Persson's whole screen image was a patriarchal one in which the concept of the "people's home" was central. The message of his films was about human beings returning to nature and the soil. Although more directed towards the future, social democracy had as one of its important reference points its roots in the past and the countryside (cf. **Karl-Fredrik regerar/Karl-Fredrik Reigns*). The prime minister himself liked to attend the opening of every new Persson film.

Persson was, of course, from time to time the object of controversy. Some critics did not like the overtly antiintellectual message of his films (which sometimes remind one of Will Rogers), but their protests were in vain. Only in his last years, when his popularity was declining, in part because he no longer found appropriate roles because of his age, was he more devastatingly criticized.

FILMOGRAPHY

Actor

1927: *Kvick som Blixten* [Fast as lightning]. 1929: *Skådespelaren Edvard Persson sjunger och berättar* [Actor Edvard Persson sings and narrates] (short). 1930: *O, vilken natt* [Oh, what a night] (short); *I förskingringstider* [In times of embezzlement] (short). 1932: *Söderkåkar/Soederkaakar* [Southsiders]; *Sten Stensson Stéen från Eslöv på nya äventyr* [Sten Stensson Stéen from Eslöv on new adventures]. 1933: *Augustas lilla felsteg* [Augusta's little misstep]; *Den farliga leken* [The dangerous game] (also script); *Lördagskvällar/Loerdagskvaellar* [Saturday evenings]; *Hemliga Svensson* [Secret Svensson]. 1934: *Flickorna från Gamla Sta'n/Flickorna Fran Gamla Stan* [The girls from the Old Town]; *Kvinnorna kring Larsson/Kvinnorna Kring Larsson* [The women around Larsson]. 1935: *Tjocka släkten/Tjocka Slaekten* [Near relations]; *Larsson i andra giftet/Larsson I Andra Giftet* [Second-marriage Larsson] (also script). 1936: *Våran pojke/Vaaran Pojke* [Our boy]; *Söder om landsvägen* [South of the highway]. 1937: *Än leva de gamla gudar/Old Gods Still Live*. 1938: *Baldevins bröllop/Baldevins Brollop* [Baldevin's wedding]. 1939: *Skanör-Falsterbo/Skanor-Falsterbo*; *Djurgårdsmässan* [The Djurgården fair] (short); *Kalle på Spången/Kalle Paa Spaangen*, a.k.a. *Charlie, the Inn-Keeper*. 1940: *Blyge Anton* [Bashful Anton]; *En sjöman till häst* [A sailor on horseback]. 1941: *Soliga Solberg* [Sunny Solberg]; *En liten vit kanin* [A little white rabbit] (short); *Snapphanar* [Partisans]. 1942: *Sol över Klara/Sun over Klara*; *Stinsen på Lyckås* [The station master of Lyckås]. 1943: *Livet på landet* [Life in the country]. 1944: *Edvard Persson i karikatyren* [Edvard Persson as caricature] (short); *När seklet var ungt* [When the century was young]. 1945: *Den glade skräddaren* [The happy tailor]. 1946: *Klockorna i Gamla Stan* [The bells of the Old Town]; *Unconquered*. 1947: *Jens Månsson i Amerika* [Jens Månsson in America]. 1948: *Vart hjärta har sin saga/Each Heart Has Its Own Story*. 1949: *Sven Tusan*; *Huset nr 17* [House no. 17]. 1950: *Pimpernel Svensson/Pimpernel Svensson*. 1951: *Greve Svensson* [Count Svensson]. 1953: *Flickan från Backafall* [The girl from Backafall]. 1954: *En natt på Glimmingehus* [A night at Glimmingehus]. 1955: *Blå himmel* [Blue sky]. 1956: *Där möllorna gå . . .* [Where the windmills are running . . .].

Director, Scriptwriter, Actor

1924: *Studenterna på Tröstehult* [The students on Tröstehult]. 1925: *Den gamla herrgården* [The old mansion] (not script). 1926: *Miljonär för en dag* [Millionaire for a day]. 1927: *På kryss med Blixten* [On cruise with lightning]. 1928: *Vad kvinnan vill* [What woman wants]; *Hattmakarens bal* [The hat maker's ball].

BIBLIOGRAPHY

Holm, 1947.
Jerselius, Kjell. *Hotade reservat*. Uppsala: Filmförlaget, 1987. Doctoral dissertation.
Persson, Edvard. *Lite grann från ovan*. Stockholm: Wahlström & Widstrand, 1943. Semibiographical account.
Richter, Jan. *Edvard Persson*. Stockholm: Bonniers, 1974. Biography.

NILS POPPE (Malmö, 31 May 1908–), actor, director. Born as Nils Einar Jönsson, he was raised in poverty in the industrial city of Malmö. He made his debut in Swedish cinema at the end of the 1930s, appearing disguised as a bear in the historical farce *Adolf Armstarke/Adolf Armstrong*. However, he soon became a popular comedian in a long string of farces that were common fodder in the Swedish cinemas of the 1940s. While the films were often uneven, Poppe's performances were usually outstanding. After directing two features with himself as actor, he struck a mother lode when he invented the cinematic figure Bom. The first Bom film, *Soldat Bom* [Soldier Bom], was one of the greatest successes in the cinema of the 1940s. It was about a young clerk, a rigid bureaucratic character, called up for military service. His obedient nature and willingness to perform any order, however absurd the consequences might be, eventually drive his superior officers into sheer madness. In the end it is only the love of a young, innocent girl that cures his follies. *Soldat Bom* was also a great success in postwar Germany. He continued to exploit the Bom character in more films in the 1950s, including one, *Dumbom* [Stupid Bom], that he directed himself. For the international audience he may, however, be best remembered as the juggler who survives the plague in *Bergman's *Det sjunde inseglet/The Seventh Seal*. The juggler is a symbol for simple and folksy art that survives all disasters. Bergman's use of Poppe had much to do with his position as a well-known and popular comedian in their native Sweden.

It is easy to characterize Poppe's comic art as socially conscious, and it is not hard to find influences from Charlie Chaplin. Both the social and Chaplin influences were evident in his directorial debut *Pengar* [Money], about a tramp who discovers all manner of absurdities and injustices during his wanderings through society. *Dumbom* is perhaps his most interesting attempt at social criticism. Here he aims at the inhuman consequences of the bureaucratic order of the new, great Swedish society where traditional human values are sacrified for the sake of technical progress. This partly reflects the 1950s and 1960s in Sweden when politicians decided to tear down the old centers of the cities to replace them with new, more functional buildings. While the old quarters may have been slums, the new housing was hardly a better alternative, considering its inhospitable expanses of concrete. In some way Poppe's film foreshadows the critical tide of the 1960s and 1970s. The antimodernist standpoint of *Dumbom* and his other films is not unique. The entire rural genre reflects the same issue. His satiric visions of bureaucratic and rigid civil servants are similar to Bergman's exploration of the theme in his films. Nevertheless, Poppe's comic art is without a doubt very personal and to be admired.

FILMOGRAPHY

Actor

1937: *Adolf Armstarke/Adolf Armstrong*; *Vardag i varuhuset* [An ordinary day in the department store] (short); *Skicka hem nr. 7/Skicka Hem Nr. 7* [Send home no. 7]. 1939: *Adolf i eld och lågor* [Adolf all fired up]; *Spöke till salu* [Ghost for sale]; *Melodin från Gamla stan* [The melody from Old Town]; *Den modärna Eva* [The modern Eve] (NCF). 1940: *Kronans käcka gossar* [The crown's brave lads]; . . . *som en tjuv om natten* [. . .

like a thief in the night]; *Karusellen går* [The merry-go-round goes around]; *Beredskaps-pojkar* [Mobilization boys]. 1942: *Tre glada tokar* [Three happy nuts]; *Tre skojiga sko-jare* [Three tricky tricksters]. 1943: *Som fallen från skyarna*, a.k.a. *Professor Poppes prilliga prillerier* [As fallen from the skies, a.k.a. Professor Poppe's nutty nuttiness]; *Det spökar, det spökar . . .* [Ghost! Ghosts! . . .]; *Aktören* [The actor] (also script); *Det går som en dans* [It goes like a dance] (NCF). 1945: *Sten Stensson kommer till stan* [Sten Stensson comes to town]; *Blåjackor* [Bluejackets] (also script). 1947: *Stackars lilla Sven* [Poor little Sven] (also script); *Tappa inte sugen* [Don't lose heart] (also script). 1948: *Soldat Bom* [Soldier Bom] (also script). 1949: *Greven från gränden* [The count from the alley] (also script); *Pappa Bom* [Daddy Bom] (also script). 1951: *Tull-Bom* [Bom in the customs barrier] (also script). 1952: *Flyg-Bom* [Bom in the air] (also script). 1953: *Dansa min docka* [Dance, my doll] (also script). 1955: *Stampen* ["Uncle's"]; *Ljuset från Lund.* [The light from Lund]. 1956: *Skorpan* [The biscuit] (also script). 1957: *Det sjunde in-seglet/The Seventh Seal.* 1958: *Flottans överman* [More than a match for the navy] (also script). 1959: *Bara en kypare* [Only a waiter] (also script); *Lejon på stan* [A lion in town]. 1960: *Djävulens öga/The Devil's Eye.* 1963: *Sten Stensson kommer tillbaka* [Sten Stensson returns] (also script). 1964: *Nils Poppe Show* (TVD).

Director, Scriptwriter

1946: *Pengar—en tragikomisk saga* [Money—a tragicomical tale]; *Ballongen* [The bal-loon]. 1953: *Dumbom* [Stupid Bom]. 1967: *Lorden från gränden* [Me and my gal] (TVD).

BIBLIOGRAPHY

Holm, 1947.
Norström, Björn. "Nils Poppe komiker med livssyn." *Filmrutan*, no. 4 (1966): 232–237.
Sima, Jonas. "Skratta sig till sanning." *Filmrutan*, no. 4 (1966):238–240. Interview.
Wigardt, Gaby. *Poppe i ljus och mörker*. Stockholm: Svenska förlaget, 1998.

FRIDOLF RHUDIN (Munkfors, 10 Oct. 1895–6 Mar. 1935), actor. Originally a tailor and amateur theater actor, he appeared as a bit player in a couple of films before becoming a leading actor in director *Gustaf Edgren's first films. These soon made him a star, and for a brief period Fridolf Rhudin was the most popular and highly paid Swedish film actor. His acting career lasted from the late 1920s until 1934. It is of course impossible to speculate what he might have achieved if he had not died prematurely in the winter of 1935. His death and funeral became an event of national mourning, and he has never been forgotten. His films are constantly revived on the television afternoon shows, and gramophone recordings of his spoken sketches belong to a popular cultural heritage still being cultivated.

While Rhudin's career may have been comparatively short, it coincides with a key period in the transition of the Swedish society from a traditional agrarian society to a modern industrial state. The real key to Rhudin's popularity is that he embodied all the hopes and fears linked with these developments. He per-sonified the country boy, a seemingly witless yokel who proved to be smarter than the city folk in the long run. He gave comfort to those in the audience who felt bewildered in the new, functional Swedish society. *Simon i Backabo* [Simon of Backabo], his last and most successful film, is a great example. Directed by Edgren, Rhudin plays a young farmer who inherits a small farm but is cheated by a couple of city slickers. On the verge of losing his property he travels to Stockholm and then to other areas of the world, rescuing, in a chain of improbable events, the Swedish gold reserves. Eventually he makes a triumphant return to Stockholm, where he is hailed as a hero, and returns to his native county where he saves his farm in the nick of time. These events could easily be interpreted as a symbolic depiction of Sweden being saved from the grips of the world depression by the common sense of a simple country boy guided by timeless, rural virtues.

FILMOGRAPHY

1920: *Mästerman* [Masterman]; *Carolina Rediviva*. 1922: *Fröken på Björneborg* [The young lady of Björneborg]. 1923: *Närkingarna* [The people of Närke]. 1924: *Flickan från Paradiset* [The girl from paradise]; *Folket i Simlångsdalen* [The people of Simlång valley]. 1925: *För hemmet och flickan* [For home and girl]; *Styrman Karlssons flammor* [First-mate Karlsson's sweethearts]. 1926: *Hon, han och Andersson* [She, he and Andersson]. 1927: *Spökbaronen* [The ghost baron]; *Den sørgmuntre barber* [The tragicomic barber]. 1928: *Svarte Rudolf* [Black Rudolf]. 1929: *Konstgjorda Svensson* [Artificial Svensson]. 1930: *Kronans kavaljerer* [Cavaliers of the crown]. 1931: *Falska miljonären* [The false millionaire]; *Skepp ohoj!* [Ship ahoy!]. 1932: *Pojkarna på Storholmen* [The boys of Storholmen]; *Muntra musikanter* [Jolly musicians]. 1933: *Fridolf i lejonkulan* [Fridolf in the lion's den]; *Hemliga Svensson* [Secret Svensson]. 1934: *Simon i Backabo* [Simon of Backabo].

BIBLIOGRAPHY

Boken om hela Sveriges Fridolf. Stockholm: Åhlen & Åkerlund, 1935.
Manns, Thorsten. "Fridolf Rhudin, genial komiker och individualist." *Filmrutan* no. 2 (1966): 92–94.

TUTTA ROLF (Oslo, 7 Oct. 1907–26 Oct. 1994), actress. Rolf was born as Solveig Jenny Berndtzen. She already had some stage acting experience when she met the Swedish revue king Ernst Rolf, when he staged a production in Oslo. They married and moved to Stockholm. Just after her husband's death, she became a film actress and went to Hollywood in the mid-1930s, where she married choreographer Jack Donahue. She was inactive in film after 1940. After her divorce from Donahue in the late 1940s she was for a while married to director *Hasse Ekman.

Tutta Rolf was the sparkling star of many of *Gustaf Molander's best films in the 1930s. Her real breakthrough came with *Vi som går köksvägen/Vi Som Gar Koeksvaegen* [We who use the servant's entrance], where she played an idle upper-class girl who on a bet with her fiancé takes a job as a servant in disguise. She meets another boy, a working-class lad who is an inventor and wants to become an engineer, and falls in love with him instead. The film was a tremendous success, with the same story later being remade in Hollywood as *Kitchen's Entrance* in 1934. While Tutta Rolf did not act in many movies, she did put a distinct mark on the Swedish films of the 1930s. She embodied a new, more modern type of woman. Her acting style was usually on the verge of being ironically distanced. However, she could also portray more sensitive roles, as in *Dollar*, where she was memorable as a fragile woman, longing for tenderness and constantly on the verge of a mental breakdown.

FILMOGRAPHY

1930: *Paramount on Parade* (Swedish version). 1932: *Kärlek och kassabrist* [Love and deficit]; *Vi som går köksvägen/Vi Som Gar Koeksvaegen* [We who use the servant's entrance]; *Lyckans gullgossar* [Lucky devils]. 1933: *Kära släkten/Kaera Slaekten* [Dear family]; *En stille flirt.* [A quiet flirt] (Norwegian version). 1934: *En stilla flirt* (Swedish version); *Fasters millioner* [Auntie's millions]. 1935: *Dressed to Thrill*; *Swedenhielms/Swedenhielms*; *Under falsk flagg* [Under false flag]. 1936: *Rhythm in the Air*; *Äventyret* [The adventure]. 1937: *O.H.M.S.* (Great Britain)/*You're in the Army Now* (United States); *Sara lär sig folkvett/Sara Laer Sig Folkvett* [Sara learns manners]. 1938: *Den stora kärleken* [The great love]; *Dollar/Dollar*. 1939: *Ombyte förnöjer* [A pleasant change]; *Valfångare/The Whalers*.

CHRISTINA SCHOLLIN (Stockholm, 26 Dec. 1937–), actress. Educated at the Royal Dramatic Theater School, Schollin gave sexual liberation in the Swedish cinema of the 1960s a female face when she starred opposite *Jarl Kulle in the films *Änglar, finns dom?/Love Mates* and *Käre John/Dear John*. Both films did extremely well at the box office, both in Sweden and abroad. Times changed, though, and today she plays very different roles. Her latest cinema role was as the unhappy German wife of the alcoholic Uncle Carl in *Bergman's *Fanny och Alexander/Fanny and Alexander*. More important, she has established herself as a domestic soap opera queen. Her role as a tough businesswoman in *Varuhuset* [The department store] earned her the epithet as Sweden's "Angela Channing." She can play very funny roles; in the comedy serial *Irma och Gerd* she was terrific as an old and very mean, upper-class lady. Currently she plays a lead role as a rather tragic middle-aged woman in the long-running series *Tre kronor* [Three crowns].

FILMOGRAPHY

1956: *Swing it, fröken!* [Swing it, miss!]. 1958: *Avsked* [Farewell] (TVD). 1959: *Raggare!* [Hot-rod teenagers]; *Sängkammartjuven* [The bed chamber thief]. 1960: *Kärlekens decimaler* [Decimals of love]; *Bröllopsdagen* [The wedding day]. 1961: *Änglar finns dom?/Love Mates*. 1962: *Biljett till paradiset* [Ticket to paradise]; *Nils Holgerssons underbara resa/The Wonderful Adventures of Nils*. 1964: *Bröllopsbesvär/Wedding Swedish Style; Käre John/Dear John*. 1965: *Den nya kvinnan* [The new woman] (TVD); *Niklasons* (TVMS). 1966: *Ormen/The Serpent*; *Yngsjömordet/Woman of Darkness*; *Operation Argus* (TVMS); *Adamsson i Sverige* [Adamsson in Sweden]. 1967: *Elsk . . . din næeste, a.k.a. Vergiss nicht deine Frau zu küssen* [Love your neighbor]; *"Tofflan"–en lyck-*

lig komedi [Henpecked]. 1968: *Lekar i kvinnohagen* [Games in the woman's playground] (TVD); *Hennes Meget Kongelige Høyhet* [Her royal highness]; *Mysinge Motell* (TVDS). 1970: *Song of Norway*. 1971: *Leka med elden* [Playing with fire] (TVD); *Vill så gärna tro* [Want so much to believe]. 1972: *Den längsta da* [The longest day] (TVM). 1973: *Mumindalen* [The Moomin valley] (TVDS). 1975: *Garaget* [The garage]. 1976: *De Lyckligt lottade* [The well situated] (TVDS). 1978: *Dante—akta're för hajen!* [Dante—beware of the shark!]. 1979: *Charleys tant* [Charley's aunt] (TVD); *Linus eller Tegelhusets hemlighet* [Linus, or The secret of the brick house]; *Katitzi* (TVMS). 1981; *"Svartskallen"* ["The black skull"] (TVM). 1982: *Sova räv* [Deceptive sleeping] (TVM); *Fanny och Alexander/Fanny and Alexander*.[1] 1983: *Polskan och puckelryggen* [The Polish woman and the hunchback] (TVD); *Barn i stan* [Children in the city] (TVM). 1986: *De två saliga/The Blessed Ones* (TVM); *Gösta Berlings saga* [The legend of Gösta Berling] (TVM). 1987–1989: *Varuhuset* [The department store] (TVDS). 1988: *Familjen Schedblad* [The Schedblad family] (TVM). 1994–1999: *Tre kronor* [Three crowns] (TVDS). 1997: *Irma och Gerd* (TVDS). 1998: *Jobbet och jag* [The job and me] (TVDS).

NOTES

1. Longer version for television in 1984, with limited cinema release in 1983.

VIVEKA SELDAHL (Stockholm, 15 Mar. 1944–), actress. Seldahl was educated at the state school of stage art and has worked on various stages including the municipal theaters in Göteborg and Stockholm. She made her film debut, after many successful years on the stage, rather late in her career. She had some television parts before being on film; she was acclaimed in her role as the village whore in *Raskens* in which she starred opposite her husband, *Sven Wollter. Her first film role in *s/y Glädjen* [S/S Joy] earned her a Gold Bug. Since then she has, on various occasions, demonstrated her ability to portray mature, sensitive, but not always nice women. She demonstrated this when she played the bigoted wife of the village big shot in *Änglagård/House of Angels*. In quite a different part, she was a Polish immigrant woman who falls victim to the social authorities in the television movie *Guldburen* [The golden cage] and gave a very strong performance.

FILMOGRAPHY

1965: *Verandan* [The veranda] (TVD). 1969: *Berndt och Anita* [Berndt and Anita] (TVM). 1973: *Då är man nog ganska rädd* [Then you are rather scared] (TVMS). 1974: *Två sätt att skrämma en flicka* [Two ways to frighten a girl] (TVM). 1976: *Raskens* (TVMS); *Tarzan är död* [Tarzan is dead] (TVM). 1982: *Ett hjärta av guld* [A heart of gold] (TVM). 1983: *Indiankojan* [The Indian hut] (TVMS). 1984: *Taxi-bilder* [Taxi pictures] (TVMS); *Polisen som vägrade ge upp* [The policeman who refused to give up]. 1986: *Bumerang* [Boomerang] (TVM). 1989: *Säkra papper* [Secure papers] (TVM); *s/y Glädjen* [S/S Joy]. 1991: *Guldburen* [The golden cage] (TVMS); *Fasadklättraren* [The cat burglar] (TVMS); *Facklorna* [The torches] (TVMS). 1992: *Grodlarven* [The frog caterpillar] (short); *Änglagård/House of Angels*. 1993: *För brinnande livet* [For dear life] (short); *Den gråtande ministern* [The crying minister] (TVMS). 1994: *Änglagård—andra sommaren* [House of angels—the second summer]; *Crack of Dawn* (short). 1995: *Alfred.* 1996: *Harry och Sonja* [Harry and Sonja]; *Alla dagar, alla nätter* [All days, all nights] (TVD); *Jerusalem; Juloratoriet* [The Christmas oratorio]. 1997: *Heta lappar* [Secret notes] (short); *Hammarkullen eller Vi ses i Kaliningrad* [Hammarkullen, or See you in Kaliningrad] (TVMS); *Kenny Starfighter* (TVM, voice only); *Lida pin* [Suffering] (short). 1999: *Vägen ut* [The way out]; *Lusten till ett liv* [The lust for a life]; *Insider* (TVM); *Mamy Blue—er riktiga mamma* [Mamy Blue—Your real mammy].

BIBLIOGRAPHY

Capolicchio, Lydia. "Jag är inte lätt att leva med." *Expressen*, 3 Mar. 1996. Interview.

AWARD

GB 1989

ALF SJÖBERG (Stockholm, 21 June 1903–17 Apr. 1980), director. Sjöberg is important in Swedish film history, and he is often regarded by critics and film historians as one of the most important directors. While this is to some degree true, his most important efforts were on the stage. As a film director he was rather uneven, putting, like most film directors with stage experience, much stress on the visual. This emphasis can in the right context lead to extraordinary results, as in his film **Hets/Torment*, but it can also bring on sheer emptiness, like his most famous disaster *Barabbas*. Sjöberg's very conscious style worked very well with young *Ingmar Bergman's feverish and expressionist accusations against a patriarchal and closed school system. When the same style was applied to Nobel Prize winner Pär Lagerkvist's deep, philosophical reflections on Jesus Christ and his surroundings, Sjöberg's effort was literally buried in sand and darkness. In *Den blomstertid . . .* [This blossomtime . . .], to take another example, the visual greatness just underlines the emptiness of the script.

One might conclude that Sjöberg was heavily dependent on the right scripts. In **Himlaspelet/The Heavenly Play* Sjöberg's style matched the script, written by Rune Lindström, who also starred in the lead. The blend of solid earthiness— the film pays heavy tribute to traditional agrarian romanticism—and religious fantasy suited Sjöberg's style. The script was important in his most famous and perhaps most valuable contribution, *Fröken Julie/Miss Julie*, where he achieved the right balance between form and content. In this film Sjöberg stressed the lyrical qualities in Strindberg's play and let the mystery of the midsummer's night—another important theme in Nordic cinema—be central to the film.

Fröken Julie was the high point of Sjöberg's film direction career. The rest of the 1950s and the 1960s were much less successful. *Barabbas* was a failure, and the historic tale *Karin Månsdotter* was yet another disappointment. His filming of Vilhelm Moberg's account of an actual legal scandal in *Domaren* [The judge] was undermined by too much irrelevant symbolism. Sjöberg tried in vain to persuade the producers to let him make a film based on Sara Lidman's harsh stories about settlers in northern Sweden, which would perhaps have suited him better. Another of Sjöberg's unfinished dreams was to bring the great romantic Almqvist's fantasy *Drottningens juvelsmycke* [The queen's diadem] to the silver screen.

Sjöberg was a pioneer in Swedish television drama when he staged one of its earliest productions, *Hamlet*, in 1955. The result is still remarkable, especially considering the utterly primitive technical conditions he had to cope with.

FILMOGRAPHY

Actor

1925: *Ingmarsarvet* [Ingmar's inheritance]. 1928: *Ådalens poesi* [The poetry of Ådalen].

Director, Screenwriter

1929: *Den starkaste* [The strongest]. 1940: *Med livet som insats* [Life at stake]; *Den blomstertid...* [This blossomtime...]. 1941: *Hem från Babylon* [Home from Babylon]. 1942: *Himlaspelet/The Heavenly Play, a.k.a. Road to Heaven*. 1944: *Kungajakt* [Royal hunt]; *Hets/Torment*. 1945: *Resan bort* [The journey away] (also actor). 1946: *Iris och löjtnantshjärta* [Iris and the lieutenant]. 1949: *Bara en mor* [Only a mother]. 1951: *Fröken Julie/Miss Julie*. 1953: *Barabbas*. 1954: *Karin Månsdotter*. 1955: *Vildfåglar* [Wild birds]; *Hamlet* (TVD, director only). 1956: *Sista paret ut* [Last pair out]. 1959: *Stängda dörrar* [No exit] (TVD, director only). 1960: *Domaren* [The judge]. 1966: *Ön* [The island]. 1969: *Fadern* [The father].

BIBLIOGRAPHY

Cowie, Peter. "Extracts from an Interview with Ingmar Bergman." *Monthly Film Bulletin* (April 1983):84–85.

Lundin, Gunnar. *Filmregi Alf Sjöberg*. Lund: Dahlin & Wedholm, 1979. Dissertation.

Lundin, Gunnar, and Jan Olsson, *Regissörens roller. Samtal med Alf Sjöberg*. Lund: Liber, 1976. Interview book.

Wright, Rochelle. "Nature Imagery and National Romanticism in the Films of Alf Sjöberg." *Scandinavian Studies* 70, no. 4 (Winter 1998):461–476.

AWARDS

Cannes 1951: Grand Prix (*Miss Julie*)

GB 1966

VILGOT SJÖMAN (Stockholm, 2 Dec. 1924–), director. Sjöman began as a novelist and entered the world of film with an adaptation of his own novel *Lektorn* (made as *Trots* [Defiance]) about a grammar school pupil and his problems. This angry young man eventually had the chance to direct a film of his own when Swedish film began its rejuvenation process, prompted by the 1963 film reform. He soon became a celebrity for challenging old-fashioned morals and various taboos. The film *491*, from a novel by Lars Görling, was first banned because of some provocative sex scenes. This caused a heated debate, not only in the newspapers but in society as a whole. It was not just sex that caused the controversy; the implicit rejection, in this film about juvenile delinquency, of the traditional well-meaning politics concerning undisciplined youth also sparked debate. The film was eventually released after some cuts. Sjöman's films became the center of a heated public debate again when he made his two "color" films about curious Lena traveling through Swedish society searching for trends and patterns of life.

After some competent and honest features in the first half of the 1970s, Sjöman's career seems to have declined. The only exception is perhaps *Linus*, a sensitive depiction of a young boy and his adventures. Sjöman's attempt to make a provocative film about sexual minorities, *Tabu* [Taboo], was a total disaster in all respects. The film was partly financed by Swedish television, which never showed it. Sjöman's stagings for television have been somewhat more successful. His latest attempt to return to the big screen was the biographical account of Alfred Nobel. Despite its ambitions, this film turned out to be more of a monument than a real, living picture. It is just too much like the many lavish but impersonal productions that have become fashionable in contemporary European filmmaking.

FILMOGRAPHY

Director, Scriptwriter

1952: *Trots* [Defiance] (script only). 1958: *Lek på regnbågen* [Playing on the rainbow] (script only). 1962: *Älskarinnan/The Swedish Mistress.* 1964: *491* (director only); *Klänningen/The Dress.* 1966: *Syskonbädd 1782/My Sister, My Love.* 1967: *Negressen i skåpet* [The Negress in the cupboard] (episode in *Stimulantia*); *Jag är nyfiken—gul/I Am Curious (Yellow)* (also actor). 1968: *Jag är nyfiken—blå/I Am Curious (Blue)* (also actor); *Skammen/The Shame* (actor only); *Resa med far* [Journey with father] (docu., short). 1969: *Ni ljuger/You're Lying* (also actor). 1970: *Lyckliga skitar* [Lucky devils]. 1971: *Troll* (also actor). 1973: *Jambo* (docu.). 1974: *En handfull kärlek* [A handful of love]; *Bröderna Karlsson* [The Karlsson brothers] (docu., short); *Älskade Jeanette McDonald* [Beloved Jeanette McDonald] (docu., short). 1975: *Garaget* [The garage]. 1977: *Tabu* [Taboo]; *Tofsen* [The tassel] (TVD). 1978: *Linus eller Tegelhusets hemlighet* [Linus, or The secret of the brickhouse]; *Kristoffers hus* [Kristoffer's house] (script only). 1981: *Jag rodnar* [I blush]. 1982: *Pelikanen* [The pelican] (TVD, director only). 1983: *Här har ni hans liv!* [Here is his life!] (TVD); *Brevet till Lotta* [The letter to Lotta] (docu., short). 1984: *Adoptionen* [The adoption] (TVD, director only); *Hur ska det går för Pettersson?* [What will become of Pettersson?] (TVDS, director only). 1987: *Malacka*; *En flicka kikar i ett fönster* [A girl looks in a window] (TVM). 1988: *Oskuld och sopor* [Innocence and garbage] (docu., short). 1989: *Fallgropen* [The pitfall]. 1990: *Ett äktenskap i kris* [A marriage in crisis] (TVDS); *Mannen i buren* [The man in the cage] (docu., short). 1992: *Självporträtt* [Self-portrait] (docu.). 1995: *Alfred*.

BIBLIOGRAPHY

Björkman, 1977.
Georgakas, Dan, and G. Crowdus. "Art Is Born at the Frontiers of Taboo." *Cineaste* 8, no. 2 (Fall 1977):12–19. Interview.
Löthwall, Lars-Olof, ed. *Sjöman: Modern Swedish Cinema.* Vol. 1. Stockholm: Swedish Film Institute, 1974.

Sjöman, Vilgot *Mitt personregister. Urval 98.* Stockholm: Natur och kultur, 1998.
Sjöman, Vilgot. *Oskuld förlorad.* Stockholm: Författarförlaget, 1988.

AWARD

GD 1971

VICTOR SJÖSTRÖM (Silbodal, 20 Sept. 1879–3 Jan. 1960), actor, director. Sjöström was born in the western province of Värmland. His father, a businessman, immigrated to the United States, eventually bringing the rest of his family with him. After a brief period in America young Victor returned to Sweden and spent a part of his youth in Uppsala, where he attended grammar school. At sixteen he began acting in a touring company touring the Finnish and Swedish countryside, eventually becoming quite well known. In 1912 he was signed by Svenska Bio when they moved from Kristianstad to Stockholm. For the next decade he directed and acted in over thirty films before leaving for Hollywood. His Hollywood career was more successful than that of *Mauritz Stiller. Sjöström returned to Sweden with the advent of sound film. He directed only two more films: in Sweden, the rather theatrical *Markurells i Wadköping* [The Markurells of Wadköping] (which for economic reasons was also made in a German version); and in Great Britain, *Under the Red Robe*. However, he had many important acting parts in Swedish film of which the last, in *Bergman's *Smultronstället/Wild Strawberries*, might be regarded the best of his film acting career. In 1943 he was appointed artistic adviser at Svensk Filmindustri, where he was able to support the young Ingmar Bergman, then engaged as scriptwriter. Bergman has, in turn and on many occasions, paid reverence to the old master, Sjöström.

Sjöström and Stiller are often portrayed as a pair. In truth they stood in contrast to each other. Sjöström depicted psychological dimensions in much greater depth and, from the very beginning, demonstrated a greater social consciousness. Although many of his early films have been dismissed as having little or no content, they are still quite interesting. Unfortunately, most of his early work was lost in a 1941 warehouse fire. It is clear, though, that the evident social consciousness in one of his surviving early melodramas—*Ingeborg Holm*—was not an exception. Many of his early films dealt with the life and poor conditions of the lower social classes. The stories were strongly moral in their tone, playing on the theme that honesty always pays in the end. This reflected a common worldview in contemporary Swedish society.

Sjöström also paved the way for the recognition of cinema as art in the late 1910s. Although the term *Golden Age* to describe the period between 1917 and 1923 is now disputed, there is no doubt that Sjöström was part of a trend toward making fewer but better films with larger budgets, often based on the works of recognized authors. The premiere of *Terje Vigen/A Man There Was*, based on a poem by Henrik Ibsen, in January 1917 was an important event. This film was followed by a string of even more successful, popular adaptations of the works of Selma Lagerlöf, whose interest in human psychology, landscape, and soul seems to have suited Sjöström perfectly.

The trend against big and lavish productions aimed at the international market that came after 1920 and the founding of Svensk Filmindustri did not please Sjöström. Both he and Stiller abandoned the Swedish film industry. Sjöström easily adapted to the Hollywood standard, and films like *He Who Gets Slapped* and *The Wind* are much in the tradition of his best Swedish work.

FILMOGRAPHY

Actor

1912: *De svarta maskerna* [The black masks]; *I livets vår/The Springtime of Life*. 1913: *Barnet* [The child]; *Vampyren* [The vampire]; *När kärleken dödar* [When love kills]. 1914: *För sin kärleks skull* [For his love's sake]. 1917: *Thomas Graals bästa film/Wanted—A Film Actress* [Thomas Graal's best film]. 1918: *Thomas Graals bästa barn/Marriage à la Mode* [Thomas Graal's best child]. 1934: *Synnöve Solbakken*. 1935: *Valborgsmässoafton/Walpurgis Night*. 1937: *John Ericsson—segraren vid Hampton Roads/John Ericsson—Victor at Hampton Roads*. 1939: *Gubben kommer* [The old man's coming]; *Mot nya tider* [Toward new times]. 1941: *Striden går vidare* [The battle goes on]. 1943: *Det brinner en eld* [There's a fire burning]; *Ordet* [The word]. 1944: *Kejsaren av Portugallien* [The emperor of Portugallia]. 1947: *Rallare* [Railroad workers]. 1948: *Jag är med eder . . .* [I am with you . . .]. 1949: *Farlig vår* [Dangerous springtime]. 1950: *Till Glädje/To Joy*; *Kvartetten som sprängdes* [The quartet that split up]. 1952: *Hård klang* [The clang of the pick]; *Kärlek* [Love]. 1955: *Männen i mörker* [Men in the dark]. 1956: *Les evadés*. 1957: *Smultronstället/Wild Strawberries*.

Director

1912: *Ett hemligt giftermål eller bekännelsen på dödsbädden/A Ruined Life* (short); *Trädgårdsmästaren/The Broken Springrose*.[1] 1913: *Äktenskapsbyrån* [The marriage bureau] (short); *Löjen och tårar* [Smiles and tears] (short); *Lady Marions sommarflirt* [Lady Marion's summer flirtation] (short); *Blodets röst* [The voice of the blood] (also actor); *Ingeborg Holm* (also script); *Livets konflikter* [Life's conflicts] (also actor);[2] *Miraklet* [The miracle]. 1914: *Kärlek starkare än hat/The Poacher* (short); *Prästen/The Clergyman*; *Halvblod* [Halfbreed]; *Dömen icke* [Judge not]; *Bra flicka reder sig själv* [A good girl fends for herself] (also script, short); *Gatans barn* [Children of the street] (also script, actor); *Högfjällets dotter* [Daughter of the highlands] (also script, actor, short). 1915: *Strejken* [The strike] (also script, actor); *En av de många* [One of the many] (also script, short); *Sonad skuld* [Debt redeemed] (also script); *Det var i maj* [It was in May] (also script, short); *Landshövdingens döttrar/The Governor's Daughters* (script); *Skomakare, bliv vid din läst/Cobbler, Stick to Your Last* (also script); *I prövningens stund* [In time of trial] (also script, short); *Judaspengar/The Price of Betrayal* (short). 1916: *Skepp som mötas* [Ships that meet]; *Havsgamar/The Sea Vultures*; *Hon segrade* [She won] (also script, actor, short); *Dödskyssen/The Death Kiss* (script, actor); *Thérèse/Therese* (also script). 1917: *Terje Vigen/A Man There Was* (also actor); *Tösen från Stormyrtorpet/The Girl from the March Croft* (also script). 1918: *Berg-Ejvind och hans hustru/You and I* (also script, actor). 1919: *Ingmarsönerna* [Sons of Ingmar] (also script, actor). 1920: *Hans nåds testamente* [His grace's will] (also script); *Klostret i Sendomir* [The monastery of Sendomir] (also script); *Karin Ingmarsdotter* [Karin Ingmar's daughter] (also script, actor); *Mästerman* [Masterman] (also actor). 1921: **Körkarlen/The Stroke of Midnight*, a.k.a. *The Phantom Chariot* (also script, actor); *Vem dömer/Mortal Clay*. 1922: *Det omringade huset* [The house surrounded] (also script); *Eld ombord* [Fire on board] (also script, actor). 1924: *Name the Man*; *He Who Gets Slapped* (also script); *Confessions of a Queen*. 1925: *The Tower of Lies*. 1926: *The Scarlet Letter*. 1927: *The Wind*; *The Divine Woman*. 1928: *The Masks of the Devil*. 1929: *A Lady to Love/Die Sehnsuch jeder Frau* (German version). 1930: *Markurells i Wadköping*; *Väter und Söhne* (German version). 1936: *Under the Red Robe*.

BIBLIOGRAPHY

Forslund, Bengt. *Victor Sjöström: His Life and Work*. New York: Zoetrope, 1988.
Gillett, John; Bergman, Ingmar: "Sjöström." *Sight & Sound* (Spring 1960):97–98. Two obituaries.
Hood, Robin [Idestam-Almquist, Bengt]. *Den svenska filmens drama. Sjöström Stiller*. Stockholm: Åhlén & Söner, 1939.
Pensel, Hans. *Seastrom and Stiller in Hollywood*. New York: Vantage Press, 1969.
Turner, Charles L. "Victor Seastrom." *Films in Review* (May 1960): 266–277; (June–July 1960): 343–355.

NOTES

1. Banned in Sweden.
2. The film was started by Stiller.

STELLAN SKARSGÅRD (Göteborg, 13 June 1951–), actor. His first acting experience was with the children's theater in Malmö. He became quite a star with the Swedish audience when he acted as the young rascal in the lead of the television serial *Bombi Bitt och jag*, based on a novel by Fritiof Nilsson Piraten. However, he failed to get accepted by the state school for stage art. This did not stop him from realizing his wish to become an actor. Without formal education in theater, he has managed to establish himself as one of the leading male actors in Sweden and has become an international celebrity. He was a regular on the Royal Dramatic stage for many years until he quit in protest. At the beginning of his career he was not so particular about his film parts. He acted in some soft pornography and other low-quality films in the 1970s until he developed a fear of the camera, rather like stage fright. When he returned to the big screen in *Hans Alfredson's *Den enfaldige mördaren* [The simple-minded murderer], he won the critics' approval and earned himself several awards. He regards this role as a village idiot in *Den enfaldige mördaren* as one of the most important in his career. It is typical of a large proportion of his productions. He has played all types of oddballs and lunatics, including his minor appearance, as a mad Russian submarine officer, in the international thriller *The Hunt for Red October*. His portrayal of the Danish painter Søren Krøyer in *Kjell Grede's *Hip Hip Hurra!* was another oddball role. Skarsgård has, however, also shown other dimensions. He played Raoul Wallenberg in another Grede film. Above all, he established himself as a star in the Swedish audience's eye when he starred as Commander Carl Gustaf Hamilton, Swedish military agent with a license to kill, in a row of films: *Täcknamn Coq Rouge* [Codename Coq Rouge], *Förhöret* [The interrogation], and *Den demokratiske terroristen* [The democratic terrorist]. Although he has described himself as a normal guy, he says that he likes to play unsympathetic characters. He has also said that he learned much about acting from *Alf Sjöberg. His two young sons, Gustaf and Alexander, have begun to act as child actors and have already appeared in several films.

FILMOGRAPHY

1968: *Bombi Bitt och jag* [Bombi Bitt and I] (TVMS). 1971: *Den byxlöse äventyraren* [The adventurer without pants] (TVMS). 1972: *Strandhugg i somras* [Go ashore last summer]; *Firmafesten* [The company party]; *Magnetisören* [The magnetizer] (TVD); *5 døgn i august* [Five days in August]. 1973: *Bröllopet* [The wedding]; *Anita*; *Åttonde budet* [The eighth commandment] (short). 1974: *Inkräktarna* [The intruders]. 1977: *Kalkonen* [The turkey] (TVM); *Som man bäddar* [You have made your bed] (TVD short); *Tabu* [Taboo]; *Hemåt i natten* [Homewards in the night]. 1981: *Kyssen* [The kiss] (short); *Babels hus* [The house of Babel] (TVMS); *Skärp dig älskling!* [Straighten up, darling!] (TVD); *Olsson per sekund* [Olsson per second] (TVM). 1982: *Den enfaldige mördaren* [The simple-minded murderer]. 1983: *Farmor och vår herre* [Grandma and our Lord] (TVMS); *P & B*; *Hustruskolan* [School for wives] (TVD). 1984: *Åke och hans värld/Åke and His World*. 1985: *Den tragiska historien om Hamlet—prins av Danmark* [The tragic story of Hamlet—prince of Denmark] (TVM); *August Strindberg ett liv* [August Strindberg a life] (TVMS); *Noon Wine* (TVM); *Falsk som vatten* [False like water]; *Pelle Svanslös i Amerikatt* [Pelle no-tail in America] (voice only). 1986: *Ormens väg på hälleberget/The Serpent's Way*. 1987: *Jim och piraterna Blom* [Jim and the Blom pirates]; *Friends*; *Hip Hip Hurra!* 1988: *The Unbearable Lightness of Being*; *Vargens tid* [Time of the wolf]; *The Perfect Murder*, *Familjen Schedblad* [The Schedblad family] (TVMS). 1989: *s/y Glädjen* [S/S Joy]; *Täcknamn Coq Rouge* [Codename Coq Rouge]; *Vildanden* [The wild duck] (TVD); *Kvinnorna på taket* [The women on the roof]; *Förhöret* [The interrogation] (TVM). 1990: *S*M*A*S*H* (TVMS); *The Hunt for Red October*; *Parker Kane* (TVM); *God afton, herr Wallenberg/Good Evening, Mr. Wallenberg*. 1991: *Oxen/The Ox*. 1992: *Den demokratiske terroristen* [The democratic terrorist]; *Wind*. 1993: *Kådisbellan/The Slingshot*; *Sista dansen* [Last dance]. 1994: *Rapport till himlen* [Report to heaven] (TVMS). 1995: *Jönssonligans största kupp.* [The Jönsson gang's biggest coup]; *Kjærlighetens kjøtere* [The mongrels of love]; *Hundarna i Riga* [The dogs in Riga]. 1996: *Harry & Sonja* [Harry and Sonja]; *Breaking the Waves*. 1997: *My Son the Fanatic*; *Insomnia*; *Riget II* [The Kingdom II]; *Tranceformer* (docu.); *Good Will Hunting*; *Amistad*. 1998: *Glasblåsarns barn* [The glassblower's children]; *Ronin*; *Savior*. 1999: *Deep Blue Sea*.

BIBLIOGRAPHY

Lundgren, H. "Stellan Skarsgård." *Kosmorama*, no. 183 (Spring 1983):32–33.

AWARDS

Berlin 1982: Silver Bear (*Den enfaldige mördaren*)
GB 1982
GB 1989

MAURITZ STILLER (Helsinki, 17 July 1883–8 Nov. 1928), director. Stiller and *Victor Sjöström are often mentioned in connection with the so-called Golden Age of Swedish silent cinema. While the notion of a Golden Age is now disputed, it does have some traces of the truth. While the pair were responsible for a great share of the total output of feature films in the 1910s, with only *Georg af Klercker matching their productivity, their filmmaking style and subject matter were very different. Stiller was closer to af Klercker in his preference for sensational melodrama. Stiller was also, above all, the modernist of Swedish silent cinema, both in terms of his content and in his style.

Stiller was born in Finland when it was still part of Russia. He was part Russian, part Jew, and it is said that he moved to Stockholm to avoid his military service. When he arrived in Sweden, he already had a solid record of experience from working in the Helsinki theaters. He soon became well known and respected in the Stockholm theater world, and he was appointed manager of Intima teatern. At the same time, he was offered a film directorship at Svenska Bio, which he accepted.

His first films were not very successful. They were shelved for several years before being released, which has caused some confusion among film historians trying to establish his filmography. In any case, he soon found the touch, and his first great success was *De svarta maskerna* [The black masks], a sensational espionage melodrama with a thrilling climax in which the fleeing hero and heroine walk a burning tightrope. This type of action was continentally inspired, especially by Danish and French adventure/action melodramas. Such later films as *Det röda tornet* [The red tower] and *Madame de Thèbes/Madame de Thebes* were of a similar genre.

Stiller, in his early years, did not get as much attention from Swedish reviewers as Sjöström. It was only in the late 1910s that he was taken more seriously (though he often got remarks like "good direction"), which coincides with the period when film production took a more respectable, more cultural turn. Like Sjöström, Stiller began doing literary adaptations of the turn-of-the-century romanticist authors. Stiller, however, was much more liberal in his adaptations, rousing, in the case of the *Gunnar Hedes saga/The Blizzard*, the vigorous opposition of its author, Selma Lagerlöf. Stiller rather freely interpreted Lagerlöf in the last grand film of the so-called Golden Age of Swedish silents, *Gösta Berlings saga/The Legend of Gösta Berling*.

Gösta Berlings saga made a star of Greta Garbo. This perhaps explains why Stiller was also lured to Hollywood. He was not as successful there as Sjöström, but his stay was not the failure it is often reputed to be. At least one film, *Hotel Imperial*, is remarkable even by today's standards. He returned to Sweden, but his career was halted by his untimely death. It is impossible to speculate whether or not he would have found a place in the nationalistic cinema of the 1930s. In any case, the modernistic legacy of Stiller is manifest in the films of *Gustaf Molander, who had scripted some of Stiller's films in the 1910s.

FILMOGRAPHY
Director, Screenwriter

1912: *Mor och dotter* [Mother and daughter] (also actor, short); *Trädgårdsmästaren/The Broken Springrose* (script only, also actor);[1] *De svarta maskerna* [The black masks] (short); *I livets vår/The Springtime of Life* (actor only); *Den tyranniske fästmannen/The Tyrannical Fiancé* (also actor, short). 1913: *Barnet* [The child] (director only, short); *Vampyren* [The vampire] (short); *När kärleken dödar* [When love kills] (short); *När larmklockan ljuder* [When the alarm bell tolls] (director only, short); *Den okända/The Girl from Abroad*; *På livets ödesvägar* [On life's roads of destiny] (director only); *Livets konflikter* [Life's conflicts] (director only);[2] *Den moderna suffragetten/The Modern Suffragette* (short); *Gränsfolken/Brother against Brother* (director only); *En pojke i livets strid* [A boy in the battle of life] (director only, short);[3] *Mannekängen* [The mannequin] (short).[4] 1914: *Bröderna* [The brothers] (short); *När svärmor regerar* [When mother-in-law reigns] (also actor, short); *För sin kärleks skull* [For his love's sake]; *Kammarjunkaren* [The valet] (script only, short); *Stormfågeln* [The stormbird] (director only); *Skottet/The Shot* (director only, short); *Det röda tornet* [The red tower] (short). 1915: *När konstnärer älska* [When artists love] (director only); *Lekkamraterna* [Playmates] (short); *Madame de Thèbes/Madame de Thebes* (director only); *Hans hustrus förflutna/His Wife's Past* (director only); *Hans bröllopsnatt* [His wedding night] (director only); *Mästertjuven/The Master Thief* (director only); *Hämnaren/The Avenger* (director only); *Minlotsen* [The mine pilot] (director only, short); *Dolken* [The dagger].[5] 1916: *Lyckonålen* [The lucky pin] (short); *Kärlek och journalistik/Love and Journalism* (director only, short); *Kampen om hans hjärta* [The struggle for his heart] (director only, short); *Vingarna/The Wings* (also actor); *Balettprimadonnan/Wolo Czawinka* [The ballet primadonna] (director only). 1917: *Thomas Graals bästa film/Wanted—A Film Actress* [Thomas Graal's best film] (director only); *Alexander den store/Alexander the Great*. 1918: *Thomas Graals bästa barn/Marriage à la Mode* [Thomas Graal's best child] (director). 1919: **Sången om den eldröda blomman /The Song of the Scarlet Flower*; *Herr Arnes pengar/Sir Arne's Treasure*, a.k.a. *The Treasure of Arne*, a.k.a. *The Three Who Were Doomed*. 1920: *Fiskebyn* [The fishing village] (director only); **Erotikon/Just like a Man*. 1921: *Johan*; *De landsflyktige/In Self Defence*. 1923: *Gunnar Hedes saga/The Blizzard*. 1924: *Gösta Berlings saga/The Legend of Gosta Berling*. 1926: *The Temptress* (director only, replaced by Fred Niblo); *Hotel Imperial* (director only). 1927: *The Woman on Trial* (director only); *The Street of Sin* (director only, replaced by Joseph von Sternberg).

BIBLIOGRAPHY

Hood, Robin [Idestam-Almquist, Bengt]. *Den svenska filmens drama. Sjöström Stiller*. Stockholm: Åhlén & Söner, 1939.
Pensel, Hans. *Seastrom and Stiller in Hollywood*. New York: Vantage Press, 1969.
Robertson, Jo Anne. "Mauritz Stiller." *Monthly Film Bulletin* (Dec. 1977):272.
Werner, Gösta. *Mauritz Stiller: ett livsöde*. Stockholm: Prisma, 1991.
Werner, Gösta. *Mauritz Stiller och hans filmer. 1912–1916*. Stockholm: Norstedts, 1969.
An attempt to reconstruct the missing films of Stiller until 1916.

NOTES

1. Banned in Sweden.
2. Started by Stiller but completed by Sjöström.

3. Never released.
4. Never released.
5. Banned in Sweden.

PETER STORMARE (Arbrå, 27 Aug. 1953), actor, director. He was born as Peter Storm, but when he entered theater school, there was already one student there with that name, so Peter changed his family name. After graduation he worked at the Royal Stage, where he became *Ingmar Bergman's protégé; Bergman regarded Peter an outstanding actor, free from mannerisms and overacting. This led Peter to an international career when Bergman made a staging of *Hamlet* in the United States in 1988 and brought his Royal Dramatic Theater ensemble with him. Peter's international roles have mainly been as a heavy, like the homicidal character in *Fargo*, and he doesn't mind these roles. As he has explained in interviews, when he was a youngster going to the movies, he always preferred the villains instead of the clean-shaven heroes. His role in Ingmar Bergman's television movie *Larmar och gör sig till* [Fussing and fuming], however, is quite the opposite, as he plays a consumptive and weak teacher attending the cinema show, which at first is a disaster but later becomes a triumph for the magic art of acting. Here he is a nice and humane person speaking dialect taken directly from the folksy drama that Bergman always secretly admired.

FILMOGRAPHY

Actor

1982: *Studenten* [The student] (TVM); **Fanny och Alexander/Fanny and Alexander.*[1] 1983: *Spanarna* [The searchers] (TVMS). 1986: *Seppan* (TVM); *Den frusna leoparden* [The frozen leopard]; *Bumerang* [Boomerang] (TVM). 1987: *Mälarpirater* [Pirates of Lake Mälaren]. 1990: *Lite skit på händerna* [A little dirt on the hands] (TVM); *Awakenings*. 1991: *Riflessi in un cielo scuro*; *Freud flyttar hemifrån* [Freud moves away from home]; *Förr i världen* [In the past] (TVM, short). 1992: *Från de döda* [From the dead] (TVM, short); *Damage*. 1993: *Backanterna* [The Bacchae] (TVD); *Morsarvet* [Mother's inheritance] (TVM). 1995: *No Man's Land* (TVM). 1996: *Fargo*; *Somewhere in the City*; *Le polygraphe*; *Ett sorts Hades* [A kind of Hades] (TVD); *Swift Justice* (TWM, one episode). 1997: *The Lost World. Jurassic Park*; *Playing God*; *Larmar och gör sig till* [Fussing and fuming] (TVM). 1998: *Hamilton/Commander Hamilton*; The Big Lebowski; *Seinfeld* (TVM, one episode); *Mercury Rising*; *Armageddon*. 1999: *Eight Millimeter*; *Amor nello specchio; Purgatory* (TVM); Circus.

Director

1992: *Luciafesten* [The Lucia party] (TVM).

BIBLIOGRAPHY

Rogoff, Gordon. "Peter Stormare. Hamlet the Swede." *The Village Voice*, 21 June 1988.

NOTE

1. Longer version for television in 1984, with limited cinema release in 1983.

ARNE SUCKSDORFF (Stockholm, 3 Feb. 1917–), director. Sucksdorff was a sickly child, the son of a wealthy merchant growing up in a religious home. His background may explain his attraction to nature's solitude. He was for a short while a zoology student and then a fine arts student. He also studied theater in the Germany of the 1930s. In the late 1930s he finally found his real interest when he acquired a camera; he soon won a photography contest and became a skillful still photographer. In 1940 he was hired by the small, newly started film company Folkfilm to make documentaries and newsreels. The company soon folded, but Sucksdorff quickly found another job at Svensk Filmindustri in their department for short documentaries. During the following years, he made a string of widely seen documentaries that were shown in the movie theaters in conjunction with the main feature. Sometimes these cinematic preludes were more favorably received than the main attraction.

In the beginning of the 1950s he began to plan a very ambitious project: to make a whole feature about a lynx roaming through Sweden. Initial financial support came from future UN General Secretary Dag Hammarskjöld, who was an early activist and supporter of environmental issues. However, Sucksdorff became seriously ill, and the project was abandoned, with footage that had already been shot being integrated into a new film—*Det stora äventyret/The Great Adventure*. This film was about two young boys who catch an otter, and was shot on the farm where Rune Waldekranz, producer at Sandrews, had been born. When Svensk Filmindustri was hesitant in their sponsorship of Sucksdorff's project, Sandrews supported the film. It was an unexpected artistic and financial triumph.

With this success, Sucksdorff was inspired to continue with more feature documentaries. He traveled to India to make *En djungelsaga/The Flute and the Arrow*, which was also successful. After this his fortunes turned. In the beginning of the 1960s, he made a more conventional feature about a lonely, nature-loving boy who is harassed by his comrades. *Pojken i trädet* [The boy in the tree] proved to be a disaster in box office terms, and the critics also did not like it. A young assistant, *Stefan Jarl, joined this production and was later to carry on Sucksdorff's cinematic legacy. With this disappointment it became practically impossible for Sucksdorff to make any more films in Sweden. Embittered, he moved to Brazil where he made the semidocumentary *Mitt hem är Copacabana* [My home is Copacabana] about street children living on the big beach of Rio de Janeiro. This has been his last film, and he now spends much of his time as an environmental crusader.

Sucksdorff is a clear example of a documentarist who stretches the boundaries of the genre. His films are more than anything philosophical statements. One might label him a romantic attached to the irrational and rather pessimistic "life philosophy" of the late nineteenth century. Nature is in its grandeur beyond humankind and their activities, and human beings can never understand the inner meaning of nature. With the main theme of *Det stora äventyret*, even the innocent child, who can perhaps be close to the inexplicable riddle of nature, can never catch the inner truth. Humanity is obliged to submit to the forces of nature and life itself.

FILMOGRAPHY

Documentary Shorts

1940: *Augustirapsody* [Rhapsody of August]. 1941: *Din tillvaros land* [The land of your being]; *En sommarsaga* [A summer tale]. 1942: *Vinden från väster* [The wind from west]. 1943: *Sarvtid* [Time of reindeer-thief]. 1944: *Trut!* [Gull!]; *Gryning* [Dawn]. 1945: *Skuggor över snön* [Shadows over the snow]. 1947: *Människor i stad/People in the City*; *Den drömda dalen* [The dreamt valley]. 1948: *En kluven värld* [A divided world]; *Uppbrott* [Breaking up]. 1949: *Strandhugg* [Go ashore]. 1950: *Ett hörn i norr* [A corner in the north]. 1951: *Indisk by* [Indian village]; *Vinden och floden* [The wind and the river].

Newsreel Series

1940–1943: *Junexjournalen* (produced by Folkfilm).

Features

1953: *Det stora äventyret/The Great Adventure* (also actor). 1957: *En djungelsaga/The Flute and the Arrow*. 1961: *Pojken i trädet* [The boy in the tree]. 1965: *Mitt hem är Copacabana* [My home is Copacabana].

BIBLIOGRAPHY

Edström, Mauritz. *Sucksdorff—främlingen i hemmaskogen*. Stockholm: PAN/Norstedts, 1968.
de la Roche, Catherine. "Filmmaker on His Own." *Films and Filming* (Nov. 1954): 11.

AWARDS

AA 1948: Best Foreign Short (*People in the City*)

Cannes 1954: International Prize (*The Great Adventure*)

GB 1965

GB 1993

KARIN SWANSTRÖM (Norrköping, 13 June 1873–5 July 1942), actress, director, producer. Swanström is not one of the most well-known names in Swedish film, and few film historians or other writers mention her. If they do, the opinions are generally unfavorable, as in the memoirs of actress *Birgit Tengroth, where Swanström is portrayed in a rather derogatory manner. The films she directed in the 1920s were not that significant. She was better at acting the roles of respectful, old, upper-class ladies, and her portrayal sometimes verged on the whimsical. She also played a memorable role in *Swedenhielms*, where she was the faithful housekeeper "Mutti" Boman, a down-to-earth antipode to the dreaming genius Swedenhielm.

Despite her anonymity, Swanström was important—and not only because she was one of the few female directors in her time. She functioned as a kind of "éminence grise" at the film factory of Svensk Filmindustri in the 1930s. As artistic manager and producer, she was to a high degree responsible for the choice of topics to be filmed. From her earlier experience as an actress and a manager of a touring theater company, she knew what would be successful with a broad audience. She favored the highly polished salon comedy that became common fodder at Svensk Filmindustri in the 1930s. Swanström was also responsible for scouting new talents for the company, and among other things, she convinced director *Gustaf Molander to screen test a young, unknown actress called *Ingrid Bergman.

FILMOGRAPHY

Actress

1921: *De landsflyktige/In Self Defence*. 1923: *Hemslavinnor* [House slaves]; *Anna-Clara och hennes bröder* [Anna-Clara and her brothers]; *Boman på utställningen* [Boman at the exhibition] (also director). 1924: *Gösta Berlings saga/The Legend of Gosta Berling*; *Unga greven tar flickan och priset* [The young count wins the girl and the prize]. 1925: *Skeppargatan 40* [No. 40 Skipper Street]; *Kalle Utter* (also director); *Flygande Holländaren* [The flying Dutchman] (also director); *Styrman Karlssons flammor* [First-mate Karlsson's sweethearts]. 1926: *Flickan i frack* [The girl in tails] (also director); *Flickorna Gyurkovics* [The Gyurkovics girls]. 1927: *Hans engelska fru/Discord*; *Bara en danserska* [Only a dancer]: *Förseglade läppar/Sealed Lips*; *Spökbaronen* [The ghost baron]; *En perfekt gentleman/A Husband by Proxy*. 1928: *Pariserskor/The Doctor's Women*; *Hans Kunglig Höghet shinglar* [His royal highness does the shingles]; *Gustaf Wasa*. 1930: *När rosorna slå ut/Nar Rosorna Sla Ut* [When the roses bloom]. 1931: *Lika inför lagen* [Equals under the law]; *Generalen* [The general]; *Trådlöst och kärleksfullt* [Wireless with love]; *Trötte Teodor/Troette Teodor* [Tired Teodor]; *En natt/En Natt* [One night]; *Längtan till havet/Marius* [Longing for the sea]. 1932: *Halvvägs till himlen* [Halfway to heaven]; *Svarta rosor* [Black roses]; *Svärmor kommer* [Mother-in-law's coming]; *Sten Stensson Stéen från Eslöv på nya äventyr* [Sten Stensson Stéen from Eslöv on new adventures]; *Vi som går köksvägen/Vi Som Gar Koeksvaegen* [We who use the servant's entrance]. 1933: *Giftasvuxna döttrar* [Marriageable daughters]. 1934: *Fasters millioner* [Auntie's millions]. 1935: *Swedenhielms/Swedenhielms*; *Kärlek efter noter* [Love to music]; *Äktenskapsleken* [The marriage game]. 1936: *Bröllopsresan*. [The wedding trip]; *På Solsidan/On the Sunnyside*; *Släkten är värst* [Unfriendly relations]; *Äventyret* [The adventure]; *Familjens hemlighet* [The secret of the family]. 1937: *Ryska snuvan* [The Russian flu]. 1938: *Den stora kärleken* [The great love]; *Styrman Karlssons flammor* [First-mate Karlsson's sweethearts]. 1939: *Sjöcharmörer* [Sea charmers]. 1940: *Stål* [Steel]; *Juninatten/A Night in June*. 1942: *Morgondagens melodi* [Melody of tomorrow].

BIBLIOGRAPHY

Gerhard, Karl. "Kungliga svenskar." *Vecko-Journalen*, no. 9 (1941):12–13, 32–33, 42.

MAX VON SYDOW (Lund, 19 Apr. 1929–), actor. He was born as Carl Adolf von Sydow, the son of a professor of antiquities in the university town of Lund. He began while quite young in amateur theater and assumed his nickname Max after a character in a flea circus in which he performed during his military duty. He later gave his memoirs the title *Loppcirkus* [Flea circus]. He was accepted by the Royal Dramatic Theater School in Stockholm in 1948, and after graduation, he began to act on various municipal stages. Von Sydow regards these as his real learning and training years. At the Malmö Municipal Theater in the mid-1950s he became part of *Ingmar Bergman's ensemble. The lead role in *Det sjunde inseglet/The Seventh Seal* brought him international fame and was the start of a very successful career. Since then he has had an international career mixing filmmaking with stage performing, and it is no understatement that he is internationally Sweden's best-known actor. In 1988 he made his debut as a film director with an adaptation of Herman Bang's novella *Ved vejen/Katinka*; while not a masterpiece, it is an unpretentious, entertaining, moving, and honestly illustrated classic.

His huge, blond appearance has made him suitable for the most varied screen parts. In his very first film roles he was typecast as a farmhand, and his part in *Jan Troell's *Utvandrarna/The Emigrants* reflects these early performances. He has played such different roles as Jesus Christ, hired assassins, archvillains, and Nazis. In Woody Allen's *Hannah and Her Sisters* he was a neurotic artist filled with Nordic gloom verging on parody. Although he has used his brighter, more comical side in the film *Äppelkriget* [The apple war], von Sydow has complained that directors seldom use these aspects of his talent.

Bergman has described von Sydow as a vigorous type in full control of his performing art. He often plays psychopathic roles. Many of von Sydow's Bergman performances have been of similar type—the tormented modern man in search of faith in a seemingly empty universe. Von Sydow is somewhat inspired by the Stanislavsky school of acting. He tries to penetrate the character he is to perform, understand him, and find some element that the audience can sympathize with or at least have some understanding of. His favorite type of director is therefore the type that sets von Sydow's fantasy in motion.

FILMOGRAPHY

1949: *Bara en mor* [Only a mother]. 1951: *Fröken Julie/Miss Julie*. 1953: *Ingen mans kvinna* [No man's woman]. 1956: *Rätten att älska* [The right to love]. 1957: *Det sjunde inseglet/The Seventh Seal*; *Herr Sleeman kommer* [Mr. Sleeman is coming] (TVD); *Prästen i Uddarbo* [The vicar of Uddarbo]; *Smultronstället/Wild Strawberries*. 1958: *Nära livet/Brink of Life*; *Spion 503* [Spy 503]; *Rabies* (TVD); *Ansiktet/The Magician* [The face]. 1960: *Jungfrukällan/The Virgin Spring*; *Bröllopsdagen* [The wedding day]. 1961: *Såsom i en spegel/Through a Glass Darkly*. 1962: *Nils Holgerssons underbara resa/The Wonderful Adventures of Nils*; *Älskarinnan/The Swedish Mistress*. 1963: *Nattvardsgästerna/Winter Light* [The communicants]. 1965: *The Greatest Story Ever Told*; *Uppehåll i myrlandet* [Stopover in the marshland] (episode in *4×4*); *The Reward*. 1966: *Hawaii*; *The Quiller Memorandum*; *Här har du ditt liv/Here's Your Life*. 1967: *The Diary of Anne Frank* (TVM). 1968: *Vargtimmen/Hour of the Wolf*; *Svarta palmkronor* [Black palm trees]; *Skammen/The Shame*. 1969: *Made in Sweden*; *En passion/The Passion of Anna*. 1970: *The Kremlin Letter*. 1971: *The Night Visitor*; *Utvandrarna/The Emigrants*; *Beröringen/The Touch*; *I själva verket är det alltid något annat som händer* [In reality something else always happens] (TVM); *Äppelkriget* [The apple war]; *I havsbandet* [By the open sea] (TVM); *Ingmar Bergman* (docu.). 1972: *A Search for Strindberg* (TVM);

Nybyggarna/The New Land; *Embassy*. 1973: *Kvartetten som sprängdes* [The quartet that split up] (TVMS); *The Exorcist*. 1974: *Steppenwolf*. 1975: *Ägget är löst/Egg, Egg, A Hard-boiled Story*; *Trompe l'œil*; *Three Days of the Condor*; *The Ultimate Warrior*. 1976: *Cuore di Cane*; *Foxtrot*, a.k.a. *The Other Side of Paradise*; *Cadaveri eccellenti/Illustrious Corpses*; *Voyage of the Damned*; *Il deserto dei Tartari*. 1977: *Exorcist II: The Heretic*; *March or die*; *Gran bollito*, a.k.a. *La signora degli orrori*. 1978: *Brass Target*. 1979: *The Hurricane*, a.k.a. *Forbidden Paradise*; *A Look at Liv* (docu.). 1980: *La mort en directe/Death Watch*; *Flash Gordon*. 1981: *She Dances Alone*; *Professione: figlio*, a.k.a. *Bugie bianche*; *Victory*, a.k.a. *Escape to Victory*. 1982: *Conan the Barbarian*; *Ingenjör Andrées luftfärd/The Flight of the Eagle*. 1983: *Le cercle des passions*; *Strange Brew*; *Never Say Never Again*; *Jugando con la muerte/Target Eagle*. 1984: *Le dernier civil* (TVM); *The Soldier's Tale* (voice); *Samson and Delilah* (TVM); *Dreamscape*; *George Stevens. A Filmmaker's Journey* (docu.); *Dune*. 1985: *Kojak: The Belarus File* (TVM); *Christoforo Colombo/Christopher Columbus* (TVM); *Codename: Emerald*; *The Last Place on Earth*; *Il pentito*; *Quo Vadis* (TVM). 1986: *Hannah and Her Sisters*; *Gösta Berlings Saga* [The legend of Gösta Berling] (TVMS); *The Second Victory; Oviri/The Wolf at the Door*; *Duet for One*. 1987: *Pelle Erobreren/Pelle, the Conqueror*. 1988: *Ved vejen/Katinka* (director only); *Familjen Schedblad* [The Schedblad family] (TVM); *Kyndelmisse* [Candlemas] (short). 1989: *Red King, White Knight*. 1990: *Mio caro dottor Gräsler*, a.k.a. *The Bachelor*; *Una vita scellerata*; *Father*; *Hiroshima: Out of the Ashes* (TVM); *Awakenings*. 1991: *A Kiss before Dying*; *Bis ans Ende der welt/To the End of the Earth*; *Oxen/The Ox*; *Den goda viljan/The Best Intentions* (TVM).[1] 1992: *Europa/Zentropa*; *Dotkniecie reki/The Silent Touch*; *Young Indiana Jones Chronicles* (TVM, one episode). 1993: *Och ge oss skuggorna* [And give us the shadows] (TVD); *Morfars resa* [Grandpa's voyage]; *Needful Things*; *Time Is Money*. 1994: *A che punto è la notte* (TVM); *Radetskymarsch* (TVM); *Onkel Vanja* [Uncle Vanya] (TVD). 1995: *Citizen X*; *Atlanten* [The Atlantic] (docu.); *Judge Dredd*. 1996: *Hamsun*; *Jerusalem*; *Enskilda samtal/Private Confessions* (TVM). 1997: *En frusen dröm* [A frozen dream] (docu., voice); *Hostile waters* (TVM); *Die Bibel—Solomon*, a.k.a. *Salomon* (TVM). 1998: *What Dreams May Come*. 1999: *Snow Falling on Cedars*.

BIBLIOGRAPHY

Cowie, Peter. *Max von Sydow: From the Seventh Seal to Pelle the Conqueror*. Stockholm: Swedish Film Institute, 1989.
Gallagher, J. "Max von Sydow on Ingmar Bergman." *Films in Review* (May 1988): 286–287.
Gow, Gordon. "The Face of the Actor." *Films and Filming* (July 1976): 10–15. Interview.
Sydow, Max von. *Loppcirkus*. Stockholm: Brombergs, 1989.

AWARDS

AAN 1989: Best Actor (*Pelle, the Conqueror*)

GB 1987

GB 1988

GB 1996

NOTE

1. Theatrically released in 1992 in an edited version.

BIRGIT TENGROTH (Stockholm, 13 July 1915–21 Sept. 1983), actress. Originally a trained ballet dancer, she received a steady engagement with Svensk Filmindustri in 1932, where she remained until the late 1930s. She acted for various companies during the 1940s, and her film career ended in 1950. She became a writer, and her literary debut in 1948—a collection of short stories entitled *Törst* [Thirst]—caused some controversy owing to its open-minded treatment of women's sexuality. This became, in the following year, the basis for *Ingmar Bergman's film of the same title. For a period she was married to Danish prime minister Jens Otto Kragh. After her divorce she continued her writing career, which includes works of a more autobiographical character.

Tengroth was quite young when she made her film debut. In the 1930s she was mainly typecast as the fresh and righteous young girl living next door. She was obviously very popular with the youthful audience. When *Ingrid Bergman made her screen debut she was at first unfavorably compared to Tengroth. Tengroth also played various down-to-earth country girl roles, such as Ebba in *Per Lindberg's *Gläd dig i din ungdom* [Rejoice in thy youth], where she embodied the pastoral ideal, fresh as a summer morning. However, if one looks more carefully at her movies one senses a trace of fragility and sensitivity somewhere beneath the surface. This is confirmed in her later literary work, where she writes about her earlier film work with bitterness and contempt (not least for some of the leading persons in the 1930s film industry).

FILMOGRAPHY

1926: *Mordbrännerskan* [The lady incendiary]. 1927: *Hin och smålänningen* [Old Nick and the Smålander]. 1928: *Synd* [Sin]. 1932: *Hans livs match* [The game of his life]; *Pojkarna på Storholmen* [The boys of Storholmen]. 1933: *Bomans pojke* [Boman's boy]; *Giftasvuxna döttrar* [Marriageable daughters]; *Vad veta väl männen-*[What do men know-]. 1934: *Atlantäventyret* [The Atlantic adventure]; *Sången om den eldröda blomman* [The song of the scarlet flower]. 1935: *Ungkarlspappan/Ungkarlspappan* [Bachelor daddy]; *Flickornas Alfred* [Ladies' man Alfred]; *Ebberöds bank* [The Ebberöd bank]. 1936: *Kungen kommer* [The king is coming]; *Vårt bygge på hem och samhälle* [Our construction of home and society] (NCF); *Annonsera!* [Advertise!]; *Johan Ulfstjerna*; *Familjens hemlighet* [The family secret]. 1937: *O, sen så'n natt!* [Oh, what a night]; *Pappas pojke* [Daddy's boy]. 1938: *Sockerskrinet* [The sugar box] (NCF); *Dollar/Dollar*. 1939: *Gubben kommer* [The old man's coming]; *Gläd dig i din ungdom* [Rejoice in thy youth]; *Oss baroner emellan* [Between us barons]. 1940: . . . *som en tjuv om natten* [. . . like a thief in the night]; *Västkustens hjältar* [Heroes of the West Coast]; *Karl för sin hatt* [A real man]. 1941: *Så tuktas en äkta man* [The taming of a husband]; *En man för mycket* [One man too many]. 1942: *Jacobs stege* [Jacob's ladder]; *Rospiggar* [Roslagers]; *Kan doktorn komma?* [Can you come, doctor?]. 1943: *I brist på bevis* [For lack of evidence]; *Katrina/Katrina*; *På liv och död* [A life or death matter]; *Natt i hamn* [Night in port]; *Sonja*. 1944: *Skogen är vår arvedel* [The forest is our heritage]; *På farliga vägar* [On dangerous ways]. 1945: *Mans kvinna* [Man's woman]. 1946: *Ödemarksprästen* [The wilderness parson]. 1947: *Dynamit* [Dynamite]; *Krigsmans erinran* [A soldier's oath]. 1948: *Synd* [Sin]. 1949: *Törst/Three Strange Loves* [Thirst]. 1950: **Flicka och hyacinter* [Girl with hyacinths].

BIBLIOGRAPHY

Tengroth, Birgit. *Jag vill ha tillbaka mitt liv*. Stockholm: Bonniers, 1972.

INGRID THULIN (Sollefteå, 27 Jan. 1929–), actress, director. Thulin was born in a small town in northern Sweden, a fact that has had some importance for her career. She returned to this milieu when she made her autobiographical feature, *Brusten himmel/Broken Sky*. She had a poor and insecure adolescence and was quite young when she moved to Stockholm to attend a secretarial school. She preferred dancing lessons and acting, and, discovered by a stage director, she was engaged by the Norrköping Municipal Theater. She was then accepted by the Royal Dramatic Theater School in 1948 and spent the next three years there. In 1948 she also made her screen debut, in a propaganda feature for the Swedish Communist Party; this was not out of political conviction but because she needed a job. While engaged at the Malmö Municipal Theater in the mid-1950s she met *Ingmar Bergman and became one of the most frequent performers in his films. Her work with Bergman included several television roles. In the 1960s she began an international career, working mostly in Italy where she has resided since then. She has also worked as a theater pedagogue and was for a long while married to Harry Schein, a longtime chairman of the Swedish Film Institute.

Ingrid Thulin's memoirs do not reveal many of her inner feelings about acting as an art. Despite her somewhat uncertain childhood, she became a secure and determined person, showing the strength common to women of northern Sweden. Bergman, whose ideal of a perfect woman is the strong motherly type, tended to cast Thulin into intellectual roles, which for Bergman are always heartless and cold. Unlike the actresses who personified Bergman's ideal, she often performed the roles of childless and loveless creatures, as, for example, in *Nära livet/Brink of Life* (about abortion), **Smultronstället/Wild Strawberries*, *Tystnaden/The Silence*, and *Viskningar och rop/Cries and Whispers*. Thulin herself thinks that she is better suited for the more ambiguous and psychological roles. Her own film, *Brusten himmel/Broken Sky*, reveals other dimensions. This depiction of her childhood and home province is quite sensual and moving. The performance of *Thommy Berggren, as the father who prefers to be out in the wilderness fishing, is a very sensitive portrayal.

FILMOGRAPHY

Actress

1948: *Känn dej som hemma* [Just feel at home] (NCF); *Dit vindarna bär* [Where the winds take you]. 1949: *Havets son/Son of the Sea*; *Kärleken segrar* [Love wins out]; *Vi bygger framtiden* [We build the future] (NCF). 1950: *Hjärter Knekt* [Knave of hearts]; *När kärleken kom till byn* [When love came to the village]. 1951: *Leva på "Hoppet"* [Living on "Hope"]. 1952: *Möte med livet* [Encounter with life]; *Kalle Karlsson från Jularbo* [Kalle Karlsson from Jularbo]. 1953: *En skärgårdsnatt* [A night in the archipelago]; *Göingehövdingen* [The chieftain of Göinge], 1954; *I rök och dans* [Dance in the smoke]; *The Model from Holland* (TVM, episode in *Foreign Intrigue*); *The Third Partner* (TVM, episode in *Foreign Intrigue*); *Witness at Large* (TVM, episode in *Foreign Intrigue*); *Två sköna juveler* [Two beautiful jewels]. 1955: *The Diplomat* (TVM, episode in *Foreign Intrigue*); *Danssalongen* [The dance hall]; *Hoppsan!* [Whoops!]. 1956: *Foreign Intrigue*; *Pettersson i Annorlunda* [Pettersson in Different Country] (NCF). 1957: *Aldrig i livet* [Not in your life]; *Missförståndet* [The misunderstanding] (TVD); *Smultronstället/Wild Strawberries*. 1958: *Nära livet/Brink of Life*; *Gasljus* [Gaslight] (TVD); *Ansiktet/The Magician* [The face]. 1959: *Älska* [Making love] (TVD); *Vår oförde son* [Our unborn son] (TVD). 1960: *Domaren* [The judge]. 1961: *Syskon* [Siblings] (TVD); *The Four Horsemen of the Apocalypse*; *La perdita dell'innocenza*, a.k.a. *Agostino*; *Intermezzo* (TVM). 1963: *Nattvardsgästerna/Winter Light* [The communicants]; *Tystnaden/The Silence*; *Ett drömspel* [A dream play] (TVD); *Sekstet* [Sextet]; *The Incurable One* (TVM). 1964: *Der Film der Niemand Seht* (short). 1965: *Die Lady/Games of Desire*; *Return from the Ashes*. 1966: *La guerre est finie/The War Is Over*; *Nattlek/Night Games*. 1967: *Domani non siamo più qui*. 1968: *Vargtimmen/Hour of the Wolf*; *Badarna* [The Bathers]; *Adelaide*, a.k.a. *Fino a farti mali*. 1969: *Riten/The Ritual* (TVM); *Un diablo bajo la almohada*. 1970: *La Caduta degli dei*, a.k.a. *Götterdämmerung/The Damned*. 1971: *N. P. il segreto*; *La corta notte delle bambola di vetro*; *Viskningar och rop/Cries and Whispers*. 1973: *La sainte famille*; *Puccini* (TVM). 1974: *En handfull kärlek* [A handful of love]; . . . *e cominciò il viaggio nella vertigini*. 1975: *Catalepsis*; *La cage*; *Monismanien 1995* [Monismania 1995]; *Mosè*, a.k.a. *Moses the Lawgiver* (TVM);[1] *Salon Kitty*. 1976: *L'Agnese va a morire*. 1977: *The Cassandra Crossing*. 1978: *Deux affreux sur le sable/It rained all night the day I left*. 1981: *L'attesa* (TVM). 1984: *Efter repetionen/After the Rehearsal* (TVM). 1985: *Il corsaro*, a.k.a. *Der Freibuter* (TVM). 1987: *Il giorno prima*, a.k.a. *Côntrole*. 1988: *Cuore di mamma*. 1989: *La trappola* (TVM). 1992: *La casa del sorriso*; *Faccia di lepre*.

Director

1965: *Hängivelsen* [Devotion] (short). 1978: *En och en/One and One*.[2] 1982: *Brusten himmel/Broken Sky*.

BIBLIOGRAPHY

Forslund, 1995.
"Ingrid Thulin Comments on Visconti." *Dialogue on Film*, no. 3 (1972):15–27.
Thulin, Ingrid. *Någon jag kände*. Stockholm: Norstedts, 1992.

AWARDS

Cannes 1958: Best Actress (*Brink of Life*)

GB 1964

NOTES

1. Shown in cinemas in edited version in 1976.
2. Codirector and coproducer with *Erland Josephson and Sven Nykvist.

JAN TROELL (Malmö, 23 July 1931–), director. Troell is one of the more prolific directors to have appeared on the Swedish film scene during the film reform at the beginning of the 1960s. Originally a schoolteacher and skilled still photographer, he won a contest for amateur filmmakers in 1959. Then he made a series of short documentaries for Swedish television. This background helps explain certain traits in his films, especially the sense of "documentarism" in his features. Many of his films are based upon real events or persons and characterized by a strong feeling for social issues. With his recent, long, critical film "essay" on contemporary Sweden, *Sagolandet* [Fairytale land], he returned to this genre.

As a film director he was immediately successful with his first full-length feature, an adaptation of Nobel Prize winner Eyvind Johnson's autobiographical writings **Här har du ditt liv/Here's Your Life*. He had even more success with Vilhelm Moberg's literary epic about Swedish immigration to America in the late nineteenth century. The first of the two films, **Utvandrarna/The Emigrants*, was the top-grossing Swedish film of the 1970s. Troell's sense for documentary-style lyrical narration is evident in all these works.

His career has not, however, been without failures. His personal and poetic tale about a music lover in *Bang!* confused the critics and was a disaster among cinemagoers. He was lured to Hollywood after his success with the Moberg epics, but his ability and talent seem to have gotten lost in the American film industry machine. Neither *Hurricane* nor *Zandy's Bride* did as well as his former films. Returning to Sweden, he made a film about engineer Salomon August Andrée's disastrous attempt to fly to the North Pole in 1897 in an air balloon, which did somewhat better. This material was better suited to his kind of filmmaking. The film is in some ways a commentary on the role of masculinity in our modern society.

Sagolandet, his three-hour-long "documentary" critique of modern Swedish society discussing the decline of the welfare state, is an expression of Troell's view that the welfare state creates obstacles for persons to develop their own abilities. This was not a popular view. Troell caused even more controversy when he made a film, based on real events, about two Finnish youngsters murdering three people in a churchyard in northern Sweden. Many attempts were made to stop the project, which was eventually realized with the name *Il Capitano*. In it he presents a very dark view of modern Sweden that serves as background to the two youngsters' flight. The background is a literal clear-cut wasteland, a mental image of a country of cold, heartless people, which confronts both the audience and the protagonists. The film was both a critical and financial failure. His latest film, a biographical account of author and Nobel Prize winner Knut Hamsun, has been more successful.

FILMOGRAPHY

Director, Scriptwriter

Short Documentaries

1959: *Sommarhamn* [Summer harbor]; *Stad* [Town]. 1961: *Sommartåg* [Summer train];

Nyårsafton på Skånska slätten [New Year's Eve in Skåne]. 1962: *De kom tillbaka* [They came back]; *Båten* [The ship]; *Den gamla kvarnen* [The old mill]; *En broder mer* [One more brother]. 1963: *Porträtt av Åsa* [Portrait of Åsa]; *Johan Ekberg*. 1964: *Trakom*; *Vår i Dalby* [Spring in Dalby]. 1975: *Nålsögat—en film om möjligheter* [The needle's eye—a film about possibilities]. 1994; *Dansen* [The dance]; *I provinsens ljus* [In the light of the countryside]. 1997: . . . *och barnen i äppelträdet* [. . . and the children in the apple tree]; *En frusen dröm* [A frozen dream].

Features

1962: *Pojken och draken* [The boy and the kite] (short); *Barnvagnen* [The pram] (script only). 1965: *Uppehåll i myrlandet* [Stopover in the marshland] (episode in *4×4*). 1966: *Här har du ditt liv/Here's Your Life*. 1968: *Ole, dole, doff* [Eeny, meeny, miny, moe]. 1971: *Utvandrarna/The Emigrants*. 1972: *Nybyggarna/The New Land*. 1973: *Gamen* [The vulture] (TVD, director only). 1974: *Zandy's Bride*, a.k.a. *For Better, For Worse*. 1977: *Bang!* 1979: *Hurricane*, a.k.a. *Forbidden Paradise*. 1982: *Ingenjör Andrées luftfärd/The Flight of the Eagle*. 1988: *Sagolandet* [Fairytale land] (docu.). 1991: *Il Capitano*. 1996: *Hamsun*.

BIBLIOGRAPHY

Berglund, Lars. "Mördare med kaniner i bagaget." *Chaplin*, no. 236 (1991):17–19.
Björkman, 1977.
Forslund, Bengt. "Till fantasins försvan." *Filmrutan*, no. 1 (1988):2–5.
Löthwall, Lars-Olof, ed. *Troell: Modern Swedish Cinema*. Vol. 2. Stockholm: Swedish Film Institute, 1975.
Silberman, Robert. "Il Capitano." In Hedling, 1998.

AWARDS

GB 1967

Berlin Golden Bear 1968 (*Ole, dole, doff*)

AAN 1972: Best Foreign Film (*The Emigrants*)

AAN 1973: Best Film, Best Script, Best Direction (*The Emigrants*)

AAN 1973: Best Foreign Film (*The New Land*)

AAN 1983: Best Foreign Film (*The Flight of the Eagle*)

GB 1988

GB 1991

Berlin Silver Bear 1992 (*Il Capitano*)

GB 1996

SIGURD WALLÉN (Tierp, 1 Sept. 1884–20 Mar. 1947), actor, director. Wallén belongs to the large group of folksy, rather unsophisticated filmmakers and actors so common in Sweden and characteristic of Swedish cinema in the prosperous years of the 1930s extending into the late 1950s. His most popular characterizations are of the kinds of figures that Albert Engström immortalized in his writings: the weatherworn fisherman living in the Stockholm archipelago or the poor, honest, hardworking small farmer of Småland, the Swedish province most symbolic for its essential Swedishness. Wallén embodied as such the Swedish "myth," a nostalgia for the old agrarian society in our modern, transient times that has persisted for many decades. His great popularity can be explained in these terms. His popularity was further bolstered by his public readings of Engström's short stories on stage and radio. These readings may have contributed to the great popularity of the films. The films *Rospiggar* [Roslagers], Sandrews's most popular film in the 1940s, and *I mörkaste Småland* [In darkest Småland] were based on Engström's stories. Wallén was an outspoken Social Democrat, which might also have contributed to his popularity, especially as he embodied the virtues and ideals of the "people's home" policy launched by the Social Democratic government in the 1930s. These sentiments are, for example, evident in the film **Karl-Fredrik regerar/Karl-Fredrik Reigns*. Two of his directorial efforts in the late 1930s also voice his Social Democratic opinions. *Med folket för fosterlandet/Med Folket Foer Fosterlandet* [With the people for the fatherland] is a historic chronicle that strongly suggests that history has come to an end with Social Democratic rule and the formation of the welfare state. Wallén also appeared in many of the propaganda features produced by the party for various election campaigns.

FILMOGRAPHY

Actor

1911: *Stockholmsfrestelser eller ett Norrlandsherrskaps äventyr i de sköna syndernas stad* [Stockholm's temptations, or The adventures of a Norrland party in the town of the sweet sins] (short); *Blott en dröm* [Just a dream] (short); *Stockholmsdamernas älskling* [The Stockholm ladies' darling] (short). 1912: *Systrarna* [The sisters] (short). 1915: *Kal Napoleon Kalssons bondtur* [Kal Napoleon Kalsson's stroke of luck] (short). 1917: *Tösen från Stormyrtorpet/The Girl from the Marsh Croft*; *Alexander den store/Alexander the Great*. 1918: *Berg-Ejvind och hans hustru/You and I*. 1919: *Ingmarssönerna* [Sons of Ingmar]; *Hans nåds testamente* [His grace's will]. 1920: *Thora van Deken*. 1928: *Gustaf Wasa*. 1930: *Fridas visor* [Frida's songs]. 1931: *Röda dagen/Roeda Dagen* [The red day]; *Skepparkärlek* [Skipper's love]. 1932: *Hans livs match* [The game of his life]; *Svarta rosor* [Black roses]; *Kärlek och kassabrist* [Love and deficit]; *Vi som går köksvägen/Vi Som Gar Koeksvaegen* [We who use the servant's entrance]. 1933: *Bomans pojke* [Boman's boy]; *Pettersson & Bendel/Pettersson & Bendel*. 1934: *Karl-Fredrik regerar/Karl Fredrik Reigns*. 1935: *Swedenhielms/Swedenhielms*; *Kärlek efter noter* [Love to music]; *Smålänningar* [The people of Småland]. 1936: *Janssons frestelse* [Jansson's temptation]; *Alla tiders Karlsson* [All-time Karlsson]; *Bombi Bitt och jag* [Bombi Bitt and I]. 1937: *Konflikt* [Conflict]; *Katt över vägen* [Cat crossing the road] (short); *John Ericsson—segraren vid Hampton Roads/John Ericsson—Victor at Hampton Roads*. 1938: *En kvinnas ansikte/A Woman's Face*; *Du gamla du fria/Du Gamla, Du Fria* [Thou old, thou free]. 1939: *Adolf i eld och lågor* [Adolf all fired up]; *Sjöcharmörer* [Sea charmers]. 1940: *. . . som en tjuv om natten* [. . . like a thief in the night]; *Juninatten/A Night in June*; *Stora famnen* [With open arms]; *Ett brott* [A crime]; *Karl för sin hatt* [A real man]. 1941: *Livet går vidare* [Life goes on]. 1942: *Rospiggar* [Roslagers]; *Det är min musik . . .* [That's my music . . .]. 1943: *Kvinnor i fångenskap* [Women in captivity]; *Flickan är ett fynd.* [The girl's a find]; *Natt i hamn* [Night in port]; *I mörkaste Småland*

[In darkest Småland]. 1944: *Släkten är bäst* [Family's family after all]; *Hans livs lopp* [The race of his life] (NCF). 1945: *Brott och straff/Crime and Punishment*. 1946: *Välkomna till oss* [Welcome to us] (NCF); *Saltstänk och krutgubbar* [Salt spray and old salts]; *När ängarna blommar* [When the meadows blossom].

Director

1922: *Anderssonskans Kalle* [Andersson's Kalle]. 1923: *Anderssonskans Kalle på nya upptåg* [New pranks of Andersson's Kalle]; *Friaren från landsvägen* [The suitor from the highway] (also script and actor). 1924: *Halta Lena och vindögde Per* [Limping Lena and cross-eyed Per] (also actor); *Dan, tant och lilla fröken Söderlund* [Dan, auntie and little Miss Söderlund]; *Grevarna på Svansta* [The counts at Svansta]. 1925: *Hennes lilla majestät* [Her little majesty]. 1926: *Dollarmillionen* [The million dollars]; *Farbror Frans* [Uncle Frans]; *Ebberöds bank* [The Ebberöd bank]. 1927: *Drottningen av Pellagonien* [The queen of Pellagonia]. 1928: *Janssons frestelse* [Jansson's temptation] (also script and actor). 1929: *Ville Andesons äventyr* [Ville Andeson's adventures]. 1932: *Pojkarna på Storholmen* [The boys of Storholmen] (also script and actor); *Lyckans gullgossar* [Lucky devils] (codirector *Ivar Johansson, also script and actor). 1933: *Giftasvuxna döttrar* [Marriageable daughters] (also script and actor); *En natt på Smygeholm* [A night at Smygeholm]. 1934: *Anderssonskans Kalle* [Andersson's Kalle]; *Pettersson-Sverige* (also actor). 1935: *Munkbrogreven/The Count of Monk's Bridge* (also actor, codirector *Edvin Adolphson); *Ebberöds bank* [The Ebberöd bank] (also script). 1936: *Samvetsömma Adolf/Samvetsoemma Adolf* [Adolf, conscientious objector]; *Landet för folket* [The land for the people] (NCF, also actor); *Skeppsbrutne Max* [Shipwrecked Max]. 1937: *Adolf Armstarke/Adolf Armstrong*; *Familjen Andersson/Familjen Andersson* [The Andersson family] (also actor); *Vi går landsvägen* [We walk along the highway] (also actor). 1938: *Två år i varje klass* [Two years in each grade] (also actor); *Med folket för fosterlandet/Med Folket Foer Fosterlandet* [With the people for the fatherland] (also script and actor); *Sigge Nilsson och jag* [Sigge Nilsson and I] (also actor); *Kloka gubben* [The wise old man] (also actor). 1939: *Mot nya tider* [Toward new times] (also actor). 1940: *Kronans käcka gossar* [The crown's brave lads] (also script and actor); *Karusellen går . . .* [The merry-go-round goes round . . .] (also actor); *Beredskapspojkar* [Mobilization boys] (also actor). 1941: *Nygifta* [Just married] (also actor); *En fattig miljonär* [A poor millionaire] (also actor). 1944: *Hemsöborna* [The people of Hemsö] (also script and actor); *Vår herre luggar Johansson/Johansson Gets Scolded* (also actor); *Skeppar Jansson* [Skipper Jansson] (also script and actor). 1945: *Änkeman Jarl* [Widower Jarl] (also script and actor).

BIBLIOGRAPHY

Wallén, Sigurd *Revydags. Tystnad, tagning, kameran går*. Stockholm: Medéns, 1944. Autobiography.

BO WIDERBERG (Malmö, 8 June 1930–1 May 1997), director. Originally a novelist, Widerberg made his way into Swedish film life as an angry young man. In 1962 he published the book *The Vision in Swedish Cinema*, a sharp and polemic attack on the contemporary Swedish cinema in which he claimed it was false and unrealistic. He even vigorously attacked *Ingmar Bergman, who, in the eyes of Widerberg, was a provincial artifact.

After writing a script for one of *Jan Troell's first shorts, Widerberg was given the chance to direct a feature of his own. Although it was only moderately successful, he was given another chance with *Kvarteret Korpen/Raven's End. This was a real breakthrough with critics and the audience. The film has recently been voted best film ever in Swedish film history by the younger critics. After his second feature his career has been one of ups and downs. *Elvira Madigan*, a love story about a pair of doomed lovers, based on the true story of a young lieutenant eloping with a circus performer and then eventually committing suicide together, was successful. He also had some success with the films *Ådalen 31* and *Joe Hill*, but a film based on Knut Hamsum's novel *Victoria* ended in total disaster. Completed after many years of controversy and delay, the film was a total flop. In the meantime he did have another success with his police film *Mannen från Mallorca* [The man from Majorca]. Except for the 1981 aborted film project *Rött och svart*, planned in collaboration with his favorite actor *Thommy Berggren, Widerberg was for a long time inactive in the film industry. Instead, he devoted himself to, among other things, television, for which he made well-received versions of such stage classics as *A Streetcar Named Desire* and *Death of a Salesman*. In 1996 he successfully returned to the silver screen with *Lust och fägring stor/All Things Fair*.

Historical events and themes were common in Widerberg's films. *Raven's End* looked back to the 1930s when the "people's home" was being established. A few years later he portrayed the tragic events in Ådalen, where, in 1931, striking workers were shot at and five people were killed. Although the film has a pastoral setting, which might remind one of his tale of *Elvira Madigan*, the film has dark tones. Intertwined with the main events is a love story involving a working boy and the daughter of the factory's manager. While this element in the story line follows the traditions of 1930s Swedish cinema, the twist at the finish, where things do not end well, does not. One could label this film as belonging to the loss of innocence genre. The last line of the film is a remark that equality is still to be fulfilled in Sweden.

Elvira Madigan was an international success, and it is also about the loss of innocence. Widerberg constantly returned to this theme. One good example is the somewhat underrated *Ormens väg på hälleberget/The Serpent's Way*, a fantastic tale set in the nineteenth century about poor settlers in northern Sweden. They are threatened by a greedy shopkeeper making unreasonable demands and are saved by some supernatural happenings that have a touch of magic realism. The theme is also evident in his last film, *Lust och fägring stor/All Things Fair*. In it a young schoolboy in the 1940s has a love affair with his schoolteacher, and it ends with negative consequences. Real historical events are used as symbols: While the story is reaching its conclusion, the schoolboy's brother is killed in a submarine accident, an event that actually occurred during World War II.

FILMOGRAPHY

Director, Scriptwriter

1962: *Pojken och draken* [The boy and the kite] (script only, short). 1963: *Barnvagnen* [The pram]; *Kvarteret Korpen/Raven's End*. 1965: *Kärlek 65* [Love 65]. 1966: *Heja Roland* [Come on, Roland]. 1967: *Elvira Madigan/Elvira Madigan, Historien om Barbara* [The story of Barbara] (actor only). 1968: *Den vita sporten* [The white game] (docu., as a member of collective "Group 13"). 1969: *Ådalen 31/Ådalen '31*. 1970: *Tvåbarnsmor, väntande hennes tredje* [Mother of two children, expecting a third] (docu., short). 1971: *Joe Hill/Joe Hill*. 1974: *Fimpen* [Stubby]. 1976: *Mannen på taket/Man on the Roof* (director only). 1979: *En handelsresandes död* [Death of a salesman] (TVD). 1981: *Missförståndet* [The misunderstanding] (TVD); *Linje lusta* [A streetcar named desire] (TVD, also actor); *Mannen från Mallorca* [The man from Majorca]. 1986: *Ormens väg på hälleberget/The Serpent's Way*. 1987: *Victoria.*[1] 1988: *En far* [A father] (TVD). 1989: *Vildanden* [The wild duck] (TVD). 1990: *Hebriana* (TVD). 1992: *Efter föreställningen* [After the performance] (TVD). 1995: *Lust och fägring stor/All Things Fair*. 1997: *Emma—åklagare* [Emma—district attorney] (TVMS, actor only).

BIBLIOGRAPHY

Björkman, 1977.

AWARDS

Cannes Silver Palm 1969 (*Ådalen '31*)

AAN 1970: Best Foreign Film (*Ådalen '31*)

Cannes Silver Palm 1972 (*Joe Hill*)

AAN 1996: Best Foreign Film (*All Things Fair*)

Berlin Silver Bear 1996 (*All Things Fair*)

NOTE

1. The film was produced at the end of the 1970s and shown at the Cannes festival in 1979 in a version that Widerberg had not authorized. After much legal trouble, the film was completed and had its "official" premiere in 1987.

SVEN WOLLTER (Göteborg, 11 Jan. 1934–), actor. Born in Göteborg, he is the product of the political climate in that city. He is, on the one hand, well known as an outspoken radical left-winger; on the other hand, he has been called "the sexiest man in Sweden." Between these extremes lies a well-acclaimed character actor of contemporary Swedish film and television. He made quite a name for himself in the 1960s when he was one of the leads in the television film of the Strindberg classic *Hemsöborna* [The people of Hemsö]. Wollter almost crushed the hearts of his Swedish audience when he starred as the ex-soldier Rasken in a television serial based on one of Vilhelm Moberg's novels. This serial had the highest ratings ever in Swedish television history. Wollter's low, gravelly voice brings authority to the various roles of men of importance that he has acted since then. He was the village big shot in *Änglagård/House of Angels* (where he starred opposite his wife *Viveka Seldahl). He was also entrusted with one of the leading parts, as the doctor, in Tarkovsky's Swedish venture *Offret/The Sacrifice*. He recently was Alfred Nobel in the film of the same name, which was a flop in spite of Wollter's fine acting.

FILMOGRAPHY

1959: *Ryttare i blått* [Rider in blue]. 1965: *Som ringer på vattnet* [Like rings on water] (short); *Vågen* [The wave] (short). 1966: *Hemsöborna* [The people of Hemsö] (TVMS); *Woyzeck* (TVD). 1967: *Drottningens juvelsmycke* [The queen's diadem] (TVDS); *Vår i September* [Spring in September] (TVD); *Glassmenangeriet* [The glass menagerie] (TVD); *Jämsides* [Side by side] (TVD); *Jag är nyfiken-gul/I Am Curious (Yellow)*; *Den nakne mannen och mannen i frack* [The naked man and the man in tails] (TVD). 1968: *Repetitionen* [The rehearsal] (TVD); *Regeln och undantaget* [The rule and the exception] (TVD); *I samma rum* [In the same room] (TVD); *Exercis* [Drill] (TVM); *Jag älskar Du älskar* [I love, you love]. 1971: *Kommissarie Migrän leker med döden* [Inspector Migraine plays with death] (TVM, short); *När Arne larmade brandkåren* [When Arne called the fire department] (TVMS); *Spelaren* [The gambler] (TVM). 1972: *Sandlådan* [The sand box] (TVD). 1973: *Ett köpmanshus i skärgården* [A merchant's house in the archipelago] (TVMS); *Då är man nog ganska rädd* [Then you are rather scared] (TVMS); *Krocken* [The crash] (TVM); *Har vi inte alltid haft det bra?* [Haven't we always been comfortable?] (TVM). 1974: *Jourhavande* [Doctor on duty] (TVMS); *Galenpannan* [The madcap] (TVM); *Domaren* [The judge] (TVD); *Rymmare* [Runaways] (TVM). 1975: *Gyllene år* [Golden years] (TVMS); *Den vita väggen* [The white wall]. 1976: *Raskens* (TVMS); *Mannen på taket/The Man on the Roof*. 1978: *Vem tillhör världen?* [To whom belongs the world?]; *Strandfyndet* [The find on the beach] (TVMS). 1979: *Linus eller Tegelhusets hemlighet* [Linus, or The secret of the brick house]; *Charlotte Löwensköld*.[1] 1981: *Sista budet* [The last command]; *Kallocain* (TVD). 1983: *Jakob smitaren* [Jacob the runaway]; *Nilla* (TVMS); *Profitörerna* [The profiteers] (TVMS). 1984: *Sista leken* [The last game]; *Mannen från Mallorca* [The man from Majorca]. 1985: *Havlandet* [Sea land]. 1986: *Offret/The Sacrifice*; *I lagens namn* [In the name of the law]. 1987: *Ein Treffen mit Rimbaud*; *En film om kärlek* [A film about love]; *Friends*. 1988: *Enkel resa* [One-way journey]; *Sweetwater*. 1989/1991: *Tre kärlekar* [Three loves] (TVMS). 1989: *Husbonden* [The master] (TVMS). 1990: *Smykketyven* [The jewelry thief]. 1991: *Guldburen* [The golden cage] (TVMS); *Facklorna* [The torches] (TVMS). 1992: *Violbukten* [The violet bay]; *Änglagård/House of Angels*. 1993: *Dockpojken* [The doll boy]. 1994: *Änglagård—andra sommaren* [House of angels—the second summer]. 1995: *Rallaren* [The railroad worker] (short); *Alfred*; *Mördare utan ansikte* [Murderer without a face] (TVMS); *Magisk cirkel* [Magic circle] (TVD). 1996: *Jerusalem*. 1997: *Genom eld och vatten. Sagan om Polhem och Linné* [Through fire and water. The tale of Polhem and Linné] (TVM); *Hjerteflimmer* [Heart flickers] (TVM). 1998: *Den tatuerade änkan* [The tattooed widow] (TVM); *Ögat* [The eye]; *Ivar Kreuger* (TVM). 1999: *Sally* (TVMS); *Art* (TVD); *The 13th Warrior*.

BIBLIOGRAPHY

Wollter, Sven, and Maja-Britta Mossberg. *Bakljus*. Stockholm: Norstedts, 1994.

AWARD

GB 1984

NOTE

1. In longer version for television in 1981.

MAI ZETTERLING (Västerås, 24 May 1925–17 Mar. 1994), actress, director. Her family immigrated to Australia but returned after a few years when she was quite young. Zetterling spent her early years in Stockholm. According to her memoirs, she was not happy, and it was hard for her to adjust to a normal life. After finishing her schooling, she had various small jobs in shops and became interested in theater acting. She joined a theater club and got a small part in one of the better second-rank theaters in Stockholm. There she was discovered and taken care of by one of the more prolific independent theater teachers, Calle Flygare, who ran a famous school. He gave Zetterling lessons for free, and eventually she was accepted at the Royal Dramatic Theater School, where she was recognized as a great talent. Soon thereafter she had a breakthrough with her role in *Hets/Torment*. This led to an international engagement with Basil Dearden on his film *Frieda*, when he came to Stockholm to make tests. Zetterling made some more films in Sweden, including *Ingmar Bergman's *Musik i mörker/The Night Is My Future*, before settling down in Great Britain. There she had mostly insignificant film parts.

When she met her new husband, writer David Hughes, in 1958, her interest had shifted to making films, and they made a string of documentaries for British television. *The Prosperity Race* was a critical overview of the Swedish welfare state and was widely acclaimed. She was then hailed for the short *The War Game*, whereupon she had the chance to make a feature in Sweden. This feature, *Älskande par/Loving Couples*, was a sensational debut in which she demonstrated both her maturity and talent with the medium. It was based on a novel by Agnes von Krusenstjerna about three women in a maternity ward and their memories. It had been scandalous in the 1930s due to its frankness about sexuality. Her second film, *Nattlek/Night Games*, largely inspired by Fellini and Bergman, caused a scandal at the Venice Festival of 1966. After this she had difficulties. The film critics were critical of her film *Flickorna/The Girls*, perhaps because this modern, feminist variation of the old Lysistrate theme was before its time. The French writer Simone de Beauvoir liked the film and wanted Zetterling to film her *Le deuxieme sexe*; however, nothing came of this—just one of Zetterling's aborted projects. Her final completed feature was *Amorosa*, a feature about Agnes von Krusenstjerna's life. Zetterling spent most of her last years in France.

Her memoirs reveal a very sensitive and observant personality. As an actress she partly personified the Swedish blond, most evidently in *Driver dagg, faller *regn/Sunshine Follows Rain*. One critic compared her to the Nordic summer night with its seductive dusk and clear-minded dawn. Maybe this reflected her choice of career: to be an actress. According to her memoirs, acting was an act of revelation; it let her see light after many years of sorrow and darkness. The experience of light she felt shines through in many of her film parts. As a film director she showed great interest in the feminist cause and giving voice to the repressed woman. She did this with a style that can be described as both clever and conscious.

FILMOGRAPHY

Actor

1941: *Lasse-Maja*. 1942: *Doktor Glas*.[1] 1943: *Jag dräpte* [I slew]. 1944: *Hets/Torment*; *Prins Gustaf*. 1946: *Iris och löjtnantshjärta* [Iris and the lieutenant]; *Driver dagg, faller regn/Sunshine Follows Rain*. 1947: *Frieda*. 1948: *Musik i mörker/The Night Is My Future*, a.k.a. *Music in Darkness*; *Nu börjar livet* [Now life starts]; *Quartet*; *Portrait of Life/The Girl in the Painting*. 1949: *The Bad Lord Byron*; *The Lost People*. 1950: *The Romantic Age/Naughty Arlette*. 1951: *Blackmailed*; *Hell in Soldout*. 1952: *Tall Headlines/The Frightened Bride*. 1953: *The Ringer*; *Desperate Moment*. 1954: *Knock on Wood*; *Dance Little Lady*. 1955: *A Price of Gold*; *Sail with the Tide* (TVM). 1956: *Ett dockhem/Of Love and Lust* [A doll's house]. 1957: *Seven Waves Away: All in the Family* (TVM). 1958: *The Truth about Women*; *Lek på regnbågen* [Playing on the rainbow]. 1959: *Jet Storm*. 1960: *Faces in the Dark*; *Piccadilly Third Stop*. 1961: *Offbeat*. 1962: *Only Two Can Play*; *The Main Attraction*; *The Master Builder* (TVM). 1963: *The Bay of St. Michel/Patterns of Plunder*; *The Man Who Finally Died*. 1965: *Lianbron* [The bridge of vines]. 1975: *Mon coeur est rouge*. 1978: *Stulet nyår* [Stolen new year] (TVM, short). 1990: *Hidden Agenda*; *Witches*. 1993: *Morfars resa* [Grandpa's voyage].

Episodes in Series

The Invisible Man (1959); *Danger Man* (1962); *Eleventh Hour* (1963).

Director, Scriptwriter

1960: *The Polite Invasion* (TV docu.). 1961: *Lords of Little Egypt* (TV docu.). 1962: *The Prosperity Race* (TV docu.). 1963: *The Do-It-Yourself Democracy* (TV docu.); *The War Game* (short). 1964: *Älskande par/Loving Couples*. 1966: *Nattlek/Night Games*. 1968: *Doktor Glas/Doctor Glas*; *Flickorna/The Girls*. 1971: *Vincent the Dutchman*. 1973: *The Strongest* (episode in *Eight Visions*). 1976: *Vi har många namn/We Have Many Faces* (TVM, also actor). 1977: *Månen är en grön ost* [The moon is a green cheese] (short). 1978: *Of Seals and Men* (docu.). 1979: *Mai Zetterling's Stockholm* (short). 1981: *Love* (one episode). 1982: *Scrubbers*. 1986: *Amorosa*. 1990: *Sunday Pursuit* (short).

BIBLIOGRAPHY

Björkman, 1977.
Forslund, 1995.
Holm, 1947.
Koskinen, Maaret. "Syskonsjälar. Mai Zetterling och Agnes von Krusenstjerna." *Chaplin*, no. 203 (1986):62–65.
Zetterling, Mai. *All Those Tomorrows*. London: Jonathan Cape, 1985.

AWARD

Venice 1947: Best Actress (*Iris and the Lieutenant*)

NOTE

1. Role cut out before premiere.

FILMS

ÄNGLAGÅRD/HOUSE OF ANGELS. This film is about a young woman named Fanny who becomes, to her surprise, the sole heir of a farm, Änglagård, when her maternal grandfather, a man she does not know, dies as a result of a strange accident. Until this point Fanny has made her living as a low-class cabaret artist, working on the continent with a vague, mysterious leather-clad man named Zac. Their sudden appearance in the village for the grandfather's funeral sends shock waves through the congregation, putting the village's low tolerance level for outsiders to a severe test. Many of them react with distaste and try to get rid of the odd, and in their eyes, unsuitable couple. The tensions are made explicit when Fanny and Zac invite some friends from the city. A couple of hostile village youngsters even try to set fire to the farm. In the end, though, Fanny and the villagers arrive at a truce, especially when one of the large estate owners discovers that he might be her real father. When Fanny, in the end, returns to the continent, she and the estate owner reconcile, with her promise to sell the timber on her farm to him.

This film was a big success with both the critics and the audience, which was rather surprising, as it had been made in obscurity and without a big marketing campaign before its release. It touched the inner feelings of the audience; it is reported that it was hailed by standing ovations in some cinemas. It is not hard to see why. The cinematography is beautiful, reminding one of earlier Swedish pastoral films and demonstrating that the pastoral still triggers deep emotions in contemporary Sweden. It resembles the classic *Hon dansade en sommar/One Summer of Happiness* where, like Göran, Fanny first feels ill at ease but then gradually feels that she belongs when she learns more about her real roots in the village, symbolized by the farm. And although she leaves the farm in the end, she knows that it is a place on earth she can always return to. The essential message of the film is that the traditional ideas of the countryside and a rural home are far from dead, no matter how internationalized and urbanized we pretend to be. The film is perhaps ultimately a fable about the Swedish people's home in relation to a larger Europe. It suggests that it might be possible to belong to one's native district in Sweden and the larger world at the same time. Paradise is not lost; it can, in fact, be regained over and over again.

CREW

Director and Script: *Colin Nutley. Cinematographer: Jens Fischer. Sound: Lasse Liljeholm, Eddie Axberg. Music: Björn Isfält. Art Director: Ulla Herdin. Wardrobe: Sven Lundén. Editor: Perry Schaffer. Producer: Memfis Film & Television, Sveriges Television (Göteborg), Svenska Filminstitutet, Danmarks Radio, Norsk Rikskringkasting.

CAST

*Helena Bergström (Fanny), Rikard Wolff (Zac), *Sven Wollter (Axel Flogfält), *Viveka Seldahl (Rut, his wife), Jakob Eklund (Mårten, their son), Ernst Günther (Gottfried), Tord Peterson (Ivar), *Per Oscarsson (Fanny's grandfather), Reine Brynolfsson (Flemming, parson), Ing-Marie Carlsson (Eva Ågren), Jan Mybrand (Per-Ove Ågren), Peter Andersson (Ragnar Zetterberg).

PREMIERE

Swedish: 21 Feb. 1991

New York: 6 Aug. 1993

BIBLIOGRAPHY

Fredriksson, Helena, David Häggmark, and Sara Larsson. "Nomader i hembygden." *Filmhäftet*, no. 85 (1994):29–38.

ÄPPELKRIGET **[THE APPLE WAR].** This film follows the theme "paradise threatened and restored." It is a variation on the common, old Swedish film theme complete with the pastoral setting. The film is set in the southwest part of the southern province of Skåne. A German capitalist with the striking name Volkswagner plans to build a huge recreation park, "Deutschneyland," in the midst of the loveliest of all landscapes. He is supported by some of the local businessmen and a crooked politician. The people living on or near this pastoral land are against the plan. A young boy is discovered to have supernatural powers and is able to contact various subterranean beings who inhabit the land. He wakens a huge giant, and they, together with the fairies and a few others, stop the threat. The film ends in a pastoral setting with all the "good people" gathered together on a green field, celebrating their victory.

Despite an utterly simple story line, style, and direction, this modern fairy tale was immensely popular with both the audience and the film critics. While the popularity of the production team of *Hans Alfredson and *Tage Danielsson contributed to the film's success, the main reason was the perfect timing of the film. The film's release coincided with the growing concern with environmental issues. The destruction of the cities during the "Record Years" (also the title of a critical 1969 documentary feature) of the 1960s had awakened people to the fact that irreplaceable values were at stake. This was most profoundly symbolized when, in the spring of 1971, protesters in Stockholm stopped the cutting of a few elms that were to be removed for a subway entrance. In the same year the farmers' cooperative movement newspaper coined the expression "the green wave" to describe the movement of people leaving the big cities to settle in the countryside. While, in reality, there were not many in the green wave, the associated protest had great symbolic value. Both the elm protest and the green wave led to changes in official environmental policies. Just five years later the Center Party (the former Farmer's League Party) did very well on a platform promising, among other things, a halt to the building of new nuclear power plants.

Although *Äppelkriget* was hardly an important contribution to Swedish film art, it has become a minor classic, even being honored with a postage stamp in the centennial year of film in 1995. It is heavily dependent on the usual pastoral tradition of Swedish film, with all the traditional symbols and icons. The cinematography is, as usual, beautifully breathtaking. "National poet" Evert Taube wrote the musical theme and the title song, "Änglamark" [Ground of angels], which was also hugely popular. "Änglamark" is today a brand name for a series of ecological products. Taube is among the people in the last sequence of the film.

CREW

Director: Tage Danielsson. Script: Hans Alfredson, Tage Danielsson. Cinematographer: Lars Svanberg. Sound: Christer Furubrand. Music: Evert Taube. Art Director: Ulf Axén. Wardrobe: Inger Pehrsson. Editor: Wic' Kjellin, Mikael Holéwa. Producer: Svenska Ord, Svensk Filmindustri.

CAST

Per Grundén (Jean Volkswagner), *Gösta Ekman [Jr.] (Sten Wall), Per Waldvik (Hans Nilsson), Yvonne Lombard (Kerstin Gustafsson), Monica Zetterlund (Anna), Håkan Serner (Eberhard), Hans Alfredson (Severin), Birgitta Andersson (Luft-Hanna), Martin Ljung, *Max von Sydow, Tage Danielsson (Anna's cousins).

PREMIERE

Swedish: 18 Dec. 1971

BIBLIOGRAPHY

Löthwall, Lars-Olof. "Allvarligt samtal med humorister." *Chaplin*, no. 111 (1971):295–296. Interview.
Nilsson, Björn. "Äppelkriget." *Chaplin*, no. 112 (1972):32. Review.

ÅSA-NISSE. Every film-producing country has a more or less burlesque sort of film that is so tied to local culture that it is incomprehensible to foreign viewers.

The *Åsa-Nisse* film series belongs to this genre; it is considered low culture and is flogged mercilessly by the critics. The series is based on the character Åsa-Nisse, a kind of Swedish hillbilly character. A total of twenty films were produced between 1949 and 1969. The first two films were met by the critics with some tolerance; the rest were slaughtered, sometimes with only a few lines. One classic review consisted of just three words: "Go in peace!" The criticism is deserved; the films are badly directed, and the acting is exaggerated. The effect of their shoestring production budgets is always visible. Yet despite what the critics said, more than 1 million Swedes annually chose to watch these films in the 1950s. When the films were shown in small cinemas in remote areas, they were almost the cinema event of the year. The films are still frequently shown on the various television channels. While not without significance in Swedish film history, the *Åsa-Nisse* series is mainly a sociological phenomenon.

The beginning of the series coincided with the heyday of the Swedish postwar rural film. This was a time of turbulent change in Swedish society. The migration from the country to the city was at its peak. The modernization of everyday life resulted in drastic changes to physical living conditions with profound psychic consequences. Many people felt that they did not fully belong to the new society; they experienced a kind of alienation in the midst of the welfare. While it was of course impossible to reverse these changes, the dreams of an old agrarian society became all the more marketable.

The makers of the *Åsa-Nisse* films chose a middle point between modernity and the past. The main, good characters are certainly from the countryside, whereas the people from the city are usually associated with being overly smart, criminal, and so on. Not all new and modern things are bad, however. Åsa-Nisse himself is an inventive person, always interested in all kinds of mechanical devices, automobiles, and the like. There are also always sympathetic characters from the world of modern society and the big city. While the films might ridicule certain aspects of modern living and thinking, they also bridge the cultural gulf between the traditional and the new.

In the 1960s the films changed, reflecting Swedes' adjustment to the new, modern reality. The pastoral nostalgia that was almost obligatory in the first films gradually disappeared, and only the farcical elements remained. The films became more and more mechanical. The sense of repetition coupled with the general decline of the film market (and the death of so many small cinema theaters) probably contributed to the series' end. The producers tried to compensate by incorporating popular artists from the youth culture in the plot, but this did not help in the long run. Finally, popular actors John Elfström and Artur Rolén, who always played the main characters, grew older and older. When they were replaced in the very last film of the series, it proved to be a total disaster.

FILMOGRAPHY

1949: *Åsa-Nisse*. 1950: *Åsa-Nisse på jaktstigen* [ÅN out hunting]. 1952: *Åsa-Nisse på nya äventyr* [ÅN on new adventures]. 1953: *Åsa-Nisse på semester* [ÅN on holiday].

1954: *Åsa-Nisse på hal is* [ÅN on thin ice]. 1955: *Åsa-Nisse ordnar allt* [ÅN fixes everything]. 1956: *Åsa-Nisse flyger i luften* [ÅN blows up]. 1957: *Åsa-Nisse i full fart* [ÅN at full speed]. 1958: *Åsa-Nisse i kronans kläder* [ÅN in army uniform]. 1959: *Åsa-Nisse jubilerar* [ÅN celebrates]. 1960: *Åsa-Nisse som polis* [ÅN as a policeman]. 1961: *Åsa-Nisse bland grevar och baroner* [ÅN among counts and barons]. 1962: *Åsa-Nisse på Mallorca* [ÅN on Majorca]. 1963: *Åsa-Nisse och tjocka släkten* [ÅN and close relatives]. 1964: *Åsa-Nisse i popform* [ÅN in pop form]. 1965: *Åsa-Nisse slår till* [ÅN strikes again]. 1966: *Åsa-Nisse i raketform* [ÅN in outer space]. 1967: *Åsa-Nisse i agentform* [ÅN secret agent]. 1968: *Åsa-Nisse och den stora kalabaliken* [ÅN and the big tumult]. 1969: *Åsa-Nisse i rekordform* [ÅN breaks all records].

BIBLIOGRAPHY

Nordberg, Carl-Eric. "Noter kring Åsa-Nisse." *Vår lösen*, no. 8 (1971):495–503.

DRIVER DAGG, FALLER REGN/SUNSHINE FOLLOWS RAIN. This film was one of the most successful films of the 1940s. It was the rural melodrama that set the pace for the whole genre in postwar Swedish cinema. It was probably seen by between 2 and 3 million viewers in its time, an amazing figure for a small country like Sweden. It was based on a prize-winning 1943 novel by teacher Margit Söderholm, and Svensk Filmindustri was, from the beginning, interested in bringing it to the screen. Despite managing director Carl-Anders Dymling's doubts over its "light" content, veteran director *Gustaf Edgren was eventually allowed to direct the film.

The plot is rather conventional, originating in large part from rural, European storytelling traditions. Some of the stories of the same genre that precede it are Gottfried Keller's classic *Romeo und Julia auf dem Dorfe* and Sweden's own national play *Värmlänningarna* [The people of Värmland]. In the story a farmer's daughter, Marit, falls in love with fiddler and half gypsy Jon. Her father opposes their relationship and tries to force her to marry another young man, Mats, a farmer's son and the inheritor of a neighboring farm. On the eve of the wedding Marit flees to join Jon. They spend a summer in the woods, but when winter comes, they are forced to return to the village. The story has a happy ending, however. It so happens that Jon is also an inheritor of a farm—his mother was in fact the woman that Marit's father was once to have married but who also escaped with a gypsy. Marit's father eventually gives his blessing to Marit and Jon's union. This story line is typically Swedish, a happy fusion between love, faith in the traditions of one's forefathers, and such tangible things as the soil. The heritage of the Swedish forefathers is, of course, a cornerstone of the whole agrarian ideology.

The Swedish title alludes to a medieval ballad. The ballad is about the love between a knight and fairy, and it ends unhappily. It counterpoints the action in the film, giving a romantic flavor rife with folkloric content. The symbolism includes the use of such old standards as waterfalls and running water. These are sometimes given mythical dimensions when serving as a testing ground for the hero, who needs to overcome the hazards of the rapids to show his mastery.

As usual for this genre, there are many beautiful nature scenes. All of this contributed to the film's success. It is still a popular afternoon rerun on television.

CREW

Director: Gustaf Edgren. Script: Gustaf Edgren, Gardar Sahlberg, Oscar Rydqvist, after a novel by Margit Söderholm. Cinematographer: Martin Bodin. Sound: Sven Hansen. Art Director: Arne Åkermark. Editor: Tage Holmberg. Producer: Svensk Filmindustri.

CAST

*Alf Kjellin (Jon), *Mai Zetterling (Marit), Sten Lindgren (Germund, her father), Anna Lindahl (Elin), *Hilda Borgström (Kerstin), Ulf Palme (Mats), Hugo Hasslo (Knut), Inga Landgré (Barbro).

PREMIERE

Swedish: 26 Dec. 1946

New York: 28 Sept. 1949

EROTIKON/JUST LIKE A MAN. This is an elegant story about an old, absentminded professor, living with his young, sweet niece, and a young, unattended wife who is being pursued by admirers. The niece shares her uncle's passion for insects, and based on their friendship, she is the one who resolves all the misunderstandings in the family. Finally, when the professor's wife abandons him, the niece consoles him with his favorite dish.

The plot, based on a play by Hungarian Ferenc Herczeg, at the time a popular author, is thin and insignificant. The film is most interesting for its direction, the mise-en-scène for which *Mauritz Stiller was provided resources to make an extravagant, spirited comedy. The Royal Opera House was used for filming one of the seduction scenes. *Erotikon* is also filled with icons and symbols for the new modernity; one of the admirers is an airman, at the time a new and sensational profession.

It has been claimed, not without controversy, that this film inspired another director of "cynical comedies," Ernst Lubitsch. In fact, Lubitsch had already directed such films in the 1910s and had showed his mastery of the genre. At the same time, Stiller also worked in this style in such films as *Kärlek och journalistik/Love and Journalism* and the two films about Thomas Graal. *Erotikon* was just the perfection of his style. In any case, the film was very successful on the international market. This might, in the long run, have proven fateful for the Swedish film industry. When Svensk Filmindustri later continued to aim at the international market without Stiller, the results were rather disappointing.

CREW

Director: Mauritz Stiller. Script: Mauritz Stiller, Arthur Nordén, after the play *A Kék róka* by Ferenc Herczeg. Cinematography: Henrik Jaenzon. Art Director: Axel Esbensen. Wardrobe: Carl Gille. Choreography: Carina Ari. Producer: Svensk Filmindustri.

CAST

Anders de Wahl (Leo Carpentier, professor), Tora Teje (Irene, his wife), Karin Molander (Marthe, his niece), Elin Lagegren (Irene's mother), *Lars Hanson (Preben Wells, sculptor), Vilhelm Bryde (Felix, baronet), Bell Hedqvist (his girlfriend), Torsten Hammarén (Sidonius, professor), Vilhelm Berndtson (Jean), Stina Berg (faithful old servant).

PREMIERE

Swedish: 8 Nov. 1920

FÄNGELSE/THE DEVIL'S WANTON, a.k.a. *PRISON.* An old man, Paul, walks into a film studio. Paul is a teacher who has been admitted from a mental asylum and presents Martin, a young director who once was his pupil, with a film idea he wants him to realize. The film will be about earth as hell and the devil's final triumph, but no one will be aware of this. Martin is skeptical. Then the perspective changes to a parallel story about Martin's friend, the author Thomas, who has a stormy marriage. Thomas talks about a streetwalker, Birgitta-Carolina, he has met. He became interested in her and wanted to write about her. Later he has a discussion with his wife about the meaninglessness of life. Thomas suggests to his wife they commit joint suicide, but she hits him on the head. When he wakes up, he thinks he has killed her, but this is, in fact, not true. Now homeless, Thomas meets Birgitta-Carolina again, and together they move into a lodging house. Later they sit together in the attic and watch an old silent farce about Death scaring people. She tells him about a dream about a "human forest" she has experienced. Birgitta-Carolina leaves Thomas and returns to her pimp, Peter, with whom she had a newborn child that Peter and Birgitta-Carolina's sister had killed. Birgitta-Carolina is brutally tortured with a burning cigarette by one of Peter's friends, and she commits suicide in the basement. The perspective switches back to the film studio where Martin is discussing the original idea with Paul. The director says that the whole idea is impossible. Thomas is now reconciled with his wife.

It is hard to encapsulate the complex plot line of this film. It is a film about a film about which it was said that it could not be made, but that feat has actually been realized, for we spectators are able to see it right in front of us. The title *Fängelse* [Prison] not only alludes to a pessimistic view of life but also mirrors the complexity of the narrative. One story—the old teacher in the film studio—encloses another story—Thomas and his life—which encloses yet a third story—the symbolic dream of Birgitta-Carolina—like a series of Chinese boxes.

This film, in part a rather black comedy, was the first film in which *Ingmar Bergman could independently pursue his own ideas. His first film, *Kris* [Crisis], had been a disaster; but with the aid of producer *Lorens Marmstedt, Bergman managed to stay on. When Bergman suggested the film, Marmstedt was convinced that this would not be a film with a big audience. He let Bergman make it on the condition that it be made on a shoestring budget. One can say that Bergman developed most of his thematic world in this early, overlooked film. It deals with themes of a nonexisting God and existence on earth. That life itself—here described as a span between birth and death—is important. The mood of this film strongly resembles such later films as *Det sjunde inseglet/The Seventh Seal*.

It has been said that Bergman actually wanted to be an acknowledged writer or at least be accepted by the literary elite. This film is in its style and content rather close to the literary school of Sweden's so-called 40-talisterna (The Fortyiers), a modernist and experimental tendency with a preference for the symbolic. The influence of French existentialism, which found fertile ground in Swedish cultural life, can also be seen in the film, although Bergman was skeptical of existential philosophy taken as a whole. On the surface, *Fängelse* expresses a pessimistic view—the devil really rules the world. Upon further scrutiny, it is also possible to see a dimension of hope in it. Thomas and his wife do in the end realize that love and togetherness are what matters most. Birgitta-Carolina's suicide is depicted so that it is possible to see a ray of hope glimmering in the midst of the darkness. Her tragedy lies in the fact that she is forced to deny her real love for Thomas.

Fängelse can, together with *Törst/Three Strange Loves*, be viewed as a farewell, a temporary one at least, to the pessimism of the 1940s. After these films, Bergman returned to more earthly matters, to his "rose" period, with the so-called summer films.

CREW

Director and Script: Ingmar Bergman. Cinematographer: Göran Strindberg. Sound: Olle Jakobsson. Music: Erland von Koch. Art Director: P. A. Lundgren. Editor: Lennart Wallén. Producer: Lorens Marmstedt/Terraproduktion.

CAST

Doris Svedlund (Birgitta-Carolina Söderberg), *Birger Malmsten (Thomas), Eva Henning (Sofi, his wife), *Hasse Ekman (Martin Grandé, film director), Stig Olin (Peter, Birgitta-Carolina's "fiancé"), Irma Christenson (Linnéa, Birgitta-Carolina's sister), *Anders Henrikson (Paul), Marianne Löfgren (Signe Bolin, hostess), Anita Blom (Anna, Signe's cousin's daughter),[1] Arne Ragneborn (Anna's fiancé), Curt Masreliez (Alf, Peter's friend), Birgit Lindqvist (a guest at the lodging house), Kenne Fant (Arne, actor), Inger Juel (Greta, actress).

PREMIERE

Swedish: 19 Mar. 1949

New York: 4 July 1962

BIBLIOGRAPHY

Qvist, Per Olov. "Dömda till frihet." *Filmhäftet*, no. 62 (1983):11–25.
See also Birgitta Steene, 1987, under Ingmar Bergman.

NOTE

1. This role has been wrongly attributed to Birgit Lindqvist in all existing Bergman filmographies so far. Lindqvist, however, has another small part in the film.

FANNY OCH ALEXANDER/FANNY AND ALEXANDER. The story centers around two children living with their family in a residential town. Their father is an actor, and they have a busy social life, involving many relatives. The father dies, and when their mother marries the bishop, things change completely for the children. The contrast between the gaiety of their old home and the coldness of their new one is striking and frightening. The bishop is very stern and unjustly punishes Alexander very severely for lying. The children are later rescued from the grips of the bishop by an antique dealer and are brought back to a more normal life. At the end, the family is gathered together again to celebrate the birth of two new children to their big family.

This was *Ingmar Bergman's triumphant return to Swedish cinema, after leaving for Germany in 1976 when he had been accused, but was later acquitted, of tax evasion. When he left Sweden he had almost sworn that he would never work in his native country again. When he returned he decided to make a cinematic testament of his native land. *Fanny och Alexander* is partly an autobiographical account, with events and persons taken from his childhood. The magnificent apartment is similar to one situated in Uppsala, where his grandmother lived. The bishop might have some of Bergman's father's traits, but as always with Bergman, one can never be sure. In his autobiography *The Magic Lantern*, he describes how he was punished by his father; this might also be pure fantasy if his siblings' version of events is correct. Whether true or not, the main thing is that it is faithful to the fantasies of the film's audience.

The film sums up many of the themes and motifs of Bergman's earlier works. It shows his love for the theater and how with the help of the theater he can create dreams and fantasies. On several occasions the film pays homage to Strindberg's play *Ett drömspel* [A dream play] with its blend of fiction and reality. The theme in both this play and Bergman's film is that there is no real difference between the two. This is evident in the antique shop scenes, where the children wait after their escape from the bishop's house.

Another important element in the film is its celebration of life. Bergman has often struggled with such eternal questions as the meaning of life and the fear of death. He resolves these questions by pointing out that meaning is rendered by our activities, especially life in community with others and the recurrence of life when a new human being is born. Nature also plays a part as a source of strength. In this regard Bergman is deeply rooted in the traditions of Nordic filmmaking.

CREW

Director and Script: Ingmar Bergman. Cinematographer: Sven Nykvist. Sound: Owe Svensson. Art Director: Anna Asp. Wardrobe: Kristina Markoff. Editor: Sylvia Ingmarsson. Producer: Jörn Donner for Cinematograph, Svenska Filminstitutet, Sveriges Television, Gaumont, Personafilm, Tobis Film.

CAST

Gunn Wållgren (Helena Ekdahl), *Allan Edwall (Oscar Ekdahl), *Ewa Fröling (Emilie Ekdahl), Bertil Guve (Alexander), Pernilla Allwin (Fanny), *Börje Ahlstedt (Carl), *Christina Schollin (Lydia), *Jarl Kulle (Gustaf Adolf), Mona Malm (Alma), *Pernilla Wallgren [-August] (Maj), *Erland Josephson (Isak Jacobi), Mats Bergman (Aron), Stina Ekblad (Ismael), *Jan Malmsjö (Edvard Vergerus), Kerstin Tidelius (Henrietta Vergerus), Marianne Aminoff (Blenda Vergerus), *Harriet Andersson (Justina), *Lena Olin (Rosa), *Gunnar Björnstrand (Landahl).

PREMIERE

Swedish: 17 Dec. 1982; longer (5-hour) version, 17 Dec. 1983; TV, 25 Dec. 1984

New York: 16 June 1983

BIBLIOGRAPHY

Corliss, Richard, and William Wolf. "God, Sex and Ingmar Bergman." *Film Comment* 19, no. 3 (May–June 1983):13–17.
Koskinen, Maaret. "Teatern som metafor." *Chaplin*, no. 189 (1983):260–263.
Marker, Lise-Lone, and Fredrik J. Marker. "The Making of Fanny and Alexander." *Films and Filming* (Feb. 1983):4–9.
McLean, Theodore. "Knocking on Heaven's Door." *American Film* 8, no. 8 (June 1983): 55–61.
Quart, Barbara, and Leonard Quart. "Fanny and Alexander." *Film Quarterly* 37, no. 1 (Fall 1983):22–27.
See also Birgitta Steene, 1987, under Ingmar Bergman.

AWARDS

AA 1984: Best Foreign Film, Photography, Art Direction, Costumes

AAN 1984: Best Direction, Script

FLICKA OCH HYACINTER [Girl with hyacinths]. A young and lonely woman, Dagmar Brink, commits suicide. She apparently had no relatives or friends. In a farewell note, she gives away her few belongings to her neighbors, an author and his wife. They are puzzled by her fate and begin to investigate her life. They collect clues and encounter people she had relationships with. These include: an alcoholic painter who was once married to her and had painted a portrait of her; a popular singer with whom she had a love affair; and an officer. Finally it seems that they discover the explanation of her tragic fate, although it is not clear that they have really understood it. She once had had a love affair with a red-haired woman, Alex (whom they first thought was male). Alex had moved to France during the war and had possibly been acquainted with French collaborators. Dagmar experienced this as an act of betrayal, and when she learned about it, she hung herself, alone, in her apartment.

It is a simple story with a narrative structure à la *Citizen Kane*. This film is generally regarded as *Hasse Ekman's best. He was often accused of having no important ideas of his own, especially in comparison with young, rising star *Ingmar Bergman. These constant comparisons evidently hurt Ekman and perhaps put obstacles in his way. He was not successful when he occasionally tried to "compete" with Bergman. This film, however, was successful. Ekman created a mood and atmosphere that are extraordinary, and above all, he elicited very fine performances from his actors. Anders Ek is brilliant as the painter who constantly oscillates between self-pity and aggressiveness. The painter is the genius who painted Dagmar's portrait, "Girl and Hyacinths," but who is drowning his talent in liquor.

Ekman has often depicted loneliness and lonely people in the midst of Swedish society, the only solution to which is togetherness. Unfortunately and all too often, people discover this truth when it is already too late. Ekman's portrayal of this phenomenon gives his films a sense of sentimental, bittersweet beauty. This is certainly true of both *Flicka och hyacinter* and another of his best films, *Ombyte av tåg* [Changing trains].

CREW

Director: Hasse Ekman. Script: Hasse Ekman. Cinematographer: Göran Strindberg. Sound: Olle Jakobsson. Music: Erland von Koch. Art Director: Bibi Lindström. Editor: Wic' Kjellin. Executive Producer: Lorens Marmstedt. Producer: Terraproduktion.

CAST

Eva Henning (Dagmar Brink), Ulf Palme (Anders Wikner, author), *Birgit Tengroth (Britt, his wife), Anders Ek (Elias Körner, artist), Marianne Löfgren (Gullan Wiklund), Gösta Cederlund (von Lieve, banker), Karl-Arne Holmsten (Willy Borge, singer), *Keve Hjelm (Stefan Brink, captain), Anne-Marie Brunius ("Alex"), Björn Berglund (Lövgren, police superintendent).

PREMIERE

Swedish: 6 Mar. 1950

HÄR HAR DU DITT LIV/HERE'S YOUR LIFE. The story starts in 1914 with fourteen-year-old Olof leaving his foster home to begin a journey through early twentieth-century northern Sweden. Olof finds various jobs, in a log-driving operation, in a brickworks, at a sawmill, and eventually in a cinema. There he meets the anarchist Fredrik, who makes him politically conscious, and the daughter of a blacksmith, with whom he has his first sexual experience. At the cinema Olof begins to distribute socialist newspapers, and when the cinema owner demands that Olof stop this, he quits his employment and takes a job with the railroad. There, together with a comrade, he begins to organize the workers, but when they try to make the workers strike, they are dismissed. At the end of the film, in 1918, Olof is on the road again, this time to the south of Sweden.

This three-hour-long epic is based on the autobiographical writings of Eyvind Johnson, later honored with the Nobel Prize in literature. It is a broad panorama of living conditions in northern Sweden during World War I. It reflects change, especially with the growing labor movement. It concentrates on the fate of a young man in his transition years from youth to manhood, to mirror the society as a whole. The final farewell scene where Olof heads south hints at a prosperous future in a land governed by the labor movement. The film is told in the typical style of *Jan Troell with pictures both lyrical and filled with meaning. As a debut, it was extraordinary.

The production was a bold venture, and producer Bengt Forslund claims that it was helped by the new spirit of the 1963 film reform. The film's cinematic forerunner was a short, *Uppehåll i myrlandet* [Stopover in the marshland], with *Max von Sydow in the lead, based on one episode from Eyvind Johnson's novel. The short was part of Troell and Forslund's plan for a longer film based on the same material. The short's good reception helped the larger project. While the board of Svensk Filmindustri was initially uncertain if the film would be successful, it received very good reviews and did well with the audience.

CREW

Director: Jan Troell. Script: Bengt Forslund, Jan Troell. Cinematographer: Jan Troell. Sound: Leif Hansen. Music: Erik Nordgren. Art Director: Rolf Boman. Props: Karl Erik Tonemar. Wardrobe: Knut Nylén. Editor: Jan Troell. Executive Producer: Bengt Forslund. Producer: Svensk Filmindustri.

CAST

Eddie Axberg (Olof Persson), Gudrun Brost (the foster mother), Ulla Akselson (Olof's mother), Bo Wahlström (Olof's big brother), Rick Axberg (Olof's little brother), Holger Löwenadler (Kristiansson), Göran Lindberg (Olsson), Tage Sjögren (Lund), *Allan Edwall (August), Anna Maria Blind (the woman in the tale), Birger Lensander (the manager of the brickworks), Max von Sydow (Smålands-Pelle), Ulf Palme (Larsson), Jan-Erik Lindqvist (Johansson), Börje Nyberg (the manager of the sawmill), *Gunnar Björnstrand (Lundgren, cinema owner), Signe Stade (Maria), Stig Törnblom (Fredrik), Åke Fridell (Nicke Larsson, traveling projectionist), Ulla Sjöblom (Olivia), Friedrich Ochsner (the blacksmith), Catharina Edfeldt (Maja, his daughter), Ulla Blomstrand (Efresina), Bengt Ekerot (Byberg), *Per Oscarsson (Niklas).

PREMIERE

Swedish: 26 Dec. 1966

New York: 19 Dec. 1968

BIBLIOGRAPHY

Filmfacts 11 (1968): 507–508. Summary of American reviews.
Kaufmann, Stanley. *Figures of Light*. New York: Harper & Row, 1971.

HETS/TORMENT. Jan-Erik is in his final year of high school. One of his teachers is the sadistic Latin lecturer nicknamed "Caligula," who rules his classes with fear and terror. Caligula has a young mistress, Bertha, who works in a tobacconist's shop. By coincidence Jan-Erik gets to know Bertha and learns that she is under the spell of the sadistic Caligula. He eventually has an affair with her. Bertha suddenly dies from what turns out to be natural causes, and a hysterical Caligula is acquitted of wrongdoing by a police inquiry. In his sadistic anger, Caligula reports Jan-Erik's affair with Bertha to the school principal, in response to which Jan-Erik hits Caligula. Jan-Erik is expelled, and while his old classmates finish their courses and pass their exams, Jan-Erik can only watch from a distance. Jan-Erik falls out with his parents and moves away from their haute bourgeois home to settle in Bertha's apartment. The school principal visits Jan-Erik and attempts in vain to reconcile Jan-Erik with his parents. One day, sometime later, Jan-Erik finds Caligula in the stairs outside the apartment. Caligula is now a pitiful creature, begging for forgiveness. Jan-Erik ignores him and walks out into the sun. At the end of the film Jan-Erik seems at peace with himself, watching the city from above.

No film caused as much debate in its time. It was scripted by the young *Ingmar Bergman, who in part used his own school experiences to condemn an old-fashioned and authoritarian school system. There was controversy about whether Bergman had exaggerated the behavior of one of his former teachers on whom the role was apparently modeled. Bergman had in fact only known him a short while. The bigger debate dealt with the school system. The screening of the film was accompanied in almost every town by public debates involving teachers, parents, and pupils. The newspapers were filled with articles, editorials, and letters to the editors, and the teachers' association journal attacked the film vigorously.

The huge controversy indicates that the timing of the film was perfect. While the film was ostensibly about the school system and much of the debate dealt with schooling, the film is a depiction of the threats inherent to an authoritarian society. This was especially topical with the ongoing events in Sweden's southern neighbor, Germany. It must be remembered that Sweden was heavily influenced by German culture and lifestyles before World War II and that a lot of Swedes admired Germany even when the Nazi regime was in power. Bergman, too, confessed when he was older his admiration of German culture and Nazism when he visited Germany as a teenager in the early 1930s, and the film might be regarded as an attempt, by Bergman, to come to terms with this. The film can be seen as a warning against such authoritarian tendencies and reflects a break that was going on in Swedish cultural life. In the wake of the defeat of

Germany and Nazism, the cultural orientation moved toward Anglo-Saxon and especially American culture. When *Hets* appeared in late 1944, this process was already occurring. The young generation, especially, felt that it was natural to oppose the old order, and the film was for the young audience something of a liberation symbol. In box office terms it was one of the most successful of the decade. With the shift in Sweden's cultural orientation the film also forebodes the disintegration of the patriarchal order around which Swedish society had been built until that time. With these cracks the notion of the "people's home" was also being eroded.

The film is packed with symbolic details that emphasize these changes in Swedish society. *Alf Sjöberg directed the film in his usual stylized, partly expressionistic manner, which heavily underlines the atmosphere of fear and the uneasiness of the school. The set of Jan-Erik's home is filled with symbols of rigid conservatism and closeness. Caligula is played by actor Stig Järrel, who often had been typecast in previous films in rather odd and sometimes psychotic character roles. The Caligula character was directly linked to Nazism—or at the very least, extreme right-wing conservatism—when he is seen reading the infamous *Dagsposten*, a newspaper identified with these views.

CREW

Director: Alf Sjöberg. Script: Ingmar Bergman. Cinematographer: Martin Bodin. Sound: Gaston Cornelius. Art Director: Arne Åkermark. Editor: Oscar Rosander. Producer: Svensk Filmindustri.

CAST

Stig Järrel (Caligula), *Alf Kjellin (Jan-Erik), *Mai Zetterling (Bertha), Olof Winnerstrand (the principal), Gösta Cederlund (Pippi, teacher), Stig Olin (Sandeman), Jan Molander (Pettersson), Olav Riégo (Jan-Erik's father), Märta Arbin (Jan-Erik's mother), *Gunnar Björnstrand, Richard Lund (teachers).

PREMIERE

Swedish: 2 Oct. 1944

New York: 21 Apr. 1947

BIBLIOGRAPHY

See Birgitta Steene, 1987, under Ingmar Bergman.

AWARD

Cannes Grand Prix 1946

HIMLASPELET/THE HEAVENLY PLAY. This film is set in seventeenth-century Dalarna (Dalecarlia). In this lovely landscape young Mats and his fiancée Marit dream of their future as farmers when Mats will take over his father's farm. The whole situation changes suddenly and dramatically when Marit is charged with sorcery and burned at the stake. Mats embarks on a long, convoluted journey to heaven to reverse these unjust events, and he eventually meets the Lord himself, an ordinary, friendly old man. At the conclusion Mats returns to his father's house, where Marit is waiting for him.

This very simple fantasy of heaven and hell has had many predecessors. These included such writers as John Bunyan and others who have described the religious experience as a voyage. This film is a very solid depiction of this genre; its style is taken from a special type of naive folkloric painting that is typical of the Dalarna region of Sweden. Dalarna was the main inspiration ground for the turn-of-the-century romanticism of Swedish art and literature and inspired the first great film works of the late 1910s based on the writings of Selma Lagerlöf. It is not difficult to understand why this particular area inspired Swedish romantics. It was a province of small, free farmers living in a pastoral landscape, maintaining their traditions into the early twentieth century. It was the perfect breeding ground for the peasant idealization that was at the core of the same Swedish romanticism. Many of the same generalizations can be made of the neighboring province Hälsingland, the setting for a later smash hit of the same rural, romantic genre, *Driver dagg, faller regn/Sunshine Follows Rain*.

Himlaspelet was written and filmed during the darkest years of the early 1940s when the Nazi threat seemed invincible, and Sweden was making many concessions to the mighty German power now surrounding it. This agrarian fantasy can be seen as an act of mental resistance to this threat. One can perhaps understand the depiction of the behavior of the villagers participating in the burning of Marit as a critique of the Swedish concession policy. Another contemporary film set in the agrarian past, *Rid i natt!* [Ride this night!], following a novel and play by Vilhelm Moberg, expresses a similar theme. In *Himlaspelet*, Mats does for a while fall victim to the spirit of the times when he cheats a blind man of a copper ore to start a prosperous business. He becomes a rich and hard old man whose soul seems lost in the dark shadows; but, in a final gesture of grace, his eyes are reopened, and he is redeemed of his sins. He is reborn into his youth and returns to his home, where Marit is now waiting for him outside.

Writer Rune Lindström, who also acted in the lead as Mats, was then a young theologian. He then became one of the more prolific scriptwriters of 1940s and 1950s Swedish film. The theme of "paradise lost and regained" recurs in most of his writing. At the end of *Himlaspelet* we see a restored paradise in accordance with the agrarian romanticism typical of Lindström. The script *Människors rike* [Realm of man], although set in a contemporary milieu, is one typical example. The conclusion of *Himlaspelet* is one of the more beautiful and memorable in Swedish film history; Mats stands outside his farm with Marit and says, "You God, I am home at last."

CREW

Director: *Alf Sjöberg. Script: Rune Lindström, Alf Sjöberg, from a play by Rune Lindström. Cinematographer: Gösta Roosling. Sound: Per-Olof Pettersson. Art Director: Arne Åkermark. Editor: Oscar Rosander. Producer: Wive Film.

CAST

Rune Lindström (Mats), Eivor Landström (Marit), *Anders Henrikson (Godfather), Holger Löwenadler (King Solomon), Gudrun Brost (his girl), Emil Fjellström (Old Jerk, the devil), Arnold Sjöstrand (Juvas Anders, the painter), Gunnar Sjöberg (the angel), Björn Berglund (Josef), Inga-Lilly Forsström (Mary), Hugo Björne (Jonah), Nils Gustafsson (the blind man), *Anita Björk (Anna).

PREMIERE

Swedish: 21 Dec. 1942

New York: 8 Oct. 1944

BIBLIOGRAPHY

Laura, David J de. "Road to Heaven." In *Film Notes of Wisconsin Film Society*, ed. A. Lennig. Madison: Wisconsin Film Society, 1960.

HON DANSADE EN SOMMAR/ONE SUMMER OF HAPPINESS. This film depicts how Göran, who has just graduated, spends his summer holiday out in the country. In the beginning he is hesitant to stay on his uncle's farm, but when he meets the young and innocent Kerstin, he changes his mind. He gradually starts to love life in the countryside. He becomes involved in a local youth club where, among other things, there are some theater activities. When the summer is over Göran returns to the city only to abandon his studies at the technical school and go back to the countryside that now fills his imagination. He reunites with Kerstin, who has been sent away from the village by her stern and religiously minded foster parents to protect her from Göran. Their meeting is the most famous nude swimming scene in Swedish film, which, hinting at their subsequent sexual intercourse on the shore, becomes a metaphor for Göran's complete assimilation into the countryside, the natural paradise of his dreams. In the youth club they successfully perform the leading parts of the old national play *Värmlänningarna* [The people of Värmland], and their lives seem complete. On the way home, though, Göran's motorcycle is knocked off the road, and Kerstin is killed. The film concludes with her funeral, which is also the starting point of the film.

This is perhaps Sweden's most widely seen film ever. Besides being a hit in Sweden, it was very successful all over the world, sometimes for different reasons in different countries. In many places it was appreciated for being erotically liberated. In East Germany it received official approval as antireligious propaganda. Whatever the reasons for the initial interest, its main attraction seems to have been its portrayal of a natural paradise in the summer light of the far north. The film is about a lost paradise; its narrative form and structure, in which the action is related as a flashback with a peculiar ending, give it a paradoxical hope. The film hovers between the real and surreal when, at the funeral, we see Göran running down to the shore to sit on the jetty and look out into the reeds (which conjure the earlier nude swim). He suddenly hears Kerstin's voice inside him, begging him never to forget her. Kerstin still seems to be alive; the lost paradise seems to go on.

Especially with the funeral, the film can also be interpreted as a mourning ceremony for the Swedish countryside whose old form was rapidly vanishing in the postwar years; the old peasant society was dying, just as Kerstin did. The paradoxical ending assures the viewer, though, that everything will live on, if only in the collective memory of the society. All this was underlined by Göran Strindberg's cinematography. The breathtaking visual language of the film successfully captures the magic spell of a bright summer night and the pastoral landscape. This has made the film a true classic in contemporary Swedish cinema that can still engage new generations of viewers.

CREW

Director: *Arne Mattsson. Script: Volodja Semitjov, Olle Hellbom, from the novel *Sommardansen* by Per Olof Ekström. Cinematographer: Göran Strindberg. Sound: Olle Jakobsson. Music: Sven Sköld. Art Director: Bibi Lindström. Editor: Lennart Wallén. Producer: Nordisk Tonefilm.

CAST

Ulla Jacobsson (Kerstin), Folke Sundqvist (Göran), *Edvin Adolphson (Anders, Göran's uncle), Irma Christenson (Sigrid), John Elfström (the parson), Erik Hell (Torsten), Sten Lindgren (Göran's father), Nils Hallberg (Nisse), Gösta Gustafson (Fredrik, Kerstin's uncle), Berta Hall (Anna, his wife).

PREMIERE

Swedish: 17 Dec. 1951

New York: 21 Mar. 1955

BIBLIOGRAPHY

Sarris, Andrew. "One Summer of Happiness." *Film Culture* 1, no. 3 (May–June 1955): 26.

AWARD

Berlin Golden Bear 1952

HUGO OCH JOSEFIN [**Hugo and Josefin**]. The story centers around two children living in the country, Josefin and Hugo. Josefin is the neglected daughter of a parson and his embittered wife. The father is only occupied with his sermons and is literally never visible in the film, whereas the mother does not seem to care about her daughter. Hugo is a child of somewhat unclear origin, and his father is in prison for refusing to do his military service. Josefin and Hugo happen to meet when Hugo begins school, and together they experience all kinds of sometimes rather frightening adventures. They become acquainted with the parson's new gardener, Gudmarsson, who becomes their friend. At the end of the film Gudmarsson eventually has to leave and loads his truck with furniture. The children force him to stop and want him to unload the furniture. He stops packing for a while and tells them a tale about people who always have to say good-bye. He leaves the children in the middle of the night. In the last shot, he begins to cry as he drives away, and the windshield wipers of his truck seem to wipe away his tears.

This rather poetic and fantastic depiction of children and their world of fantasy caused some debate when it appeared. Many asked whether this was a film for children or a film about children, especially as the children's audience could hardly have comprehended the deep, existential questions raised in it. Many children did not and reacted negatively to the film. It might have been better suited for somewhat older children with their questions about the existence of God and the necessary break with the innocence of childhood. Although Josefin's father is a minister, she experiences God as an abstraction or an absent being, just as her father is also absent from her life. Hugo, more concretely, acts as her savior in school when he defends her against the other mean children. Gudmarsson (*Gud* meaning "God" in Swedish) appears as a revelation. He is a friendly old man with a beard just like many children would imagine a personified God to appear. The ending of unavoidable and eventual breakup has a double dimension, an end to the fantasy world in the children's minds and a concomitant step into young adulthood.

One might say that this film is an important forerunner to a recent trend that Birgitta Steene has described as the making of "adult children's films," films about children and their childhood aimed mainly at a grown-up audience. Some obvious examples are *Åke och hans värld/Åke and His World* and **Fanny och Alexander/Fanny and Alexander*. These films are perhaps based on a need to raise some kind of religious or at least religiously colored questions in an otherwise secular society, where material needs have been fulfilled, but the spiritual is not addressed. A return to childhood makes it easier to spell out such fundamental questions, as childhood contains the symbolic values of purity and naturalness.

Some of **Kjell Grede's later films also concern a fatherless society in which the patriarchal order of the "people's home" is cracking. In some ways Grede has set out on the same path as **Bergman, who has obviously inspired Grede's cinematic style. Grede is perhaps even more liberal in his use of symbols. He once even stated: "Reality is an insult!" While the symbolic concept functions in *Hugo och Josefin*, Grede seems to have become lost in a jungle of irrelevant symbolism in some of his later films.

CREW

Director: Kjell Grede. Script: Kjell Grede, Maria Gripe, after the novels of Maria Gripe. Cinematographer: Lasse Björne. Sound: Lennart Engholm. Music: Torbjörn Lundquist. Props: Jutta Ekman. Wardrobe: Eva-Lisa Nelstedt. Editor: Lars Hagström. Producer: Göran Lindgren/Sandrews.

CAST

Fredrik Becklén (Hugo), Marie Öhman (Josefin), Beppe Wolgers (Gudmarsson), Inga Landgré (Josefin's mother), Helena Brodin (the schoolmistress), Bellan Roos (Lyra, the lonely woman), Karl Carlsson (Karl Carlsson), Tord Stål (Josefin's father—voice only).

PREMIERE

Swedish: 16 Dec. 1967

New York (Film Festival): 29 Sept. 1968

INGEBORG HOLM. Ingeborg is married to a young shopkeeper with whom she has small children. Their future seems prosperous and bright, but her husband falls ill and dies. Ingeborg must engage an assistant to run the shop, who mismanages it, and the store goes bankrupt. Ingeborg is forced to seek financial assistance from the poor board and must accept the placement of her children in a foster home while she is employed in a make-work institution for the poor. When she is not allowed to see her children, she runs away but is caught and brought back again. The years pass; Ingeborg grows older and is eventually hospitalized. In the end, one of her sons, who has become a sailor, returns to meet his now mentally ill mother. Despite her illness she does recognize her son.

This melodrama is an early example of a socially conscious theme found in many of *Victor Sjöström's productions and in much of Swedish cinema. It was the first Swedish film to cause a public debate, and it eventually contributed to a change in welfare legislation. The film is based on a play by teacher Nils Krok (1906) who had worked with the poor board in Helsingborg. Sjöström had earlier become familiar with the play when he was a touring actor, and he had staged it on one of his tours. The film idea evolved when Sjöström had to find an appropriate subject for actress *Hilda Borgström, who was under contract and had nothing else to do. Right after the premiere a representative from the poor board vigorously attacked the film and claimed that its contents were inaccurate. Both Krok and Sjöström replied, with Krok maintaining that there were still many social evils that remained unsolved. The events that followed the film bore him out; the welfare law was soon improved.

Besides the burning social questions it addressed, the film is of great cinematic value. Sjöström's style was quiet and realistic, with a maturity that was well ahead of its time. Although the film industry in Sweden had only just been established, the film's narrative style and storytelling mode were well realized. Sjöström made great use of deep-angle shots to make rooms vivid and avoid the usual flatness. Sjöström's characteristic gentleness with his actors resulted in a type of subtle, controlled acting that underlines the seriousness of the film. Reading the critiques of his other films of the time, which were lost in a 1941 fire, one gets the impression that this film was typical of his mature filmmaking style, even though his other films seem to have involved lighter material.

Ingeborg Holm contributed to both the solution of an important social problem and the liberation of film as a medium.

CREW

Director: Victor Sjöström. Script: Nils Krok, after his own play. Cinematographer: Henrik Jaenzon. Producer: Svenska Biografteatern.

CAST

Hilda Borgström (Ingeborg Holm), Aron Lindgren (her husband/Erik, her son as grown-up), Eric Lindholm (shop clerk), Georg Grönroos (attendant at the poorhouse), William Larsson (sheriff), Richard Lund (doctor).

PREMIERE

Swedish: 27 Oct. 1913

BIBLIOGRAPHY

Hedling, Erik, and Anna Meeuwisse. "Filmen som agitator." *Bokbox*, no. 93 (Dec. 1987): 15–23.

INTERMEZZO. The main character, Holger Brandt, is an internationally re-nowned violinist, and the beginning of the film sees him returning home to Sweden after a long tour with the pianist Thomas. Thomas wants to retire from touring to stay home. He has a new pupil, Anita, a talented young piano player who is invited to Holger's home and leaves Holger spellbound by her playing and her appearance. He works to persuade her to accompany him around the world in place of Thomas. Eventually she does go with him, becoming his mistress. He abandons his wife and children, and they have a time of happiness touring around Europe. His wife seeks a divorce, but unable to cut all his Swed-ish ties, he is reluctant to sign the divorce papers. When Anita receives a large grant, Holger sets her free and drifts, now alone, through continental Europe. At one point in Paris he hears a Swedish sailor talking about his homesickness, and Holger decides to return to his family. Just after returning, he stands outside the school his daughter Anne-Marie attends. When she comes out of the school's entrance, she recognizes her father and hurries across the street and is hit by a truck. She is brought to the hospital critically injured, but she survives. While they are waiting in the hospital, Holger is reconciled with his reluctant wife and his son Åke.

This melodrama did very well internationally, bringing world fame to *Ingrid Bergman. David O. Selznick later bought the rights to the film and remade it, again with Ingrid Bergman, now starring opposite Leslie Howard as Holger. The original film is, however, generally considered the better of the two. It stands as proof to *Gustaf Molander's craftsmanship and delicate treatment of the film medium.

The film has complex inner meaning. It is easy to interpret the film as a modern version of *Faust*, which is underlined by *Gösta Ekman's ability to act the role of Holger as a dreamer and seeker of eternal youth. Holger is the artist desiring unbounded creativity, willing to sell his soul and his family's happiness. One might say that his impresario Charles, who pushes him to continue touring, plays the role of Mephisto. The important scene at home where Holger encounters Anita and they begin to play together can be viewed both as a prison, tying him to a domesticity, and as a cathedral, where he may express his heavenly ambitions. Another Faustian scene is his encounter with Anita outside the royal palace, when they look into the moving water filled with ice floes. He expresses the wish to just be swept away by the irresistible and irrational forces of life. Finally, there is an interesting scene toward the end when he and Anita are in Switzerland and a picture of the aging Holger is overlaid by flowers and a picture of him in his youth. This is a clever illustration of Holger's tragic, Faustian character.

According to the rules set by bourgeois society, theirs is an impossible love and life. It is the tragic fate of Holger that he is doomed to part from Anita and, with her departure, lose his dreams of eternal youth. Molander often deals with the theme of "the missed opportunity," and he does so in this film. Moreover, Holger must somehow be punished and pay in the end. He does so by almost causing the death of his darling little daughter, who, in the beginning of the film, is an innocent admirer of Anita and cannot understand why her mother rejects the other woman.

CREW

Director: Gustaf Molander. Script: Gustaf Molander, Gösta Stevens. Cinematographer: Åke Dahlqvist. Sound: Terrence Wendt. Music: Heinz Provost. Art Director: Arne Åkermark. Editor: Oscar Rosander. Producer: Svensk Filmindustri.

CAST

Gösta Ekman [Sr.] (Holger Brandt), Inga Tidblad (Margit, his wife), Ingrid Bergman (Anita Hoffman), Erik "Bullen" Berglund (Charles), Hugo Björne (Thomas Stenborg), *Hasse Ekman (Åke Brandt), Britt Hagman (Ann-Marie Brandt), *Anders Henrikson (Swedish sailor).

PREMIERE

Swedish: 16 Nov. 1936
New York: 24 Dec. 1937

JAG ÄR NYFIKEN—GUL; JAG ÄR NYFIKEN—BLÅ/I AM CURIOUS (YELLOW); I AM CURIOUS (BLUE). This film caused a sensation when it appeared in the late 1960s. This was not, at least in Sweden, because it contained some provocative sex scenes, although some people condemned these (there is a sexual intercourse scene in front of the royal castle in Stockholm). It was mainly controversial because of its content and form. This was not an ordinary film; *Vilgot Sjöman freely mixed the fictive and the documentary. The rather thin plot is about a young girl, Lena (Nyman), exploring contemporary Swedish society together with her boyfriend Börje. She interviews, among other persons, Olof Palme, then minister of education and later to become prime minister. She also does real interviews with people who have just arrived at the airport from vacations in Spain, then ruled by Franco. Her fictitious father had been a fighter on the Republican side in the Spanish civil war but had returned after just three weeks. She confronts him to make him own up to his failure. During these scenes the film contains a controversial shot of her piercing the eyes of a portrait of Franco (this, in reality, almost led to legal action on the grounds of insulting a foreign head of state). Between the documentary actions she has a rather stormy and sexually active relationship with Börje. He, like her father, sometimes behaves like a male chauvinist.

The film was mainly controversial for its depiction of certain aspects of Swedish society that were officially ignored; there were still bad social conditions despite the official myths surrounding the welfare society. The film showed the "cracks" in the "people's home," that Sweden was still a class society despite all the social democratic rhetoric to the contrary. The film also showed that modernity had not reached all areas of Sweden. There were still parts living in a past world. This is particularly evident in the *Blue* film where Lena extended her voyage to northern Sweden with its vast wilderness and deep forests. These parts of the two films echo the romanticism and mysticism of nature from Swedish film of the past.

The first—*Yellow*—part of the film proved to be an extraordinary success; more than 1.3 million moviegoers saw it in Sweden, and it caused a huge debate in the newspapers. The *Yellow* part was initially banned as offensive by U.S. customs authorities, but when it was finally released there, it was an even larger success than in Sweden. The *Blue* part was more moderately successful and did not cause as much controversy.

CREW

Director: Vilgot Sjöman. Script: Vilgot Sjöman. Cinematographer: Peter Wester. Assistant: Andreas Bellis. Sound: Tage Sjöborg. Music: Bengt Ernryd. Editor: Wic' Kjellin. Producer: Göran Lindgren/Sandrews.

CAST

Lena Nyman (Lena), *Börje Ahlstedt (Börje), Peter Lindgren (Rune, Lena's father), Vilgot Sjöman (Vilgot Sjöman), Chris Wahlström (Rune's woman—only the *Yellow*), Marie Göranzon (Börje's wife), Magnus Nilsson (Magnus), Ulla Lyttkens (Ulla), Holger Löwenadler (the king—only the *Yellow*), Olof Palme (himself—only the *Yellow*), Anders Ek (nonviolence trainer—only the *Yellow*), *Sven Wollter (captain—only the *Yellow*), Sonja Lindgren (Sonja Lindgren—only the *Blue*), Bertil Wikström (Bertil Wikström—only the *Blue*), Hans Hellberg (Lena's former lover—only the *Blue*), Bim Warne (Lena's former lover's girlfriend—only the *Blue*), Gunnel Broström (the woman on the island—only the *Blue*).

PREMIERE

Swedish: 9 Oct. 1967 (*Yellow*); 11 Mar. 1968 (*Blue*)

New York: 10 Mar. 1969 (*Yellow*); 20 May 1970 (*Blue*)

BIBLIOGRAPHY

I Am Curious (Yellow)—The Complete Scenario of the Film by Vilgot Sjöman. New
    York: Grove Press, 1969.
I Am Curious (Blue)—A Film by Vilgot Sjöman: The Complete Scenario. New York:
    Grove Press, 1970.
Sjöman, Vilgot. *I Was Curious: Diary of the Making of a Film*. New York: Grove Press,
    1969.

KALLE PÅ SPÅNGEN/KALLE PAA SPAANGEN, a.k.a. *CHARLIE, THE
INN-KEEPER*. Kalle is the keeper of the inn "Spången," where he lives in a
rather miserable marriage with his dominating wife. He conceals the fact that
one of the servant girls is in reality his daughter, born out of wedlock. Besides
being afraid of this being revealed, he is also being threatened by state representative Högberg (a Swedish "landsfiskal," a combination of local police and
representative of the tax authorities). Högberg is not pleased with the way Kalle
is running his inn and demands that Kalle "modernize"; otherwise, Kalle will
lose his permit to serve liquor (which was, in fact, severely restricted in Sweden
at that time). Högberg has a son, Gösta, who is an irresponsible young man on
the verge of becoming a serious juvenile delinquent. During a wedding at the
inn, Gösta steals a wallet, for which one of the servant girls is blamed and
arrested. The truth does come through with Kalle making a gallant speech in
front of the court to make Gösta confess his guilt. At the same time the truth
about Kalle's daughter is also revealed, and Kalle is reconciled with his wife.
The deceit cleared away, their marriage is now blessed with a little son, and
Gösta, too, is redeemed and has his own family.

This film is of a folksy, melodramatic style that had been done many times
before in Swedish film and on the Swedish stage. Despite this, it proved to be
a smash hit and was one of the most popular Swedish films ever. There are
many reasons for this, one being the presence of actor *Edvard Persson in the
lead as the innkeeper Kalle, who was at that time the most popular Swedish
actor. Timing was also an important factor; the film was made just before the
outbreak of World War II when there was no doubt that there would be a great
war in Europe. The only questions were when and if Sweden would be involved.

The film acknowledges the threat of war but provides a reassurance that all
will end well. It takes its symbols from the agrarian-pastoral ideals that form
such a distinctive and important core in Swedish cinema. When Högberg threat-
ens the inn, Kalle states that he still has his farm, inherited from a long string
of forefathers. The film and especially the character Kalle are a strong defense
of old-fashioned values. It fiercely attacks modernity and the modern state, per-

sonified by Högberg. This "neo-Rousseauian" fantasy blames modern society for evils such as war and destruction. Kalle makes the claim that a human being who is resting on a green pasture cannot and does not invent new, more deadly weapons. Adding to all these themes is the patriarchal authority that Edvard Persson brought to the film,

The film concludes in pastoral harmony to convince the audience that all will end well. At the outbreak of the war, Prime Minister Per Albin Hansson stated that "our preparedness is good." He probably did not mean military readiness, which was in fact in a rather shaky state. What he probably meant was that Sweden was ready on a spiritual level. *Kalle på Spången* demonstrates this. The film was also shown in neighboring Denmark, then already occupied by Germany. Rather ironically, despite the blood-and-soil message that no Nazi could oppose, the film was seen as a resistance symbol.

CREW

Director: Emil A. Pehrsson. Script: Henry Richter, Theodor Berthels, Edvard Persson. Cinematographer: Olle Ekman. Sound: Gösta Bjurman. Music: Nathan Görling; Alvar Kraft, Lasse Dahlqvist (songs). Editor: Emil A. Pehrsson. Producer: Europa Film.

CAST

Edvard Persson (Karl Jeppsson), Bullan Weijden (Berta, his wife), John Degerberg (Sjölund), Carl Ström (Högberg), Tord Bernheim (Gösta), Mim Persson (Stina), Annita Gyldtenungae (Karin, Karl's daughter), Walter Sarmell (Olle).

PREMIERE

Swedish: 4 Nov. 1939

New York: 26 Jan. 1940

EN KÄRLEKSHISTORIA [A LOVE STORY]. This is a story of two teenagers depicting all the tenderness and uncertainty of adolescent love. We meet the two central characters in company with their peer group, driving their mopeds around and around as part of a teenage ritual. The two, Pär and Annika, belong to different social classes. He is from a rather poor home, whereas her father is a successful refrigerator salesman. In Annika's home all emotions are dead; they are visited by her aunt, a bitter woman growing old. The film climaxes at an outdoor party thrown by both families with the usual Swedish ingredients of crayfish and alcohol. During the night much hidden bitterness and frustration are let loose as the members of Annika's and Pär's families quarrel with themselves and each other. The atmosphere becomes hostile, and Annika's father, tired of life, disappears into the morning fog but shows up again in the final shots.

This is truly a film about emotions, or, rather, the lack of them, in the welfare state. While the parents' generation has been materially successful, the price has been a void between the generations where people are unable to communicate.

The generation of Pär's grandfather has been shunted into hospitals where they sit completely abandoned and alone. While their children do on occasion visit, they do so only out of duty. The young children, too, live their own lives with little meaningful contact with their parents.

While *En kärlekshistoria* might be seen as a criticism of the welfare society, it is in fact an appeal to people to start to take care of each other and develop a sense of solidarity. *Roy Andersson belongs to the leftist generation of the late 1960s, and his aim was to move past present-day problems by pointing a way to the future. Andersson is a remarkable filmmaker, able to depict delicate social and emotional matters and atmosphere distinctly and precisely. Almost everything is perfect in the acting and visual style. His perfectionism became an obstacle in his second film, *Giliap*, another black depiction of alienation with utopian hopes for a better way of living. *A Love Story* was unexpectedly successful with the audience; *Giliap*, in contrast, was a failure.

CREW

Director: Roy Andersson. Script: Roy Andersson. Cinematographer: Jörgen Persson. Sound: Owe Svensson. Music: Björn Isfält. Props: Lars Wallén. Wardrobe: Per Lekang, Maj Eriksson. Editor: Kalle Boman. Executive Producer: Waldemar Bergendahl, Rune Hjelm, Kalle Boman. Producer: Europa Film.

CAST

Rolf Sohlman (Pär), Anne-Sofie Kylin (Annika), Bertil Norström (John, Annika's father), Margreth Weivers (Elsa, Annika's mother), Lennart Tellfeldt (Lasse, Pär's father), Gunnar Ossiander (Pär's grandfather), Anita Lindblom (Eva, Annika's aunt), Maud Backéus (Gunhild, Pär's mother), Björn Andrésen, Christer Hellquist, Nils Söderlund (the gang).

PREMIERE

Swedish: 24 Apr. 1970

BIBLIOGRAPHY

Koskinen, Maaret. "Konsten att återbörda tingen till synligheten: Roy Anderssons *En kärlekshistoria*." In Hedling, 1998.
Löthwall, Lars-Olof. "En historia om Roy Andersson." *Chaplin*, no. 99 (1970):119–120. Interview. Review by Torsten Manns in the same issue.

KARL-FREDRIK REGERAR/KARL-FREDRIK REIGNS. This film is set at the turn of the century and begins with farm laborer Karl-Fredrik Pettersson being thrown off the Björnhammar estate for political agitation among the other laborers. He leaves defiantly, making his way down a big avenue, playing the "Internationale" on his accordion. The film then jumps forward to the early 1930s. Karl-Fredrik is now a politician and a Social Democratic member of the Parliament, preparing for the general election, which is expected to bring the party to power. His grown-up daughter, as radical as Karl-Fredrik had been earlier, is a left-wing journalist who writes articles to inflame the workers on today's Björnhammar estate. Then she meets Olof, who—unknown to her—is the young heir to the estate, and falls helplessly in love. This modern, rational woman begins to undergo profound changes under the influence of this not-so-practical, dreamy young man. They are estranged for a while when she learns his true identity, but Karl-Fredrik's faithful housekeeper reunites them. Olof, in the meantime, has taken over the now nearly bankrupt Björnhammar. The banks refuse to lend him money, and his only hope is the new government, in which Karl-Fredrik has become minister of agriculture. Will he help the new owner of the estate from which Karl-Fredrik was once expelled in such a humiliating way? The final answer is yes. He explains why in a speech that even convinces Olof's aristocratic mother to reach out a conciliatory hand.

From a political point of view, this is a key film of the 1930s. It appeared just one year after the Social Democratic government came to power and a cooperation policy with the Farmer's League Party had been introduced. One of the scriptwriters was Social Democrat member of Parliament John Sandén. The Social Democratic Party had to establish its credentials as being sufficiently nationalistic in the political turbulence of the early 1930s. The nationalistic rhetoric that saturates this film symbolized the Social Democratic shift in priorities from class struggle to political cooperation. The "Internationale" changes from being a symbol of resistance in the beginning of the film to becoming a tool used by "un-Swedish" agitators at the end. The aim of the new politics was to disarm both the political Right and the Left to establish a solid majority in the middle. This was the reasoning behind the "people's home" policy that was to dominate Sweden for many decades. The people's home concept is very evident in the film. When Karl-Fredrik first disapproves of his daughter's affair, her talk about Björnhammar as "home" causes him to give in, despite what had happened before. The film symbolizes the new Sweden being built through the cooperation of the different classes and with the fusion of emotional and rational thinking, all based on firm Swedish soil. One potent symbolization of this is Karl-Fredrik's stop in the fields, while on the way to the estate, where he thoughtfully caresses the ears of wheat. In his speech at the end of the film, he says that all Swedes despite their class have physical and spiritual roots in the Swedish soil.

CREW

Director: *Gustaf Edgren. Script: Oscar Rydqvist, Gustaf Edgren, John Sandén. Cinematographer: Åke Dahlqvist, Martin Bodin. Sound: Anders Djurberg. Music: Eric Bengtson. Art Director: Arne Åkermark. Editor: Rolf Husberg. Producer: Svensk Filmindustri.

CAST

*Sigurd Wallén (Karl-Fredrik Pettersson), Gull-Maj Norin (Lena, his daughter), Björn Berglund (Olof), Pauline Brunius (Olof's mother), Dagmar Ebbesen (Augusta, Karl-Fredrik's housekeeper), Carl Ström (Eriksson), Hugo Björne (Olof's father), Eric Abrahamson (Öberg, newspaper editor).

PREMIERE

Swedish: 3 Mar. 1934

New York: 1 Feb. 1938

BIBLIOGRAPHY

Sjögren, Olle. "Per Albin regerar." *Ord & Bild*, nos. 1–2 (1972):43–53.

KARRIÄR [CAREER]. Monika Hall is a young aspiring actress, touring with a third-rate theater company. When their bus breaks down on the road, they are forced to stop in a small town where the aging star of the company, Nanna, happens to have an old lover, the manager of the steel mill. He is not at home, but his son gives the company a guided tour around the mill, where Monika happens to meet a young worker, Erik. The following day they meet again and talk about their future career plans. Erik is planning to be an engineer, and Monika, of course, wants to be a famous actress. They keep in contact and on one occasion Monika lies to him on the telephone, telling him that she now has the leading part in *Romeo and Juliet*. When Erik visits unexpectedly she manages to persuade the real actress in the role to let her play Juliet just this one evening. The performance reveals that she is more talented than the original actress, which causes a split in the company. Monika and Nanna leave the company and move to Stockholm, where Nanna persuades another former lover to sponsor a new theater production with them. Nanna, however, has growing problems with alcoholism, and the opening night is a disaster. Monika tries in vain to rescue the situation. Despite this catastrophe Monika's talent is discovered, and she receives an engagement at the Royal Dramatic Theater. The years pass and Monika eventually returns to Erik's hometown on a tour. They meet and straighten out all their mutual misunderstandings. They have both attained their goals: Erik is now an engineer, and Monika is famous in her profession. They decide to become a couple. Erik, though, wonders in the end if it really was that important to work so hard for a career.

This film can be regarded as the ultimate depiction of the notion of the "people's home." The male lead, Erik, embodies the male dream of climbing the social ladder, from being just a young working man to becoming a real builder and designer of the new Swedish society. The merging of the two main characters also points to another aspect of this utopia: the necessity of bringing the rational and the pleasurable together. One might say that the film shows a kind of magic triangle of love, labor, and nature in one happy combination. *Karriär* is typical of its time, for it is possible to find the same pattern in many other films of the 1930s. The final scene is pastoral, with the two lovers sitting together in a green pasture with a steel mill in the background. It summarizes the meaning of the whole movie as a utopic state of being where nature and technology are in perfect harmony. This was the modernist ideal of 1930s Sweden.

What really makes the film work, and why it can be regarded as one of the finest films of the 1930s, is *Schamyl Bauman's delicate work with the direction of the actors. It is a good example of his intimate style, with frequent use of close shots and very low-key acting. The acting is quite unlike the exaggerated style that so often spoiled older Swedish films. Bauman had actress *Signe Hasso in her first big role in the underrated *Häxnatten* [Witches' night]. With *Karriär*, she became as big a star as the character she personified in the film.

CREW

Director: Schamyl Bauman. Script: Franz Winterstein, after an idea by Börje Larsson. Cinematographer: Hilmer Ekdahl. Sound: Sven Josephson. Music: Jacques Armand [Olof Thiel]. Editor: Rolf Husberg. Producer: Irefilm.

CAST

Signe Hasso (Monika Hall), Sture Lagerwall (Erik Norrby), Tollie Zellman (Nanny Hög-felt), Carl Barcklind (Ferdinant Sund), Ruth Stevens (Karin Lund), Olof Widgren (Helge Berg), Olof Sandborg (manager of the Royal Dramatic Theater).

PREMIERE

Swedish: 11 Oct. 1938

BIBLIOGRAPHY

Soila, 1991.

KÖRKARLEN/THE STROKE OF MIDNIGHT, a.k.a. *THE PHANTOM CHAR-IOT.* David Holm has a miserable life, spending most of his time drinking with various companions. The story begins on New Year's Eve with David and two of his pals sitting and drinking in a churchyard. David remembers an old acquaintance, Georges, who died exactly one year before on New Year's Eve. A person who dies on the last day of the year, he says, is condemned to serving death by driving a death chariot. David starts a quarrel, and one of his companions hits him over the head with a bottle. David experiences what he takes to be death and watches in horror as the death chariot comes. It is, in fact, driven by Georges who tells David about his sorrowful duties. Georges reminds David about his earlier life and how he ruined it by becoming a drinker. He tells how David's younger brother accidentally killed someone when he was intoxicated and that this marked the beginning of David's decline. He was abandoned by his wife, and he turned into a hard and bitter man. Even the efforts of Edit, a self-sacrificing young sister of the Salvation Army, to help him were treated with contempt. He even deliberately infected her with tuberculosis. An attempt by a Salvation Army officer, an ex-drinker and sometime drinking buddy of David's, to reconcile David with his wife also failed. Georges brings David to Edit's deathbed and then to David's wife who is on the verge of committing suicide together with their little children. David wakes up to rush home and save them in the nick of time. At the end he repents and prays, "Oh God, let my soul be ripe before it can be harvested."

This story is at first sight a simple reformation melodrama, and the film has certainly been used for temperance propaganda purposes on many occasions. What is remarkable about the film is its refined storytelling technique and its mature psychology. *Victor Sjöström shows his mastery in directing his actors and, above all, himself in the lead as David Holm. It is a good example of Sjöström's intimate style, using, for example, close shots to tighten the screen space. *Ingmar Bergman holds that *Körkarlen* is one of the films that has influenced him most profoundly. Bengt Forslund writes that Sjöström put much of himself and his father into the David Holm character. Sjöström settles his own past with his depiction of the "weak" side of masculinity and the "strong" side of femininity. David is such a vivid character with his transformations from a handsome, careless hobo to an evil, ruined man and finally to a soulful, repenting sinner. The physically weak and consumptive Edit is perhaps the strongest character in the film. She has a determined and flaming soul that finally triumphs.

The production of the film was rather difficult. Sjöström received much aid from Selma Lagerlöf to realize the structurally complicated script. The story takes place on different time levels: in the past, in the present, and in a dream world. The cinematography work was complicated by the double exposure shots of the death chariot. While the technique was not new, having been used before by *Klercker and *Stiller, it was considerably more refined. In some cases, cinematographer Julius Jaenzon let the same piece of film roll through the camera four times in a row to get the right result. The film was an overwhelming success, both in Sweden and abroad, and contributed to Sjöström's international fame.

CREW

Director: Victor Sjöström. Script: Victor Sjöström, after a novel by Selma Lagerlöf. Cinematographer: Julius Jaenzon. Art Director: Axel Esbensen, Alexander Bakó. Producer: Svensk Filmindustri.

CAST

Victor Sjöström (David Holm), *Hilda Borgström (his wife), Tore Svennberg (Georges), Astrid Holm (Edit, nurse), Lisa Lundholm (Maria, nurse), Tor Weijden (Gustafsson), Concordia Selander (Edit's mother), Einar Axelsson (David's brother), Nils Arehn (preacher in the prison).

PREMIERE

Swedish: 1 Jan. 1921

New York: 4 June 1922

BIBLIOGRAPHY

Florin, Bo. "Körkarlen—en stilstudie." *Filmhäftet*, nos. 89–90 (1997):22–31.

KVARTERET KORPEN/RAVEN'S END. This film is set in Sweden's third largest city, Malmö, in 1936. It revolves around a working-class family living in the poor neighborhood "Raven's End." The father is an unemployed alcoholic, the mother must earn money as a charwoman, and the son, Anders, dreams of being an author. Anders's girlfriend gets pregnant and wants to get married, but he hesitates and asks his parents for advice. In the argument that ensues, the intoxicated father accuses his wife of being the cause of his and the family's misery. It turns out that she had been unfaithful once. She also tells Anders that she once had to have an abortion because of their poverty. Anders begs her to vote for the Social Democratic Party in the forthcoming elections so that their lives may improve. In the end, Anders decides to break with his milieu, his home, and his fiancée. He goes to Stockholm to a meeting at the publishing house where his work has hitherto been refused.

The film does not contain much action; it is more a record of the atmosphere and feelings of this time, a crucial point in Swedish contemporary history. Although the Social Democrats had already been in power for four years, Swedish society was still marked by poverty among the working class. The unemployment rate was still high, and the welfare state was still a utopian goal. This film is remarkable in that it captures all these problems and brings them alive on the screen. The viewer can feel the misery and the sense of both degradation and pride among the working class. *Bo Widerberg makes good use of sound to create atmosphere. While Anders is talking with his parents and when he is walking across the yard, one can hear the radio in the background carrying Hitler's speeches and accounts from the Berlin Olympics. This strongly hints that Social Democratic policies were still far from being consolidated and that political victory in the next elections was uncertain.

Widerberg pleads for a more realistic and sociological film art in his book *Vision in Swedish Film*. Many of his ideals were taken from British kitchen-sink realism. *Kvarteret Korpen* is obviously inspired by these ideals. Widerberg is above all an observer who leaves the spectator to reach his or her own conclusions. When Anders breaks with his milieu (and eventually his social class), one must ask oneself if this is just an individual emancipatory action or if it is good for the working class as a whole. It was a common view in the 1930s (reflected in the films of the time) that an individual from the working class could pursue a career taking him into a better social class without betraying working-class solidarity. In fact, such individual efforts were supported by leading Social Democrats. When Widerberg raised this question again, almost thirty years later, the answer was not so certain. Maybe he is hinting in *Kvarteret Korpen* at what he later makes clear in other films: that Sweden still was an unjust class society despite thirty years of Social Democratic rule.

CREW

Director: Bo Widerberg. Script: Bo Widerberg. Cinematographer: Jan Lindström. Sound: Sven Fahlén. Set Design: Einar Nettelbladt. Editor: Wic' Kjellin. Producer: Europa Film.

CAST

*Thommy Berggren (Anders), *Keve Hjelm (the father), Emy Storm (the mother), Christina Frambäck (Elsie), Ingvar Hirdwall (Sixten), Agneta Prytz (the neighbor), Nina Widerberg (Nina), Louise Gustafsson (Anders's girlfriend), Fritiof Nilsson Piraten (the author in the waiting room).

PREMIERE

Swedish: 26 Dec. 1963

New York: 21 May 1970

BIBLIOGRAPHY

Aghed, Jan. "Kvarteret Korpen." *Svensk filmografi* 6 (1977): 163–165:

AWARD

AAN 1965: Best Foreign Film

MÄNNISKORS RIKE **[REALM OF MAN].** This film is a continuation of *På dessa skuldror* [On these shoulders], one of the first postwar films to deal with contemporary rural problems. The first film is about a farmer's son, Kjell, who returns to his home to rejuvenate his ancestral farm. However, when his father dies in an accident, he is forced to leave because he cannot afford to pay his greedy brothers' shares. Embittered, he moves to a smaller farm, where he continues to struggle on his little piece of land. He has a quarrel with one of his brothers, Aron, who has married into a more prosperous farm. Aron eventually develops a bad conscience and offers Kjell a loan to buy the ancestral farm since the new owner, a doctor from the city, cannot manage it. At first Kjell turns down the offer, but his wife reminds him of his duties to the village, their expected child, and their forefathers. In the final scene the two brothers reconcile in the summer night while standing on a hill overlooking the village.

These two films, based on the novels of popular author Sven Edvin Salje, were cooperative ventures between Nordisk Tonefilm and the publishing house LT, the latter owned by the farmers' cooperative movement. The underrated Salje has been the leading chronicler of the drastic changes to small farms in the postwar period. In just one decade, their number was halved. *På dessa skuldror* and, above all, *Människors rike* reflect this revolution, maintaining optimistically, despite the changes, that the countryside still has a future. It lies in the cooperation among rural people. Reconciliation is a major Salje theme, and this is emphasized in Rune Lindström's script. As in Lindström's *Himlaspelet/The Heavenly Play*, about paradise lost and regained, there are, as the titles imply, strong Christian overtones in the two films. Kjell is a kind of Christ-like figure who bears the burden and fate of his fellow villagers on his shoulders. He is a guide who, by preserving the heritage of his forefathers, the cornerstone of agrarian romanticism, lets the others see the light. *Människors rike* is thematically completely pastoral. Göran Strindberg's cinematography is very lyrical, and the final scene when the two brothers meet in the bright summer night is very moving. The two films proved to be an unexpected success with the audience; each film was seen by approximately 1 million viewers.

CREW

Director: Gösta Folke. Script: Karl Fredrik Björn, Rune Lindström. Cinematographer: Göran Strindberg. Sound: Olle Jakobsson. Music: Erland von Koch. Art Director: Bibi Lindström. Editor: Lennart Wallén. Producer: Nordisk Tonefilm.

CAST

Ulf Palme (Kjell), *Anita Björk (Birgit, his wife), Erik Hell (Aron), Märta Arbin (Inga, their mother), Ragnvi Lindbladh (Sonja, Aron's wife), Oscar Ljung (Andreasson), Artur Cederborgh (Sonja's father), Hanny Schedin (Sonja's mother), Jan-Erik Lindqvist (Janne, farmhand).

PREMIERE

Swedish: 19 Sept. 1949

MITT LIV SOM HUND/MY LIFE AS A DOG. This film is about twelve-year-old Ingemar Johansson in the years 1958 and 1959. It is not a happy time for him, as his mother is in the hospital for consumption, and he has been sent away to his uncle in Småland. Moreover, his best friend, a dog, has been taken away from him. Things do not turn out so badly, though, for his uncle is rather eccentric, as are the other persons living in the small community. Ingemar is an optimist, always trying to see things from a brighter side. Imagine, he thinks to himself, how much worse things are for the space dog, Laika, who orbits the earth with no hope of returning. Ingemar meets the girl Saga and begins to feel his first emotional attachment to the opposite sex. The film ends with everyone listening to the radio when Ingemar's namesake wins the world champion title in heavyweight boxing.

This film summarizes two important trends or themes in contemporary Swedish film. The first is the search for the missing father. Ingemar's real father is somewhere abroad, and the uncle serves as a substitute. The second is that of nostalgia for a notion of community with all its attendant symbols. The film plays on strong feelings of community; the Swedes in the late 1950s had common goals around which to gather, which today seem absent. The most obvious symbols of this are the sights and sounds of the late 1950s that saturate the film. One hears the radio reports from Sweden's final in the 1958 world soccer championship and the 1959 bout between Ingemar Johansson and Floyd Patterson, both magic moments in contemporary Swedish sports history. The film is crammed with more bits of nostalgia (some of these can be found in a nostalgia book written in 1986 by *Lasse Hallström's old television colleague *Lasse Åberg).

This film was regarded by Swedish critics as Hallström's best film, and they awarded him their critics prize in 1986. The film was also widely acclaimed internationally, not least in the United States, where the New York film critics appointed it the best foreign film of 1987. It also received the Golden Globe award the following year. It did well at the box office, being one of the most successful foreign films in the American market in 1987. *Mitt liv som hund* served as a springboard for Hallström into American filmmaking.

CREW

Director: Lasse Hallström. Script: Lasse Hallström, "Brasse" Brännström, Reidar Jönsson, Pelle Berglund, after a novel by Reidar Jönsson. Cinematographer: Jörgen Persson. Sound: Eddie Axberg. Music: Björn Isfält. Art Director: Lasse Westfeldt. Wardrobe: Inger Pehrsson. Editor: Susanne Linnman, Christer Furubrand. Executive Producer: Waldemar Bergendahl. Producer: Svensk Filmindustri.

CAST

Anton Glanzelius (Ingemar Johansson), Anki Lidén (Ingemar's mother), Tomas von Brömssen (the uncle), Manfred Serner (Ingemar's brother), Melinda Kinnaman (Saga), Kicki Rundgren (Ulla), Lennart Hjulström (the artist), Ing-Marie Carlsson (Berit), Leif Ericsson (Sandberg).

PREMIERE

Swedish: 13 Dec. 1985

New York: 2 May 1987

BIBLIOGRAPHY

Milne, Tom. "Mitt liv som hund." *Monthly Film Bulletin* (April 1987):117–118.

AWARDS

GB 1985

AAN 1988: Best Direction and Best Script Based on Other Medium

1939. The film begins in a small village close to the Norwegian border just before the outbreak of World War II. With the declaration of war, things change for a village family. The father is called up for military service. When the Germans occupy Norway, a refugee is seen being shot down at the border. Annika, the daughter, goes to Stockholm to find a job, where she happens to meet Berit, a self-assured young woman who helps Annika adjust to the much tougher life in the big city. Annika gets a job as a waitress and then meets Bengt, a handsome young athlete from an upper-class family. They marry, but her happiness does not last long. He reveals ugly sides of his personality, obviously the result of his upbringing with an authoritarian father. He rapes Annika. She first takes refuge in Berit's apartment and finally returns to her home in Värmland.

This three-hour-long epic was meant to celebrate the seventy-year anniversary of Svensk Filmindustri and commemorate the outbreak of World War II fifty years before. Before making the film Svensk Filmindustri asked people to contribute their wartime reminiscences. Many contributions were received from ordinary people around Sweden, and these were molded into a script that became the basis of the film. The reaction to the film was rather uneven. Many critics did not like it, while the audience seems to have been pleased; and more than half a million Swedes paid their tribute at the box office.

While the film might suffer from uneven direction, this alone cannot explain the hostility of the critics. Instead the hostility might be explained by the fact that the film turned out to be something different than the expected piece of nostalgia. On the surface the film is a careful reconstruction of the so-called preparedness time; it is a triumph for the property department. Other than this the film contains little sentimental sweetness. It crushes some of the myths that surround this period and society at that time. The interclass marriage, a commonly glorified theme in Swedish film history, is used to reveal a sharply divided, class-oriented society. The concept of Sweden as a "people's home" is attacked and completely undermined by this dark view of Swedish society. The film is shot from a feminine perspective, which makes it even more interesting. Bengt is as authoritarian as his father, an unpleasant upper-class character who seems to be a Nazi. Bengt cannot stand the friendship between Annika and Berit, especially when Annika cannot give him a child. When Annika is forced to leave Bengt, she has nothing left to return to. The countryside, the traditional site of humane values in Swedish cinema, has also lost its innocence because of the war. The film ends in total uncertainty about the future and with an ambiguity that really mirrors the time and feelings of those who lived through it.

CREW

Director: Göran Carmback. Script: "Brasse" Brännström, with the aid of Catti Edfeldt and Kjell Sundstedt. Cinematographer: Jens Fischer. Sound: Wille Peterson-Berger, Jean-Frédéric Axelsson. Music: Anders Berglund. Art Director: Lasse Westfeldt, Jimmy McGann. Wardrobe: Inger Pehrsson. Editor: Susanne Linnman. Executive Producer: Waldemar Bergndahl, Lennart Wiklund. Producer: Svensk Filmindustri, Svenska Filminstitutet, Sveriges Television.

CAST

Helene Egelund (Annika), Ingvar Hirdwall (Olof, her father), Anita Ekström (Ella, her mother), *Per Oscarsson (Isak, her grandfather), *Helena Bergström (Berit), Johan Ulveson (Harald), Willie Andéason (Gustaf), Per Morberg (Bengt), *Keve Hjelm (Alfred, his father), Anita Wall (Cecilia, his mother).

PREMIERE

Swedish: 25 Dec. 1989

BIBLIOGRAPHY

Qvist, Per Olov. "Folkhemmets sönderfall." *Filmhäftet*, nos. 69–70 (1990):45–50.

RONJA RÖVARDOTTER **[RONJA, THE ROBBER'S DAUGHTER]**. Ronja and Birk are children from two feuding families. The families live in different parts of the same castle, and the children often yell challenges and insults at each other. Ronja and Birk, however, fall in love, and with the gulf separating their feuding families, they have to meet in secret in the forest surrounding the castle. The two children spend a summer there living in a cave away from their parents' hostilities, which they can no longer endure. At the end of the film the two families are forced to reconcile to face the threat of foreign warriors.

Although set in the Middle Ages, this film, based on one of Astrid Lindgren's most popular children's stories, deals with modern topics. Since the 1950s, Astrid Lindgren's writing have provided material for a long string of successful children's films. They are, with their action and adventure scenes, of course, directed toward a young audience. But *Ronja Rövardotter* was also a film for an adult audience. Ronja's father Mattis does correspond to the masculine ideal of the time period when the film was made. Just like engineer Andrée in *Ingenjör Andrées luftfärd/Flight of the Eagle*, he is fundamentally weak. He acknowledges and expresses his inner feelings when he cries.

The most important dimension of the film is the mythical one. It belongs to a long row of Swedish films inspired by the experience of nature. Like **Hon dansade en sommar/One Summer of Happiness* or many of **Ingmar Bergman's films, the film deals with the idea of a last summer of innocent childhood spent in nature before entering adulthood. Sometimes the summer is marked by tragedy, the loss of a loved one (such as in *Hon dansade en sommar* or Bergman's *Sommarlek/Illicit Interlude*). In other cases, such as in this film, the transition is happier. The film does, though, have its moments of fear and anxiety when Ronja is confronted by the various spiritual beings in the forest, symbolizing her awakening sexual feelings and conscience. The film also contains many visual and thematic allusions to turn-of-the-century romanticism. Many shots duplicate the famous late nineteenth-century painting *Our Land*. The film also deals with more modern, ecological issues. It provides the lesson that one must be careful with and considerate of mother nature.

CREW

Director: *Tage Danielsson. Script: Astrid Lindgren, after her own novel. Cinematographer: Rune Ericson. Sound: Christer Furubrand. Music: Björn Isfält. Art Director: Ulf Axén. Wardrobe: Lenamari Wallström. Producer: Svensk Filmindustri, Svenska Ord, Norsk Film, Betafilm.

CAST

Hanna Zetterberg (Ronja), Dan Håfström (Birk), *Börje Ahlstedt (Mattis), Lena Nyman (Lovis, Ronja's mother), *Per Oscarsson (Borka, Birk's father), Med Reventberg (Undis, Birk's mother), *Allan Edwall (Skalle-Per, Mattis's father).

PREMIERE

Swedish: 14 Dec. 1984

AWARD

Berlin Silver Bear 1985

SÅNGEN OM DEN ELDRÖDA BLOMMAN [THE SONG OF THE SCARLET FLOWER]. The story has a simple plot line. Olof, the son of a wealthy peasant, loves to fool around with the girls serving on the farm, which results in a quarrel with his father. As a result he leaves his home to join a gang of log drivers, continuing to seduce every girl he meets. One day he meets Kyllikki, daughter of another well-to-do-farmer, who is able to resist him. She tells Olof that he must complete a dare if he is to get a rose from her, a symbol of her love. Olof, challenged by a rival, performs a daredevil, spectacular log race through a hazardous rapid. Later, in a coast town, Olof encounters one of his former sweethearts at a brothel. This causes him to reflect upon his so-far carefree life, which prompts him to return home. On his way home he proposes to Kyllikki and wins her hand despite her father's opposition. Olof and Kyllikki marry, but the former rival manages to awaken Olof's jealousy by hinting that Kyllikki is not a virgin. In the end this is resolved when Kyllikki challenges Olof's double standard.

The story is based on a 1905 novel by Finnish author Johannes Linnankoski (a pseudonym for Vihtori Peltonen). This was mainly inspired by Swedish turn-of-the-century romanticism in general and Selma Lagerlöf in particular. Written very impressionistically, there is much room for free interpretation. The story has been filmed on three different occasions in Sweden (and twice in Finland: by *Teuvo Tulio in 1938 and *Mikko Niskanen in 1971). The three Swedish versions—by *Mauritz Stiller in 1919, *Per-Axel Branner in 1934, and *Gustaf Molander in 1956—are very different, reflecting the time periods in which each version was made. They were all very successful at the box office.

Stiller's version is very free in its interpretation. It reflects the time period in the wake of late nineteenth- and early twentieth-century "national romanticism." His film is filled with lyrical photography of the landscape and stars *Lars Hanson as an uncomplicated, daredevil seducer. The 1934 Branner version is more psychological. It puts a heavier stress on the moral development of Olof, played by *Edvin Adolphson. He has to overcome the "bad seed," the genetic inheritance from the father. One might say that this version reflects Branner's interest in depicting the youth question in his films. He portrays the liberation of a young man associated with growing out of irresponsibility and becoming mature and grown up. This fits perfectly with the main trend of 1930s film, with its stress on the themes of youth and modernity, the young generation being the future of the country. This generation was to be responsible for building the new society, "the people's home." Branner's version has spectacular cinematography of nature and landscape, sometimes used symbolically. Wild rapids reflect stormy youth, and a quiet river, the tranquillity of maturity.

Gustaf Molander, who had originally scripted Stiller's version, made the third version. It is more an artifact, a kind of pastische, part of a last, grand revival of postwar rural drama. It is more down to earth than the other versions, having been scripted by Rune Lindström, who stressed the basic theme of agrarian romanticism—the need to preserve the earth inherited from the forefathers. The Branner version concludes with a shot of Olof, Kyllikki, and their newborn child, reflecting the final maturity of Olof; it is typical of the nativity propaganda of its time. Molander's version, in contrast, closes with a shot of Olof welcoming Kyllikki home to the farm of his father. This is quite representative of the "green" thread in films of this genre in the postwar period. These were, perhaps, a challenge to the rapid transition of Swedish society in the 1950s and 1960s.

CREW—FIRST FILMING

Director: Mauritz Stiller. Script: Gustaf Molander, Mauritz Stiller. Cinematographer: Ragnar Westfelt, Henrik Jaenzon. Music: Armas Järnefält. Art Director: Axel Esbensen. Producer: Svenska Biografteatern.

CAST—FIRST FILMING

Lars Hanson (Olof Koskela), Axel Hultman (Olof's father), Louse Fahlman (Olof's mother), Greta Almroth (Annikki), Lillebil Christensen (Elli), Edith Erastoff (Kyllikki), Hjalmar Peters (Kyllikki's father).

PREMIERE—FIRST FILMING

Swedish: 14 Apr. 1919

CREW—SECOND FILMING

Director: Per-Axel Branner. Script: Ragnar Hyltén-Cavallius. Cinematographer: Julius Jaenzon. Sound: Gustaf Gyllby. Art Director: Arne Åkermark. Editor: Rolf Husberg. Producer: Wive.

CAST—SECOND FILMING

Edvin Adolphson (Olof), John Ekman (Olof's father), Gertrud Pålsson-Wettergren (Olof's mother), Aino Taube (Annikki), Gull-Mai Norin (Maikki), Inga Tidblad (Kyllikki), Sven Bergvall (Kyllikki's father), *Birgit Tengroth ("Dark-Eye"), *Anders Henrikson (Antti).

PREMIERE—SECOND FILMING

Swedish: 12 Nov. 1934

CREW—THIRD FILMING

Director: Gustaf Molander. Script: Rune Lindström. Cinematographer: Åke Dahlqvist. Sound: Lennart Unnerstad. Music: Erland von Koch. Art Director: P. A. Lundgren. Editor: Oscar Rosander. Producer: Svensk Filmindustri.

CAST—THIRD FILMING

*Jarl Kulle (Olof), Erik "Bullen" Berglund (Olof's father), Linnéa Hillberg (Olof's mother), Ann-Marie Gyllenspetz (Annika), Ulla Jacobsson (Elli), *Anita Björk (Kyllikki), Edvin Adolphson (Kyllikki's father), Ingvar Kjellson (Falk), Marianne Bengtsson (Maria).

PREMIERE—THIRD FILMING

Swedish: 19 Dec. 1956

BIBLIOGRAPHY

Soila, Tytti. "Five Songs of the Scarlet Flower." *Screen* 35, no. 3 (Fall 1994): 265–274.

SMULTRONSTÄLLET/WILD STRAWBERRIES. Isak Borg is an aged physician who is about to go to the university city of Lund to be honored on the fiftieth anniversary of his doctorate. Before leaving he has a strange dream; in it he walks around an empty city. He sees, among other thing, a huge clock without hands, and he sees himself lying in a coffin. He is accompanied on his journey to Lund by his daughter-in-law Marianne. They stop at his old home where he seems to doze off and, dreamlike, enters the world of his childhood. He stands in the door and watches his family and how his sweetheart Sara is seduced by his brother. He quits dozing, and the two continue their journey, picking up some young people on the road. One of them, a young girl also called Sara, is remarkably similar to the Sara of his childhood. They visit other people, among them Isak's very old mother, who presents him with some old things, including an old watch without hands. The two young men they had earlier picked up have a fierce discussion about whether God exists, which Isak mediates. Then Isak has another strange dream where he is scrutinized by an examiner who passes the sentence: Isak lacks emotions and can therefore not pass his exam. Finally they arrive in Lund. Isak's son Evald, Marianne's husband, is also a physician and seems to be a mirror of his father. He is cold and emotionless, and their marriage is both childless and unhappy. In the evening Isak is greeted by Sara before they leave. Isak has a final dream, once again recalling his childhood. The final scene is one of harmony and happiness where his parents are fishing and the rest of the family are about to leave on a sailing trip.

This film, which has often been analyzed, follows a classic, common pattern, especially in the religious literature, of the "homo viator," the man who travels. An old man gives a final account of his life, a psychoanalytical voyage filled with all the obvious symbols of, among other things, the fear of timeless death. However, there is also a strong sense of coming to terms with death, an end to a long struggle of many personal anxieties. Much of this lies in the thought of being reborn, that life has a continuity. The two Saras represent such an "unending" life span. The end of life is also seen as a return to the innocence of childhood.

The wild strawberries in the title have an important role as an earthly, cyclical symbol. These appeared in *Bergman's first film, *Kris* [Crisis]—but were cut in the final version—and at the end of *Det sjunde inseglet/The Seventh Seal*. With this symbolization Bergman demonstrates his link to the pastoral tradition in Swedish cinema. These two films, along with *Smultronstället*, follow, at least on a psychic level, a pattern common to Swedish films, that of paradise lost and regained.

CREW

Director and Script: Ingmar Bergman. Cinematographer: Gunnar Fischer. Sound: Aaby Wedin. Music: Erik Nordgren. Art Director: Gittan Gustafsson. Editor: Oscar Rosander. Producer: Svensk Filmindustri.

CAST

*Victor Sjöström (Isak Borg), *Gunnar Björnstrand (Evald, his son), *Ingrid Thulin (Marianne, Evald's wife), *Bibi Andersson (Sara), Folke Sundqvist (Anders), Björn Bjelfvenstam (Viktor), Jullan Kindahl (Agda, Isak's housekeeper), Gunnar Sjöberg (Sten Alman), Gunnel Broström (Berit, his wife), Naima Wifstrand (Isak's mother), Per Sjöstrand (Sigfrid Borg), Gio Petré (Sigbritt Borg), *Gunnel Lindblom (Charlotta Borg), Sif Ruud (Aunt Olga), Gertrud Fridh (Karin, Isak's wife), Åke Fridell (Karin's lover), *Max von Sydow (gas station owner).

PREMIERE

Swedish: 26 Dec. 1957

New York: 22 June 1959

BIBLIOGRAPHY

Andersson, Lars Gustaf. "Smultronstället och Homo viator-motivet." *Filmhäftet*, no. 62 (1988): 26–39.
Bergman, Ingmar. *Wild Strawberries*. London: Lorimer, 1970. Script.
See also Birgitta Steene, 1987, under Ingmar Bergman.

AWARDS

Berlin Golden Bear 1958: Best Film

AAN 1960: Best Script

UNGA HJÄRTAN [YOUNG HEARTS]. Marianne is a seventeen-year-old girl from an haute bourgeois home. Her parents live in an unhappy marriage and decide to send her to a confirmation preparation course in the countryside. There she meets a young man from a neighboring farm, Hans, and despite her resistance—because he is already engaged—they fall helplessly in love. Then comes news that her father has been seriously hurt in an automobile accident, and Marianne discovers that her father has for a long time had a young mistress, not much older than she. Marianne, after much agony, decides to break with Hans, and on their confirmation day, Marianne tries in vain to reconcile with

Hans's fiancée. Marianne and Hans part, and the viewer is left uncertain as to whether Marianne will stay with her mother or become engaged to her cousin Stellan, with whom she had had an earlier relationship.

This tight little youth melodrama is virtually unknown today; it is hardly mentioned in Swedish film history. It is a simple and straightforward story, but it is interesting because, unlike others of its time, it addresses youth questions. It provides more evidence that the mid-1930s constituted an important transition time in Swedish cinema and society. Youth questions have long been regarded as post–World War II phenomena. While it is true that we now have a distinctive youth culture, often identified with mass consumption, we must remember that it is much older than this. Just after World War I the topic of youth as a cultural entity was being discussed, and research on youth and adolescent phenomena was already in full swing.

Unga hjärtan focuses on events that can be attributed to the transition from childhood to adult life. It deals with the discovery of physical love with all its sweetness and pain. It also deals with overcoming narcissism. Marianne is seen to be strongly tied to her father. Her discovery of his infidelity is both a painful blow and an inspiration to be free of her childish self by taking the painful, obligatory step into womanhood.

The film confirms *Per-Axel Branner's sensitivity to both the medium of film and young actors and actresses. One writer has hailed him as a youth specialist, which both this film and another of his films, *Ungdom av i dag*, confirm. These two films are perhaps the first in the Swedish cinema to give a wholly modern view of the teenager as distinct from other groups.

CREW

Director: Per-Axel Branner. Script: Martin Rogberg, Per-Axel Branner. Cinematographer: Valdemar Christensen. Sound: Henning O. Petersen. Music: Otto Lington. Editor: Valdemar Christensen, Carl H. Petersen. Producer: Svenska AB Nordisk Tonefilm, Nordisk Tonefilm A/S.

CAST

Anne-Marie Brunius (Marianne), Märta Ekström (Marianne's mother), Gabriel Alw (Marianne's father), Håkan Westergren (Hans), Georg Blickingberg (the parson), Frank Sundström (his son), Wanda Rothgardt (Anna), Ingrid Robbert (Birgit, Hans's fiancée), Inga-Bodil Vetterlund (Margit).

PREMIERE

Swedish: 22 Oct. 1934

UTVANDRARNA/THE EMIGRANTS. This film depicts the wave of immigration from Sweden to the United States that from the 1860s until the 1910s took upward of 1 million Swedes to a new and hoped-for better future. If one considers that Sweden only had a few million inhabitants at the time, one can imagine the effects this had on Swedish society. The film is based on Vilhelm

Moberg's novels, which, with their realistic depiction that included foul language, caused some anger when they were written in the 1940s and 1950s. The story centers around the small farmer Karl Oskar, his wife, and his brother. He has inherited a small farm but sees no future in laboring in his stone-filled fields where the harsh climate can at any time destroy his hopes of a meager harvest. He and several others from the same village in southeast Småland reflect on their various needs to emigrate: being poor, experiencing religious intolerance, or being social outcasts. They decide to leave, and after a long journey, they arrive at the promised land. Karl Oskar and his family eventually settle in Minnesota. There life there is depicted in the sequel *Nybyggarna/The Good Land*.

Many directors wanted to make a film with this rich, epic material, including John Ford. Moberg at first turned down these offers and eventually decided on *Jan Troell; after seeing his epic *Här har du ditt liv/Here's Your Life*, he was convinced that Troell was the man to do it. *Utvandrarna* turned out to be one of the costliest projects in Swedish film history. Fortunately it was also one of the most successful Swedish films of the 1970s despite the critics' mixed reactions. Some thought that the film's plot was a little too disjointed, that its epic structure had been lost. Other critics pointed out that Troell had, with his use of forceful images, captured the moods and sentiments extraordinarily.

These ostensibly contradictory interpretations might be part and parcel of an integrated whole. These factors are perhaps those that make up the Swedish national epic. The lack of a tight action-oriented, American-style plot is a strength, for it allows for a Swedish drama style beholden to the rural, visually rich—with which Swedes identify. This style allows access to another element of Swedish national patriotism—the ability of the Swede to endure and live with rural poverty—as the great romantic Almqvist described it in his classic 1838 essay about the importance of poverty in Sweden. For contemporary Swedes, watching these wretched conditions of the past reminds them of their strength and endurance in the face of adversity. The film also was successful in the United States, being nominated for several Academy Awards. For an American audience the film might have served as a reminder of the ideals that built their nation, especially important given the social unrest surrounding the Vietnam War.

CREW

Director: Jan Troell. Script: Jan Troell, Bengt Forslund. Cinematographer: Jan Troell. Sound: Sten Norlén, Eddie Axberg. Music: Eric Nordgren. Art Director: P. A. Lundgren. Wardrobe: Ulla-Britt Söderlundh. Props: Peter Høimark. Editor: Jan Troell. Executive Producer: Bengt Forslund. Producer: Svensk Filmindustri.

CAST

*Max von Sydow (Karl Oskar Nilsson), Liv Ullmann (Kristina, his wife), Eddie Axberg (Robert, his brother), Pierre Lindstedt (Arvid, farmhand), *Allan Edwall (Danjel, Kristina's uncle), Monica Zetterlund (Ulrika, prostitute), *Hans Alfredson (Jonas Petter), Aina

Alfredsson (Oskar's mother), Svenolof Bern (Oskar's father), Gustaf Färingborg (Brusander, parson), Åke Fridell (Aron), Bruno Sörwing (Lönnegren), Ulla Smidje (Inga-Lena), Agneta Prytz (Fina Kajsa), Halvar Björk (Anders Månsson).

PREMIERE

Swedish: 8 Mar. 1971

New York: 24 Sept. 1972

BIBLIOGRAPHY

Forslund, Bengt. "Oförglömliga filmdagar med Vilhelm Moberg." *Vecko-Journalen*, no. 34 (1973):20–21, 50–51. Gives the story of the production.
Kanfer, Steven. "The Emigrants: A Dream Survives." *Time*, 4 Dec. 1972.
Utvandrarna. Booklet published by Svensk Filmindustri and Emigrantinstitutet, 1970.

AWARDS

AAN 1972: Best Foreign Film

AAN 1973: Best Film, Best Director, Best Actress, Best Script

Golden Globe 1973: Best Foreign Film

GENERAL BIBLIOGRAPHY

Andersson, Gunder. "Ragneborn, Holmsen, Kjellgren och tidsandan. Om ungdom på glid i ett välfärdssamhälle på marsch." In *Svensk filmografi*. Vol. 5, 1950–1959. Stockholm: Svenska Filminstitutet, 1984. Essay on the films about juvenile delinquents in the 1940s and 1950s.

Andersson, Ing-Mari. "Arbetarrörelsen och valfilm." *Chaplin*, no. 170 (1980):199–204. Essay on the propaganda features produced by the Social Democratic Party. Beware of some factual errors.

Bengtsson, Bengt. "Folkhemskritiker eller sensationsfilmare? En återblick på 'ungdomsfilmaren' Egil Holmsen." *Filmhäftet*, nos. 69–70 (1990):24–32. Essay on one of the most interesting makers of films about problematic youth in the postwar cinema.

Bengtsson, Bengt. *Ungdom i fara—ungdomsproblem i svensk spelfilm 1942–1962*. Stockholm: Stockholms Universitet, 1998. Dissertation on youth and juvenile delinquency in Swedish postwar films.

Björkin, Mats. *Amerikanism, bolsjevism och korta kjolar: filmen och dess publik i Sverige under 1920-talet*. Stockholm: Aura, 1998. Dissertation on Swedish films and film culture in the 1920s.

Björkman, Stig. *Film in Sweden. The New Film Directors*. South Brunswick, NJ: A. S. Barnes, 1977. Collection of essays on some contemporary Swedish filmmakers.

Bono, Francesco, and Maaret Koskinen, eds. *Film in Sweden*. Stockholm: Svenska Institutet, 1996. Essays on contemporary Swedish film. Contains useful bibliography.

Broström, Jonas. "I krigets slagskugga: Sverige." In *Der Zweite Weltkrieg im Skandinavischen Film. International Edition*. Vol. 22. Lübeck: Nordische Filmtage, 1980. Useful and well-researched account of Swedish film during World War II.

Cowie, Peter. *Swedish cinema, from Ingeborg Holm to Fanny and Alexander*. Stockholm: Svenska Institutet, 1985. One of a few general studies in English; unfortunately, rather shallow.

Film Comment. Vol. 6, no. 2 (Summer 1970). Special issue. Film in Sweden.

Florin, Bo. *Den nationella stilen. Studier i den svenska filmens guldålder.* Stockholm: Aura, 1997. Dissertation on style in the cinema of the so-called Golden Age, 1917–1924.

Forslund, Bengt. "Åttiotalets svenska filmverklighet." *Chaplin,* no. 196 (1985):9–11. Reflections made by a producer who has worked in Swedish film since the 1960s. Also see his valuable comments on individual films in *Svensk filmografi,* vol. 7.

Forslund, Bengt. *Bengt Forslund presenterar filmstjärnor. En bok om svenska skådespelare i världen.* Stockholm: Alfabeta, 1995. Short articles about Swedish actresses with international careers.

Fullerton, John. "AB Svenska Biografteatern: Aspects of Production 1912–1920." In *Current Research in Film: Audiences, Economics and Law.* Vol. 1, ed. Bruce A. Austin. Norwood, NJ: Ablex, 1985.

Furhammar, Leif. *Filmen i Sverige. En historia i 10 kapitel.* Höganäs: Wiken, 1991. Revised edition, 1998. Written by former professor at chair, this is the best general history so far, although it sometimes lacks in analysis.

Furhammar, Leif. *Folklighetsfabriken. Porträtt av ett svenskt filmbolag.* Stockholm: PAN-Norstedts, 1979. Study of one of the minor companies, Svensk Talfilm, producer of, among other things, the *Åsa-Nisse* movies.

Furhammar, Leif. "Svensk dokumentärfilmshistoria från PW till PW." *Filmhäftet,* nos. 38–40 (1982). Overview of Swedish documentary from the 1920s until the 1950s.

Gay, James Paul. "Red Membranes, Red Banners." *Sight & Sound* 41, no. 2 (Spring 1972):94–98. Essay on the political cinema of the early 1970s (Bergenstråhle, Troell, Sjöman, and others).

Geber, Nils-Hugo. "Den problematiska svenskheten." *Filmhäftet,* no. 53 (May 1986):4–14. On the problem to define a specific national Swedish cinema.

Gillett, John. "Swedish Retrospect." *Sight & Sound* 43, no. 3 (Summer 1974):152–153. On the rediscovery of, among other things, Georg af Klercker.

Hagman, Ingrid. "Den frånvarande fadern." *Chaplin,* no. 241 (Sept.-Oct. 1992):14–19. Essay on the "absent father" in some new Swedish films.

Hedling, Erik, ed. *Blågult flimmer. Svenska filmanalyser.* Lund: Student Litteratur, 1998. Valuable but somewhat uneven anthology with analysis of Swedish films from various times.

Holm, Crick. *På tu man hand med filmidoler.* Stockholm: Medéns, 1947. Articles about actors.

Idestam-Almquist, Bengt. *När filmen kom till Sverige. Charles Magnusson och svenska bio.* Stockholm: Norstedts, 1959. Detailed pioneer study on the beginning of Swedish film.

Idestam-Almquist, Bengt. *Svensk film före Gösta Berling.* Stockholm: PAN-Norstedts, 1974. A sample of articles on early Swedish cinema.

Jeune cinéma. No. 57 (Sept.–Oct. 1971). Special issue "Cinéastes suedoises."

Jungstedt, Torsten. *Kapten Grogg och hans vänner. Om Victor Bergdahl, Emil Åberg, M. R. Liljeqvist och Paul Myrén som alla var med om den tecknade svenska stumfilmen.* Stockholm: Proprius, 1977. The only study on early Swedish animation film.

Kolaja, Jiri. "Swedish Feature Films and Swedish Society." *Hollywood Quarterly* 5, no. 2 (1950):189–194.

Lachmann, Michael, and Hauke Lange-Fuchs. *Film in Skandinavien 1945–1993*. Berlin: Henschel, 1993.

Lennerhed, Lena. "Fäbodjäntan och hennes systrar-om 70-talets pornografiska biograffilm." In *Svensk filmografi*. Vol. 7, 1970–1979. Stockholm: Svenska Filminstitutet, 1989. Essay on the erotic films of the 1970s.

Liljedahl, Elisabeth. *Stumfilmen i Sverige—kritik och debatt. Hur samtiden värderade den nya konstarten*. Stockholm: Proprius, 1975. Doctorale dissertation on early Swedish film criticism.

Lindström, Lars. "Svenska Bio från Kristianstad till Lidingön." In *Svensk filmografi*. Vol. 1, 1897–1919. Stockholm: Svenska Filminstitutet, 1986. Detailed study on the early company Svenska Bio.

Norlin, Margareta. *Children's Film in Sweden*. Stockholm: Swedish Institute, 1990.

Olsson, Jan. *Från filmljud till ljudfilm. Samtida experiment med Odödlig teater, Sjungande bilder och Edisons Kinetophon 1903–1914*. Stockholm: Proprius, 1986. On early experiments with sound and film in Sweden.

Olsson, Jan. "Liebe macht blind and Frans Lundberg. Some Observations on National Cinema with International Ambitions." *Film History* 3, no. 4 (1989):307–316.

Olsson, Jan. *Sensationer från en bakgård. Frans Lundberg som biografägare och filmproducent i Malmö och Köpenhamn*. Stockholm/Stehag: Symposion, 1988. Well-researched study on early film producer Frans Lundberg.

Olsson, Jan. *Svensk film under andra världskriget*. Lund: Liber, 1979. Dissertation on Swedish film during World War II.

Olsson, Jan, ed. *I offentlighetens ljus*. Stockholm/Stehag: Symposion, 1990. Collection of essays on early Swedish film. Illustrated (in color) with posters of almost all Swedish films until 1929.

Osten, Gerd. *Den nya filmrealismen*. Stockholm: LTs förlag, 1956. Collection of essays on the films of the 1950s.

Östergren, Klas. "Brottsplats: Folkhemmet. Femtiotalets svenska deckar-och thrillerfilm." In *Svensk filmografi*. Vol. 5, 1950–1959. Stockholm: Svenska Filminstitutet, 1984. Well-written essay on the various attempts in Sweden to make films within the detective and thriller genres.

Paulus, Alfred. *Schwedische Filmproduktion 1955–1963. Analyse ihrer Voraussetzungen und Tendenzen*. Tübingen: Gunter Narr, 1984.

Qvist, Per Olov. "Bort från byn och hem igen. Storstaden i svensk film." *Filmhäftet*, nos. 55–56 (Dec. 1986):35–59. Essay on the country versus city theme in Swedish film.

Qvist, Per Olov. *Folkhemmets bilder. Modernisering, motstånd och mentalitet i den svenska 30-talsfilmen*. Lund: Arkiv, 1995. Study on the Swedish cinema in the 1930s and its relation to politics and society.

Qvist, Per Olov. "Jakten efter den försvunna svenskheten." *Filmhäftet*, no. 53 (May 1986):15–39. Essay on Swedish film and Swedish mentality.

Qvist, Per Olov. *Jorden är vår arvedel. Landsbygden i svensk spelfilm 1940–1959*. Uppsala: Filmhäftet, 1986. Dissertation on the Swedish rural postwar cinema.

Qvist, Per Olov. "Paradise Lost and Regained." In *Nordic Landscopes. Cultural Studies of Place*, ed. Anders Linde-Laursen and Jan Olof Nilsson. Copenhagen: Nordic Council of Ministers, 1995.

Qvist, Per Olov. "Svensk film upptäcker hembygden." *Filmrutan*, no. 3 (1992):2–9. Essay on some films of the early 1990s and how they depict the Swedish community.

Qvist, Per Olov. "Vår beredskap var god." *Filmkonst* 3 (1990):171–192. Essay on the Swedish cinema during World War II.

Reinholds, Jan. *Bio i Sverige 1900–1975. Marknad för fotografiska skådespel.* Lerum: Reinholds Text & Förlag, 1986. Study from an economic-historic point of view.

Reinholds, Jan. *Filmindustri 1900–1975. Tekniska genombrott och produktion av fotografiska skådespel.* Lerum: Reinholds Text & Förlag, 1986.

Revue du cinema, La. Image et son. No. 263 (Feb. 1970). Special issue "Le cinéma suedois."

Rodin, Gösta. *Den svenska filmens glada 30-tal.* Stockholm: Nordisk bokindustri ab, 1976. Memoirs by one of the directors in the 1930s.

Rönnberg, Margaretha. *En lek för ögat. 28 filmberättelser av Astrid Lindgren.* Uppsala: Filmförlaget, 1987. Study of the various film adaptations of Astrid Lindgren's novels and stories.

Schein, Harry. "Det hände på 60-talet." In *Svensk filmografi.* Vol. 6, 1960–1969. Stockholm: Svenska Filminstitutet, 1977. A not-too-objective but interesting essay on the cinema of the 1960s written by the former chairman of the Film Institute.

Schein, Harry. *I själva verket. Sju års filmpolitik.* Stockholm: Norstedts, 1970. A detailed account of the film politics in the 1960s.

Schein, Harry. *Schein.* Stockholm: Bonniers, 1980. Autobiography.

Sjögren, Olle. *Den goda underhållningen. Nöjesgenrer och artister i Sveriges radio och TV 1945–1995.* Stockholm: Stiftelsen etermedierna i Sverige, 1997. Historical chronicle about entertainment in Swedish radio and television that gives useful facts about the background of later filmmakers such as Hans Alfredson, Tage Danielsson, Lasse Hallström, and Lasse Åberg.

Sjögren, Olle. "Den komiska strömkantringen. Några funderingar kring revoltfirande, bakrus och skrattfest i svensk film." *Chaplin,* no. 180 (1982):120–127. Essay on the new Swedish film comedy of the 1970s and early 1980s.

Sjögren, Olle. "Det blågula stjärnbaneret." *Filmhäftet,* nos. 83–84 (1993): 3–82. Long essay on the influence of American cinema and culture on Swedish film.

Skånska kinematografen. En bok om film i Skåne och skånska filmare. Sydsvenska Dagbladets årsbok 1977. Malmö: Sydsvenska Dagbladet, 1976. Collection of articles on filmmakers and artists from the province Skåne. Some about the earliest Swedish film production in Kristianstad.

Soila, Tytti. *Kvinnors ansikte. Stereotyper och kvinnlig identitet trettiotalets svenska filmmelodram.* Stockholm: Institutionen för teater och filmvetenskap, Stockholms Universitet, 1991. Dissertation on the image of women in the films of the 1930s.

Soila, Tytti. "Sweden." In *Nordic National Cinema,* ed. T. Soila, A. Söderbergh-Widding, and G. Iversen. London: Routledge, 1998.

Statens offentliga utredningar (SOU). Official government investigations. Do often contain valuable statistics and other facts about the film industry and the film audience.

1942: *Betänkande med förslag rörande statligt stöd av svensk filmproduktion,* no. 36. Stockholm: Ecklesiastikdepartementet.

1945: *Ungdomen och nöjeslivet,* no. 22. Stockholm: Justiedepartementet.

1951: *Statligt stöd åt svensk filmproduktion,* no. 1. Stockholm: Finansdepartementet.

1951: *Filmcensuren. Betänkande 1,* no. 16. Stockholm: Ecklesiastikdepartementet.

1952: *Barn och film*, no. 51. Stockholm: Ecklesiastikdepartementet.

1956: *Vissa ändringar i nöjesbeskattningen*, no. 23. Stockholm: Finansdepartementet.

1959: *Filmstöd och biografnöjesskatt*, no. 2. Stockholm: Finansdepartementet.

1969: *Filmen-censur och ansvar*, no. 14. Stockholm: Utbildningsdepartementet.

1970: *Samhället och filmen. Del 1. Samhällsstödda biografer. Filmstudios. Barn-
film. Filmbranchen och TV*, no. 73. Stockholm: Utbildningsdepartementet.

1972: *Samhället och filmen. Del 2. Film och TV-undervisning. Kortfilm*, no. 9.
Stockholm: Utbildningsdepartementet.

1973: *Samhället och filmen. Del 3. Den svenska filmbranchen. Film och mervär-
desskatt: Filmarbetarnas villkor. Filmstöd utomlands*, no. 16. Stockholm: Utbildningsdepartementet.

1973: *Samhället och filmen. Del 4. Slutbetänkande*, no. 53. Stockholm: Utbildningsdepartementet.

Steene, Birgitta. "The Image of the Child in Swedish Cinema." *Current Sweden*, no. 365
Stockholm: Swedish Institute, 1988.

Sundgren, Nils Petter. *The New Swedish Cinema*. Stockholm: Svenska institutet (Sweden
Books), 1970.

*Svensk Filmindustri tjugofem år. En bok om filmproduktion och biografrörelse utgiven
till jubiléet av AB Svensk Filmindustri*. Stockholm: Svensk Filmindustri, 1944.
Collection of articles about major Svensk Filmindustri.

Svensk filmografi. Vols. 1–8. Edited by Lars Åhlander and Jörn Donner. Stockholm:
Svenska Filminstitutet, 1977–1997. Ambitious project to present all hard facts
and comprehensive information on Swedish film from the beginning until today.
Unfortunately, the printed volumes are often rather unreliable concerning factual
information. Much of this has been corrected in the CD-ROM edition (1996–,
available on PC and Mac) that so far covers all films until mid-1996.

Svensson, Arne. *Den politiska saxen. En studie i Statens Biografbyrås tillämpning av
den utrikespolitiska censurnormen sedan 1914*. Stockholm: Institutionen för teater
och filmvetenskap, Stockholms Universitet, 1976. Dissertation about the Swedish
Board of Censorship and how it acted in accordance with Swedish foreign policy.

Timm, Mikael. "Mot publiken, ur samtiden . . . Den svenska filmens 70-tal." In *Svensk
filmografi*. Vol. 7, 1970–1979. Stockholm: Svenska Filminstitutet, 1989. Essay
on trends in Swedish cinema of the 1970s.

Waldekranz, Rune. "Anna Hofman-Uddgren. Sveriges första kvinnliga filmregissör."
Chaplin, no. 196 (1983):117–121. About the first woman film director in Sweden.

Waldekranz, Rune. "Kriser och kransar i 50-talets svenska film." In *Svensk filmografi*.
Vol. 5, 1950–1959. Stockholm: Svenska Filminstitutet, 1984. Essay on the cinema
of the 1950s, written by a former producer at Sandrews.

Werner, Gösta. "Svenska Bios produktionspolitik fram till 1920." In *i Rörande bilder.
Festskrift till Rune Waldekranz*, ed. Leif Furhammar, Kjell Jerselius, and Olle
Sjögren. Stockholm: Norstedts, 1981. Gives valuable facts on production at and
economy of Svenska Bio.

Widerberg, Bo. *Visionen i svensk film*. Stockholm: Bonniers, 1962. Polemical attack on
contemporary Swedish cinema.

Wright, Rochelle. *The Visible Wall: Jews and Other Ethnic Outsiders in Swedish Films*.
Carbondale: Southern Illinois University Press, 1998.

GENERAL INFORMATION

FILM MUSEUM

Svenska Filminstitutet (Swedish Film Institute)
  P. O. Box 27 126
  S-102 52 Stockholm
  Phone: (land code Sweden) 8–665 11 00
  Home page: http:// www.sfi.se
  Film archive, library, stills archive. A separate film museum is planned.

FESTIVALS

Göteborgs Film Festival
  P. O. Box 7079
  S-402 32 Göteborg
  Phone: (land code Sweden) 31–41 00 45
  Appointed "official" film festival of Sweden. Annually in January–February.

Stockholm Film Festival
  P. O. Box 3136
  S-103 62 Stockholm
  Phone: (land code Sweden) 8–677 50 00
  Annually in November.

Umeå Film Festival
  P. O. Box 43
  S-901 02 Umeå
  Phone: (land code Sweden) 90–13 33 56
  Annually in September.

Uppsala Film Festival
  P. O. Box 1746
  S-751 47 Uppsala
  Phone: (land code Sweden) 18–12 00 25
  Annually in October (only short films).

EDUCATION

Dramatiska Institutet
  P. O. Box 27 090
  S-102 51 Stockholm
  Phone: (land code Sweden) 8–665 13 00
  Handles the professional training of film directors, and so on.

UNIVERSITY EDUCATION

Institutionen för filmvetenskap (Department of Film Science)
  Stockholms Universitet
  P. O. Box 27 062
  S-102 51 Stockholm
  Phone: (land code Sweden) 8–674 70 00

ASSOCIATION

Svenska Teaterförbundet (Swedish Actors Equity Association)
  P. O. Box 12 170
  S-112 94 Stockholm
  Phone: (land code Sweden) 8–785 03 30
  Organizes actors as well as other film workers.

FILM JOURNALS

Filmhäftet
  c/o Michael Tapper
  Lilla Fiskaregatan 10
  S-222 22 Lund

Filmkonst
  P. O. Box 7079
  S-402 32 Göteborg

Film & TV
P. O. Box 2068
S-103 12 Stockholm

Filmrutan
P. O. Box 82
S-851 02 Sundsvall

FINNISH CINEMA

PREFACE

The effort of introducing the cinema of a small, distant country is half doomed in advance. Just as with Bulgarian, Norwegian, or Venezuelan cinema, almost nothing is known about Finnish cinema outside the country's borders. I can only guess that a foreign spectator approaches Finnish films as if they were a science fiction experience. As with most small countries, the Finnish cinema is mostly rather provincial, relegated to immediate oblivion even in its own surroundings. In other respects a cinema such as Finland's can be seen as some kind of shadow history of more advanced or productive film countries—someone once compared the stylistic nearness of Teuvo Tulio's brilliantly original melodramas of the 1930s to the Czech cinema of the same period.

The national cinema clearly needs a spearhead—much as the Swedish cinema had on many occasions, first during the silent era with *Victor Sjöström and *Mauritz Stiller, then from the 1950s onward with *Ingmar Bergman (and *Alf Sjöberg), then again with the "new wave" and directors such as *Bo Widerberg and *Jan Troell. Moreover, all along the Swedish cinema was blessed with many exported talents—Greta Garbo, *Ingrid Bergman, Zarah Leander. Finland, with no clearly defined "Golden Age" (reminiscent of the Swedish silent era) to show, had only the late-coming and lonely exception of Aki Kaurismäki's personal achievement and its legend at least among the West European and always alert Japanese cinephiles, which again has—almost strangely—proved sufficient to arouse a revived interest in old Finnish cinema.

Names like Valentin Vaala and Matti Kassila, never much remarked upon in their heyday, have been "found" in a real sense at long last. Next, owing to the research of some "objective" foreign historians who have taken the trouble to carefully compare Swedish and Finnish film history, a surprising fact has been discovered: At least at certain times—1936–1939, 1940–1945, certain periods of the 1950s, the years of the "new wave" in the 1960s—Finnish cinema has been as vivid and creative as the better-known Swedish cinema of the period.

Of course, artistic success is not the only point. Cinema constitutes a secret history. It combines the observations and inner feelings of any given country. This is especially so in certain countries, among them, perhaps, Finland, a country situated between East and West, capitalism and socialism (a now-vanished system but a reality for most of the century). It is quite difficult, even impossible, to get the history of Finland straight without taking the cinema into consideration. Film has always aroused a kind of heightened interest, reflected in the fact that a nation of 4 million inhabitants could produce 30 feature films in one year (1955); so popular cinema—comedy, melodrama—was in a very true sense a dialogue between the people and their time.

As we well know, with the sole exception of Hollywood, even the best of comedies rarely pass abroad—even "commedia all' italiana," the fabulous phenomenon of the 1950s and 1960s, became known in foreign countries only in a fragmented way, and very great comedians such as Karl Valentin (Germany), Voskovec and Werich (Czechoslovakia), Cantinflas (Mexico), and Totò (Italy) remain almost as unknown abroad as the very Finnish Esa Pakarinen. How to estimate its impact, then? We know that in Finland more than a tenth of the nation—sometimes every fifth person—went to see some of the 1930s and 1940s farces; today they command incredible spectator numbers every time they are shown on television. Yet they go unviewed by foreign film specialists— who, incidentally, might gain through them a much closer look at the essence of Finnish cinema (and through it, Finland's national characteristics) than by concentrating solely on a handful of canonized "classics."

INTRODUCTION

THE 1920s

The very first Finnish feature film was *Salaviinanpolttajat* [The moonshiners], produced in 1907; after this dozens of films were completed in the 1910s. All of them seem to have vanished. This is regrettable for many reasons, above all because "the hidden history" of a country that in 1917 had gained her independence and in 1918 had experienced a bitter civil war is now lost—the flavor of a distinct period that feature films often manage to capture remarkably. Until 1917 Finland was under Russian rule; in Helsinki, new Russian and Swedish films were shown promptly upon their release.

There is no doubting the provincialism of early Finnish cinema; there was no equivalent "Golden Age" of the Swedish and Danish cinema here. Thus the 1920s—when cinematic history had already been made in other parts of the world for a quarter of a century—were to be the birth and the cradle of Finnish cinema in the best and most beguiling sense. Our young, independent Finland was to now have her own picture album. We can just begin to imagine the excitement in a cinema caused by a documentary showing familiar locations in a slightly new way or by an excerpt of a play presented in the new cinematic language.

The cinema of the 1920s was the beginning of a meaningful dialogue. In those days cinema was a very popular art of great immediacy; each new film was seen by audiences of hundreds of thousands. So people were, in a way, taking a stand in the darkness of a theater, and it was a way well suited to the quiet populace of a very quiet country.

From the very beginning, Finnish cinema was intimately connected to the best literature in the land. Many a vernacular literary classic became in the course of years also a classic of the cinema; one outstanding example is the first cinematic version of Aleksis Kivi's play *Nummisuutarit [The village shoemakers], written in the 1860s. Its inspired director *Erkki Karu was also the founder of Suomi-Filmi, the country's first major production company, and its director as a matter of course.

There were not too many fine entities in the films of the 1920s—the highlights were rather in certain emotionally charged scenes or moments or looks; there were budding film stars, and initial lineaments of a variety of film genres could be detected. All this was brought into being by prominent directors like Teuvo Puro, Woldemar Wohlström, and above all, by Erkki Karu. Films produced in those days were dramas of contemporary life, in which the main attraction was the title of the film or the subject matter, or comedies with urban settings (a surprising fact in a country that was still predominantly agrarian), and even military farces. For example, the film Meidän poikamme [Our boys] (Karu, 1929) deals with a serious issue—the army of the young republic—behind a lighthearted surface, naive humor, and evasive movements.

Many actors, who were to make a career in cinema later on, were being seen on screen for the first time, quite often in idyllic images in the middle of rural landscape. We can well imagine the thrill when big cameras and other film equipment were being dragged into the virgin countryside. This was how those precious, touching images of a land that is with us no more were captured; these modest images have preserved for us "the Finland of our dreams."

THE 1930s

It was in the 1930s that Finnish cinema really took off. It was then that it developed into a real "film industry," which meant for a small country, in many ways, imitating others. It was—seen from the point of view of themes and style—on the one hand, something original and, on the other, a reflection of what was being done in Germany, Czechoslovakia, England, and Sweden. Here, the 1930s turned out to be quite dramatic; our cinema began in a virtual void of mediocrity, then attained maturity in less than ten years, reaching the best achievements it was ever to have. This development was arrested in the very last month of the decade by the Winter War, shattered by blackouts and decreasing production.

When sound was introduced in the early 1930s, Finnish cinema shared the same difficulties filmmakers were facing everywhere. Very little was being produced—only some trivial, pathetic, primitive films, which in no way hinted at the standards attained in 1939. This year might well be the very best year in the history of cinema, not only globally but also in Finland. In that year Finnish studios produced very compelling and professional entertainment; we saw the release of our all-time sports classic Avoveteen [Towards a new horizon] (Orvo Saarikivi, 1939), which was made while the nation was awaiting the arrival of the 1940 Olympics, as well as Vihreä Kulta [Green gold] (*Valentin Vaala,

1939), an early ideological drama set in Lapland and promoting "green values" even then. Along with spirited yet rather mindless comedies, films with an exceptionally powerful message were being produced; these were based on historical events but intended for the day. Quite often, they voiced a rather aggressive attitude concerning our relationship with our neighbor in the East. In 1934, Suomi-Filmi gained a rival when Suomen Filmiteollisuus (SF), another "major production company," was founded. Both studios produced a crucial ideological drama in 1939, and it is significant that the head of each studio directed his own film: *Helmikuun manifesti* [February manifesto] was directed by *Toivo Särkkä, and *Risto Orko directed *Aktivistit* [Activists].

The pioneering company Suomi-Filmi was going through some rough periods under the leadership of Erkki Karu, whose ideas might have been a bit too artistic. Now, Risto Orko, a young director emerging from a completely different field, sharpened up the production, and within a year he directed *Siltalan pehtoori* [The foreman of Siltala farm], the first Finnish film to gain an audience of 1 million. He quickly appointed Valentin Vaala the company's chief director. Vaala's long career is quite stunning, both for its versatility and for its standards. His lifework includes films such as the tentative urban comedies *Vaimoke* [Surrogate wife] and *Mieheke* [Surrogate husband], the first of the *Niskavuori* films, which was to begin a remarkable series of family dramas, and *Juurakon Hulda* [Hulda of Juurakko] with its explicit feminist stance (this film was later to be produced in Hollywood under the title *Farmer's Daughter*). Further, he directed films about the life of lumberjacks, as well as historical dramas—his films were always made with style and an understanding of the secrets of unadulterated cinema.

The other Finnish "mogul," T. J. Särkkä, also started as a dilettante in the world of cinema. His career was to encompass fifty feature films; his first was released in 1935 when he was already forty-five years old. SF, in contrast to Suomi-Filmi, was a kind of mouthpiece for agrarian Finland; it was a haunt where the carryings-on of country yokels got a showing. It was also the production unit that promoted the laid-back genre of serial films.

In this mini Hollywood of Finland, all the ingredients were to be found: the different genres of cinema, the scripts and the stories, and commercial fervor. At the same time, some memorable films were being engendered by revolutionaries and by individuals cruising outside the system. Among them were the very young *Teuvo Tulio, who in the early 1930s was called "Finland's Valentino," and notably *Nyrki Tapiovaara, the director of *Juha* and *Varastettu kuolema* [Stolen death]. Tapiovaara's career came to an abrupt end when he was killed in the Winter War; at the time, his fifth film, *Miehen tie* [A man's way], had been only partially shot. He will remain in Finnish cinema as a symbol of unfulfilled promise.

Again, the 1930s were the first true era of stardom. Among the unforgettable romantic stars of those days were *Tauno Palo, *Ansa Ikonen, *Regina Linnanheimo, Helena Kara, and Irma Seikkula. Comedians such as Aku Korhonen, Kaarlo Angerkoski, and Siiri Angerkoski were stars in their own right as well.

THE 1940s

The 1940s, the time of the war and the years to follow, formed a unique success story in the history of Finnish cinema: Practically every single new film shown was seen by some 400,000 people. This meant that the two major studios, SF and Suomi-Filmi, became well established, and we can now talk about a Finnish film industry. Those years also offered numerous small companies opportunities to try their luck, even if the result might be only one single film or maybe two. Yet the obstacles could be monumental: Right through the decade there were shortages of materials of all kinds. For once the question became whether the studios could obtain enough raw film rather than whether audiences could be tempted to the theaters. The most popular film of all, *Kulkurin valssi* [The vagabond's waltz] (1941), was seen by the amazing figure of more than 1 million Finns, in other words, by one of every four people in the country's population.

The psychological effect of cinema was powerful. The flow of images not only offered an opportunity for escapism, but it also demonstrated that life was still going on despite all the hardships. The scope of almost all the films released in those years, as well as the charisma of the stars, was quite exceptional. The early 1940s—the war years—were for Finnish cinema one of the best periods of all, whereas the decade's end was a weird concoction in which certain directors—like Suomi-Filmi's Valentin Vaala and *Ilmari Unho—could one day release one of the finest Finnish films, then soon after produce something quite absurd. There is no question: A certain panic could be sensed in the air that this Golden Age was not going to last forever.

THE 1950s

The 1950s constituted the last full decade of Finnish "industrial" film. In its early years, a third large company, Fennada, was founded; in the meantime, Suomi-Filmi, the oldest of the companies, had already started to slow its production, clearly aware of the fact that a severe crisis was getting closer. SF, the largest of the companies and piloted by T. J. Särkkä, accelerated its production in such a frenzied way that at times it seemed to lack sanity. The most celebrated of SF's accomplishments were folksy comedies (*rillumarei*). At the same time, young director *Matti Kassila attempted to do in Finland something similar to what *Ingmar Bergman was achieving in Sweden. *Tuntematon sotilas* [The unknown soldier] (*Edvin Laine, 1955) is a testimony to the collective creativity operating before the end of the decade, and it forebodes the emerging hegemony of television and a sunset for the entire cinema industry.

Cinema—in both its good and bad manifestations—perhaps unconsciously recorded in an inimitable way how this predominantly agrarian country was becoming urbanized. It delineated this process with all of its complex consequences. The two comedians "Pekka and Pätkä," the lumberjack films, and the endless Niskavuori family dramas deal with this theme in a variety of ways. It seems quite likely that the majority of films produced in the 1950s were of inferior quality, especially those released in the last years of the decade, when a certain angst about survival was beginning to prevail. This fear was somehow reflected in production values, as funding preconditions were becoming ever more meager. Still, the 1950s constituted the final decade of cinema that to the audiences of those days (and to the future generations as well) represented the "true and real" cinema; thus, it is quite apparent that the period has been too easily undervalued. Even run-of-the-mill films made in the 1950s will still be discussed in forty years' time.

Traditional cinema had now reached maturity, and simultaneously the first signs of a modest stirring of "the new wave" could be detected.

THE 1960s

The 1960s can be divided in two distinct parts. In the early years, the producers pretended that the Golden Age was still with them. The three major companies were still alive—SF especially was frantically active. The result was a breathless final gallop, a huge number of films, if we indeed are permitted to call all of them films. Quality was often hard to find in these productions, which were mainly churned out by one gifted director, *Aarne Tarkas, who wasted his talent in these mindless efforts. The end came in the mid-1960s when T. J. Särkkä sold out the entire production of his company to television. The result was immediate inflation. People were now able to see Finnish films for free, so cinemas attracted only a fraction of the audiences of earlier days.

Now the only major production company continuing to produce feature films was Fennada Film, which had been founded back in the 1950s. The initiative had passed to the hands of new men and new companies. The model was often a company built around one talented director, as in the case of *Maunu Kurkvaara or *Risto Jarva (and his company Filminor) or *Jörn Donner, who, after beginning a promising career as a director in Sweden, had come back to Finland in the mid-1960s. *Mikko Niskanen, whose career commenced at the time of the change from old to new, became a notable portrayer of young people. He began by directing three war films. The greatest trauma in Finnish society, war, was still a very rarely broached subject in Finnish cinema. A large part of the new cinema had to struggle to survive in the conditions and atmosphere created by the State Film Prizes, an award system begun in 1962. It now had become cruelly obvious that it was no longer possible to produce films in a small country like Finland without some kind of public support system.

THE 1970s

In the thickening atmosphere of the early 1970s, the winds of freedom of the 1960s could still be felt—few of the newcomers to the cinematic world could guess that their first film was to be the only film they were ever going to make. There were experiments in new forms—imaginative but often insubstantial work. Then in 1974 the black hole of national film production was reached: Only two feature films were produced, both of them substandard.

By now, television had captured for good the cinema audiences of this little country, and it might be seen as a sign of the times that the finest feature film of the decade, Mikko Niskanen's *Kahdeksan surmanluotia* [Eight deadly shots] (1972), was produced on television; very few people went to see it in cinemas.

The most popular films could still attract audiences of around 700,000, which means one in six Finns. The most successful producer, comedian *Spede Pasanen, made numerous slapdash yet altogether riotous films in which Vesa-Matti Loiri in the leading role created the notorious character of Uuno Turhapuro (Mr. Emptybrook), who is a beer-swilling elemental Finn and the embodiment of masculine sloth. For many years, the entire institution of cinema rested on such films, and they kept the national film production financially above water. Yet these films were careless enough to eliminate even the modest criteria; even the worst products of old times had some signs of being "real films" in comparison to the brave new video-dominated age.

The second commercially successful production was *Rauni Mollberg's first film, *Maa on syntinen laulu* [The earth is a sinful song], which was also duly recognized abroad. Otherwise, theater attendance was at its lowest level ever— even the most talented suffered, as did Risto Jarva, who died tragically in a car crash. At one end of the scale, there was the "art film," always struggling in its efforts to gain recognition; and at the other end was the popular film in its most outrageous and uncontrolled manifestation.

THE 1980s

After the shaky 1970s, Finnish cinema in the new decade stretched ahead in a sea of unpredictability or even some kind of superfluity. Now only rarely could audiences of the previous decades be attained. And while the main cause of complaint was the minuscule audience, a lot of thought was given to what could be done about it. In the 1940s, an average audience of any Finnish film was about 400,000, that is, one in ten Finns; in the 1980s, each local film was seen by only 10,000 or 20,000 individuals out of a population of 5 million. And even these figures began to decline in the 1990s. The gulf between popular cinema and art cinema was becoming ever more tragic. The audiences and critics alike were still under the spell of the "bush theater."

The great characters of the previous generation were now making their final movies: Edvin Laine, who had already lost his touch, and Mikko Niskanen, who now found himself in an urbanized Finland that had abandoned its rural background. There were some big productions filmed on war: Jaakko Pakkasvirta's *Pedon merkki* [Sign of the beast] (1982) was a powerful epic, Rauni Mollberg brought out a new version of *Tuntematon sotilas* [The unknown soldier] (1985), and Pekka Parikka directed *Talvisota* [The Winter War] (1989)—probably the least notable but certainly the most popular of the 1980s war films.

Even if the audiences were very small, many films were produced; for instance, in 1985 the total number of new releases reached an astounding thirty. Among these were several experimental oeuvres, but no new Fellini or Bergman emerged. Yet, now as always, cinema rendered an enduring record of the period: The series of Anssi Mänttäri (this poor man's Fassbinder) films, which were practically ignored by contemporary audiences, will certainly prove to be a real sociological and cultural treasure trove for anyone researching the 1980s in the years to come.

And right in the middle of all this we come across the *Kaurismäki brothers, the first real international breakthrough of Finnish cinema. They started out together; the elder brother Mika directed, whereas the manuscript was written by Aki. *Matti Pellonpää, a talented actor who some ten years later came to be nominated the "best actor in Europe," naturally appeared in the main role. Then the brothers went separate ways, and their respective careers as directors progressed like thrillers. If it were not for them, the 1980s would have been something like the last frontier. It is also probable that there would not have been any Finnish cinema at all without the hugely successful *Turhapuro* series produced by popular comedian Spede Pasanen. These films offered a composite image of the self-admiration and self-pity of the everyday Finnish man; and just like the main character, a true sloth of a man, the nation was falling into decay, for by the end of the decade, Finland, which had once called itself the "Japan of Europe," woke up to find itself in an entirely transformed reality.

THE 1990s

Seldom has the pendulum of our national cinema swung so vehemently between appreciation and denigration as it did in Finland in the 1990s: From international acclaim to total apathy, it moved; from triumphal exhilaration, it swept to feelings of defeat and pretension. There have been countless articles in our press lamenting the state of national cinema, claiming it was totally irresponsible, even superfluous. And yet there have been moments of glory— notably thanks to Aki Kaurismäki. His *Leningrad Cowboys Go America* has become a cult movie. *Boheemielämää/La viè de bohème*, a film based on Henry Murger's classic novel and indeed acted in French, has even succeeded in moving the French. And his latest, *Kauas pilvet karkaavat* [Drifting clouds], has been a hit all over Europe. *Markku Pölönen's *Kivenpyörittäjän kylä* [The last wedding] clearly signaled a return to the rural themes cinema audiences had been awaiting—here we go again, and this time with a distinct nostalgic flavor. At the same time, stark urban themes bear testimony to an ever harsher existence and show a country in the grips of a severe economic crisis; one of the most heart-rending is Veikko Aaltonen's contribution *Tuhlaajapoika* [The prodigal son]. Quite often it is the films made for television that are most telling in dealing with these issues. In the 1990s, as so often in the past, Finnish cinema is in search of its soul, stuck between talent and routine, caught between the old and the new, fluctuating between moments of insight and total irresolution.

There is something that has veritably enriched Finnish cinema in the 1990s, and that is the increasingly central position women directors have achieved therein. *Pirjo Honkasalo has been active in the movie sector ever since the 1970s. In the early 1980s, she, along with Pekka Lehto, directed the noteworthy historical film *Tulipää* [Flame top], and since then she has been involved in the direction of fine documentaries. The glass ceiling was broken. Päivi Hartzell (*Lumikuningatar* [The snow queen]), Kaisa Rastimo, and other fresh female talent of the 1990s have unquestionably lent a new and original perspective to Finnish cinema.

NOTES TO THE FILMOGRAPHIES

ORDER OF FILMS

The date of a film is normally the release year according to the international filmography standard. For Finnish productions, these are the dates given by Filmografia Fennica.

ENGLISH TITLES

The italicized titles given are originally in English. When an italicized title appears after a slash, this means that the original English title differs from the Finnish title. All translations of film titles appear in brackets. The translations are those recommended by Filmografia Fennica (until 1970) or by the production companies (after 1970).

AWARDS

I have restricted myself to major European festivals (Cannes, Berlin, Venice), the annual European Film Award Felix, and the Finnish annual prize Jussi.

BIBLIOGRAPHIES

I have used abbreviated citations. Full bibliographic information is given in the "General Bibliography" at the end of this part.

LIST BY CAREER

DIRECTORS

Erik Blomberg

Jörn Donner

Roland af Hällström

Pirjo Honkasalo

Risto Jarva

Erkki Karu

Matti Kassila

Aki Kaurismäki

Mika Kaurismäki

Maunu Kurkvaara

Edvin Laine

Markku Lehmuskallio

Hannu Leminen

Rauni Mollberg

Mikko Niskanen

Risto Orko

Pertti (Spede) Pasanen

Antti Peippo

Markku Pölönen

Lasse Pöysti

Ville Salminen

Toivo Särkkä

Nyrki Tapiovaara

Aarne Tarkas

Teuvo Tulio

Ilmari Unho

Valentin Vaala

ACTORS/ACTRESSES

Kristiina Halkola

Ansa Ikonen

Leo Jokela

Lea Joutseno

Edvin Laine

Regina Linnanheimo

Rauni Mollberg

Kati Outinen

Esa Pakarinen

Tauno Palo

Pertti (Spede) Pasanen

Matti Pellonpää

Lasse Pöysti

Joel Rinne

Esko Salminen

Ville Salminen

Elina Salo

Kari Väänänen

CINEMATOGRAPHERS

Antti Peippo

Timo Salminen

AUTHORS

Mika Waltari

Hella Wuolijoki

ACTORS, ACTRESSES, DIRECTORS, CINEMATOGRAPHERS, AUTHORS

ERIK BLOMBERG (Helsinki, 18 Sept. 1913–12 Oct. 1996), director. Blomberg became interested in photography when he was still a schoolboy. Later he studied the field both in England and in France, where he had the opportunity to acquaint himself with the film studios of the 1930s. Already his first camera work was being noted: the ceaselessly heaving sea swell in the film *VMV 6* (1936) and the visual multifariousness of early twentieth-century Helsinki in *Nyrki Tapiovaara's (later a close associate) *Varastettu kuolema* [Stolen death] (1937). Blomberg was a key figure of the "image-conscious" generation in Finnish cinema; after many years behind the camera (some of them spent in Sweden in the late 1940s) shooting feature films and documenting the war, at last he felt ready to take up directing. So ready was he that *Valkoinen peura* [The white reindeer] (1952) is, along with *Tuntematon sotilas* [The unknown soldier], the most celebrated film of the "old" Finnish cinema. Its magic is born out of a powerful landscape, through which emerges a mystic, atavistic sequence of events. The affinity between eroticism and violence is an established theme much employed in horror movies, but the way in which Blomberg and the other "auteur" of this film, his actress wife and dramaturg Mirjami Kuosmanen, express the essence of angst, fear, and cruelty beneath an ostensibly folkloric and exotic imagery is cinema art at its most subjective.

The two adaptations of literary works that followed *Valkoinen peura* are the most ingenious achievements of their kind in Finland. One of them is *Kun on tunteet* [When there are feelings], a dramatization based on Maria Jotuni's short stories, and the other, *Kihlaus* [The betrothal], a folksy comedy by Aleksis Kivi, expanded into a full-length film. In *Kun on tunteet*, the overlapping of individual stories and the tales and characters meandering therein offer a multilayered expedition into a precise period, into the consciousness, sexual roles, and social dynamism therein. With a delightful touch of whimsey, Blomberg creates a kind of "candid camera cinema," giving us for once something to gape at: The corps of actors present us with an all-time Finn parade, a festive cavalcade of virtuosi.

Altogether, Blomberg directed only about half a dozen feature films (the last being a Finnish-Polish coproduction, *Hääyö* [The wedding night], 1958), but he also made a great number of documentaries, commissioned films, and educational films, as well as newsreels, which turn out to be among the best of their kind. In 1965, Blomberg directed his first film for television and continued to work in this new medium, specializing in themes dealing with the history of the eighteenth and nineteenth centuries.

FILMOGRAPHY

1952: *Valkoinen peura* [The white reindeer]. 1954: *Kun on tunteet* [When there are feelings]. 1955: *Miss Eurooppaa metsästämässä* [Hunting for Miss Europe]; *Kihlaus* [The betrothal/The engagement]. 1962: *Hääyö/Noc poslubna* [The wedding night] (co-prod. with Poland).

JÖRN DONNER (Helsinki, 5 Feb. 1933–), director, producer. Donner is a man of many talents. He is not only a film producer and director but also a critic, a journalist, a member of both the Finnish and European Parliaments, and the author of excellent books on Berlin and *Ingmar Bergman. He directed a few short films in Finland before beginning a career as a film director in Sweden. The most important of the four films he made in Sweden are the first and the last, *En söndag i september* [A Sunday in September] and *Tvärbalk* [Rooftree] (1965); their merit lies in a certain ability to capture intimate moments and a talent to ironically record idiosyncrasies of our habits and customs. Afterward, Donner made a sequence of films in Finland; they aroused controversy, scandal, enthusiasm, even contempt. The best of these is the first; *Mustaa valkoisella* [Black on white] has preserved its position as a sociological documentation of a salesman struggling on the threshold of burnout and the impending breakup of his middle-class marriage; the stage of conflict is invariably the bed—whose bed it is seems to be less important. *Naisenkuvia* [Portraits of women] (1969) is a laid-back "cinema verité" film focusing again on the middle classes. Its main character, a producer of pornographic movies, is played with certain self-mockery by Donner himself (he also played the main role in *Mustaa valkoisella*). The film was released at the same time as the notable documentary *Perkele! Kuvia Suomesta* [Fuck off! Images of Finland], which Donner filmed in various parts of Finland and in which the country's powerful and poor speak their minds.

If such films offered an insight into Finnish erotic culture and inhibitions, Donner had lost a lot of his grasp already in his early 1970s film *Anna*, with Harriet Andersson (the star of his Swedish films) in the main role once more. Donner's later films *Miestä ei voi raiskata* [Men can't be raped] and *Dirty Story* combine the trends of his Swedish and Finnish period, but since their release, he has been totally occupied by activities in other fields of society. And as time goes by, he seems to pay less and less attention to film production, which, after all, was his first interest.

FILMOGRAPHY

Director

1963: *En söndag i september* [A Sunday in September] (Sweden); *Att älska* [To love] (Sweden). 1965: *Här börjar äventyret* [Adventure starts here] (Sweden). 1967: *Han-hon* [He-she] (episode for *Stimulantia*, Sweden); *Tvärbalk* [Rooftree] (Sweden). 1968: *Mustaa valkoisella* [Black on white]. 1969: *Sixtynine*. 1970: *Naisenkuvia* [Portraits of women]. 1971: *Anna* (Sweden); *Perkele! Kuvia Suomesta* [Fuck off! Images of Finland] (docu.). 1972: *Hellyys* [Tenderness]. 1975: *Baksmälla/Krapula* [Hangover]. 1976: *Three Scenes with Ingmar Bergman* (docu.). 1978: *The Bergman File* (docu.); *Miestä ei voi raiskata* [Men can't be raped]. 1985: *Dirty Story*.

AWARD

Jussi 1968

KRISTIINA HALKOLA (Kuusankoski, 3 June 1945–), actress. Halkola was one of the last actors to work in the Finnish cinema for a monthly salary (FJ-Filmi, 1967–1969). Afterward, she worked for the Television Theatre for seven years. She was the most emblematic representative of the dynamism of the 1960s in Finland; paradoxically, she could be considered the last "star" of the era of studio production even though she obviously represented the new trends in the movies. Her unrestrained yet subtle talent portraying emotions made her an absolute smash in *Käpy selän alla* [Under your skin]; likewise, it rendered the young girl in *Mustaa valkoisella* [Black on white] a real, frank, yet touching character, turning the rebellious girl in *Punahilkka* [Little Red Riding Hood] into a living, breathing creation. In more recent years, too, she has acted in many good roles, and in the early 1970s, she was one of the "queens" of Finnish political song. Later on, Halkola was the chairman of the radical wing of the Finnish Communist Party.

FILMOGRAPHY

1965: *Vaaksa vaaraa* [The edge of danger/Close to danger]. 1966: *Tunteita* [Feelings]; *Tänään olet täällä* [Today you are here]; *Käpy selän alla* [Under your skin/Skin skin]. 1967: *Lapualaismorsian* [Girl of Finland]. 1968: *Mustaa valkoisella* [Black on white]; *Punahilkka* [Little Red Riding Hood]. 1988: *Lauran huone* [Laura's room] (short).

AWARD

Jussi 1967

ROLAND AF HÄLLSTRÖM (Lempäälä, 23 July 1905–21 Feb. 1956), director. Hällström was a theater director, film critic, and cinema director in the 1930s, but he gained prominence only from the late 1940s onward, when the last decade of his life was starting. When he died, at the film festival in Karlovy Vary, he had just been acclaimed, ironically, "a young promising director from Finland."

There was radiance in Hällström's personality, but at the same time a certain kind of unevenness seemed to be almost an in-built quality. He was in the true sense of the word an unfulfilled artist; there seemed to be hiding some delicate secrets under the surface of his oftentimes melodramatic films. Hällström's best film from the 1940s, *Pikajuna pohjoiseen* [The Northern Express], is also his first larger work, a combination of fatalistic drama and extremely accurate and realistic observation. *Noita palaa elämään* [The witch comes back to life] from the early 1950s is one of the very few Finnish horror movies; it is almost shameless and very likely a "bad" film, but it is beguiling in how it blends melodrama and sensational elements, one of which was nudity, in those quite puritanical days of the 1950s.

Hällström's four last films are all adaptations of Finnish national literature; he took up with an exceptionally fresh and expressive touch these works that until then had been treated rather mechanically. This is especially true of *Ryysyrannan Jooseppi* [Joseph of Ryysyranta] (1955), whose scope of expression and register would have been a real event, whatever theme, but here they had a notable effect because films describing the proletariat are usually doomed to be merely one dimensional. Here for once we have a film that brings the poor under intense aesthetic observation and where also irony and humor flourish on different levels. The entire film is dominated by an authentic grasp of imagery. And it does not come as a surprise when we are told that the film crew and set designers carried on heated discussions of Victor Hugo's *Les Miserables* and its attendant romanticism during the production: Mere misery and mere depiction of misery are not enough in themselves. Roland af Hällström is one of the directors who "died with his boots on"; he collapsed with a heart attack two days before the shooting of the film *Lain mukaan* [According to the law] was finished.

FILMOGRAPHY
Director

1938: *Paimen, piika ja emäntä* [Cowherd, maid and housewife]. 1939: *Vänrikki Stoolin tarinat* [The tales of Ensign Steel]. 1940: *Simo Hurtta*. 1946: *Houkutuslintu* [The decoy]. 1947: *Pikajuna pohjoiseen* [The Northern Express]. 1948: *Läpi usvan* [Through the fog]. 1949: *Hornankoski* [The rapids of hell]; *Vain kaksi tuntia* [Only two hours]. 1950: *Hallin Janne* [Halli's Johnny]. 1951: *Ylijäämänainen* [Stolen love]; *Tukkijoella* [The log drivers]. 1952: *Suomalaistyttöjä Tukholmassa* [Finnish girls in Stockholm]; *Noita palaa elämään* [The witch comes back to life]. 1953: *Saariston tyttö* [The girl from the Skerries]; *Kolmiapila* [The clover]; *Miljonäärimonni* [The millionaire recruit]; *Kuningas kulkureitten* [Vagabond king]. 1954: *Putkinotko* [Pipe hollow]. 1955: *Ryysyrannan Jooseppi* [Joseph of Ryysyranta]; *Poika eli kesäänsä* [The boy lived up his summer]. 1956: *Lain mukaan* [According to the law].

AWARD

Jussi 1948

PIRJO HONKASALO (Pori, 22 Feb. 1947–), director. Honkasalo no doubt possesses a special talent that has lent unity to her career. Her distinctive and extremely individualistic style is clearly marked in her documentaries as well as in her feature films—be the subject the turbulent student years of the late 1960s and the early 1970s, the historical epic in a rural setting, or love-hate ambivalence toward the windy and muddy city of Helsinki. *Tulipää* [Flame top] and *Da Capo*, made along with Pekka Lehto, were seen as being rather empty extravaganzas; however, they foretold a genre that was to be Honkasalo's specialty—the cinema of remembrance and subconsciousness, that borderland between reality and dream. These themes achieve a totality of personal expression in her documentaries—specifically in a form "that transcends documentary" as her fine trilogy *Mysterion, Tanjuska ja 7 perkelettä* [Tanjuska and the 7 demons], and *Atman* splendidly evince.

FILMOGRAPHY

1976: *Ikäluokka* [Their age/age class] (short, codir. Pekka Lehto); *Swastika* (short, codir. Pekka Lehto). 1979: *Kainuu 39* [Two forces] (codir. Pekka Lehto). 1980: *Tulipää* [Flame top] (codir. Pekka Lehto). 1983: *250 grammaa* [250 grammes—a radioactive testament] (short, codir. Pekka Lehto). 1985: *Da Capo* (codir. Pekka Lehto). 1991: *Mysterion* (doc.). 1993: *Tanjuska ja 7 perkelettä* [Tanjuska and the 7 demons] (doc.). 1996: *Tallinnan Tuhkimo* [The Cinderella of Tallinn] (codir. Merja Pensala, docu.); *Atman* (docu.). 1998: *Tulennielijä* [Fire-eater].

AWARDS

Jussi 1980

Jussi 1981

ANSA IKONEN (St. Petersburg, 19 Dec. 1913–23 May 1989), actress. Ikonen was the first actress in Finland to become a true film star and "a face loved by the camera" in the best sense of the cliché. She started out as an assistant in the theater and was employed by the National Theatre from 1935 until 1978. It was also in 1935 that she almost by chance began a screen career, during which she acted opposite *Tauno Palo, the greatest of Finnish screen idols, in about a dozen films. These films have attained the status of legend, among them: *Vaimoke* [Surrogate wife], *SF-paraati* [SF parade], and above all, *Kulkurin valssi* [The vagabond's waltz], the greatest of the hits made in the war years, and *Isän vanha ja uusi* [Father's new and ex] (1954), in which Ikonen showed the skills of a mature actress. As did many other actors of the "old school," she played her last film roles at a time when the Golden Age of Finnish cinema was approaching its end, and that as early as 1961. The last film director to work with Ikonen was the American Don Siegel.

FILMOGRAPHY

1934: *Minä ja ministeri* [Me and the cabinet minister]; *Meidän poikamme ilmassa—me maassa* [Our boys in the air—we on the ground]. 1935: *Syntipukki* [The scapegoat];

Kaikki rakastavat [Everybody's in love]. 1936: *Vaimoke* [Surrogate wife]. 1937: *Ja alla oli tulinen järvi* [And below was a fiery lake]; *Koskenlaskijan morsian* [The logroller's bride]; *Kuin uni ja varjo* [Like dream and shadow]; *Kuriton sukopolvi* [The unruly generation]. 1938: *Olenko minä tullut haaremiin* [Have I entered a harem?]; *Rykmentin murheenkryyni* [The black sheep of the regiment]. 1939: *Jumalan tuomio* [God's judgement]. 1940. *Serenaadi sotatorvella oli sotamies Paavosen tuurihousut* [Serenade with a war trumpet]; *SF-paraati* [SF parade]; *Runon kuningas ja muuttolintu* [The king of poets and the bird of passage]; *Oi, kallis Suomenmaa* [Finland, our dear native land]. 1941: *Kulkurin valssi* [The vagabond's waltz]; *Täysosuma* [Bull's eye]. 1942: *Uuteen elämään* [To a new life]; *Rantasuon raatajat* [The toilers of Rantasuo]. 1943: *Tyttö astuu elämään* [The girl goes out into the world]. 1944: **Vaivaisukon morsian* [The wooden pauper's bride]; *Nainen on valttia* [The woman is the trump]; *Suomisen Olli rakastuu* [Olli falls in love]. 1945: *Nokea ja kultaa* [Crime and gold]. 1947: *Pikku-Matti maailmalla* [Little Matti out in the wide world]; **Pikajuna pohjoiseen* [The Northern Express]. 1948: *Laitakaupungin laulu* [Song of the city outskirts]. 1949: *Jossain on railo* [The crevice]. 1950: *Professori Masa* [Professor Masa]. 1951: *Gabriel, tule takaisin* [Gabriel, come back]; *Vihaan sinua—rakas* [Darling, I hate you]. 1952: *Kulkurin tyttö* [The vagabond's girl]. 1953: *Tyttö kuunsillalta* [The girl from Moon Bridge]. 1955: *Rakas lurjus* [Beloved rascal]; *Isän vanha ja uusi* [Father's new and ex]. 1956: *Ratkaisun päivät* [Days of decision]. 1958: *Äidittömät* [The motherless ones]. 1961: *Miljoonavaillinki* [Short by a million]. 1987: *Rusinoita* [Raisins] (short).

AWARD

Jussi 1944

RISTO JARVA

RISTO JARVA (Helsinki, 15 July 1934–16 Dec. 1977), director, producer. Jarva met his death in a car accident in December 1977, the night after the successful premiere of his film *Jäniksen vuosi* [The year of the hare]. He had time to finish only eleven full-length films; nonetheless, they form an exceptionally coherent whole. Nature and man's relationship to nature were the undisputed concern of this man who had initially studied engineering. This concern was at the root of all his films, regardless of their subject matter. In his early short films Jarva began with the basic elements: color, rhythm, shape, movement. The first of his feature films was *Yö vai päivä* [Night or day] (together with Jaakko Pakkasvirta, 1962); with its lyrical images of forest in the rain, glitter of water, blue-tinged verdure—thus began his account of Finnish nature in its profoundest sense. *Jäniksen vuosi* fifteen years later announced that the circle was now complete.

Jarva had always been faithful to the things he considered important: In *Onnenpeli* [Game of chance] the weight is on debate and the sheer joyfulness of life with summer Helsinki as the backdrop, whereas in **Työmiehen päiväkirja* [The worker's diary] Jarva makes an almost pedantic effort to tie the individual tightly with history, then carries on to admit charitably that all people do have a right to their arguments (this is underlined by the final love scene merging triumphantly with a starry sky and the galaxies). In *Ruusujen aika* [Time of roses], Jarva paints a picture of Finland of the future (in 2012); while it is a horror scenario of all the things the director hopes will not happen, at the same time it allows us a glimpse of hope. *Yhden miehen sota* [One man's war] is particularly wrenching with its melancholy landscape on the outskirts of the city, that no-man's land of the unemployed and small-time entrepreneurs struggling with their endless problems; it is an ambiguous landscape of both hope and despair immortalized by the camera of the masterly *Antti Peippo.

One of Jarva's principal films, *Kun taivas putoaa* . . . [When the heavens fall . . .] (1972), strikes a slightly different note in his mode of production. It is melodrama, a satirical, stylistically almost vulgar tale from the world of scandal magazines—here is the director's dark side. When this film and *Yhden miehen sota* were met by the scorn of cinema audiences and critics (as well as their prejudices), Jarva turned with staunch determination to a lighter genre—the world of comedies, with which he made himself quite comfortable. It might well be that these "alternative comedies" of his were related to Jacques Tati's philosophy—or might have been, had he had time to develop the genre. *Loma* [The vacation] (1976) is a kind of "Grand Hotel" in a holiday paradise; a large group of Finnish tourists arrive in the sunny south, where Antti Litja—the unforgettable hero of Jarva's late films—has accidentally landed; actually, he had been on his way to the Alps to do some skiing. *Jäniksen vuosi* [The year of the hare] (1977) tells the story of an advertising man who opts out of the rat race. It shows how a modern gets back to nature, where his closest friend turns out to be a small hare. The story of man's defection is much used in the new cinema, and Jarva has made his own very personal and touching version of it.

FILMOGRAPHY

Director

1962: *Yö vai päivä* [Night or day] (codir. Jaakko Pakkasvirta). 1964: *X Paroni* [Baron X] (codir. Jaakko Pakkasvirta and *Spede Pasanen). 1965: *Onnenpeli* [Game of chance]. 1967: *Työmiehen päiväkirja* [The worker's diary]. 1969: *Ruusujen aika* [Time of roses]. 1970: *Bensaa suonissa* [Rally]. 1972: *Kun taivas putoaa* . . . [When the heavens fall . . .]. 1973: *Yhden miehen sota* [One man's war]. 1975: *Mies joka ei osannut sanoa ei* [The man who couldn't say no]. 1976: *Loma* [The vacation/Holidays]. 1977: *Jäniksen vuosi* [The year of the hare].

AWARDS

Jussi 1964–1965

Jussi 1967

Jussi 1970

Jussi 1977

LEO JOKELA (Hausjärvi, 24 Jan. 1927–11 May 1975), actor. Jokela began his working life as an engine driver, no less, then studied at the theater school, after which he chose to become a cinema makeup man because of his shyness. There, he was almost accidentally introduced first to small roles and then to ever bigger parts; later minor parts and short appearances in a great number of films made him a cult figure in the way that is familiar in the cinema of every single country. Primarily, Jokela was a fantastic actor, his performances could be outrageously funny, and many of the minor characters he created (especially in *Aarne Tarkas's films) are unforgettable.

FILMOGRAPHY

1949: *Kanavan laidalla* [At the edge of the canal]. 1950: *Orpopojan valssi* [The orphan's waltz]; *Köyhä laulaja* [The poor singer]; *Maija löytää sävelen* [Maija finds the right tune]. 1951: *Lakeuksien lukko* [It happened in Ostrobothnia]; *Tukkijoella* [The log drivers]. 1952: *Noita palaa elämään* [The witch comes back to life]. 1953: *Kuningas kulkureitten* [Vagabond king]; *Alaston malli karkuteillä* [The nude on the run]. 1954: *Kovanaama* [The tough guy]; *Sininen viikko* [Blue Week]; *Laivaston monnit maissa* [Naval recruits on shore leave]; *Putkinotko* [Pipe hollow]; *Hilman päivät* [Hilma's name day]; *Olemme kaikki syyllisiä* [We're all guilty]; *Laivan kannella* [On deck]; *Leena*. 1955: *Näkemiin Helena* [Farewell, Helena]; *Ryysyrannan Jooseppi* [Joseph of the ragged shore/Joseph of Ryysyranta]; *Tähtisilmä* [Starry eyes]; *Sankarialokas* [Conscript hero]; *Säkkijärven polkka* [Säkkijärvi Polka]; *Villi Pohjola* [The wild north]. 1956: *Lain mukaan* [According to the law]; *Jokin ihmisessä* [Somethin in people]; *Tyttö lähtee kasarmiin* [The girl in the barracks]; *Elokuu* [Harvest month]; *Rintamalotta* [Girls at the front]. 1957: *Kuriton sukupolvi* [Wild generation]; *Taas tyttö kadoksissa* [Another girl lost]; *Vääpelin kauhu* [The sergeant's nemesis]; *Syntipukki* [Scapegoat]. 1958: *Kulkurin masurkka* [The vagabond's mazurka]; *Asessorin naishuolet* [The assessor's troubles with women]; *Paksunahka* [Thick skin]; *Sotapojan heilat* [The soldier boy's sweethearts]; *Pieni luutatyttö* [The little girl with the broom]; *Sven Tuuva* [Soldier Sven]. 1959: *Kovaa peliä Pohjolassa* [Playing a hard game up north]; *Ei ruumiita makuuhuoneeseen* [No bodies in the bedroom]; *Punainen viiva* [The red line]; *Pekka ja Pätkä mestarimaalareina* [Pete & Runt, Master painters]; *Lasisydän* [The glass heart]; *Iskelmäketju* [Hit parade]. 1960: *Isaskar Keturin ihmeelliset seikkailut* [The wonderful adventures of Isaskar Keturi]; *Pekka ja Pätkä neekereinä* [Pete & Runt, Negroes]; *Kaks' tavallista Lahtista* [Two ordinary guys]; *Kankkulan kaivolla* [At the well]; *Komisario Palmun erehdys* [Police Inspector Palmu's mistake]; *Autotytöt* [Car girls]; *Opettajatar seikkailee* [The school marm on a road to adventure]; *Iloinen Linnanmäki* [Fun at the amusement park]; *Molskis, sanoi Eemeli, molskis!* ["Kerplunk," Emil said]. 1961: *Tähtisumua* [Stardust]; *Minkkiturkki* [The mink coat]; *Olin nahjuksen vaimo* [I was a poke's wife]; *Tyttö ja hattu* [The girl and her hat]; *Kaasua, komisario Palmu!* [Step on the gas, Inspector Palmu!]; *Oksat pois...* [No trifling]; *Kultainen vasikka* [The golden calf]; *Pikku Pietarin piha* [Little Peter]; *Kertokaa se hänelle...* [Tell it to her...]. 1962: *Älä nuolase...!* [Don't count your chickens...!]; *Taape tähtenä* [Stardom]; *Tähdet kertovat, komisario Palmu* [The stars will tell, Inspector Palmu]; *Vaarallista vapautta* [Dangerous freedom]; *Yö vai päivä* [Night or day]. 1963: *Villin Pohjolan kulta* [Gold from the Wild North]; *Turkasen tenava!* [Confounded brat!]. 1966: *Johan nyt on markkinat!* [What the devil!]; *Rakkaus alkaa aamuyöstä* [Love begins in the small hours]. 1967: *Pähkähullu Suomi* [Crazy Finland]. 1968: *Noin seitsemän veljestä* [About seven brothers]; *Vain neljä kertaa* [Four times only]. 1969: *Näköradiomiehen ihmeelliset siekailut* [The marvelous adventures of a TV man]; *Leikkikalugangsteri* [Toy gangster]; *Vodkaa, komisario Palmu* [Vodka, Inspector Palmu]. 1970: *Speedy Gonzales—noin 7 veljeksen poika* [Speedy Gonzales, son of about seven brothers]. 1971: *Saatanan radikaalit* [Damned radicals]; *Kahdeksas veljes* [The eighth brother]. 1974: *Viu-hah-hah-taja* [The whizzer].

LEA JOUTSENO (Helsinki, 6 Nov. 1910–20 June 1977), actress. Joutseno was working as a translator at Suomi-Filmi when she was "discovered"—almost accidentally—and came to be for a whole decade the brightest star in the company. She was a good representative of a breed of actress typical of that epoch— that is, the war years—portraying sharp-tongued, emancipated authoresses as well as the heroines of the popular and lighter writers, such as Hilja Valtonen and Kersti Bergroth (nom de plume Tet). Joutseno was a witty comedienne, who, as time went by, took more and more to writing the manuscripts and dialogue of her own films. She had the rare presence of mind to quit the limelight at a time when her star was still shining brightly. In an interview done in the 1970s, she gave a sample of her biting self-mockery: "I was never a beauty-queen, just another pretty face, who in the course of time has been converted into a matron resembling a swollen sausage."

FILMOGRAPHY

1937: *Juurakon Hulda* [Hulda of Juurakko]. 1938: *Niskavuoren naiset* [The women of Niskavuori]. 1939: *Vihreä kulta* [Green gold]. 1940: *Kersantilleko Emma nauroi?* [Was it the sergeant Emma laughed at?]; *Poikani pääkonsuli* [My son, the consul general]. 1941: *Morsian yllättää* [The bride springs a surprise]. 1942: *Varaventtiili* [Safety valve]; *Hopeakihlajaiset* [Silver betrothal anniversary]. 1943: *Neiti Tuittupää* [Miss Hothead]; *Tositarkoituksella* [With serious intent]. 1944: *Dynamiittityttö* [Dynamite girl]. 1945: *Vuokrasulhanen* [A hired fiancé]. 1946: *Viikon tyttö* [Girl of the week]. 1948: *Kilroy sen teki* [Kilroy was here].

AWARD

Jussi 1945

ERKKI KARU (Helsinki, 10 Apr. 1887–8 Dec. 1935), director. Karu was the man who laid the foundations of Finnish cinema; he was the founder of two major film companies and the director of a larger number of silent films than anyone else in Finland. He was the one who brought the country's past and present, its countryside and towns, its reality and dreams, to the silver screen, either via cinematic tales or literary adaptations. His main work, *Nummisuutarit [The village shoemakers], reflected his theater background; however, he translated theatrical clichés in an uninhibited and creative manner into the language of cinema. The artistic high point in Karu's life was the year 1923, when he directed *Koskenlaskijan morsian* [The logroller's bride], a film about lumberjacks, and the outrageous farce *Kun isällä on hammassärky* [When father has toothache]. Later, he made mainly unadorned and genuinely folksy cinema, but he was quite limited psychologically and rather monotonous in his means of expression, so that in his films there is not a great variety of styles representing the different genres of cinema art.

He was often patriotic to the point of chauvinism: Several of his films close with the Finnish flag flying, and the three *Meidän poikamme* [Our boys] films were unrestrained propaganda for the defense forces. From the beginning to the end, these films are a mixture of something depressingly banal and yet genuinely inspired. The second in the series, *Meidän poikamme merellä* [Our boys at sea], was, despite its pathetic plot, the first true Finnish musical—thanks to the presence of the popular singer Georg Malmsten and his pals.

Karu was always in spirit a foolhardy entrepreneur, and the nadir of his exertions was the plan he promoted in the 1920s to build the first skyscraper in Helsinki—right in the middle of a severe economic depression, whose effects also snuffed out Karu's work at Suomi-Filmi, the company he had founded in 1919. Nonetheless, he was not downhearted, and two years before his premature death, he founded another company, SF (Suomen Filmiteollisuus), which was to become the most productive company of the country. When it was launched, Karu stated: "However well farce and light music are doing, each country needs her own national theatre, in the true sense of the word." This is "the secret" of Karu's greatness—the core of emotional and straightforward popular cinema with unmistakable rural overtones.

FILMOGRAPHY

1920: *Sotagulashi Kaiun häiritty kesäloma* [War profiteer/Kaiku's disrupted summer vacation]; *Ylioppilas Pöllövaaran kihlaus* [Student Pöllövaara's betrothal]. 1922: *Finlandia* (docu., codir. Eero Leväluoma). 1923: *Koskenlaskijan morsian* [The lumberjack's bride/The logroller's bride]; *Nummisuutarit* [The village shoemakers/The heath cobblers]; *Kun isällä on hammassärky* [When father has toothache]. 1924: *Myrskyluodon kalastaja* [The fisherman of Storm Skerry]. 1925: *Suvinen satu* [Summer fairytale]. 1926: *Muurmannin pakolaiset* [Fugitives from Murmansk]. 1927: *Runoilija muuttaa* [The poet moves]. 1928: *Nuori Luotsi* [The young pilot]. 1929: *Meidän poikamme* [Our boys]. 1931: *Tukkipojan morsian* [The logdriver's bride]. 1933: *Meidän poikamme merellä* [Our boys at sea]; *Voi meitä! Anoppi tulee* [The mother-in-law cometh!]; *Ne 45000* [Those 45,000]. 1934: *Meidän poikamme ilmassa, me maassa* [Our boys in the air]. 1935: *Syntipukki* [The scapegoat]; *Roinilan talossa* [On the Roinila farm].

MATTI KASSILA (Keuruu, 12 Jan. 1924–), director. Kassila made his debut in the early 1950s; he proved to be the most important new arrival in Finnish cinema for the entire decade, and later evaluation has classified his films as evergreen. He was a survivor of the Golden Age and one who knew exactly what he was doing. His breakthrough came with *Radio tekee murron* [The radio commits a burglary] (1952); it started a delightfully novel and absurd new genre of comedy as it recorded an actual chain of events: A popular radio reporter was doing a burglary and broadcast it while it was actually happening. This film was followed in rapid succession by a variety of others, which make up the core of Kassila's reputation. *Hilmanpäivät* [Hilma's name day] and *Pastori Jussilainen* [The Reverend Jussilainen] are true cinematic drama adaptations; here, Kassila conceives the whole world as the stage and the essence of nature as a spiritual landscape; he also manages to tune the actors into the very same spirit. His is the talent to deepen the psychological makeup of the protagonists and to construct multilayered group pictures.

Tyttö kuunsillalta [The girl from the Moon Bridge] (1954) is an imaginative telephone drama: Two elderly people begin to build a relationship—they have been lovers in their youth—on the telephone; he does recognize her. If this film plays with the elements of memory and associations, *Sininen viikko* [Blue week] (1954) definitively dramatizes over the present: It is the eternal triangle in which the splendor and eroticism of Finnish summer darken into tragedy. It was this film that gave grounds for talk about the "emergence of a Finnish *Ingmar Bergman." *Elokuu* [Harvest month] (1956) is one in a series of films based on novels by F. E. Sillanpää; while the previous adaptations (*Tulio, *Tapiovaara, *Vaala) stressed pantheistic notions, Kassila unveils the disillusion of an old and resigned author. Producing such a successful series of films requires a correct combination of many contrasting elements. Country and town, folk comedy and the high society milieu, popular culture (and we don't mean *rillumarei* foolery!), and the subtlest touches of "high culture"—all these ingredients seemed attainable to the young and enterprising director. Kassila's subsequent films did not achieve the same good grasp, admittedly; however, *Lasisydän* [Heart of glass] (1959) is a delectable comedy dealing with modern, fashionable trends both sarcastically and affectionately; it is an ironic presentation of the great days of Finnish industrial design. Kassila's most popular films were released from 1960 onward, a sequence of detective stories built around an arrogant and unwittingly comical figure of a police inspector; in fact, the four *Komisario Palmu* [Police Inspector Palmu] films created quite a unique type of detective story, truly enchanting as a combination of earnest criminal investigation and outrageous parody. Masterful actors make all this work, but the main factor was that Kassila was able to employ full blast his personal talents while developing this style; his weight has always been maintained by those films that are both light and entertaining while observing "important" themes unobtrusively.

With the exception of the Palmu films (the last was released in 1959), suddenly it seemed that Kassila was a has-been—all of his films up to the mid-1980s were rather uninteresting. Then came a surprise, *Ihmiselon ihanuus ja kurjuus* [The glory and misery of human life], a film once again based on a novel by Sillanpää. It is a reflection on the countryside that is no longer what it used to be, a report on wasted talent and on the unavoidable wretchedness of human life—all the themes that have been omnipresent as subtexts in Kassila's works, even in the films that superficially appear absurd and innocuous.

FILMOGRAPHY

1949: *Professori Masa* [Professor Masa]; *Isäntä soittaa hanuria* [The head of the house plays the accordion]. 1950: *Maija löytää sävelen* [Maija finds the right tune]. 1951: *Lakeuksien lukko* [It happened in Ostrobothnia]; *Radio tekee murron* [The radio commits a burglary]. 1952: *Radio tulee hulluksi* [The radio goes crazy]; *Varsovan laulu* [Song of Warsaw]; *Tyttö kuunsillalta* [The girl from the Moon Bridge]. 1954: *Sininen viikko* [Blue week]; *Hilmanpäivät* [Hilma's name day]. 1955: *Isän vanha ja uusi* [Father's new and ex]; *Pastori Jussilainen* [The Reverend Jussilainen/Pastor Jussilainen]. 1956: *Elokuu* [Harvest month]. 1957: *Kuriton sukupolvi* [Wild generation]; *Syntipukki* [Scapegoat]. 1959: *Punainen viiva* [The red line]; *Lasisydän* [Heart of glass], 1960; *Komisario Palmun erehdys* [Police Inspector Palmu's mistake]. 1961: *Tulipunainen kyyhkynen* [The blood-red pigeon]; *Kaasua, komisario Palmu!* [Step on the gas, Inspector Palmu!]. 1962: *Tähdet kertovat, komisario Palmu* [The stars will tell, Inspector Palmu]; *Kolmen kaupungin kasvot* [The faces of three cities]. 1968: *Äl' yli päästä perhanaa* [Let not one devil cross the bridge]. 1969: *Vodkaa, komisario Palmu* [Vodka, Inspector Palmu]. 1970: *Päämaja* [The headquarters]. 1971: *Aatamin puvussa ja vähän Eevankin* [In Adam's clothes and a little bit in Eve's too]. 1972: *Haluan rakastaa, Peter* [I want to love, Peter]. 1973: *Meiltähän tämä käy* [It's up to us]. 1979: *Natalia*. 1984: *Niskavuori* [The tug of home/The Niskavuori family]. 1987: *Jäähyväiset presidentille* [Farewell to the president]. 1988: *Ihmiselon ihanuus ja kurjuus* [The glory and misery of human life]. 1994: *Kaikki pelissä* [Play it all].

AWARDS

Jussi 1951

Jussi 1954

Jussi 1955

Jussi 1957

AKI KAURISMÄKI (Orimattila, 4 Apr. 1957–), director. Very few Finns have ever gained international fame, but now we have Aki Kaurismäki, the first Finnish person in the field of cinema who has come close to being famous. If we are to rely on Gallup polls carried out in the streets of European capitals, Aki Kaurismäki is as well known or even better known than the composer Jean Sibelius, the runner Paavo Nurmi, the architect Alvar Aalto, or even our celebrated rally drivers. Along with his elder brother *Mika, who studied cinema in Munich, he has created the concept "Kaurismäki Finland." Aki himself never made it to the Finnish film school because he was considered to be too cynical—there really cannot be an attribute that fits him less well. In his films, Aki has depicted the marginal Finland, the world of losers and have-nots, which, seen through his eyes, becomes full of wondrous magic and heartfelt human pain, deep compassion, and humor. There is a fantastic grasp of style in his films, to which his masterly cameraman *Timo Salminen (the youngest son of director *Ville Salminen) has, without a doubt, greatly contributed. From the very start, the intimacy and minimalism of Kaurismäki's films have moved critics to describe him as the director best suited to carry on Robert Bresson's work.

Aki Kaurismäki's films can be divided roughly into three or four categories. He started in an almost megalomaniac way, making a modern version of Dostoyevsky's *Crime and Punishment*. And it turned out to be a success, as were his other "classic" films: *Hamlet liikemaailmassa* [Hamlet goes business] (1987), a nearly prophetic film about the Finland of the 1980s about to collapse in a wild vortex of financial speculation, and *Boheemielämää/La vie de bohème* (1992), based on the novel by Henry Murger. It is a delicate and poetic vision of France—even spoken in French. It is the director's approach to these literary classics that makes these films fresh and vibrant: Instead of being pompous transliterations into the language of cinema, they are presented as animated dialogues with the author colleagues of the past, as though they were live conversation partners in the now.

The "working-class trilogy" made up of *Varjoja paratiisissa* [Shadows in paradise] (1986), *Ariel* (1988), and **Tulitikkutehtaan tyttö* [The match factory girl] (1989)—along with **Kauas pilvet karkaavat* [Drifting clouds] (1996), which was made as a follow-up to the three (especially to the first one)—belongs, even in international terms, to the most sensitive descriptions of working-class milieu and proletarian identity done in recent times. They unfold in some kind of colonial Finland, a Third World Finland found in the depths of inner cities or in the distant outskirts of towns, where a resilient, authentic humanity survives by virtue of biting humor and a healthy contempt of bureaucracy and the official mode of life with its attendant con men and speculators.

The films about the Leningrad Cowboys have gained the level of cult films; they introduce "the world's worst rock'n roll band," complete with incredible cone-shaped hairstyles and spiked shoes. The series includes two full-length films and half a dozen short films, and *Total Balalaika Show* (1993) is also part of this series. It is the documentation of the amazing meeting of East and West in the concert given by the Leningrad Cowboys together with the Red Army Ensemble, consisting of 200 singers and musicians.

These films are road movies (a genre that is close to Kaurismäki), as are his quickly made "cheapies," which are among the most charming films in his production. One is *Calamari Union* (1985); it is based on an absurd anecdote and is in a brilliant way both minimalist in its reduced realization and epic when depicting a long journey through the streets of downtown Helsinki. All the characters are named Frank, several of which perish along the way. *Pidä huivista kiinni, Tatjana* [Take care of your scarf, Tatjana] (1994) is another stroke of genius, a film about a weekend of two Finnish workingmen. It takes place simultaneously in the imagined past, "in the 60's" and in a most startlingly realistic world, where the efforts of these extremely Finnish heroes to be themselves in a manic loneliness dominated by Koskenkorva vodka and Finnish tango are much affected by the presence and mentality of our Eastern neighbors.

FILMOGRAPHY

1981: *Saimaa-ilmiö* [The Saimaa gesture] (codir. Mika Kaurismäki, docu.) 1983: *Rikos ja rangaistus* [Crime and punishment]. 1985: *Calamari Union*. 1986: *Varjoja paratiisissa* [Shadows in paradise]. 1987: *Hamlet liikemaailmassa* [Hamlet goes business/Hamlet]. 1988: *Ariel*. 1989: *Leningrad Cowboys Go America*. 1989: *Tulitikkutehtaan tyttö* [The match factory girl]. 1990: *I Hired a Contract Killer*. 1992: *Boheemielämää/La vie de bohéme*. 1993: *Total Balalaika Show* (doc.). 1994: *Pidä huivista kiinni, Tatjana* [Take care of your scarf, Tatjana]; *Leningrad Cowboys Meet Moses*. 1996: *Kauas pilvet karkaavat* [Drifting clouds].

AWARDS

Jussi 1983

Jussi 1986

Jussi 1991

Jussi 1993

MIKA KAURISMÄKI (Orimattila, 21 Sept. 1955–), director. French critics have thus assessed the two Kaurismäki brothers: If the younger brother *Aki is an "auteur" (an absolute "creator" of his films), Mika is a "metteur-en-scène," a craftsman, a filmmaker in the established, the traditional, and the professional sense. Mika is the more expansive of the two; he is a professional with a touch of good old Hollywood. In Finnish cinema, he is one of the last masters of our strong storytelling tradition. While he has directed only a few films based on novels, the outcome is truly impressive—for example, *Klaani—tarina Sammakoitten suvusta* [The clan—tale of the frogs] (1984), an actual "gospel of misery," which tells of a family of criminals.

Mika Kaurismäki is an outstanding visualist and illustrator of milieus—the small becomes spectacular; large retains its human scale and intimacy. Amazonian nature, the extensive plains of Pohjanmaa, the bazaars of Istanbul, the wooden houses in the working-class neighborhood of Tampere's Pispala, that borderland of small cafes and service stations—for many people, these signify precisely that "Kaurismäki Finland." He knows how to handle that old "Suomi-Filmi" landscape and imagery in a way that is a valuable contribution to the European-based modernism. He masters a variety of styles: "realism," parody, satire, even epic.

There is no doubting that the genre he is most comfortable with is road movie; his three best films belong to this category: *Arvottomat* [The worthless] (1982), his first film made together with his brother Aki, who wrote the manuscript; *Rosso* (1985), which describes the journey of an Italian contract killer in Finland; and *Zombie ja kummitusjuna* [Zombie and the ghost train] (1991), a melancholy portrait of a musician on the road to voluntary self-destruction. "Melancholy" is also the attribute best suited to describe a typical Mika Kaurismäki landscape—a gloomy, rainy, autumnal scene with an old battered-up car in the middle of it. The structure of Mika's films is usually strong; there is vision in them, as, for instance, in *Helsinki-Napoli All Night Long* (1987), in which leading roles are occupied by characters such as a Finn driving a taxi in Berlin and Italian emigrants and in which actors such as Eddie Constantine and Samuel Fuller (with whom Mika in 1994 made the documentary *Tigrero*) appear as guest stars.

FILMOGRAPHY

1980: *Valehtelija* [The liar] (short). 1981: *Saimaa-ilmiö* [Saimaa gesture] (codir. Aki Kaurismäki, docu.). 1982: *Arvottomat* [The worthless]; *Jackpot 2* (short). 1983: *Klaani—tarina Sammakoitten suvusta* [The clan—tale of the frogs]. 1985: *Rosso*. 1987: *Helsinki-Napoli All Night Long*. 1989: *Cha, Cha, Cha*; *Paperitähti* [Paper star]. 1990: *Amazon*. 1991: *Zombie ja kummitusjuna* [Zombie and the ghost train]. 1993: *The Last Border—Viimeisellä rajalla/The Last Border*. 1999: *Tigrero—Elokuva joka ei valmistunut/Tigrero—A Film That Was Never Made*. 1996: *Condition Red—Hälytystila/Condition Red*. 1998: *Los Angeles without a Map*.

AWARDS

Jussi 1982

Jussi 1992

MAUNU KURKVAARA (St. Petersburg, 18 July 1926–), director. Kurkvaara was originally a painter, and he retained the disciplines of this profession when he began—as the first in this country—to sketch the outlines of a Finnish "new wave." He was always a skillful creator of images even though many of his other qualities left a lot to be desired, occasionally significantly so. Kurkvaara planned and directed, prepared the manuscript, and shot and edited his films from the very beginning, doing everything himself. He first worked thus with dozens of short films and later on with "drama films," the drama qualities of which he wanted definitely to do away with. He knew exactly what he was doing, as a statement from about 1960 proves: "The time of old romances has gone, society has changed. My themes came from this time, I was doing realistic things." The trilogy *Rakas* . . . [Darling . . .], **Yksityisalue* [Private property], and *Meren juhlat* [Feast at sea] is a kind of Helsinki study, seen always from different angles and at different times of the year. Kurkvaara's urban images are a synthesis of impressions, and their allure is often in sharp contrast to the cliché-ridden narration, dialogue, and character development. *Rakas* . . . effortlessly maps out the lives of young people: parallelism of work and leisure, unfulfilled plans, and plans that become reality when a baby is born to two people; maybe then the end of youth is a fact. The fashion-conscious upper middle classes are often in the foreground in Kurkvaara's films; above all, he portrays people with "mobile professions" and with "showy" lifestyles—the "surprise party" is not the only reason Kurkvaara is often seen as a single-idea imitator of Antonioni. Among his later films, *Punatukka* [Redhead] (1968) attains something of the clarity of this Italian director. Quite a few of Kurkvaara's films of the 1960s represent a rather rough pamphleteering style; however, his finest achievement, *Yksityisalue*—a film about town planning and construction—avoids this style totally. Kurkvaara left the cinema in the early 1970s and since then has directed only occasionally.

FILMOGRAPHY

1955: *Onnen saari* [Island of happiness]. 1956: *Ei enää eilispäivää* [No more tomorrows]. 1958: *Tirlittan* [Tweet tweet]. 1959: *Patarouva* [The queen of spades]. 1960: *Autotytöt* [Car girls]. 1961: *Rakas . . .* [Darling . . .]. 1962: *Yksityisalue* [Private property]. 1963: *Meren juhlat* [Feast at sea/Festival at sea]; *Lauantaileikit* [Saturday games]. 1964: *Naiset* [Women]; *Raportti eli Balladi laivatytöistä* [Report, or The ballad of the sailor's girls]. 1965: *Why* (episode from the pan-Scandinavian production *4×4*); *Kielletty kirja* [The forbidden book]. 1966: *Tänään olet täällä* [Today you are here]. 1968: *Rottasota* [The rat war]; *Miljoonaliiga* [The million dollar gang]; *Punatukka* [Redhead]. 1971: *Kujanjuoksu* [The gauntlet]. 1983: *Menestyksen maku* [A taste of success]. 1986: *Perhosen uni* [Butterfly's dream].

AWARD

Jussi 1962

EDVIN LAINE (Iisalmi, 13 July 1905–18 Nov. 1989), actor, director. Laine was for the Finnish cinema a kind of "national director chosen by God"—or at least that was the role that the director of *Tuntematon sotilas* [The unknown soldier] (1955) played with great gusto. This film is a "happening" that will eternally remain in the memory; it is based on Väinö Linna's best-seller, and it is the most significant novel ever written about war in Finland. The film was released very soon after the novel had been published and became an equally great success. It was, and still is, quite indisputable that Edvin Laine, with his theatrical background and strong personality, was in the Finland of those days the only director capable of taking up the challenge of this film. The accomplishment was also noted abroad: The realism and antiwar sentiments of Laine's oeuvre were comparable to the famous films of Pabst and Milestone. In Finland, the veneration lavished on him reached, at times, quite absurd levels.

In fact, most of Laine's films are precisely that "filmed theater" of ill-repute that Finnish cinema is so often accused of. He had a theatrical background, both as actor and director, and he continued working at the theater until the last weeks of his life. In certain genres he turned his hand to he had a lot of trouble—his comedies were often quite wooden, for instance, and melodrama under his direction became almost brutal and aggressive.

Powerful films remain clearly in the minority in Laine's production, but a few are worth remembering. His first film, *Yrjänän emännän synti* [The sin of the Lady of Yrjänä] (1943), is a small gem, a refreshing film that moves skillfully from interiors to open air and keeps demonstrating some of the fervor of "pure" cinematic expression. However, it proved to be the only one of its kind, and in the late 1940s Laine adopted social drama as his specialty. Even though none of these films functions as a unit, they all contain notable sequences, some showing traditional work techniques, which is something quite exceptional in Finnish cinema. Laine's films dealing with social problems employed realism only very indirectly, in fact, actually steering clear of it.

Prinsessa Ruusunen [Sleeping Beauty] (1949) was released right in the middle of this sequence of social dramas. It might well be the purest and most enchanting children's film ever made in Finland and a striking example of a genre one would not easily have imagined Laine attempting. Again, *Opri* (1954) is an honest and delightful film from the opposite end of the human life span; it deals with old people, their wrangling and their bitterness, behind which lurk all the disappointments of a long life. Yet shining through all this is golden humor— here representing all that is genuine and original about Laine, reminiscent of his best performances as an actor (some of them given under the direction of others).

A strange combination of the sensitive and the burlesque in Laine's films produced more stylistic blunders than films with a good balance between such conflicting elements. At the same time, most of Laine's celebrated epics were somehow "phony"—somehow they descend into triviality. However, some reveal themselves as illuminating manifestations; this is especially true of the Niskavuori family sagas. Film adaptations of three out of five plays by *Hella Wuolijoki treating this theme were directed by Laine, and particularly one of them, *Niskavuoren Heta* [Heta from Niskavuori] (1952), has become a true milestone in the Finnish cinematic tradition portraying country life. It is a rural drama, cohering remarkably all the essential elements—formal interior scenes, open-air sequences with their feel of nature, all those aspects intimately connected with the traditions observed in the country (Laine was always strong with work scenes). And all of this was held together by strong actor performances.

Unfortunately, the studio era of Finnish cinema was almost over when Laine was given the chance to direct his most ambitious epic, *Täällä pohjantähden alla* [Here beneath the Polar Star] (1968–1970), based on a series of novels by Väinö Linna, the author of *Tuntematon sotilas*. By now, Laine's style had regressed to a kind of monotonous backwoods realism, which later on was to appeal to audiences in the same reassuring way television domestic sitcoms do. Finland, that promised land of amateur actors and open-air theaters, has kept her faith in "bush theater" and its aesthetic; it is in a pantheon such as this that Laine may lay claim to a place.

FILMOGRAPHY

Actor

1944: *Sylvi*. 1945: *Anna-Liisa*. 1947: *Naiskohtaloita* [Destinies of women]. 1954: *Hilman päivät* [Hilma's name day]. 1955: *Rakas lurjus* [Beloved rascal]; *Pastori Jussilainen* [The Reverend Jussilainen/Pastor Jussilainen]. 1957: *Risti ja liekki* [The cross and the flame]; *Musta rakkaus* [Black love].

Director, Actor

1943: *Yrjänän emännän synti* [The sin of the Lady of Yrjänä]. 1945: *Ristikon varjossa* [In the shadow of the prison bars]; *Nokea ja kultaa* [Crime and gold]. 1946: *Kultainen kynttilänjalka* [The golden candlestick]. 1948: *Onnen-Pekka* [Lucky Peter]. 1951: *Vihaan sinua—rakas* [Darling, I hate you]. 1952: *Yhden yön hinta* [The price of one night].

1953: *Jälkeen syntiinlankeemuksen* [After the fall of Man]. 1958: *Sven Tuuva* [Soldier Sven]. 1960: *Myöhästynyt hääyö* [The delayed wedding night]. 1983: *Akaton mies* [How to find a wife for a farmer].

Director

1946: *Kirkastuva sävel* [The glorious melody]. 1947: *Kultamitalivaimo* [The gold med-allist's wife], *Pikku Matti maailmalla* [Little Matti out in the wide world]. 1948: *Lai takaupungin laulu* [The song of the city outskirts]; *Laulava sydän* [The singing heart]. 1949: *Ruma Elsa* [Ugly Elsa]; *Prinsessa Ruusunen* [Sleeping Beauty]; *Aaltoska organiseeraa* [Aaltonen's missus takes charge]. 1950: *Isäpappa ja keltanokka* [The old man and the youngster]; *Tapahtui kaukana* [Love north of the Arctic Circle]. 1952: *Niskavuoren Heta* [Heta from Niskavuori]. 1954: *Kunnioittaen* [With respect]; *Niska-vuoren Aarne* [Aarne of Niskavuori]; *Opri*. 1955: *Veteraanin voitto* [The veteran's vic-tory]; *Tuntematon sotilas* [The unknown soldier]. 1957: Musta rakkaus [Black love]; *Niskavuori taistelee* [The Niskavuori fights]. 1960: *Skandaali tyttökoulussa* [Scandal in the girls' school]. 1962: *Pikku suorassu* [Little Iris Klewe]; *Pinsiön parooni* [The baron of Pinsiö]. 1968: *Täällä pohjantähden alla* [Here beneath the Polar Star]. 1970: *Akseli ja Elina* [Akseli and Elina]; *Pohjantähti* [The North Star]. 1976: *Luottamus* [Trust] (codir. Victor Tregubovits). 1977: *Viimeinen savotta* [The last lumbercamp]. 1979: *Ruskan jäl-keen* [Winter of black snow]. 1986: *Akallinen mies* [The farmer takes a wife].

AWARDS

Jussi 1953

Jussi 1956

Jussi 1968

MARKKU LEHMUSKALLIO (Rauma, 31 Dec. 1938–), director. Lehmuskallio entered the world of cinema quite accidentally, yet there are not many auteurs in our cinema whose vocation is more strongly perceivable. He started out with nature documentaries, which he shot himself. Later, his works attained the qual-ity of primitive visual arts in their simplicity as in such feature films as *Antti Puuhaara* [Antti Treebranch] and *Pulakapina* [The horse "rebellion"]. However, the world of commercially produced cinema proved to be a disappointment to Lehmuskallio, and he soon chose to follow his own lonely path producing his films himself.

The first feature film he directed was *Korpinpolska* [The raven's dance] (1980). It was realized with a very small production team. The actors were all amateurs and had only supporting roles, as the theme of the film is nature and how to listen to it.

Korpinpolska was followed by *Skierril—vaivaiskoivujen maa* [Skierril—land of the dwarf birch], a film that took Lehmuskallio to Lapland, to the Sami people. His next film, *Sininen imettäjä* [Blue mammy] (1985), concentrated on an individual, a man and an artist, and on his inner reality. *Inuksuk*, shot in arctic conditions in Canada, led Lehmuskallio even further from feature films. It brought to the foreground an authentic experience—and that in a form that can be called documentary, yet it is something more: It is a remarkable synthesis of roughness and simplicity.

The two-part *Minä olen* [I am] presents the tradition of Inuit art and its present masters and helps us in understanding the way the people of the far North experience the world. The trilogy—realized in Siberia (*Poron hahmossa pitkin taivaan kaarta* [In reindeer shape across the sky], *Kadotettu paratiisi* [Paradise lost], *Jäähyväisten kronikka* [The farewell chronicle])—completes the cycle; here not only the harmony and beauty of the natural way of life are depicted but also the threats facing it.

FILMOGRAPHY

1973: *Pohjoisten metsien ääniä* [Echoes from the Nordic forests] (docu., short). 1974: *Tapiola* (docu., short). 1976: *Elämän tanssi* [Dance of life] (docu., short). 1980: *Korpinpolska* [The raven's dance]. 1982: *Skierri—vaivaiskoivujen maa* [Skierri—land of the dwarf birch]. 1985: *Sininen imettäjä* [Blue mammy]. 1988: *Inuksuk*. 1991: *Minä olen 1 & 2* [I am 1 and 2] (docu.). 1993: *Poron hahmossa pitkin taivaan kaarta* [In reindeer shape across the sky]. 1994: *Kadotettu paratiisi* [Paradise lost] (docu.). 1995: *Jäähyväisten kronikka* [The farewell chronicle] (docu.). 1997: *Anna* (docu.).

AWARD

Jussi 1980

HANNU LEMINEN (Helsinki, 5 Jan. 1910–6 June 1997), director, set designer. Leminen started out as a set designer, but during the war years, he became a specialist in directing films dealing with problems of the time, as well as melodramas. His works are mostly combinations of the two. *Tuomari Martta* [Magistrate Martta] (1943) seized on a burning-hot issue: While men were fighting on the front, women had taken on an ever greater variety of professions, and now the issue was how to get them back to the kitchen sink. When at the end of the film, Helena Kara (Leminen's wife) pleads, "Do not abandon little children" while a celestial halo of lighting effects surrounds her beautiful face, we find ourselves close to a force field—a powerful moment. **Valkoiset ruusut* [White roses] is often considered to be the film Leminen should be remembered for; it is a direct dramatization of a novel by Stefan Zweig, which Max Ophuls directed under the name *Letter from an Unknown Woman* four years later.

Thereafter came a number of sex education films, which at the time of their release were defined in Finnish with that funny-sounding title "syphilis films." On the whole, they are quite boring. Soon afterward, *Soita minulle, Helena!* [Play for me, Helena!] fortunately restored our faith in Leminen's skills. The film is based on a novel by Aino Räsänen, the queen of Finnish "women's books"; it catches in a remarkable way the most prevailing tone of the 1940s— apprehension of the fleeting nature of happiness and delusion of lasting achievements.

A new phase in Leminen's production was launched with the historical romance *Rosvo-Roope* [Rob the robber] (1950), a genre well suited to an ex–set designer! He was now concentrating on idylls from the turn of the century—it was as if his own time froze him off, so he escaped time and time again into those bygone days. *Kesäillan valssi* [A summer night's waltz] (1951) is the key film; it is also an authentic melodrama because of the central role music plays in it. Paradoxically, there was a catch in following "pure style". Leminen's undeniable skills as a set designer began to lead him into a kind of dramaturgical "never-never land"; his film craft was becoming ever neater; it was "art" in the most unremarkable sense of the word. Leminen got himself together in his very last films, which introduced some new, powerful dramaturgical elements. All too prematurely, however, he left the cinema world in 1957 to start working in a leading position for the emerging television industry.

FILMOGRAPHY

Director

1941: *Pakkorajalta Syvärille* [From the dictated border to the Svir River]; *Täysosuma* [Bull's eye]. 1942: *Avioliittoyhtiö* [Marriage, Inc.]; *Puck*. 1943: *Tuomari Martta* [Magistrate Martta]; *Valkoiset ruusut* [White roses]; *Synnitön lankeemus* [The sinless fall]. 1944: *Suurin voitto* [The greatest victory]. 1945: *Vain sinulle* [For you alone]; *En ole kreivitär* [I'm not a countess]. 1946: *Synnin jäljet* [The tracks of sin]. 1947: *Hedelmätön puu* [The barren tree]; *Tuhottu nuoruus* [Ruined youth]. 1948: *Sankari kuin sankari*; *Soita minulle, Helena!* [Play for me, Helena!]. 1950: *Rosvo-Roope* [Rob the robber]. 1950: *Amor hoi!* [Amor, ahoy!]; *Ratavartijan kaunis Inkeri* [Beautiful Inkeri and the railwayman]. 1951: *Kesäillan valssi* [A summer night's waltz]. 1952: *Hän tuli ikkunasta* [He came through the window]; *Maailmat kohtaavat* [Where the worlds meet]. 1954: *Morsiusseppele* [The bridal garland]; *Onnelliset* [The happy ones]. 1955: *Lähellä syntiä* [Close to sin]. 1956: *Riihalan valtias* [The mistress of Riihala]; *Ratkaisun päivät* [Days of decision]; *Muuan sulhasmies* [A certain suitor]. 1957: *Vieras mies* [The stranger].

AWARD

Jussi 1944

REGINA LINNANHEIMO (Helsinki, 7 Sept. 1915–24 Jan. 1995), actress. Linnanheimo started her career in 1934 under the direction of *Valentin Vaala and completed it in 1956 when only forty years old. Between these years, she pursued in fact two separate careers, a "legitimate" one consisting of several leading roles in the prestigious productions of SF (e.g., *Kaivopuiston kaunis Regina* [Beautiful Regina of Kaivopuisto] and *Katariina ja Munkkiniemen kreivi* [Catherine and the count of Munkkiniemi]) and the other in *Teuvo Tulio's melodramas—an existence wild, untamed, and one at times approaching madness (but not in her private life, of course). In the 1940s she starred in *Rakkauden risti* [The cross of love] and *Levoton veri* [Restless blood], and in the 1950s she rendered a fierce portrayal of passion in *Rikollinen nainen* [A crooked woman], *Mustasukkaisuus* [Jealousy], and *Olet mennyt minun vereeni* [You've gone into my blood], with which Linnanheimo rounded off her career. Part of her charisma is the shock of contrast: She was capable of depicting authority (in patriotic dramas), idyllic sensitivity and poetry, and a clear sense of drama. At such times it is as if her very subconsciousness illumined her face.

FILMOGRAPHY

1931: *Jääkärin morsian* [The light infantryman's bride]. 1934: *Helsingin kuuluisin liikemies* [The most famous businessman in Helsinki]. 1935: *Kun isä tahtoo*... [When father wants to ...]. 1936: *VMV 6*; *Taistelu Heikkilän talosta* [The fight over the Heikkilä mansion]; *Mieheke* [Surrogate husband]. 1937: *Nuorena nukkunut* [Silja—fallen asleep when young]. 1938: *Kiusaus* [Temptation]. 1939: *Eteenpäin—elämään* [Forward— toward life]; *Helmikuun manifesti* [February manifesto]; *Pikku pelimanni* [The little fiddler]. 1940: *Suotorpan tyttö* [The tenant farmer's girl]; *Lapseni on minun* [My child is my own]; *Yövartija vain*... [Just a night watchman]. 1941: *Kulkurin valssi* [The vagabond's waltz]; *Kaivopuiston kaunis Regina* [Beautiful Regina of Kaivopuisto]. 1942: *Onni pyörii* [The wheel of chance]; *Niin se on, poijaat* [That's how it is, boys]. 1943: *Katariina ja Munkkiniemen kreivi* [Catherine and the count of Munkkiniemi]. 1944: *Herra ja ylhäisyys* [Lord and master]; *Kuollut mies vihastuu* [The dead man loses his temper]. 1945: *Linnaisten vihreä kamari* [The green chamber of Linnais]. 1946: *Rakkauden risti* [The cross of love]; *Levoton veri* [Restless blood]. 1947: *Intohimon vallassa* [In the grip of passion]. 1949: *Hornankoski* [The rapids of hell]; *Pikku pelimannista viulun kuninkaaksi* [From the little fiddler to the king of violinists]; *Vain kaksi tuntia* [Only two hours]. 1952: *Silmät hämärässä* [Eyes in the dark]; *Rikollinen nainen* [A crooked woman]. 1953: *Mustasukkaisuus* [Jealousy]. 1956: *Olet mennyt minun vereeni* [You've gone into my blood].

AWARD

Jussi 1946

RAUNI MOLLBERG (Hämeenlinna, 15 Apr. 1929–), actor, director. Mollberg studied at the drama school in the same class as *Mikko Niskanen, and in the 1950s he worked both as director and actor in hundreds of plays. These years in the theater provided him with a fruitful foundation for future work as a film director; here he got to know Finnish provincial theaters and their actors—faces not overused on television or in the cinema. He spent years directing for television before tackling his first film, *Maa on syntinen laulu* [The earth is a sinful song], which turned out to be a great success in many countries. Mollberg's films are all based on literary works, and he treats his sources with great respect. In his best scenes he manages to capture the interplay of the interplay of thrilling dialogue with strange, startlingly comic facial expressions (as in the film *Aika hyvä ihmiseksi* [Pretty good for a human being]); at his worst, he wallows in overly explicit realism and tasteless physical exaggeration, in an inertia where no inner development can exist. In the latter case, naturalism does not really work at all, and the larger visions wane and fade away, and scenes focused on the human face become mere disparate instants. One of Mollberg's best films is a new version of Väinö Linna's *Tuntematon sotilas*, made thirty years after

*Edvin Laine's classic oeuvre. This time the leading theme is youth—young men cruelly converted to cannon fodder.

FILMOGRAPHY

Actor

1950. *Tanssi yli hautojen* [The Dance over the graves].

Director

1963: *Kuopio* (short). 1973: *Maa on syntinen laulu* [The earth is a sinful song/Earth is our sinful song]. 1976: *Turo* (short). 1977: *Aika hyvä ihmiseksi* [Pretty good for a human being]. 1978: *Kustaa Vilkuna* (short). 1979: *Tampere 200* (short). 1980: *Milka—elokuva tabuista* [Milka, a film about taboos]. 1985: *Tuntematon sotilas* [The unknown soldier]. 1990: *Ystävät, toverit* [Friends, comrades]. 1994: *Paratiisin lapset* [Children of the paradise] (also actor).

AWARDS

Jussi 1973

Jussi 1977

Jussi 1981

Jussi 1985

MIKKO NISKANEN (Äänekoski, 3 Jan. 1929–25 Nov. 1990), director. Niskanen's fifteen films make up an unusually graphic chronicle of his own lifetime: They start in his childhood years in the 1930s and then, portraying the emotions and sentiments of a great variety of people, voyage all the way to the mid-1980s. The chief theme of Niskanen's films is identical to that of Finnish society at large: the vanishing of the old agrarian world and its transformation into something else entirely. His work is so emotionally charged that the viewer is constantly aware of the director's obsessive search for his own roots. Thus, Niskanen's themes loom powerfully: growth and withering away, the identity crisis, rebellion, adjustment and reconciliation, the constant search for the meaning of life when everything seems to be slipping away.

As many as half of Niskanen's fifteen films are historical, that is, reconstructions of bygone times. His very first film, *Pojat* [Boys], deals with the war, as do the ensuing two films. This is a theme that Finnish cinema has tackled surprisingly seldom. *Pojat*, the finest of his war films, is also his first outstanding portrait of young people. It is still a traditional film (Niskanen worked shortly for Suomi-Filmi just before it closed down and also studied cinema art in Moscow), whereas *Käpy selän alla* [Under your skin] was independently produced, a manifesto of a new spirit of getting things done. This film is about four young persons' trip to the countryside in search of erotic and ideological identity, and it attained immense popularity.

Through his themes, Niskanen expressed the most intimate emotions of his own artistic self, and he did it in a straightforward, honest, gentle, nonetheless humorous spirit. The Helsinki of *Lapualaismorsian* [Girl of Finland], the village in *Syksyllä kaikki on toisin* [In the autumn, everything will be different], the countryside discovered by the urban youth in *Käpy selän alla* and then lost by the rural young in *Ajolähtö* [Gotta run!], the people going through the crisis of the 1930s, and again a new generation experiencing the crisis of the 1970s— all these specific Finnish stereotypes and the vanquished old world and the present day observed via the characters of Niskanen's films reveal volumes about their director. He was very good at discovering new, talented actors, and what we remember about his films is faces, their freshness and openness, their screen presence sans professionalism, a quality we might even call amateurishness. Another thing we recall about these films is the essence and the spirit of the time. This poetic grasp of a given period is characteristic of Niskanen; he saw himself as the "last connoisseur" of the mood prevailing at the time of transition.

Niskanen's most outstanding film is the over-five-hours-long *Kahdeksan surmanluotia* [Eight deadly shots], a tragic story about a smallholder based on real-life events. His last films are also memorable and on the same wavelength; *Elämän vonkamies* [Life's hardy men] and *Nuoruuteni savotat* [Lumber camp tales] are both film adaptations of Kalle Päätalo's incredible output of dozens of long epic novels. Once again, these films sketch out youthful expectations and how life with its cruel inevitability crushes them, every time, unfailingly.

FILMOGRAPHY

1962: *Pojat* [Boys]. 1963: *Sissit* [The partisans]; *Hopeaa rajan takaa* [Silver from across the border]. 1966: *Käpy selän alla* [Under your skin/Skin skin]. 1967: *Lapualaismorsian* [Girl of Finland]. 1968: *Asfalttilampaat* [The asphalt lambs]. 1971: *Laulu tulipunaisesta kukasta* [Song of the scarlet flower]. 1972: *Kahdeksan surmanluotia* [Eight deadly shots]. 1977: *Pulakapina* [The horse rebellion]. 1978: *Syksyllä kaikki on toisin* [In the autumn, everything will be different/In the fall everything is different]. 1982: *Ajolähtö* [Gotta run!]. 1984: *Mona ja palavan rakkauden aika* [Mona and the time of burning love]. 1986: *Elämän vonkamies* [Life's hardy men]. 1988: *Nuoruuteni savotat* [Lumber camp tales].

AWARDS

Jussi 1962

Jussi 1963

Jussi 1966

Jussi 1967

Jussi 1971

Jussi 1982

RISTO ORKO (Rauma, 15 Sept. 1899–), director, producer. Orko had followed different occupations, such as that of journalist and theater director, before, in 1934, he replaced *Erkki Karu as the managing director of Suomi-Filmi after Karu had been dismissed.

The strategy of the company now moved at a fast pace: It emerged as an urban, modern alternative to its competitor, the folksy and provincial SF, and also showed itself to be more "artistic." The essential idea was to employ a small group of talented directors and allow them utter freedom in their creative work. The first contract was signed with *Valentin Vaala, whose service to the company turned out to be the most fruitful and to last the longest. After Vaala came Orvo Saarikivi, *Ilmari Unho, and Wilho Ilmari, a well-known man of the theater. Orko's approach to his work was to aim at training his people, to raise the level of technical expertise, and to focus on artistic standards. Orko personally took on the training of his staff, and he encouraged *Leminen and Forsman to travel abroad and visit the leading European studios. Furthermore, he invited to Finland some high-ranking foreign professionals—Albert Rudling from Sweden and Charlie Bauer and Marius Reich from France. The cooperation between directors and technicians was an intimate one; it was a kind of dramaturgical symbiosis: "[R]ight throughout my career as producer there was not a single manuscript nor one detail I did not thrash out with the director," Orko relates. In a somewhat casual way, the first film school of the country operated in concert with Suomi-Filmi; its "students" were employed in the company's productions, first as extras and later on as actors.

Risto Orko acted also as principal director of Suomi-Filmi. *Siltalan pehtoori* [The foreman of Siltala farm] (1934), a romantic tale set in a country manor, was the first Finnish film to attract an audience of more than 1 million, and this meant one in four Finns saw it. The most significant of Orko's films being released toward the end of the 1930s are illuminating as evidence of the worsening political atmosphere, which was to result in two wars with the Soviet Union. First, *Jääkärin morsian* [A yager's bride] was the biggest Finnish film spectacular to be realized up to that date; it was by no means only "filmed theater" but really hums with life, thanks to music, action, good local color, and really lively acting. *Aktivistit* [Activists], a drama simultaneously reflecting historical sentiments and those of 1939, is once again much more than a mere "picture book." The majority of the films directed by Orko are light farces approaching the negligible, and the final ones, in which the leads were played by a popular comic duo of the war years, were even banned after the war as being "politically suspect."

We might say that Orko's greatest achievement was his company, Suomi-Filmi—the only "all-round movie factory" in Finland. A laboratory, quality film distribution, and the production of short films perfected the sophisticated approach to production, which might claim a few dozen of the best films ever made in Finland.

Helsinki was intended to host the 1940 Olympic Games, and it was to be Orko directing the commemorative film. The arrangements were already far advanced, and loads of cameras had arrived in Helsinki at the end of November, when the Winter War broke out between Finland and the Soviet Union. Those famous pictures that were distributed all over the world were shot with those cameras. "The war itself is the script-writer. Its manuscript is acted out on the front, or behind it,—on the home-front. All that could be recorded had to be recorded, just as long as film stock lasted. And there was this obligation to go wherever it was possible to go and wherever the cameraman dared to go. There you have it, a very simple manuscript."[1]

FILMOGRAPHY

Director

1933: *Herrat täysihoidossa* [Men in a boarding house]. 1934: *Minä ja ministeri* [Me and the cabinet minister]; *Siltalan pehtoori* [The foreman of Siltala farm]. 1936: *VMV 6*. 1937: *Ja alla oli tulinen järvi* [And below was a fiery lake]. 1938: *Jääkärin morsian* [A yager's bride/a yager's wife]; *Markan tähden* [A day as an heiress]. 1939: *Aktivistit* [Activists]. 1940: *Taistelun tie* [The road of war]; *Kyökin puolella* [In the kitchen]. 1941: *Ryhmy ja Romppainen* [Ryhmy and Romppainen]. 1943: *Jees ja just* [Yes and right away!]. 1960: *Taistelujen tie* [Road to battle]. 1980: *Tulitikkuja lainaamassa* [Out to borrow matches].

NOTE

1. Risto Orko.

KATI OUTINEN (Helsinki, 17 July 1961), actress. Outinen first made her name known in Tapio Suominen's dynamic youth movie *Täältä tullaan, elämä!* [Right on, man!] (1980), later developing into the doyenne of minimalistic, spare screen acting in *Aki Kaurismäki's films, where she often played opposite *Matti Pellonpää as the perfect foil (*Varjoja paratiisissa* [Shadows in paradise], *Pidä huivista kiinni, Tatjana* [Take care of your scarf, Tatjana]). Outinen was both hauntingly ethereal and bizarre as Ophelia in Kaurismäki's *Hamlet liikemaailmassa* [Hamlet goes business]. She has a talent to elucidate the frailty that does not quite give way; she reminds one of a tiny bird that transmits that certain inner strength. Her best-known role is that of the protagonist in Kaurismäki's *Tulitikkutehtaan tyttö* [The match factory girl].

FILMOGRAPHY

1980: *Täältä tullaan, elämä!* [Right on, man!]. 1984: *Aikalainen* [The contemporary]; *Päivää, herra Kivi* [Hello, Mr. Kivi]. 1986: *Kuningas lähtee Ranskaan* [The king goes forth to France]; *Varjoja paratiisissa* [Shadows in paradise]. 1987: *Hamlet liikemaailmassa* [Hamlet goes business/Hamlet]. 1990: *Tulitikkutehtaan tyttö* [The match factory girl]. 1994: *Pidä huivista kiinni, Tatjana* [Take care of your scarf, Tatjana]; *Kaikki pelissä* [Play it all]. 1996: *Kauas pilvet karkaavat* [Drifting clouds]. 1997: *Sairaan kaunis maailma* [Freakin' beautiful world].

AWARD

Jussi 1991

ESA PAKARINEN (Rääkkylä, 9 Feb. 1915–28 Apr. 1989), actor, singer, composer. While touring in Finland in the late 1940s, Pakarinen, a skillful musician who played the accordion like a virtuoso, won fame and huge popularity with one existentialist trick—in performance he popped his false teeth from his mouth—"and this was something that fascinated this nation with bad teeth!" In the movies he made in the 1950s, he created a sequence of splendid characters, folksy blockheads who nonetheless turned out to be quite cunning, and these were the roles he kept on playing with great success for the next forty years on tour, in shopping centers and at roofing parties. One of Pakarinen's many roles was Pekka Puupää, the most popular comic hero of the 1950s, whom he played for all of thirteen films. The name *Pakarinen* is inseparable from the so-called *rillumarei* phenomenon, a rough kind of comedy with roots deep in the countryside, which is spiced by brisk and racy musical numbers. Yet here was not mere cheery populism but rather a healthy rejoinder to the Finnish cinema comedy still weighed down by the heavy theater tradition. Some of Pakarinen's most memorable creations are the gold digger in *Rovaniemen markkinoilla* [At the Rovaniemi fair], the miner back from the States in *Lännen lokarin veli* [Mr. Coolman from the Wild West], and the jovial train conductor in *Lentävä kalakukko* [Esa "flies" to Kuopio].

FILMOGRAPHY

Actor

1951: *Rovaniemen markkinoilla* [At the Rovaniemi fair]. 1952: *Lännen lokarin veli* [Mr. Coolman from the Wild West]. 1953: *Rantasalmen sulttaani* [Adventure in Morocco]; *Lentävä kalakukko* [Esa "flies" to Kuopio]; *Pekka Puupää* [Pete Blockhead]; *Se alkoi sateessa* [It began in the rain]; *Pekka Puupää kesälaitumilla* [Pete Blockhead takes a vacation]. 1954: *Hei, rillumarei* [!Hei, Trala-lala-lalaa]; *Pekka ja Pätkä lumimiehen jäljillä* [Pete and Runt on the trail of the Abominable Snowman]. 1955: *Pekka ja Pätkä puistotäteinä* [Pete and Runt as park nannies]; *Kiinni on ja pysyy* [Caught and held fast . . .]; *Pekka ja Pätkä pahassa pulassa* [Pete and Runt in hot water]. 1957: *Pekka ja Pätkä ketjukolarissa* [Pete and Runt in a chain collision]; *Pekka ja Pätkä salapoliiseina* [Pete and Runt, detectives]; *Pekka ja Pätkä sammakkomiehinä* [Pete and Runt, frogmen]. 1958: *Pekka ja Pätkä Suezilla* [Pete and Runt in Suez]; *Pekka ja Pätkä miljonääreinä* [Pete and Runt, millionaires]. 1959: *Pekka ja Pätkä mestarimaalareina* [Pete and Runt, master painters]. 1960: *Pekka ja Pätkä neekereinä* [Pete and Runt, Negroes]. 1961: *Mullin mallin* [Helter-skelter]. 1973: *Meiltähän tämä käy* [It's up to us]. 1977: *Jäniksen vuosi* [The year of the hare]. 1978: *Runoilija ja Muusa* [Poet and muse]. 1979: *Koeputkiaikuinen ja Simon enkelit* [The test-tube adult and Simo's angels]. 1981: *Kiljusen herrasväki* [That Kiljunen family]. 1983: *Jon*. 1988: *Taavi Kassilan petos* [The betrayal].

TAUNO PALO (Hämeenlinna, 25 Oct. 1908–25 Apr. 1982), actor. Palo is the most renowned and the best-loved actor in Finnish cinema—and quite undisputably its greatest and its best. He acted in sixty-five films and almost always played the lead while simultaneously drudging away in often times gruelling work in the theater. He was endowed with a rare instinct—the quality of per-

forming equally brilliantly on the screen and on the stage. Palo mastered the
entire gamut of Finnish cinema: comedy, tragedy (however, his talent best revealed itself on the stage), melodrama. The good, the bad, and the ugly—Palo
was like a musical instrument, ready to be played however diverse the music.
He was renowned as the complete professional; at the same time, he managed
to retain that spontaneity and ability to surprise frequently seen in only amateur
actors.

Palo had the skill to combine lightweight and youthful charm with heavy-
duty acting; this virtuosity could be seen most clearly in the theater, where Palo
acted the emblematic roles of modern American drama in the stirring plays by
Miller and Williams of the late 1940s and the early 1950s. On screen, this aspect
of Palo's acting was seen in the role of a company director saddled with a
drinking problem in *Mies tältä tähdeltä* [A man from this planet] (1958). General audiences love to recall Palo for his romantic roles and as the unrivaled
lover of the popular cinema. He was also a brilliant performer in musicals, and
the love scenes played with a series of beauties over several decades make up
an immortal romantic iconography of Finnish cinema. Two films that highlight
this side of Palo's talent are *Herra ja ylhäisyys* [Lord and master] (1944)—an
adventure story with a Mexican location—and *Rosvo-Roopé* [Rob the robber]
(1950). Palo created several heroic figures projected with a marked patriotic
pathos; these characters keenly reflect emotions felt at the end of the 1930s in
Finland. Later, he acted many roles portraying deeper, more desperate emotions—the whole spectrum of man's existence. He instinctively understood the
two extremes of humanity—innocent romanticism and profound despair—and
this talent was the essence of his performances in several roles as the "loser."
Even if Palo is best remembered as a romantic hero, melancholia and a sense
of loss could be detected in his acting quite early on. (It is regrettable that Palo's
last screen role was as early as 1961; however, it was succeeded by occasional
appearances on television; actors like him were jettisoned when the era of the
film studios came to an end.)

Signs of middle age added by a few extra kilos showed quite early in Palo;
this also altered his humor, although it still remained quite winning. His acting
roles form a unity, which permits us to talk about a born "auteur"—a creator
of the most individual stripe. Just one theme proves the point: the process by
which the relationship between man and woman is triggered, and the way the
awareness of prevailing sexual roles is heightened, is particularly prominent in
Palo's acting. The uneven films on the *Niskavuori* theme survive, thanks to Palo;
he starred in four of them. Here, fundamental concerns become more important
than a story: land, instincts, responsibility, conflict in relationships between men
and women. Here the actor paints his self-portrait as a man with real emotions,
leaving the manuscript—even the director—behind. A further gift of Palo's was
to play on the erotic register at a time when a bashful tradition excluded its
explicit expression.

FILMOGRAPHY

1931: *Jääkärin morsian* [The light infantryman's bride]. 1932: *Kuisma ja Helinä* [Kuisma and Helinä]. 1934: *Helsingin kuuluisin liikemies* [The most famous businessman in Helsinki]. 1935: *Kaikki rakastavat* [Everybody's in love]. 1936: *Vaimoke* [Surrogate wife]; *Mieheke* [Surrogate husband]. 1937: *Koskenlaskijan morsian* [The logroller's bride]; *Juurakon Hulda* [Hulda of Juurakko]. 1938: *Niskavuoren naiset* [The women of Niskavuori]; *Jääkärin morsian* [A yager's bride]. 1939: *Eteenpäin—elämään* [Forward—toward life]; *Helmikuun manifesti* [February manifesto]; *Jumalan tuomio* [God's doom/The judgement of God]. 1940: *Serenaadi sotatorvella eli sotamies Paavosen tuurihousut* [Serenade with a war trumpet]; *Suotorpan tyttö* [The tenant farmer's girl]; *SF-paraati* [SF parade]; *Aatamin puvussa ja vähän Eevankin* [Dressed like Adam and a little like Eve, too]. 1941: *Kulkurin valssi* [The vagabond's waltz]; *Kaivopuiston kaunis Regina* [The beautiful Regina of Kaivopuisto]; *Onnellinen ministeri* [The lucky cabinet minister]. 1942: Onni *pyörii* [The wheel of chance]; *Avioliittoyhtiö* [Marriage, Inc.]; *Puck.* 1943: **Valkoiset ruusut* [White roses]. 1944: **Vaivaisukon morsian* [The *wooden pauper's bride*]; *Herra ja ylhäisyys* [Lord and master]. 1945: *Kolmastoista koputus* [The thirteenth knock]. 1946: *Menneisyyden varjo* [Shadow of the past]; *Viikon tyttö* [Girl of the week]; *Loviisa, Niskavuoren nuori emäntä* [Loviisa]. 1947: *Pimeänpirtin hävitys* [The destruction of Pimeäpirtti]; *Koskenkylän laulu* [The song of Koskenkylä]. 1948: *Laitakaupungin laulu* [Song of the city outskirts]; *Laulava sydän* [The singing heart]. 1949: *Rosvo-Roope* [Rob the robber]; *Kanavan laidalla* [At the edge of the canal]. 1950: *Professori Masa* [Professor Masa]; *Amor hoi!* [Amor, ahoy!]; *Härmästä poikia kymmenen* [Ten men from Härmä]. 1951: *Ylijäämänainen* [Stolen love]; *Tukkijoella* [The log drivers]. 1952: *Silmät hämärässä* [Eyes in the dark]; *Hän tuli ikkunasta* [He came through the window]; *Omena putoaa* [The apple falls]. 1953: *Maailman kaunein tyttö* [The loveliest girl in the world]; *Kolmiapila* [The clover]; *Se alkoi sateessa* [It began in the rain]; *Hilja—maitotyttö* [Hilja the milkmaid]. 1954: *Kunnioittaen* [With respect]; *Niskavuoren Aarne* [Aarne of Niskavuori]; *Kasarmin tytär* [The daughter of the regiment]; *Hilman päivät* [Hilma's name day]. 1955: *Isän vanha ja uusi* [Father's new and ex]; *Nukkekauppias ja kaunis Lilith* [The doll merchant and beautiful Lilith]; *Neiti talonmies* [Miss Janitor]; **Tuntematon sotilas* [The unknown soldier]. 1956: *Ratkaisun päivät* [Days of decision]. 1957: *Risti ja liekki* [The cross and the flame]; *Kuriton sukupolvi* [Wild generation]; *Niskavuori taistelee* [Niskavuori fights]. 1958: *Mies tältä tähdeltä* [A man from this planet]; *Verta käsissämme* [Blood on our hands]. 1959: *Kovaa peliä Pohjolassa* [Playing a hard game up north]. 1960: *Nina ja Erik* [Nina and Erik]. 1961: *Tulipunainen kyyhkynen* [The blood-red pigeon].

AWARDS

Jussi 1946

Jussi 1950

Jussi 1952

PERTTI (SPEDE) PASANEN (Kuopio, 10 Apr. 1930–), actor, director, producer. Pasanen is the popular radio and television comedian who from the mid-1960s on has produced the most successful movie farces Finland has known.

There was still a measure of cinematic ambition in his first films (*Pähkähullu Suomi* [Crazy Finland], 1967), but it soon faded when the far-reaching series about Uuno Turhapuro was launched in the early 1970s. In these films, cinematic expression is lowered, with an almost aggressive attitude toward routine television recording. However, the series has created the figure of Turhapuro (acted brilliantly by Vesa-Matti Loiri), a beer-swilling slob who bawls absurdities from his couch like an ape. He has become some kind of stereotype for the Finnish good-for-nothing idle male, who has been decaying in tandem with his country. Bob Hope is the comedian Spede sees as his model; in fact, he masters a local Finnish and yet quite personal version of the mix of the hard, angular gestures, summaries of absurd situations, and verbal virtuosity that was Bob Hope's own special talent.

FILMOGRAPHY

Actor

1954: *Laivan kannella* [On deck]. 1955: *Sankarialokas* [Conscript hero]; *Säkkijärven polkka* [Säkkijärvi polka]; *Villi Pohjola* [The wild North]. 1956: *Tyttö tuli taloon* [The girl came into the house]; *Tyttö lähtee kasarmiin* [The girl in the barracks]; *Rintamalotta* [Girls at the front]; *Anu ja Mikko* [Anu and Mikko]. 1957: *Pekka ja Pätkä ketjukolarissa* [Pete and Runt in a chain collision]; *Vääpelin kauhu* [The sergeant's nemesis]; *Pekka ja Pätkä sammakkomiehinä* [Pete and Runt, frogmen]. 1958: *Pekka ja Pätkä Suezilla* [Pete and Runt in Suez]. 1959: *Ei ruumiita makuuhuoneeseen* [No bodies in the bedroom]. 1961: *Mullin mallin* [Helter-skelter]. 1962: *Taape tähtenä* [Stardom]. 1963: *Hopeaa rajan takaa* [Silver from across the border]. 1967: *Pähkähullu Suomi* [Crazy Finland]. 1968: *Noin seitsemän veljestä* [About seven brothers]. 1969: *Näköradiomiehen ihmeelliset seikkailut* [The marvellous adventures of a TV man]; *Leikkikalugangsteri* [Toy gangster]; *Pohjan tähteet* [Leftovers from the North]. 1970: *Speedy Gonzales—noin 7 veljeksen poika* [Speedy Gonzales, son of about seven brothers]. 1973: *Uuno Turhapuro* [Numbskull Uselessbrook/Numbskull Emptybrook]. 1974: *Viu-hah-hah-taja* [The whizzer]. 1975: *Professori Uuno D. G. Turhapuro* [Professor Numbskull D(avid) G(oliath) Emptybrook]. 1976: *Lottovoittaja UKK Turhapuro* [Lottery-winner U.K.K. Emptybrook]. 1977: *Häpy endkö? Eli kuinka Uuno Turhapuro sai niin kauniin ja rikkaan vaimon* [Hapless end? Or how Numbskull Emptybrook won the hand of such a rich and beautiful lady]. 1978: *Rautakauppias Uuno Turhapuro, presidentin vävy* [Hardware dealer Numbskull Emptybrook, the president's son-in-law]. 1981: *Uuno Turhapuron aviokriisi* [The marital crisis of Numbskull Emptybrook]. 1982: *Uuno Turhapuro menettää muistinsa* [Numbskull Emptybrook loses his memory]. 1983: *Uuno Turhapuron muisti palailee pätkittäin* [Numbskull Emptybrook's memory slowly comes back]. 1984: *Uuno Turhapuro armeijan leivissä* [Numbskull Emptybrook in the army]. 1985: *Kliffaa hei!* [Cool, hey! Happy-Go-Lucky Andy and Carefree Charlie]; *Uuno Epsanjassa* [Numbskull Emptybrook in Spain]. 1986: *Uuno Turhapuro muuttaa maalle* [Numbskull Emptybrook back in the country]; *Pikkupojat* [Little boys]. 1988: *Tupla-Uuno* [Double Uuno]. 1990: *Uunon huikeat poikamiesvuodet maaseudulla* [Uuno's marvelous bachelor years]. 1991: *Uuno Turhapuro herra Helsingin herra* [Mr. Uuno Turhapuro from Helsinki]. 1992: *Uuno Turhapuro Suomen Tasavallan Herra Presidentti* [Uuno Turhapuro, Mr. President of Finland]. 1994: *Uuno Turhapuron veli* [Uuno Turhapuro's brother].

Director, Actor

1964: *X-paroni* [Baron X]. 1966: *Millipilleri* [Mill Pill]. 1971: *Hirttämättömät* [The un-hanged]; *Kahdeksas veljes* [The eighth brother]. 1979: *Koeputkiaikuinen ja Simon enkelit* [The test-tube adult and Simo's angels]. 1980: *Tup akka lakko* [To stop smoking]. 1984: *Lentävät luupäät* [Flying fools]. 1987: *Uuno Turhapuro kaksoisagentti* [Double agent Uuno Turhapuro]. 1993: *Uuno Turhapuron poika* [Uuno Turhapuro's son].

ANTTI PEIPPO (Lahti, 10 Sept. 1934–29 June 1989), director, cinematographer. Peippo, who started out as a visual artist, moved over to the cinema when he was about thirty and became *Risto Jarva's right hand as cameraman. He was a master whose flair and vision met every challenge from every cinematic mode, from comedy to melodrama, from "commissioned" films and documentaries (in this last category, the gray landscape of marginal Finland in *Yhden miehen sota* [One man's war] is great poetry) to premonitions of the future. Further, Peippo directed a series of fine short films from the early 1970s on, many of which deal with Finnish history with a rare insight; they make up an absorbing jigsaw puzzle on themes of past and present. Peippo's masterpiece is *Sijainen* [Proxy] (1989), his profound account of schizophrenia just lying in wait in the recesses of society; it was finished just a few months before his death.

FILMOGRAPHY

Director

1979: *Ihmemies* [Wonderman/The miracle man]. 1986: *Nykytaiteen museo* [The Museum of Modern Art]. 1989: *Sijainen* [Proxy] (also cinematographer).

Cinematographer

1965: *Onnenpeli* [Game of chance]. 1967: *Työmiehen päiväkirja* [A worker's diary]. 1969: *Ruusujen aika* [Time of roses]. 1970: *Bensaa suonissa* [Rally]. 1972: *Kun taivas putoaa* [When the heavens fall]. 1973: *Yhden miehen sota* [One man's war]. 1975: *Mies joka ei osannut sanoa ei* [The man who couldn't say no]. 1976: *Loma* [The vacation/Holidays]. 1977: *Jäniksen vuosi.* [The year of the hare]. 1978: *Vartioitu kylä 1944.* 1983: *Menestyksen maku* [A taste of success].

MATTI PELLONPÄÄ (Helsinki, 28 Mar. 1951–13 July 1995), actor. Pellonpää, who in 1992 was awarded the Felix prize for being "the best European actor," is the best-known actor of the new Finnish cinema. Above all, he is remembered as the central character in *Aki and *Mika Kaurismäki's films—indeed, as their alter ego. He was endowed with the magical talent of confronting us with the most fundamental and oftentimes wondrous aspects of life: greed (in the role of the agent in the Leningrad Cowboys movies), friendship (in Aki's *Varjoja paratiisissa* [Shadows in paradise] and in Mika's *Zombie ja kummitusjuna* [Zombie and the ghost train]), love (in *Pidä huivista kiinni, Tatjana* [Take care of your scarf, Tatjana]), and solidarity (in *Varjoja paratiisissa*)—all such qualities are expressed with precision and in universally understood terms. Through his talent, the most vital aspects of life are to be seen up there on the cinema screen; there we encounter the miracle of a performance by a born screen actor—one who perceives the world through a spectrum of golden humor. Pellonpää demonstrated for us the highest perfection of his profession: He convinced us that the simple secret of screen acting is "only" to be a human being. The comedian he most brings to mind is Buster Keaton, that laconic and poetic artist par excellence. In Finland, Pellonpää is preceded by a legendary "tribe" of bohemians. His most significant qualities—his laconic manner, his noncommittal bearing, and his constancy—were all mere "show"; he understood instinctively and passionately what screen acting was all about. There are scenes in his films that suggest that his register could be as multifaceted as any renaissance artist. He died just a few weeks before the shooting of *Kauas pilvet karkaavat [Drifting clouds] was due to begin; this was in July 1995 when he was only forty-four years old.

FILMOGRAPHY

1970: *Akseli ja Elina* [Akseli and Elina]. 1976: *Antti Puuhaara* [Antti Treebranch]. 1977: *Viimeinen savotta* [The last lumber camp]. 1979: *Ruskan jälkeen* [Winter of black snow]. 1981: *Valehtelija* [The liar]; *Pedon merkki* [Sign of the beast]. 1982: *Jackpot 2* (short); *Arvottomat* [The worthless]. 1983: *Regina ja miehet* [Regina and the men]; *Huhtikuu on kuukausista julmin* [April is the cruelest month]; *Rikos ja rangaistus* [Crime and punishment]. 1984: *Kello* [The clock]; *Aikalainen* [The contemporary]; *Rakkauselokuva* [Nothing but love]; *Klaani—tarina Sammakoitten suvusta* [The clan—tale of the frogs]. 1985: *Viimeiset rotannahat* [Rare, medium, well done]; *Calamari Union*; *Ylösnousemus* [The resurrection]. 1986: *Kuningas lähtee Ranskaan* [The king goes forth to France]; *Varjoja paratiisissa* [Shadows in paradise]. 1987: *Hamlet liikemaailmassa* [Hamlet goes business/Hamlet]. 1988: *Ariel.* 1989: *Cha Cha Cha*; *Leningrad Cowboys Go America*; *Kumma juttu* [Strange thing]. 1990: *Räpsy ja Dolly eli Pariisi odottaa* [Dolly and her lover]; *Kiljusen herrasväen uudet seikkailut* [The new adventures of that Kiljunen family]. 1991: *Kadunlakaisijat* [The street sweepers]; *Zombie ja kummitusjuna* [Zombie and the ghost train]. 1992: *Boheemielämää/La vie de bohéme*; *Papukaijamies* [Parrot man]. 1993: *The Last Border—Viimeisellä rajalla* [The last border]. 1994: *Pidä huivista kiinni, Tatjana* [Take care of your scarf, Tatjana]; *Leningrad Cowboys Meet Moses.* 1995: *The Iron Horsemen.*

AWARDS

Jussi 1991

Felix (European Film Award) 1992: Best Actor

MARKKU PÖLÖNEN (Eno, 16 Sept. 1957–), director. Pölönen is the one among the younger generation of directors who is expected to carry on with traditional Finnish cinema. Both critics and audiences look to him to persevere portraying the old agrarian way of life, consequently challenging the changing world and its values. He is relied on to continue the work done by such popular figures as *Edvin Laine. Pölönen's one-hour-long *Onnen maa* [The land of happiness] is a small-scale, personal, nationalistic, and subjectively romantic film—we can hear in it the director's voice and sense there a hint of the old-time al fresco dance pavillions where nature and "civilization" meet; besides, there is the reek of Koskenkorva vodka and perspiration. His greatest effort so far, *Kivenpyör-ittäjän kylä* [The last wedding], deals with the same theme, but here there is a feeling of repetition, and it seems that the original idea turned out to be a rather predictable series of follow-ups.

FILMOGRAPHY

1993: *Onnen maa* [The land of happiness]. 1995: *Kivenpyörittäjän kylä* [The last wedding].

AWARD

Jussi 1996

LASSE PÖYSTI (Sortavala, 24 Jan. 1927–), actor, director. During the war years, Pöysti was probably the most popular figure in Finland. He started his acting career at the age of fourteen in 1941 as Olli, the hugely popular son in the series of films about the family Suominen. In other parts of the world, very few young actors have survived such stardom without damage being done to their personalities, but Pöysti developed into one of the great character actors in Finland. All that the charisma and authority he possessed in his youth did to him was to enrich and embellish him as an actor. Yet for several years he was adrift, notably in the 1950s while he was pursuing a career as a film director, but when he moved over to the theater, his achievements became ever move impressive. He worked in a number of theaters, including the Dramaten in Stockholm from 1981 to 1985. Several great performances in various television dramas signaled a fresh start in Pöysti's mature years, as did his return to the cinema in powerful, charismatic roles such as the leading role in Ralf Lång-backa's *Herra Puntila ja hänen renkinsä Matti* [Mr. Puntila and his servant Matti], the police superintendent in *Kaurismäki's Klaani—tarina Sammakoitten suvusta* [The clan—tale of the frogs] done with a touch of Maigret (later, Pöysti acted this French detective brilliantly on radio), and above all the portrait of our Nobel laureate Sillanpää in *Kassila's Ihmiselon ihanuus ja kurjuus* [The glory and misery of human life]—an outstanding tour de force and an illustration of how the clarity of a child's perception can surface as the primary element in the creative work of the consummate artist.

FILMOGRAPHY

Actor

1941: *Suomisen perhe* [The Suominen family]; *Onnellinen ministeri* [The lucky cabinet minister]. 1942: *Suomisen Ollin tempaus* [Olli Suominen's stunt]. 1943: *Suomisen tai-teilijat* [The little artists of the Suominen household]. 1944: *Suomisen Olli rakastuu* [Olli falls in love]. 1945: *Suomisen Olli yllättää* [Olli pulls a surprise]. 1948: *Haaviston Leeni* [Leeni of Haavisto]; *Kilroy sen teki* [Kilroy was here]; *Hormoonit valloillaan* [Hormones on the loose]. 1949: *Ruma Elsa* [Ugly Elsa]; *Katupeilin takana* [Behind the mirror in the window·]; *Sinut minä tahdon* [It's you I want]. 1950: *Professori Masa* [Professor Masa]; *Isäpappa ja keltanokka* [The old man and the youngster]; *Rakkaus on nopeampi Piiroisen pässiäkin* [Love is even quicker than Piironen's ram]. 1951: *Vain laulajapoikia* [We songsters]; *Radio tekee murron* [The radio commits a burglary]; *Kenraalin morsian* [The general's fiancée]; *Rion yö* [A night in Rio]; *Tukkijoella* [The log drivers]; *Vihaan sinua—rakas* [Darling, I hate you]. 1952: *Kaikkien naisten monni* [The girl's very own recruit]. 1953: *2 hauskaa vekkulia* [Two funny guys]; *Miljonäärimonni* [The millionaire recruit]. 1954: *Kovanaama* [Tough guy]; *Laivaston monnit maissa* [Naval recruits on shore leave]; *Putkinotko* [Pipe hollow]. 1955: *Näkemiin, Helena* [Farewell, Helena]; *Sankarialokas* [Conscript hero]; *Miss Eurooppaa metsästämässä* [Hunting for Miss Europe]; *Villi Pohjola* [The wild North]. 1957: *Vääpelin kauhu* [The sergeant's nemesis]; *Syntipukki* [Scapegoat]. 1958: *Asessorin naishuolet* [The assessor's troubles with women]; *Sotapojan heilat* [The soldier boy's sweethearts]. 1959: *Taas tapaamme Suomisen perheen* [The Suominen family is here again]. 1960: *Justus järjestää kaiken* [Justus will take care of everything]. 1968: *Punahilkka* [Little Red Riding Hood]. 1976: *Pyhä perhe* [The Holy family]. 1979: *Herra Puntila ja hänen renkinsä Matti* [Mr. Puntila and his servant Matti]. 1984: *Klaani—tarina Sammakoitten suvusta* [The clan—tale of the frogs]; *Dirty Story*. 1986: *Kuningas lähtee Ranskaan* [The king goes forth to France]; *Näkemiin, hyvästi* [Farewell, goodbye]. 1987: *Lain ulkopuolella* [Outside the law]. 1988: *Ihmiselon ihanuus ja kurjuus* [The glory and misery of human life]. 1989: *Kukunor*. 1992: *Mestari* [The champion].

Director, Actor

1952: *Kaikkien naisten monni* [The girl's very own recruit]. 1953: *2 hauskaa vekkulia* [Two funny guys]. 1955: *Näkemiin, Helena* [Farewell, Helena]. 1958: *Asessorin naishuolet* [The assessor's troubles with women]. 1960: *Justus järjestää kaiken* [Justus will take care of everything]

Director

1952: *Ja Helena soittaa . . .* [And Helena plays on . . .]; *Salakuljettajan laulu* [The smuggler's serenade]. 1954: *Kummituskievari* [The haunted inn].

AWARDS

Jussi 1977

Jussi 1980

Jussi 1986

JOEL RINNE (Asikkala, 6 June 1897–3 Dec. 1981), actor. Rinne was the central figure in a well-known theatrical dynasty, one of the great figures of Finnish theater. His stage career began in 1918, and since 1928 until his death he worked at the National Theatre. His career in cinema lasted half a century and included altogether about sixty roles, starting with leading roles in silent films; already in them his natural mimic talent could be seen. However, it was the introduction of sound that really made him an admired film actor; he became some kind of foil to *Tauno Palo, his even more popular contemporary. Rinne's most exciting period as an actor was probably the war years, when he starred both as the hero in elegant adventure films (the Dead Man series) and as the solid figure with high principles in a number of poignant and patriotic films. One of these roles is as the author-clergyman in *Kirkastettu sydän* [The transfigured heart], a man who feels it is his duty to give his life for his fatherland. Such a role could easily appear ingratiating, but Rinne makes a success of it because of his skill at building associations. The naturalness with which he moved among sets and commanded open space is quite admirable; this grace was an inborn quality distinguishing a natural screen actor from all those whose skills derive from grinding away at lessons.

Rinne is best remembered for his role as Superintendent Palmu in the four films directed by *Matti Kassila in the 1960s. In these, he creates a character who is charismatic, authoritarian, and at the same time comical. While sketching Police Inspector Palmu, Rinne was well aware of the significance the generation of "strong old men" had taken in Finnish history: Palmu splendidly parodied these figures; among them were found some Finnish presidents.

FILMOGRAPHY

1923: *Koskenlaskijan morsian* [The logroller's bride]; *Rautakylän vanha parooni* [The old baron of Rautakylä]. 1926: *Murtovarkaus* [The burglary]. 1928: *Nuori luotsi* [The young pilot]; *Miekan terällä* [With the blade of a sword]. 1931: *Aatamin puvussa ja vähän Eevankin* [Dressed like Adam and a bit like Eve too]; *Rovastin häämatkat* [The dean's honeymoon travels]. 1932: *Olenko minä tullut haaremiin?* [Have I entered a harem?]. 1934: *Minä ja ministeri* [Me and the cabinet minister]; *Meidän poikamme il-massa—me maassa* [Our boys in the air—we on the ground]. 1936: *VMV 6.* 1937: *Ja alla oli tulinen järvi* [And below was a fiery lake]; *Kuin uni ja varjo* [As dream and shadow . . .]. 1938: *Tulitikkuja lainaamassa* [Out to borrow matches]; *Syyllisiäkö?* [Are they guilty?]; *Nummisuutarit* [The village shoemakers]. 1939: *Halveksittu* [Scorned]; *Seitsemän veljestä* [Seven brothers]. 1940: *Suotorpan tyttö* [The tenant farmer's girl]; *SF-paraati* [SF parade]. 1941: *Perheen musta lammas* [The black sheep of the family]; *Jos oisi valtaa* [If I only had the power]; *Suomisen perhe* [The Suominen family]; *Poikamiespappa* [Bachelor papa]; *Täysosuma* [Bull's eye]. 1942: *Kuollut mies rakastuu* [The dead man falls in love]; *Yli rajan* [Over the border]. 1943: *Syntynyt terve tyttö* [Born, a healthy girl]; *Miehen kunnia* [A man's honor]; *Kirkastettu sydän* [The transfigured heart]. 1944: *Kuollut mies vihastuu* [The dead man loses his temper]; *Kartanon naiset* [The women on the estate]. 1945: *Kolmastoista koputus* [The thirteenth knock]; *Valkoisen neilikan velho* [The wizard of the white carnation]. 1947: *Hedelmätön puu* [The barren tree]; *Pikku-Matti maailmalla* [Little Matti out in the wide world]. 1948: *Kilroy sen teki* [Kilroy was here]; *Hormoonit valloillaan* [Hormones on the loose]. 1949: *Kalle-Kustaa Korkin seikkailut* [The adventures of Kalle-Kustaa Korkki]. 1950: *Isäpappa ja keltanokka* [The old man and the youngster]; *Tapahtui kaukana* [Love north of the Arctic Circle]. 1952: *Yhden yön hinta* [The price of one night]; *Kuollut mies kummittelee* [The dead man walks again]. 1953: *Huhtikuu tulee* [April's coming]; *Tyttö kuunsillalta* [The girl from Moon Bridge]. 1954: *Niskavuoren Aarne* [Aarne of Niskavuori]. 1955: *Rakas lurjus* [Beloved rascal]. 1956: *Tyttö tuli taloon* [A girl came into the house]; *Muuan sulhasmies* [A certain suitor]. 1957: *Niskavuori taistelee* [Niskavuori fights]. 1960: *Komisario Palmun erehdys* [Police Inspector Palmu's mistake]. 1961: *Kaasua, komisario Palmu!* [Step on the gas, Inspector Palmu!]; *Kultainen vasikka* [The golden calf]. 1962: *Tähdet kertovat, komisario Palmu* [The stars will tell, Inspector Palmu]. 1969: *Vodkaa, komisario Palmu* [Vodka, Mr. Palmu]. 1970: *Päämaja* [The headquarters].

AWARDS

Jussi 1944

Jussi 1962

ESKO SALMINEN (Helsinki, 12 Oct. 1940–), actor. From the beginning, Salminen was doomed to be an actor, born as he was to a family with a long theatrical tradition. He started his screen career when he was still studying at the Theatre Academy, and in the 1960s, he became a youth icon in a number of harmlessly crazy movies, after which he vanished from the silver screen except for a few rare appearances in some farces. During those years he established a reputation as a celebrated young stage actor entrusted with some powerful and demanding roles: Peer Gynt, van Gogh, Danton. In the 1980s Salminen returned to the cinema, and now his roles were commensurate with his exceptional talent, whether in historical or literary spectaculars or in films made in an intimate mode, such as his portrayal of the stepfather in *Aki Kaurismäki's *Hamlet liikemaailmassa* [Hamlet goes business] or his outstanding intervention as the perverse psychiatrist in Veikko Aaltonen's *Tuhlaajapoika* [The prodigal son].

FILMOGRAPHY

1949: *Katupeilin takana* [Behind the mirror in the window]. 1958: *Sven Tuuva* [Soldier Sven]. 1959: *Pekka ja Pätkä mestarimaalareina* [Pete and Runt, master painters]. 1960: *Skandaali tyttökoulussa* [Scandal in the girls' school]; *Kaks' tavallista Lahtista* [Two ordinary guys]; *Opettajatar seikkailee* [The school marm on the road to adventure]. 1961: *Tähtisumua* [Stardust]; *Minkkiturkki* [The mink coat]; *Toivelauluja* [Songs after the heart's desire]; *Tyttö ja hattu* [The girl and her hat]; *Kaasua, komisario Palmu!* [Step on the gas, Inspector Palmu!]; *Kultainen vasikka* [The golden calf]. 1962: *Kuu on vaarallinen* [The moon is dangerous]; *Tähdet kertovat, komisario Palmu* [The stars will tell, Inspector Palmu]. 1963: *Jengi* [The gang]. 1965: *Juokse kuin varas* [Make like a thief/Run like a thief]. 1966: *Johan nyt on markkinat!* [What the devil!]; *Rakkaus alkaa aamuyöstä* [Love begins in the small hours]. 1967: *Pähkähullu Suomi* [Crazy Finland]. 1968: *Vain neljä kertaa* [Four times only]. 1970: *Speedy Gonzales—noin 7 veljeksen poika* [Speedy Gonzales, son of about seven brothers]. 1978: *Runoilija ja Muusa* [Poet and muse]. 1979: *Seitsemän veljestä* [Seven brothers]. 1981: *Pedon merkki* [Sign of the beast]. 1982: *Kuningas jolla ei ollut sydäntä* [The king who had no heart]. 1983: *Uuno Turhapuron muisti palailee pätkittäin* [Numbskull Emptybrook's memory slowly comes back]; *Apinan vuosi* [In the year of the ape]. 1984: *Niskavuori* [The tug of home/The family Niskavuori]. 1986: *Valkoinen kääpiö* [The white dwarf]; *Harmagedon*. 1987: *Hamlet liikemaailmassa* [Hamlet goes business/Hamlet]. 1988: *Pohjanmaa* [Plainlands]; *Ariel*. 1989: *Cha Cha Cha*; *Talvisota* [The Winter War]. 1991: *Vääpeli Körmy ja vetenalaiset vehkeet* [Sergeant Major Körmy and the submarine trouble]. 1992: *Tuhlaajapoika*

[The prodigal son]. 1993: *Marraskuun harmaa valo* [The gray light of November]. 1994: *Kaikki pelissä* [Play it all]; *Aapo*; *Uuno Turhapuron veli* [Uuno Turhapuro's brother].

TIMO SALMINEN (Turku, 11 July 1952–), cinematographer. Timo Salminen, son of director *Ville Salminen, is one of the most notorious cameramen in the Finnish cinema; since the early 1980s he has been devising the visual aspects for the films of the *Kaurismäki brothers. It is difficult to say to what extent the idiosyncratic aesthetic of the Kaurismäki films—their concept of space relationships, the link to the "other Finland," the hues and shades of the earth—is conjured by the director and how much of it is summoned up by the cameraman. Salminen also excels in black-and-white film. His work brings to mind the masters of the Golden Age; yet this is no mere imitation.

FILMOGRAPHY

1981: *Saimaa-ilmiö* [The Saimaa gesture]. 1982: *Arvottomat* [The worthless]. 1983: *Rikos ja rangaistus* [Crime and punishment]. 1984: *Klaani—tarina Sammakoitten suvusta* [The clan—tale of the frogs]. 1985: *Calamari Union*; *Rosso*. 1986: *Varjoja paratiisissa* [Shadows in paradise]. 1987: *Tilinteko* [The final arrangement]; *Hamlet liikemaailmassa* [Hamlet goes business/Hamlet]. 1988: Ariel. 1989: *Cha Cha Cha*; *Leningrad Cowboys Go America*; *Paperitähti* [Paper star]. 1990: **Tulitikkutehtaan tyttö* [The match factory girl]; *I Hired a Contract Killer*; *Amazon*. 1992: *Boheemielämää/La vie de bohème*; *Tuhlaajapoika* [The prodigal son]. 1993: *The Last Border—Viimeisellä rajalla* [The last border]. 1994: *Pidä huivista kiinni, Tatjana* [Take care of your scarf, Tatjana]; *Leningrad Cowboys Meet Moses*. 1995: *The Iron Horsemen*. 1996: **Kauas pilvet karkaavat* [Drifting clouds].

AWARDS

Jussi 1991

Jussi 1995

VILLE SALMINEN (Maarianhamina, 2 Oct. 1908–22 Nov. 1993), actor, director, set designer. Among Finnish cinema people, Salminen is probably the nearest specimen to what we call the Hollywood professional in the best sense of the word. He started his career in the theater as a set designer and actor and in 1937 moved over to cinema to continue in the same occupations. He directed the first of a total of thirty films in 1941 (he was a set designer in forty-five!). As Salminen remembers, among all this there was only one single production— *Evakko* [Evacuated] in the mid-1950s—that he really wanted to direct. Otherwise, he worked on whatever "the machinery" requested him to do, moving freely from one genre to another. In practically each of his films there is a sequence that shows a touch of a real master.

And that's what Salminen indubitably was—a master. Even in his mediocre films there were brilliant sequences, such as the fashion shows in *Toukokuun taika* [May magic]. And in *Rion yö* [A night in Rio], the fantastic dance scenes are full of the excitement of the exotic outside world (these effects had been created more with imagination than with money), and still all this is somehow so fundamentally Finnish. The folksy ballads (*Kaunis Veera eli Ballaadi Saimaalta* [Beautiful Veera], 1950) or the manic biographies of musicians (*Orpopojan valssi* [The orphan's waltz], 1949) approach creative madness under Salminen's direction. His career is filled with contradictions, and yet it offers delicious insights as well. The secret is in the films' all-embracing visuality.

It was only the dilemma in production policy that stopped Salminen from making really high-class Finnish cinema entertainment. *Säkkijärven polkka* [Säkkijärvi polka] and *Evakko*, both with a Karelian location—that legendary land of Finnish eccentricity and poetry—were the final reminders of his talent. When the era of the big studios came to an end, Salminen left the cinema; thereafter, he served as the head of the theater division in Finnish commercial television.

FILMOGRAPHY

Actor

1931: *Jääkärin morsian* [The light infantryman's bride]. 1932: *Kuisma ja Helinä* [Kuisma and Helinä]. 1936: *Mieheke* [Surrogate husband]. 1938: *Jääkärin morsian* [A yager's bride/A yager's wife]; *Poikamiesten holhokki* [The bachelors' ward]; *Markan tähden* [A day as an heiress]. 1939: *Aktivistit* [Activists]; *Avoveteen* [Towards a new horizon]; *Punahousut* [Red pants]. 1940: *Kyökin puolella* [In the kitchen]. 1941: *Ryhmy ja Romppainen* [Ryhmy and Romppainen]. 1943: *Jees ja just* [Yes and right away!]. 1944: *Herra ja ylhäisyys* [Lord and master]; *Kuollut mies vihastuu* [The dead man loses his temper]; *Hiipivä vaara* [Creeping danger]. 1945: *En ole kreivitär* [I'm not countess]. 1946: *Rakkauden risti* [The cross of love]; *Nuoruus sumussa* [Youth in a fog]. 1948: *Laulava sydän* [The singing heart]; *Pontevat pommaripojat* [The virile bomber boys]. 1949: *Kalle-Kustaa Korkin seikkailut* [The adventures of Kalle-Kustaa Korkki]. *Rion yö* [A night in Rio]; *Tytön huivi* [The scarf]. 1952: *Tervetuloa aamukahville eli Tottako toinen puoli* [Welcome to the Breakfast Club]. 1956: *Silja—nuorena nukkunut* [Silja—the maid]. 1958: *Paksunahka* [Thick skin]; *Sven Tuuva* [Soldier Sven]. 1961: *Tähtisumua* [Stardust]. 1968: *Täällä Pohjantähden alla* [Here beneath the Polar Star]; *Asfalttilampaat* [The Sphalt lambs]. 1979: *Ihmemies* [Wonderman/The Miracle Man]. 1984: *Klaani—tarina Sammakoitten suvusta* [The clan—tale of the frogs].

Director, Actor

1941: *Viimeinen vieras* [The last guest] (codir. Arvi Tuomi). 1945: *Mikä yö* [What a night]. 1952: *Kipparikvartetti* [The sailor quartet]. 1953: *Lentävä kalakukko* [Esa "flies" to Kuopio]. 1954: *Laivaston monnit maissa* [Naval recruits on shore leave]; *Laivan kannella* [On deck].

Director

1946: *Menneisyyden varjo* [Shadow of the past]. 1948: *Haaviston Leeni* [Leeni of Haavisto]; *Toukokuun taika* [May magic]; *Irmeli seitsentoistavuotias* [Irmeli—sweet seventeen]; *Pontevat pommaripojat* [The virile bomber boys]. 1949: *Orpopojan valssi* [The orphan's waltz]. 1950: *Köyhä laulaja* [The poor singer]; *Kaunis Veera eli Ballaadi Saimaalta* [Beautiful Veera/Ballad of Lake Saimaa]. 1951: *Kenraalin morsian* [The general's fiancée]; *Rion yö* [A night in Rio]; *Tytön huivi* [The scarf]. 1952: *Mitäs me taiteilijat* [Just we artists]. 1953: *Pekka Puupää* [Pete Blockhead]; *Lumikki ja 7 jätkää* [Snow White and the seven loggers]; *Alaston malli karkuteillä* [The nude on the run]. 1955: *Säkkijärven polkka* [Säkkijärvi polka]. 1956: *Evakko* [Evacuated]; *Anu ja Mikko* [Anu and Mikko]. 1957: *Taas tyttö kadoksissa* [Another girl lost]. 1959: *Yks' tavallinen Virtanen* [Just an ordinary Finn]. 1960: *Oho, sanoi Eemeli* [Oho! said Emil]; *Kaks' tavallista Lahtista* [Two ordinary guys]; *Molskis, sanoi Eemeli, molskis!* ["Kerplunk," Emil said]. 1961: *Toivelauluja* [Song after the heart's desire].

ELINA SALO (Sipoo, 9 Mar. 1936–), actress. Around 1960, Elina Salo set out to be the most popular screen actress in Finland; in those days her roles were typical of the light entertainment of the period. Several years on the stage were needed before Elina Salo's charisma and intensive talent were to become truly apparent on the silver screen. Already *Risto Jarva's *Työmiehen päiväkirja* [The worker's diary], the most noteworthy film of the Finnish cinema in the 1960s, was an augury of the great things to come. It was followed by roles played in Sweden, including the leading part in *Kjell Grede's film *Harry Munter*. Salo was bilingual and did most of her stage acting at the Swedish-speaking Lilla Teatern in Helsinki. A new active phase in Salo's film career began with the role of poetess L. Onerva in Jaakko Pakkasvirta's *Runoilija ja Muusa* [Poet and muse] and culminated in *Aki Kaurismäki's films, in which her performances rank among the very pinnacles of Finnish screen acting. There was a natural place for Salo in the world of Kaurismäki as her role of the mother both in *Hamlet liikemaailmassa* [Hamlet goes business] and in *Tulitikkutehtaan tyttö* [The match factory girl] demonstrates.

FILMOGRAPHY

1956: *Tyttö tuli taloon* [A girl came into the house]; *Rintamalotta* [Girls at the front]. 1957: *Herra sotaministeri* [Mr. Minister of War]. 1958: *Kulkurin masurkka* [The vagabond's mazurka]; *Sotapojan heilat* [The soldier boy's sweethearts]. 1959: *Patarouva* [The queen of spades]; *Taas tapaamme Suomisen perheen* [The Suominen family is here again]. 1960: *Justus järjestää kaiken* [Justus will take care of everything]; *Skandaali tyttökoulussa* [Scandal in the girls' school]; *Komisario Palmun erehdys* [Police Inspector Palmu's mistake]; *Iloinen Linnanmäki* [Fun at the amusement park]. 1961: *Tähtisumua* [Stardust]; *Minkkiturkki* [The mink coat]; *Kaasua, komisario Palmu!* [Step on the gas, Inspector Palmu!]; *Kultainen vasikka* [The golden calf]. 1962: *Älä nuolase . . . !* [Don't count your chickens . . .]; *Naiset, jotka minulle annoit* [The women you gave me]; *Yö vai päivä* [Night or day]. 1963: *Tie pimeään* [The road to darkness]; *Villin Pohjolan salattu laakso* [The secret valley in the wild North]. 1965: *Vaaksa vaaraa* [The edge of danger]. 1967: *Työmiehen päiväkirja* [The worker's diary]. 1970: *Bensaa suonissa* [Rally/Gas in the veins]. 1971: *Kreivi* [The count]. 1978: *Runoilija ja Muusa* [Poet and muse]. 1979: *Herra Puntila ja hänen renkinsä Matti* [Mr. Puntila and his servant Matti]. 1981: *Pedon merkki* [Sign of the beast]. 1986: *Linna* [The castle]; *Lumikuningatar* [The Snow Queen]. 1987: *Hamlet liikemaailmassa* [Hamlet goes business/Hamlet]. 1988: *Taavi Kassilan Petos* [The betrayal]. 1990: *Tulitikkutehtaan tyttö* [The match factory girl]. 1994: *Pidä huivista kiinni, Tatjana* [Take care of your scarf, Tatjana]. 1996: *Kauas pilvet karkaavat* [Drifting clouds].

AWARD

Jussi 1979

TOIVO SÄRKKÄ (Rural commune of Mikkeli, 20 Nov. 1890–9 Feb. 1975), director, producer, screenwriter. Särkkä had been working as a bank manager and a Russian-language teacher when he in the mid-1930s began at the age of forty-five to dedicate his life to cinema; he became the managing director of SF (Suomen Filmiteollisuus), the film company that has produced more films than any other in Finland. The following thirty years saw the release of 236 films, of which Särkkä directed 49 himself. This is a record for Finland as well.

SF set "authenticity" and "nationalism" as its goals. Särkkä was to add to these qualities his very own connotation—often demeaning but in most cases genuine and touchingly popular. It soon became apparent what were to become Särkkä's own special territories. One was the depicting of the province of Pohjanmaa (Ostrobothnia) as a spiritual landscape; he even made a special project of it. "Great feelings" had to be highly dramatized, and through them "the greatness of Finnish people was to gush forth." Another was a certain inborn talent for cinematic eroticism and melodrama. A third quality characteristic to Särkkä's work was a kind of fundamental Slavic tone, which can most distinctly be sensed in *Kulkurin valssi* [The vagabond's waltz]. A fourth component was good old-fashioned theatricality. Särkkä was genuinely fond of the theater, and he believed in it so intensely that the concept of cinema's idiosyncratic mode of expression probably never entered his mind; still, *Katupeilin takana* [Behind the mirror in the window], a romantic story from the turn of the century, emerges as an example of outstanding cinema. One more quality could be identified: The Särkkä concept of history was altogether romantic and "textbookish."

Särkkä loved to be surrounded by the stars, and it is one ingredient that lends his films that particular aroma of "true" and "old-fashioned" cinema that appeals to the ever new generations of movie audiences. Whatever Särkkä did he did in a great hurry, and it certainly has contributed to his huge image as the primary representative of the naive and primitive aesthetic practiced at SF. Yet there is some dreamy magic in Särkkä's best films (*Kuin uni ja varjo* [As dream and shadow], *Vaivaisukon morsian* [The wooden pauper's bride]), and the slow developments, the prolonged monologues, and the shilly-shallying dialogue of other films (such as *Tulitikkuja lainaamassa* [Out to borrow matches]) function precisely because no real effort to "create cinema" has been made.

When we reach the 1950s there is less and less to be said about Särkkä's films. A sober account of the greatest trauma of the Finnish society is given in *1918—Mies ja hänen omatuntonsa* [1918]. It was his most crucial and flawless film of the decade, when the hustle and bustle of production took practically all Särkkä's time and any chance of focus. And in many other respects, too, the 1950s were typified by a multitude of vain films. Simply put, Särkkä did not have either the patience or the skill to invest in a talented corps of directors.

That was the whole problem. SF signified a triumph of popular sentiments, but it also demonstrated a chronic lack of ambition, and its best directors (*Ville Salminen, *Matti Kassila) left the company, fed up with its too-intensive and slapdash approach to production.

The year 1955 saw the release of *Tuntematon sotilas* [The unknown soldier], the most ambitious production of SF. It was produced by Särkkä and directed by *Edvin Laine. Its financial success proved to be a trap: In order to avoid taxes, Särkkä invested the profits into careless mass production, which has more than anything else given rise to the bad reputation held by the traditional Finnish cinema. One crisis followed another, and once television had spread over the country, cinema audiences vanished. In 1964 when Särkkä sold all his films to television and closed down his company, it was a symbolic and unmistakable end to Finnish film production based on the studio system.

FILMOGRAPHY

Director, Screenwriter

1936: *Kaikenlaisia vieraita* [All kinds of visitors] (codir. Yrjö Norta); *Pohjalaisia* [The Bothnians/The Northerners] (codir. Yrjö Norta). 1937: *Kuin uni ja varjo* [As dream and shadow . . .] (codir. Yrjö Norta). 1938: *Rykmentin murheenkryyni* [The black sheep of the regiment] (codir. Yrjö Norta). 1939: *Eteenpäin—Elämään* [Forward—towards life]; *Jumalan tuomio* [God's judgement] (codir. Yrjö Norta); *Pikku Pelimanni* [The little fiddler]; *Serenaadi sotatorvella* [Serenade with a war trumpet]. 1940: *Suotorpan tyttö* [The girl from Suotorppa/The tenant farmer's girl]; *Runon kuningas ja muuttolintu* [The king of poets and bird of passage]. 1941: *Suomisen perhe* [The Suominen family]; *Kaivopuiston kaunis Regina* [Beautiful Regina of Kaivopuisto]. 1942: *Uuteen elämään* [To a new life]; *August järjestää kaiken* [August will fix everything]. 1944: *Vaivaisukon morsian* [The wooden pauper's bride]; *Sylvi; Anja tule kotiin* [Anja come back home!]. 1947: *Naiskohtaloita* [Destinies of women]; *Suopursu kukkii* [The wild rosemary blooms]. 1948: *Neljästoista vieras* [The fourteenth guest]. 1949: *Pikku pelimannista viulun kuninkaaksi* [From the little fiddler to the king of violinists]. 1950: *Katariina kaunis leski* [Katarina, the beautiful widow]. 1956: *Viisi vekkulia* [Five jolly rascals]; *Juha*. 1957: *1918—Mies ja hänen omatuntonsa* [1918]. 1961: *Miljoonavaillinki* [Short by a million]; *Kuu on vaarallinen* [The moon is dangerous]; *Me* [Us].

Director

1937: *Asessorin naishuolet* [The assessor's love troubles] (codir. Yrjö Norta); *Lapatossu* [The old railroad worker] (codir. Yrjö Norta). 1938: *Tulitikkuja lainaamassa* [Out to borrow matches] (codir. Yrjö Norta); *Olenko minä tullut haaremiin?* [Have I entered a harem?] (codir. Yrjö Norta). 1939: *Helmikuun manifesti* [The February manifesto] (codir. Yrjö Norta). 1940: *Tavaratalo Lapatossu ja Vinski* [The department store "Lapatosu and Vinski"]. 1941: *Kulkurin valssi* [The vagabond's waltz]; *Onnellinen Ministeri* [The lucky cabinet minister/The happy minister]. 1942: *Onni Pyörii* [The wheel of chance]. 1944: *Ballaadi* [Ballad]; *Suomisen Olli rakastuu* [Olli falls in love]. 1946: *Nuoruus sumussa* [Youth in a fog]. 1947: *Suomen Suurkisat 1947* [Finland's great games of 1947]. 1949: *Katupeilin takana* [Behind the mirror in the window/behind the street mirror/Behind the street scene]. 1950: *Tanssi yli hautojen* [Dance over the graves]. 1953: *Hilja, maitotyttö* [Hilja, the milkmaid]. 1955: *Rakas lurjus* [The beloved rascal]. 1958: *Pieni luutatyttö*

[The little girl with the broom]. 1959: *Kovaa peliä pohjolassa* [Playing a hard game up North]; *Taas tapaamme Suomisen perheen* [The Suominen family is here again]. 1960: *Kankkulan kaivolla* [At the well] (codir. *Aarne Tarkas). 1962: *Ihana seikkailu* [The beautiful adventure].

Screenwriter

1938: *Nummisuutarit* [The village shoemakers]. 1940: *SF-paraati* [SF parade]. 1942: *Rantasuon raatajat* [The troillers of Rantasuo]. 1943: *Hevoshuijari* [Horse swindler]; *Nuoria ihmisiä* [Young people] (codir. Ossi Elstelä); *Yrjänän emännän synti* [The sin of the Lady of Yrjänä]. 1945: *Anna-Liisa*. 1947: *Särkelä itte* [Särkelä himself]. 1948: *Haaviston Leeni* [Leeni of Haavisto]; *Toukokuun taika* [May magic]; *Irmeli seitsentoistavuotias* [Irmeli—sweet seventeen]. 1949: *Isäntä soittaa hanuria* [The head of the house plays the accordion]. 1950: *Kaunis Veera eli Ballaadi Saimaalta* [Beautiful Veera/Ballad of Lake Saimaa]. 1951: *Lakeuksien lukko* [It happened in Ostrobothnia].

AWARD

Jussi 1950

NYRKI TAPIOVAARA (Pitäjänmäki, 10 Sept. 1911–29 Feb. 1940), director. Tapiovaara is always brought up when we talk about the potential and talent of Finnish cinema. This director, who was killed at the age of twenty-nine in the Winter War two weeks before its end, has become a kind of symbol of the unrealized promise of our national cinema. He had been a cinema critic and theater director and a promoter of the very first Finnish film club (Projektio, one founder of which was Alvar Aalto) before he directed his first film, *Juha*, in 1937. This triangular drama—an older peasant whose young wife is seduced by a slick vagabond—develops into a classic cinematic tale because Tapiovaara portrays these simple people so accurately and because his concept of nature's elements is so apt. The Finnish-born *Mauritz Stiller, the second of the great directors of Swedish silent cinema, had directed the same theme in 1919.

The next film, *Varastettu kuolema* [Stolen death] (1938), dealt with Finnish pro-independence activists who were working underground in 1905. Actually, the Runar Schildt's text, on which this film is based, deals with the events of the civil war of 1918, but in the late 1930s it was still a very sensitive subject. Yet the intellectual left-wing radicalism so characteristic of Tapiovaara blossomed in this film, which contains many avant-garde and poetic climaxes reminding us of both experimental French cinema and contemporary Soviet films. The next two works were farces: *Kaksi Vihtoria* [Two henpecked husbands] is a noisy film that skillfully employs the language of parody—the Finnish "carnival mood" at its best. And *Herra Lahtinen lähtee lipettiin* [Mr. Lahtinen takes French leave] is an experimental film with that same spirited élan that René Clair's works display at their best. Tapiovaara had had a fruitful connection with theater, cabaret, painting, and literature, and all these elements contribute to this ingenious film.

Critic Helmer Adler writes of the influences in Tapiovaara's work: "Realism and great pathos, profusion and force are Slavic, style choice and intellectualism are Western." Before his untimely death, Tapiovaara directed the major part of *Miehen tie* [A man's way] (1940), which is based on a novel by F. E. Sillanpää (the Nobel Prize winner in 1939). Here we have a director who has "grown up," who masters the "classical" style in the world's most natural way. Here we have an epic film in which the countryside does not simply feature as a backdrop but develops as an internal landscape, a puzzling and controversial labyrinth of meanings.

FILMOGRAPHY

1937: *Juha*. 1938: *Varastettu kuolema* [Stolen death]. 1939: *Kaksi Vihtoria* [Two hen-pecked husbands/The two victors]; *Herra Lahtinen lähtee lipettiin* [Mr. Lahtinen takes French leave/Mr. Lahtinen takes off]. 1940: *Miehen tie* [A man's way/The way of a man] (codir. Hugo Hytönen).

AARNE TARKAS (Rural commune of Pori, 19 Dec. 1923–7 Oct. 1976), direc-tor, screenwriter. Tarkas is a phenomenon of the Finnish popular cinema of the 1950s; his career lasted fifteen years and is composed of altogether thirty-three feature films representing all possible categories. He even made Finnish west-erns, or rather "northerns," as the events in these films took place in last-chance Lapland. At first, he directed "serious"—and boring—"problem" films but then found his own field in the mind-numbing world of military farce (e.g., *Vatsa sisään, rinta ulos!* [Stomach in—chest out!] with its outrageous transvestite humor). Many of his films have good and even wonderful scenes, but on the whole, his name as early as 1960 came to be synonymous with sloppy produc-tion values. In the sunset days of the large production company SF, he was an absurd workaholic who could direct two separate films simultaneously, one in the daytime and another at night.

FILMOGRAPHY

Director, Screenwriter

1952: *Yö on pitkä* [The night is long]. 1954: *Kovanaama* [The tough guy]; *Olemme kaikki syyllisiä* [We're all guilty]. 1955: *Sankarialokas* [Conscript hero]; *Villi Pohjola* [The wild North]. 1956: *Jokin ihmisessä* [Something in people]; *Rintamalotta* [Girls at the front]. 1957: *Herra sotaministeri* [Mr. Minister of War]; *Vihdoinkin hääyö...* [The wedding night, at last!]. 1958: *Kulkurin masurkka* [The vagabond's mazurka]; *Paksun-ahka* [Thick skin]; *Sotapojan heilat* [The soldier boy's sweethearts]. 1959: *Ei ruumiita makuuhuoneeseen* [No bodies in the bedroom]; *Vatsa sisään, rinta ulos!* [Stomach in—chest out!]. 1960: *Nina ja Erik* [Nina and Erik]; *Isaskar Keturin ihmeelliset seikkailut* [The wonderful adventures of Isaskar Keturi]; *Opettajatar seikkailee* [The school marm on the road to adventure]. 1961: *Tähtisumua* [Stardust]; *Minkkiturkki* [The mink coat]; *Olin nahjuksen vaimo* [I was a poke's wife]; *Oksat pois...* [No trifling]. 1962: *Älä nuolase...!* [Don't count your chickens]; *Hän varasti elämän* [The stolen life]; *Naiset, jotka minulle annoit* [The women you gave me]. 1963: *Villin Pohjolan kulta* [Gold from the wild North]; *Turkasen tenava!* [Confounded brat!]; *Teerenpeliä* [The blackcock's game]; *Villin Pohjolan salattu laakso* [The secret valley in the wild North]. 1966: *Johan nyt on markkinat!* [What the devil!].

Director

1956: *Tyttö lähtee kasarmiin* [The girl in the barracks]. 1960: *Pekka ja Pätkä neekereinä* [Pete and Runt, Negroes]; *Kankkulan kaivolla* [At the well]. 1961: *Tyttö ja hattu* [The girl and her hat].

Screenwriter

1951: *Radio tekee murron* [The radio commits a burglary]. 1952: *Radio tulee hulluksi* [The radio goes crazy]. 1953: *Kuningas kulkureitten* [Vagabond king]. 1957: *Taas tyttö kadoksissa* [Another girl lost].

AWARD

Jussi 1951

TEUVO TULIO (St. Petersburg, 23 Aug. 1912–), director. Tulio acted the role of the Finnish Valentino in some passionate films at the end of the 1920s at the tender age of sixteen. This prince of Finnish melodrama never lost this passion. It is regrettable that three out of the four films he made in the 1930s have been destroyed, but we know that a primordial force, a veritable madness, filled the screen right from the very first films he directed. When his friend *Valentin Vaala moved over to Suomi-Filmi, which was playing the game according to the rules of the power brokers, Tulio remained true to himself to the point of absurdity and held on to his unabated primal artistic strength—also to his creative madness—right to the very end. He produced, he wrote, he staged, he edited, and naturally he directed—in other words, he did everything and did it in a way that had the charm of something "hand-made" and yet had some startling banalities on several levels. Yet it is seldom that one detail disrupts the overall visual effect of his creation. This speaks volumes of an almost manic concentration on basic principles and also of contempt for the rules of "proper art."

The typical Tulio story is the familiar one. A girl arrives from the country and is promptly seduced. Just like the movies of Cecil B. DeMille, who worked in that distant town churning out the films that manipulated the moral values of the world, Tulio first allowed his audience to see sin and lechery, and then in the second half of the film he showed repentance and wracking self-pity—thus securing box office income from two utterly different types of audiences. "Men put women on pedestals but turn them into whores."

As the story was more or less the standard one, the significance of style was so emphasized that we might begin to consider Tulio as the most daring stylist in the Finnish cinema. The contrast between light and shade was sharp; recurring images had the power to hypnotize even though their use could no doubt be exhausting (almost all Tulio's films linger on in some purposeless existence or other). Night, dreams, delirium—all are parts of a landscape of key images and mental visions, where the border between madness and mental balance is a line drawn in water. Passion is the highest life-giving force; at the same time, it possesses dark and destructive energy. One peculiar "prop" of the Finnish cinema became an essential feature in Tulio's films: the haystack, that cradle of love, that nest of sin. Another Tulio hallmark is the sharp contrast between the breathtakingly portrayed countryside (where wild races in horse-drawn carts, rivers, and shooting the rapids are always features) and the town, always seen as a kind of symphony of sin.

On one hand, Tulio's films are dominated by clouds, by silhouettes of people; they are landscapes of ideals and unadulterated erotic fervor, of all those primordial elements. On the other hand, in the course of years a melodramatic register is ever more pronounced: Crazed looks and visual overstatement arrive with such an uncompromising impact that even a hardened viewer is shocked. In the beginning, Tulio's films embraced some literary elements (*Laulu tulipunaisesta kukasta* [Song of the bloodred flower], 1938), but especially after the war the impression is both riotous and decayed—and the films emerge ever more impressive as cinema. The sheer sensual ardor of images enchants, and films like *Sellaisena kuin sinä minut halusit* [The way you wanted me] (1944), *Rakkauden risti* [The cross of love] (1946), and *Levoton veri* [Restless blood] (1946) keep introducing expressively new controversial elements: crime, jealousy, blindness, sheer decadence. The great star of these films was as a matter of course the blond, beautiful *Regina Linnanheimo, who eventually abandoned all the pretense of "normal" acting.

If it seemed that Tulio's career was by the mid-1950s (when he was just over forty years old!) veering toward irrationality, his final works sealed his incompatibility with the "cinema sector" and with the "official" art at large: The untamed bird of the Finnish cinema chose silence and total isolation.

FILMOGRAPHY

1936: *Taistelu Heikkilän talosta* [The fight over the Heikkilä mansion]. 1937: *Nuorena nukkunut* [Silja—fallen asleep when young]. 1938: *Kiusaus* [Temptation]; *Laulu tulipunaisesta kukasta* [Song of the bloodred flower/Song of the scarlet flower]. 1939: *Vihtori ja Klaara* [Jiggs and Maggie]. 1940: *Unelma karjamajalla* [The reverie in the herdman's hut]. 1944: *Sellaisena kuin sinä minut halusit* [The way you wanted me]. 1946: *Rakkauden risti* [The cross of love]; *Levoton veri* [Restless blood]. 1947: *Intohimon vallassa* [In the grip of passion]. 1949: *Hornankoski* [The rapids of hell]. 1952: *Rikollinen nainen* [A crooked woman]. 1953: *Mustasukkaisuus* [Jealousy]. 1956: *Olet mennyt minun vereeni* [You've gone into my blood]. 1962: *Se alkoi omenasta* [In the beginning was an apple]. 1972: *Sensuela*.

ILMARI UNHO (Uusikaupunki, 22 Oct. 1906–3 Apr. 1961), director. Unho had worked as an actor, a director, a theater manager, and a journalist before his patriotic chauvinism led him to Suomi-Filmi, first as a scriptwriter, then as a director. His first films were surprising in view of his earnest disposition. They were actually military farces, musicals, and light comedies. Given his undeniable talent, it is hard to credit the number of really trifling films Unho made. Among the light entertainment production of the war years we might recall his adventure comedies, in which the hero was a character called "Kuollut mies" ("the Dead Man"), acted by the charismatic *Joel Rinne. These were elegant and stylish films, and they might even be considered as a modest Finnish contribution to the wave of "film noir" in international production. Unho was at his best when working on melodrama's borderline (chief wartime films *Kirkastettu sydän* [The transfigured heart] and *Kartanon naiset* [The women on the estate]) or when recording Finnish heritage as in "Minä elän" ["I live"] (1946), a deeply felt biography of Finnish author Aleksis Kivi, or in *Härmästä poikia kymmenen* [Ten men from Härmä] (1950), a kind of Finnish western, a drama of strong men and rigid principles set in the province of Pohjanmaa.

FILMOGRAPHY

Director

1939: *Punahousut* [Red pants]. 1940: *Kersantilleko Emma nauroi?* [Was it the sergeant Emma laughed at?]; *Poikani pääkonsuli* [My son, the consul general]. 1941: *Poretta eli Keisarin uudet pisteet* [Poretta, or the emperor's new points]. 1942: *Neljä naista* [Four women]; *Kuollut mies rakastuu* [The dead man falls in love]. 1943: *Syntynyt terve tyttö* [Born, a healthy girl]; *Miehen kunnia* [A man's honor]; *Kirkastettu sydän* [The transfigured heart]. 1944: *Kuollut mies vihastuu* [The dead man loses his temper]; *Kartanon naiset* [The women on the estate]. 1945: *Kolmastoista koputus* [The thirteenth knock]; *Valkoisen neilikan velho* [The wizard of the white carnation]. 1946: "*Minä elän*" ["I live"]. 1947: *Pimeänpirtin hävitys* [The destruction of Pimeäpirtti]; *Koskenkylän laulu* [The song of Koskenkylä]. 1948: *Kilroy sen teki* [Kilroy was here]; *Ruusu ja kulkuri* [The rose and the vagabond]. 1949: *Kalle-Kustaa Korkin seikkailut* [The adventures of Kalle-Kustaa Korkki]; *Kanavan laidalla* [At the edge of the canal]. 1950: *Härmästä poikia kymmenen* [Ten men from Härmä]. 1951: *Sadan miekan mies* [The man of a hundred swords]; *Kuisma ja Helinä* [Kuisma and Helinä]. 1952: "*Jees, Olympialaiset,*" *sanoi Ryhmy* ["Give us the Olympics," said Ryhmy]; *Rengasmatka eli Peräkylän pikajuna* [Express to the back of beyond]. 1953: *Sillankorvan emäntä* [Mother or woman].

VALENTIN VAALA (Helsinki, 11 Oct. 1909–22 Nov. 1976), director. Vaala started with passion: He was only seventeen years old when he directed his first film, which he then, in dispair, chucked into the sea. Taking the leading role was the fifteen-year-old Theodor Tugai, who later on as *Teuvo Tulio aspired to become "Finland's Valentino" and who was to turn out to be one of the country's most important directors. In 1935, Vaala entered the ranks of Suomi-Filmi and remained there for the next twenty-five years as "in-house director." From the very start, he established himself as a man of many genres, first as a master of urban comedy—quite an astounding fact in a country that was still predominantly agrarian, whose cinema had found its main themes in rural landscapes. Vaala's instinct for creating stars was at once apparent, and quite a few of the leading actors and actresses he used over the years were amateurs. This was not, however, the case with *Tauno Palo and *Ansa Ikonen, who became the most popular star duo of all times in the Finnish cinema. In Vaala's most acclaimed urban comedy, *Mieheke* [Surrogate husband], the role of Palo's partner was played by Finnish American actress Tuulikki Paananen, who in the 1930s happened to be visiting Finland. Later on, she appeared in a minor role in Jacques Tourneur's oeuvre *The Leopard Man*.

Stylistically, Vaala came quite close to the "avant-garde" of the best contemporary European cinema, and as a director of comedies, he ranked in the top category. A striking feature of his work was his constant employment of female writers either for source material or as scriptwriters. In his films, the entire "untamed scamstress glow" finds its purest expression and thus unfolds a whole range of "women's films" reflecting the spirit of the times—the state of war between the sexes, which he always documented with true insight.

The most emblematic wartime actress was *Lea Joutseno, whom Vaala discovered in the film company office. She starred in eight films, and it was in these that Vaala got closest to Lubitsch, a director he had often held up as his ideal. The more "serious" heroines merit a mention as well: Vaala was, like Cukor, a director of women par excellence and also an able promoter of mimic art of true economy. His principles were: "One never acted in front of the camera" and "One has to act with restraint because the camera intensifies facial expressions. A montage that has been done correctly becomes a magic instrument that triggers the desired emotions in the audience."[1]

These urban films were followed by a transfer to the countryside and the resulting cinematic sketching of "another reality": In Vaala's films the countryside was recorded without all that archetypal plodding and all that shilly-shallying characterizing the films of other studios. The camera was on the move, and there was verve in the editing. The intense drama dealing with lumberjacks, *Koskenlaskijan morsian* [The logroller's wife], was followed by *Niskavuoren naiset* [The women of Niskavuori], the first film version in a five-part drama series by *Hella Wuolijoki; this is a powerful saga set in the province of Häme, where the location figures as a kind of Finnish counterpart to Marcel Pagnol's Provence.

The ideological tendencies of the time were also prime elements in Vaala's films and never more prominently than in the three 1930s productions, all based on Hella Wuolijoki's writings: *Niskavuoren naiset* is one, and the two others are *Juurakon Hulda* [Hulda of Juurakko] and *Vihreä kulta* [Green gold]. The films represent different genres: Seen as a whole, they are an unparalleled introduction to the language, clichés, and power dealing of the ruling class of those days. Here we see how the country was being led and upon what kind of misconceptions, illusions, and conning the first republic was being built. *Vihreä kulta* turns out to be one of the best films about Lapland; in it lovers who escape failed marriages set out for the far north, where the true values of life are still attainable.

Vaala's two chief "serious" films were released in the late 1940s: *Loviisa, Niskavuoren nuori emäntä* [Loviisa], the finest of the Niskavuori series, and

Ihmiset suviyössä [People in the summer night], which is based on the novel
and the ideas of F. E. Sillanpää, Finland's one and only Nobel Prize winner in
literature. In both, a certain "underdramatization" occurs: Sillanpää's own world
and his pantheistic cosmos are realized as cinema in the film *Ihmiset suviyössä*,
and this portrayal of a group of people is as multilayered as any of Altman's
analogous "music oeuvres." *Loviisa, Niskavuoren nuori emäntä* is dominated by
the conflict between an "amour fou" and a marriage based on possession, a
collision of dream and realism.

About 1950, most of Vaala's films were starting to show signs of a certain
unevenness, some of them turning downright forgettable; however, the old virtuosity could still be seen. In most cases, it was to be found in themes asking
if life is worth living or if humanity and true human relationships are "somewhere else"—the eternal theme of unfulfillment. *Gabriel, tule takaisin* [Gabriel,
come back], a film based on a play by *Mika Waltari, is, however, a heartless
Vaala masterpiece: a flagrant portrait of a man set out to cheat women. When
the big production crisis of the late 1950s came and Suomi-Filmi began to close
down production of feature films, Vaala was sacked, but they had to reinstate
him after a huge and heartfelt public outcry. A leading film magazine put a
question about "renewal" to Vaala. The workaholic, who mastered all the international styles, replied: "I have been abroad twice; once I spent more than a
week in Stockholm, and once I was two weeks in the Soviet Union. That's
about it."[2]

FILMOGRAPHY

1929: *Mustalaishurmaaja* [The gypsy charmer]; *Mustat silmät* [Dark eyes]. 1931: *Lav-
eata tietä* [The wide road]. 1933: *Sininen varjo eli keskiyön murha* [The blue shadow,
or The midnight murder]. 1934: *Helsingin kuuluisin liikemies* [The most famous businessman in Helsinki]; *Koustu, Fransi ja liljepekin Kalle* [Koustu, Fransi and Kalle of
Liljepek]. 1935: *Kun isä tahtoo . . .* [When father wants to . . .]; *Kaikki rakastavat* [Ev-
erybody's in love]. 1936: *Vaimoke* [Surrogate wife]; *Mieheke* [Surrogate husband]. 1937:
Koskenlaskijan morsian [The logroller's bride/Bride of the rapids shooter]; *Juurakon
Hulda* [Hulda of Juurakko]. 1938: *Niskavuoren naiset* [The women of Niskavuori]; *Sys-
mäläinen* [The man from Sysmä]. 1939: *Rikas tyttö* [The rich girl]; *Vihreä kulta* [Green
gold]. 1940: *Jumalan myrsky* [The wrath of God]. 1941: *Antreas ja syntinen Jolanda*
[Andreas and sinful Yolanda]; *Morsian yllättää* [A surprising bride]. 1942: *Varaventtiili*
Safety valve; *Keinumorsian* [The bride on the swing]. 1943: *Neiti tuittupää* [Miss Hot-
head]; *Tositarkoituksella* [With serious intent]. 1944: *Dynamiittityttö* [The dynamite girl].
1945: *Linnaisten vihreä kamari* [The green room at Linnainen Manor]. 1946: *Loviisa,
Niskavuoren nuori emäntä* [Loviisa]. 1947: *Maaret—tunturien tyttö* [Maaret—daughter
of the Fells]. 1948: *Ihmiset suviyössä* [People in the summer night]. 1949: *Jossain on
railo* [The crevice]; *Sinut minä tahdon* [It's you I want]. 1951: *Gabriel, tule takaisin!*
[Gabriel, come back!]. 1952: *Kulkurin tyttö* [The vagabond's girl]; *Omena putoaa* [The
apple falls]. 1953: *Huhtikuu tulee* [April is coming]; *Siltalan pehtoori* [The steward of
Siltala]. 1954: *Minäkö isä!* [Me, a father!]. 1955: *Minä ja mieheni morsian* [Me and my
husband's fiancée]. 1956: Yhteinen vaimomme [Our common wife]. 1957: *Nummisu-

utarit [The village shoemakers]. 1958: *Nuori mylläri* [The young miller]; *Niskavuoren naiset* [The women of Niskavuori/The women from Niskavuori]. 1960: *Taistelujen tie* [Roads to battle]. 1961: *Nuoruus vauhdissa* [Swinging youth]. 1963: *Totuus on armoton* [The truth is merciless].

AWARDS

Jussi 1945

Jussi 1947

Jussi 1952

NOTE

1. Valentin Vaala.
2. Valentin Vaala.

KARI VÄÄNÄNEN (Ivalo, 17 Sept. 1953–), actor. Väänänen is one of the most notable actors of the Finnish theater and cinema of the 1980s; he is a voyager par excellence who in his roles has been seen in the widest variety of locations— from the icy shores of the Arctic Sea (in Jaakko Pyhälä's *Jon*) on to Berlin and the Amazon in *Mika Kaurismäki's films, from Sicily to Finland in *Rosso*, in which he plays the role of a second-rate mafioso (naturally in Italian, as a consummate actor like Kari Väänänen ought to). He is an artist of great contrasts—disciplined and firm when needed (*in Klaani—tarina Sammakoitten suvusta* [The clan—tale of the frogs], the most impressive moments are created by Väänänen in his portrayal of one member of the Sammakko family); likewise in *Tuntematon sotilas* [The unknown soldier], his Lammio, "a shit-of-a-man, who upheld certain ideals when the war is on," is acted with the same kind of harshness. But he is also capable of loosening up entirely and even depicting convincingly neurotic characters. Through all this his understanding of absurd humor is never absent. Väänänen directed his first feature film, *The Vaiennut kylä* [Quiet village], in 1997.

FILMOGRAPHY

Actor

1981: *Pedon merkki* [Sign of the beast]. 1983: *Jon; Apinan vuosi* [In the year of the ape]. 1984: *Klaani—tarina Sammakoitten suvusta* [The clan—tale of the frogs]. 1985: *Viimeiset rotannahat* [Rare, medium, well done]; *Calamari Union; Ylösnousemus* [The resurrection]; *Rosso; Tuntematon sotilas* [The unknown soldier]. 1986: *Harmagedon; Näkemiin, hyvästi* [Farewell, goodbye]. 1987: *Älä itke Iines* [Gone with the mind]; *Hamlet liikemaailmassa* [Hamlet goes business/Hamlet]; *Helsinki-Napoli All Night Long*. 1989: *Cha Cha Cha; Leningrad Cowboys Go America; Kukunor; Paperitähti* [Paper star]. 1990: *Räpsy ja Dolly eli Pariisi odottaa* [Dolly and her lover]; *Amazon*. 1991: *Zombie ja kummitusjuna* [Zombie and the ghost train]. 1992: *Boheemielämää/La vie de bohème; Mestari* [The champion]; *Papukaijamies*. 1993: *Ripa ruostuu* [Ripa hits the skids]; *The Last Border—Viimeisellä rajalla* [The last border]; *Goodbye Gibraltar*. 1994: *Leningrad*

Cowboys Meet Moses. 1995: *The Iron Horsemen*. 1996: **Kauas pilvet karkaavat* [Drifting clouds].

AWARD

Jussi 1983

MIKA WALTARI (Helsinki, 19 Sept. 1908–26 Aug. 1979), author, screenwriter. Waltari is the best-known Finnish author internationally; his novel *The Egyptian* (1945) has been translated into dozens of languages, and it is still being published in new editions. This author of many books was also the most prolific writer of film scripts. His texts—whether they were written especially for a film or were adaptations of literary works—have been used in almost forty films, and only a few might be considered trifling. Just as in the case of Graham Green, Waltari's literary production can be divided into "serious" and "light entertainment," even if Waltari himself was too modest a man to define the matter in such a pretentious way. Waltari's essential qualities were inborn irony, which was present even in his most unassuming films, and genuine gentleness, which has brightened some in fact mediocre creations.

Even if the majority of Waltari's films are quite forgettable (in many cases they were commissioned films that were produced quickly), he had several "guaranteed" special fields: the intimate tale that developed into a drama of the drawing room (*Vieras mies tuli taloon* [A stranger came into the house], 1938), the light and spirited farce (*Kuriton sukupolvi* [The unruly generation], 1938), the patriotic cinema (*Oi kallis Suomenmaa* [Finland, our dear native land], 1940), the historical romance (one of the most popular films ever made in Finland—*Kulkurin valssi* [The vagabond's waltz], 1941), and finally, the black comedy (the masterpiece of this genre is the "heartless comedy" *Gabriel, tule takaisin!* [Gabriel, come back!], a tale of a womanizer, directed in 1951 by **Valentin Vaala). Some of Waltari's last films were detective stories made in the 1960s and built around the figure of Superintendent Palmu; here the city of Helsinki—an enduring and beloved theme in Waltari's productions—plays a role as important as any actor.

FILMOGRAPHY

Films Based on a Novel by Mika Waltari

1933: *Sininen varjo* [The blue shadow]. 1936: *VMV 6*. 1937: *Kuriton sukupolvi* [The unruly generation]. 1938: *Vieras mies tuli taloon* [A stranger came into the house]. 1950: *Tanssi yli hautojen* [The dance over the graves]. 1951: *Gabriel, tule takaisin!* [Gabriel, come back!]. 1952: *Omena putoaa* [The apple falls]; *Noita palaa elämään* [The witch comes back to life]. 1953: *Huhtikuu tulee* [April's coming]. 1955: *Rakas lurjus* [Beloved rascal]. 1956: *Jokin ihmisessä* [Something in people]. 1957: *Kuriton sukupolvi* [Wild generation]; *Vieras mies* [The stranger]. 1958: *Verta käsissämme* [Blood on our hands]. 1960: *Komisario Palmun erehdys* [Police Inspector Palmu's mistake]; *Myöhästynyt hääyö* [The delayed wedding night]. 1961: *Kaasua, komisario Palmu!* [Step on the gas, Inspector Palmu!]; *Miljoonavaillinki* [Short by a million]. 1962: *Tähdet kertovat, komisario*

Palmu [The stars will tell, Inspector Palmu]. 1964: *Jäinen saari* [The island of ice]. 1982: *Kuningas jolla ei ollut sydäntä* [The king who had no heart]. 1985: *Suuri illusioni* [Grand illusion].

Screenwriter

1937: *Kuriton sukupolvi* [The unruly generation]. 1938: *Vieras mies tuli taloon* [A stranger came into the house]. 1939. *Helmikuun manifesti* [February manifesto]; *Seitsemän veljestä* [Seven brothers]. 1940: *Oi kallis Suomenmaa* [Finland, our dear native land]. 1941: *Kulkurin valssi* [The vagabond's waltz]. 1942: *Onni pyörii* [The wheel of chance]. 1943: *Tyttö astuu elämään* [The girl goes out into the world]; *Nuoria ihmisiä* [Young people]. 1944: *Nainen on valttia* [The woman is the trump]. 1950: *Tanssi yli hautojen* [The dance over the graves]. 1951: *Gabriel, tule takaisin!* [Gabriel, come back!]; *Neljä rakkautta* [Four times love]. 1952: *Omena putoaa* [The apple falls]. 1953: *Maailman kaunein tyttö* [The loveliest girl in the world]. 1955: *Rakas lurjus* [Beloved rascal]. 1957: *Pikku Ilona ja hänen karitsansa* [Little Ilona and her lambkin].

AWARD

Jussi 1952

HELLA WUOLIJOKI (Helme, Estonia, 22 July 1886–2 Feb. 1954), author. Estonian-born Wuolijoki is one of the great personalities and opinion makers of Finnish culture, at times even a member of the éminence grise. In the "white" Finland of the 1930s, she was obliged to publish her novels and plays under a pseudonym, and during the war she received a prison sentence for hiding a Russian agent. After the war, in a different political climate, she was appointed head of Finnish Radio. Her greatest achievement is the chronicle of the Niskavuori family; this saga of a large farm in the province of Häme and its people over several generations has become one of the cornerstones of Finnish drama. As a private individual, Wuolijoki was both a radical and a capitalist, and it is this duality that gave her production its specific dramatic interest. Several impressive films based on her plays were made by directors *Valentin Vaala and *Edvin Laine; of these, Vaala's *Loviisa, Niskavuoren nuori emäntä* [Loviisa] (1946) is the most powerful. The themes of the Niskavuori plays were also detectable in many other films based on Wuolijoki's work: the eternal struggle between idealism and selfish greed, the conflict between generations, the dream about a great love and "another kind of life." The scenarios in Wuolijoki's dramas are so persuasive—just as in Marcel Pagnol's plays—that the development of cinematic form comes off in just about every case. Conflict is also given a convincing treatment rare in Finnish cinema, especially in films set in rural surroundings.

FILMOGRAPHY

Films Based on a Novel by Hella Wuolijoki

1937: *Juurakon Hulda* [Hulda of Juurakko]. 1938: *Niskavuoren naiset* [The women of Niskavuori]. 1939: *Eteenpäin—elämään* [Forward—toward life]; *Vihreä kulta* [Green gold]. 1945: *Vastamyrkky* [The antidote]. 1946: *Loviisa, Niskavuoren nuori emäntä* [Loviisa]. 1949: *Jossain on railo* [The crevice]. 1952: *Niskavuoren Heta* [Heta from Nis-kavuori]. 1953: *Tyttö kuunsillalta* [The girl from Moon Bridge]. 1954: *Niskavuoren Aarne* [Aarne of Niskavuori]. 1957: *Niskavuori taistelee* [Niskavuori fights]. 1958: *Nis-kavuoren naiset* [The women of Niskavuori]. 1979: *Herra Puntila ja hänen renkinsä Matti* [Mr. Puntila and his servant Matti]. 1984: *Niskavuori* [The tug of home/The family Niskavuori].

FILMS

***EVAKKO* [EVACUATED].** In the mid-1950s, *Ville Salminen directed three feature films with Karelia, that legendary borderland between Finland and Russia, as the theme. Since the war (when part of the Finnish Karelia was ceded to the USSR), this subject has been tinged with feelings of loss and tragedy in our national consciousness. *Evakko* [Evacuated] is about all this—how people and whole families were forced to flee their homes in Karelia. It is an intimate film depicting big issues on a small scale. An image of large snowflakes falling on a boat, another of a cat in a snow drift—pictures like these are key to the film. Salminen was originally a painter, and before the shooting, he used to draw the storyboard; he took on control of the style in a way that enlarges everyday naturalism into a functioning, living, and logical scheme. The outcome is a nightmarish dreamscape of delicately drawn images, of nostalgia said to be "as profound as the darkness of night."

CREW

Director and Art Director: Ville Salminen. Script: Ville Salminen, Jussi Talvi, after a novel by Unto Seppänen. Cinematographer: Unto Kumpulainen. Sound: Tuomo Kattilakoski, Gösta Salminen. Music: Harry Bergström. Editor: Nils Holm. Executive Producer: Mauno Mäkelä. Producer: Fennada-Filmi.

CAST

Santeri Karilo (Aato Nikkanen), Linda Lampinen (Ulla Nikkanen), Aino-Maija Tikkanen (Elvi Nikkanen), Eila-Kaarina Roine (Sirkka Nikkanen), Tauno Söder (Arvo Nikkanen), Kaarlo Wilska (Risto Havia), Kerttu Hämeranta (Aina Havia), Leena Korhonen (Aisa Havia), Sakari Jurkka (Otto Kiesi), Anton Soini (Tahvo Kiesi), Mirjam Salminen (Hanna Kiesi), Väinö Parviainen (Yllö), Pertti Weckström (Samu Yllö), Matti Kuusla (Salu Yllö), Matti Oravisto (Tauno Tuomaala).

PREMIERE

Finnish: 31 Aug. 1956

HÄRMÄSTÄ POIKIA KYMMENEN [TEN MEN FROM HÄRMÄ]. The film is based on an old folk ballad about two knife-wielding ruffians; the milieu is the legendary Pohjanmaa (Ostrobothnia), the province that shares many myths with the American western. It is an amazing mixture of violence, exploding macho culture, and the significance of ownership, where no mercy is shown. The conflict between the old and the new forms the basis of this film—the very best work of *Ilmari Unho as director. Here he has skillfully utilized both amateur and professional actors and treated the theme with unrestrained energy and total absence of prejudice. Here the limits of madness are exceeded, the madness that in a certain way tinges the society and its events. In the structure of films like this, one naturally follows the dialectic of uncontrolled fury and repentance, and of violence and tranquility. The roots of the strife are quite absurd; all is overwhelmed by unrestrained violence. Nonetheless, Unho has managed to compose really magical images conveying his intuitive perception of nature and its connotations.

CREW

Director: Ilmari Unho. Script: Arttu Leinonen. Cinematographer: Eino Heino. Sound: Hugo Ranta. Music: Antti Sonninen. Art Director: Ville Hänninen. Editor: Armas Laurinen. Producer: Suomi-Filmi.

CAST

*Tauno Palo (Isoo-Antti), Yrjö Kantoniemi (Iikka Rannanjärvi/Iisakki Nukari), Kalervo Nissilä (Jukka Anssi, Juho Matinpoika), Kalle Kirjavainen (rural police chief), Jussi Oksa (master of the Pouttula house), Hilkka Helinä (Katri), Kauko Helovirta (Janne, son of Isoo-Antti), Arvi Tuomi (governor), Tellervo Vasa (wife of Isoo-Antti), Juho Hannuksela (Karnaatti), Kyllikki Väre (Maija), Emmi Heikkilä (wife of Pouttula), Frans Pihlgren (master of the Pöyhönen house), Helmi Kujala (sister of Anssi).

PREMIERE

Finnish: 15 Sept. 1950

IHMISET SUVIYÖSSÄ [PEOPLE IN THE SUMMER NIGHT]. F. E. Sillanpää has been one of the luckiest—if not the luckiest—Finnish "national authors." The works of this Nobel laureate have been frequently adapted for film, and none of them is completely beyond redemption. *Tapiovaara, *Kassila, *Tulio, and *Vaala have each in their own way sought by the art of the cinema to solve the equation of the world according to Sillanpää—the author's style, his conception of time, and the complex bond between man and nature.

Ihmiset suviyössä is probably the most outstanding of these films. Just like the novel the film is something more than a story with a plot. It is a rhapsody of a northen summer night, the magic climax of summer, when human destinies meet, when love and violence, birth and death, become one. The tension between these components is quite remarkable. During one short summer night, an hour and an eternity, the weight of centuries and our life here and now unite. The film is essentially a drama about stability and the transitoriness of rural life. Debts and inheritance rights loom large here. Characters representing a variety of social strata figure also in the film, even if it is the time of summer holidays; functionaries like a midwife, doctor, policeman, and prison guard play a role in it. Communities of fate are almost existential. In this film is proclaimed the most profoundly felt bond between man and nature in Finnish cinema. And Martti Katajisto's interpretation of a young lumberjack is modern in a way that reminds us of Jean Cocteau's creations from the same period.

CREW

Director and Editor: Valentin Vaala. Script: Valentin Vaala, *Lea Joutseno, Usko Kemppi, after a novel by F. E. Sillanpää. Cinematographer: Eino Heino. Sound: Evan Englund. Music: Taneli Kuusisto. Art Director: Ville Hänninen. Executive Producer: *Risto Orko. Producer: Suomi-Filmi.

CAST

Eila Pehkonen (Helka), Matti Oravisto (Arvid), Emma Väänänen (Hilja Syrjämäki), Martti Katajisto (Nokia), Eero Roine (Jalmari Syrjämäki), Toivo Hämeranta (master of the Telaranta house), Tyyne Haarla (wife of Telaranta), Maija Nuutinen (mother-in-law), Kaisu Leppänen (Santra Mettälä), Matti Lehtelä (Jukka Mettälä), Tellervo Nokelainen (Selma Telaranta), Erkki Kalakari (Matti Puolamäki), Eero Leväluoma (policeman), Kaarlo Halttunen (doctor), Toivo Lahti (master of the house), Tarmo Manni (Iivari).

PREMIERE

Finnish: 15 Oct. 1948

KAHDEKSAN SURMANLUOTIA [EIGHT DEADLY SHOTS]. This over-five-hours-long epic by *Mikko Niskanen is the most outstanding achievement in Finnish cinema; in it the borderlines between life and cinema, life and work of art, lose all their definition. And here we encounter that sadness and that compassion that only pure art can attain.

The catalyst of this alchemy is a news report about a shocking tragedy: A cornered smallholder has shot four policemen. Out of this matter-of-fact piece of news Niskanen conjures up a film full of wondrous, spell-binding life force, full of sympathy, unadorned humanity, and a deep understanding of the lot of the humble and the poor.

As a psychological drama it is difficult to find a parallel to this film. The inner and the exterior elements are in perfect harmony; the dilemma of being an outsider in society—the main character challenges the law by steadfastly carrying on his moonshining activities—becomes here a celebration of man's will to remain free. Niskanen uncovers man's psychophysical dimensions, his wasted potential while he simultaneously identifies the core of what ethnology is capable of saying about a man. Here we have a lot of qualities that resemble directors such as Cassavetes, but Niskanen goes even further. And the portrayal of the main character by Niskanen himself is nothing other than astounding. He gives his all, absolutely, and lives this role down to the physical convulsions.

CREW

Director, Script, and Executive Producer: Mikko Niskanen. Cinematographer: Kimmo Simula, Juhani Voutilainen, Seppo Immonen, Juhani Sarro. Sound: Veijo Lehti, Kari Tamminen. Music: Erkki Ertama. Art Director: Jorma Lindfors. Editor: Jyrki Rapp. Production: Yleisradio TV1/Televisioteatteri-Käpyfilmi.

CAST

Mikko Niskanen (Pasi), Tarja-Tuulikki Tarsala (Pasi's wife), Paavo Pentikäinen (Reiska), Tauno Paananen (Tanu), Elina Liimatainen (Ellu), Ari Vainiontaus (Ari), Mauno Argillander (Manu), Kaarlo Wilska (preacher), Yrjö Liehunen (storekeeper), Ilmari Piironen (executive game director in province), Sulo Hokkanen (Sulo Kokki), Veikko Vakomies (1st man), Toini Penttinen (housewife), Kalle Kellokangas (Kalle), Veikko Paananen (2nd man), Irja Suominen (postmistress), Alpo Kuivakangas (master of the house), Eino Pekkola (neighbor), Fjalar Jarva (Fjalar Jarva), Pertti Weckström (doctor).

PREMIERE

Finnish: 15 Sept. 1972

KAUAS PILVET KARKAAVAT [DRIFTING CLOUDS]. "If I didn't make a film about unemployment now I wouldn't have the nerve to look at my face in the mirror," *Aki Kaurismäki commented at the time when Finland had been suffering for years from dramatic, structural, and—as many saw it—terminal unemployment, which had forced about half a million citizens along with their families into some kind of nonlife in this country of 5 million inhabitants. The central characters in the film are a tram driver and his head-waitress wife, who both lose their jobs. They belong to the type of losers often featured in Kaurismäki's films: They just will not give up. The film provides us with a unique portrait of small-time entrepreneurs and ordinary, modest people; we might call it an anthology of the plights unemployment inflicts on us: marital crisis and the pressures that bring people to the limits of human endurance. Yet a ray of optimism shines through all this gloom: As a group enterprise, a new restaurant is opened (reflecting that familiar slogan of the war years, "Buddies are not abandoned"). This is the vision that many critics have seen as a continuation of the Frank Capra tradition.

CREW

Director, Script, and Editor: Aki Kaurismäki. Cinematographer: *Timo Salminen. Sound: Jouko Lumme. Art Director: Markku Pätilä, Jukka Salmi. Producer: Sputnik Oy/Aki Kaurismäki.

CAST

*Kati Outinen (Ilona), *Kari Väänänen (Lauri), *Elina Salo (Mrs. Sjöholm), Sakari Kuosmanen (Melartin), Markku Peltola (Lajunen), Matti Onnismaa (Forsström), *Matti Pellonpää (child in the photograph), Pietari (Pietari, the dog), Shelley Fischer (pianist), Outi Mäenpää (Lauri's sister).

PREMIERE

Finnish: 27 Jan. 1996

AWARD

Cannes 1996 (Ecumenical Jury Special Mention)

LAULU TULIPUNAISESTA KUKASTA [SONG OF THE BLOODRED FLOWER]. This is a basic Finnish theme, from a novel by Johannes Linnankoski, and it has been filmed in Sweden three times (the first version was by *Mauritz Stiller in 1919). This is *Teuvo Tulio's earliest surviving work, and it displays threads common in his work: the story of a vagabond who wanders from girl to girl, thus attempting to flee his own feelings of emptiness. The style is sculpted: Actors are often positioned against clouds, looks (often revealing passion and rage) speak volumes, the whole erotic catalog entails a picturebook of nature and the physiognomy of man—we can detect the influence of the best Soviet cinema. "Among us there are not good ones and bad ones, but we are all longing for love" could well be the credo of a typical debate in Finnish national cinema. The film explores the fundamentals and nothing else: erotism, sin, virginity, booze, repentance, religion, the clash of moral values, the bloody network of class prejudice. Outdoor images are predominated by clouds, water, foaming rapids, rafts of logs, galloping horses—all these ever-present features in the aesthetic of Tulio's images. The portrait of the Finnish man that emerges from this film is quite ruthless: The film stresses the hysterical and boastful virginity-worship that men indulge in while hopping from bed to bed themselves.

CREW

Director, Editor, and Executive Producer: Teuvo Tulio. Script: Yrjö Kivimies, after a novel by Johannes Linnankoski. Cinematographer: Fred Runeberg. Sound: Leo Salminen. Music: Toivo Lampén. Art Director: Kosti Aaltonen.

CAST

Kille Oksanen (Olavi), Rakel Linnanheimo (Kyllikki), Mirjami Kuosmanen (Annikki), Nora Mäkinen (Elli Gaselli), Birgit Nuotio (girl with dark hair), Maire Ranius (Pihlajaterttu), Sylvi Palo (prostitute), Aku Peltonen (boss of lumber camp), Veikko Linna (master of the Moisio house), Lauri Korpela (Olavi's father), Ida Kallio (Olavi's mother), Onni Veijonen (Taro), Elli Ylimaa (midwife).

PREMIERE

Finnish: 4 Dec. 1938

BIBLIOGRAPHY

Soila, 1994. A discussion of the question of nationality with reference to the five remakes of the Scandinavian story *The Song of the Scarlet Flower* (1918, 1934, 1938, 1956, 1971).

NUMMISUUTARIT [THE VILLAGE SHOEMAKERS]. This film is based on a drama by Aleksis Kivi, a Finnish national author. It was written in the 1860s and tells the story of a simple but kindhearted country boy's journey to ask for a maiden's hand. Its quality compares to the best films being produced abroad at the time. The airy way dream and memory segments and mental images are used bestows on it a unique rhythm, which in a supreme fashion meets the challenge laid down by silent film to "translate" a work based on language into images. The most famous episode in the film is the drunken scene, the shooting of which was done in quite a novel way: The drunker the young man became, the wilder the camera swayed, swirled, and rotated. With the help of winches, cameraman Kurt Jäger and his camera were hoisted up about eight meters inside a wooden box; the rope holding the box was twisted into a kink by the people on the ground. When the rope was released, naturally it started to unwind, thus causing the box and the cameraman therein to swirl rapidly and erratically. The story goes that Jäger only agreed to climb into the box after he had been promised both extra compensation for the job and a straight drink after his return to solid ground.

CREW

Director, Editor, and Executive Producer: *Erkki Karu. Script: Artturi Järviluoma, after a drama by Aleksis Kivi. Cinematographer: Kurt Jäger. Music: Jean Sibelius, Selim Palmgren, Toivo Kuula, Oskar Merikanto. Art Director: Karl Fager. Producer: Suomi-Filmi.

CAST

Axel Slangus (Esko), Adolf Lindfors (cantor Sepeteus), Alarik Korhonen (master shoemaker Topias), Kirsti Suonio (his wife Martta), Antero Suomio (Iivari), Juho Puls (sailor Niko), Heidi Korhonen (his daughter Jaana), Aku Käyhkö (Mikko Vilkastus), Jaakko Korhonen (young blacksmith), Konrad Tallroth (master of the house), Kaarlo Kari (Martta's brother), Martti Tuukka (Antres), Sven Relander (Teemu, violin player).

PREMIERE

Finnish: 11 Nov. 1923

PIKAJUNA POHJOISEEN [THE NORTHERN EXPRESS]. This journey through a long night culminating in disaster is in structure similar to the "omnibus" series, to which the American *Grand Hotel* and *Shanghai Express* belong. Here, through a crowd of well-known actors, whose life stories are packed in a limited time and space, we see the drama of birth and death. Visually and ideologically, we are close to the fatalistic aura of French cinema.

It is difficult to conceive of a scene more redolent of the 1940s than the first few minutes of this film, shot at the railway station of Helsinki late at night. All of these people are on their way to meet their destinies. Some of them are obviously involved in dubious or even criminal matters, soon to be unravelled in the complicated and melodramatic plot formations. The flickering images of the tracks, along with the acoustic world of the train, create a cacophony of unfulfilled promises. By means of bold stylization, an almost physical relationship is created with time, which turns out to be short. At the end, there is the inevitable catastrophy; its apocalyptic madness reminds us of the films Cecil B. DeMille produced in the 1920s. "Nice" people die; some are crippled. The time of war, with all its calamities only two years earlier, has come back to the cinema screen. "We can never know when our time has come to an end."

CREW

Director: *Roland af Hällström. Script: Viljo Hela (= Roland af Hällström), Finn E. Sommerschiled, after a novel by Karen Aabyen. Cinematographer: Esko Töyri. Sound: Björn Korander, Emil Häkkänen. Music: Tapio Ilomäki. Art Director: Eero Leväluoma, Kosti Aaltonen. Editor: Tapio Ilomäki. Executive Producer: Yrjö Rannikkkko. Producer: Fenno-Filmi.

CAST

*Ansa Ikonen (Maire Kytö), Leif Wager (Reino Sompa), Tauno Majuri (Mauno Ismola), Aku Korhonen (Hugo Auvonen), Arna Högdahl (wife of mining counsellor), Sven Relander (Fjalar Lindström), Eino Kaipainen (Kaarlo Kyrö), Liisa Tuomi (dancer Miss Mona), Anja Kola (Raili Oras), Tapio Nurkka (Kalevi Oras), Arvi Tuomi (major of the Salvation Army), Kalle Viherpuu (locomotive engineer), Unto Salminen (locomotive stoker), Matti Aulos (conductor).

PREMIERE

Finnish: 29 Aug. 1947

SININEN VIIKKO [BLUE WEEK]. The primary theme of *Sininen viikko* [Blue week] is summer, a common obsessive myth of Scandinavian cinema in the 1950s (in Sweden, *Hon dansade en sommar/One Summer of Happiness* and most of *Ingmar Bergman's early films celebrate this theme). The subsidiary theme is an instant in time, in this case, one week, a segment of time dramatic in its symmetry, signifying birth and death. At the beginning of the film, we get the strong impression that this slice of life is going to be something that we all share: It is the weekend, motorboats circle at sea, the illusion of freedom is in the air, all those new consumer goods are available that have become part of even working-class existence. Stylistically (*Matti Kassila's own narration), this is the authentic, accepted voice of working-class literature.

So this is Saturday night fever in the early 1950s somewhere near the town of Kotka. A young worker begins a relationship with the wife of a middle-aged man; the strings of this eternal triangle get knotted together during a brief evening, and the "blue week" passed on an island seals the inevitable. When the week comes to a close with an open-air dance, the exposure of the illicit love affair, and the suicide of the disabled husband, the sheer melodrama of all this is less significant than its infinite ordinariness. The pressures of the working week have been gotten rid of, and Monday is always looming like a shadow—a guilt-filled moment even though it could be a beginning of a new life.

The film sharply illustrates the meeting of different social classes and erotic behavior patterns, and explores the issues of dress, word choice, and morals, of course. The opportunity for sexual joy and guilt based on Christian traditions collide. The landscape sketched by Kassila and cameraman Osmo Harkimo mirrors the mood: The key images—sea, cliff, the water lilies in a pond—unveil the simultaneous presence of happiness and death.

CREW

Director: Matti Kassila. Script: Matti Kassila, after a short story by Jarl Hemmer. Cinematographer: Osmo Harkimo. Sound: Yrjö Saari. Music: Matti Rautio. Art Director: Aarre Koivisto. Editor: Armas Vallasvuo. Executive Producer: *T. J. Särkkä. Producer: Suomen Filmiteollisuus.

CAST

Gunvor Sandkvist (Siiri Forss), Matti Oravisto (Usko Siltanen), Toivo Mäkelä (Bertel Forss), Paavo Hukkinen (Usko's 1st friend), Kauko Laurikainen (Usko's 2nd friend), Juhani Kumpulainen (agitator), Kaarlo Saarnio (usher), *Leo Jokela (Usko's 3rd friend), Maija Rautavuo (1st girl), Ulla Sandqvist (2nd girl), Armas Jokio (man on the dance floor).

PREMIERE

Finnish: 26 Feb. 1954

TULITIKKUTEHTAAN TYTTÖ [THE MATCH FACTORY GIRL]. This is a tale of a naive, melancholy young girl and her pathetic family. The father keeps swigging Koskenkorva vodka from a bottle hidden under the table, whereas the tired figure of mother hovers around in a dreamlike state, animated only by the constantly blaring television. The subtitle of the film might well be: "The Banality of Silence." Very little is being uttered in this film attempting to portray the truth behind clichés, and when someone does talk, it is something quite trivial or something that just might have fatal consequences. In its tone, the film reminds us of fairytales (the title bears a reference to Hans Christian Andersen, and the protagonist is a counterpart of the main character in a popular Finnish juvenile book), while managing to be at the same time the most prosaic film in the history of Finnish cinema. *Aki Kaurismäki has employed the language of melodrama but has reduced it to microscopically minimal dimensions. It is a laconic, even a cruel film—yet somehow it radiates a long-suppressed tenderness. In a popular poll carried out in the 1990s it was chosen to be, along with *Mikko Niskanen's *Kahdeksan surmanluotia* [Eight deadly shots], the "best Finnish movie ever."

CREW

Director, Script, and Editor: Aki Kaurismäki. Cinematographer: *Timo Salminen. Sound: Jouko Lumme. Art Director: Risto Karhula. Producer: Villealfa Filmproductions Oy/Svenska Filminstitutet.

CAST

*Kati Outinen (Iiris), *Elina Salo (mother), Esko Nikkari (stepfather), Vesa Vierikko (man), Reijo Taipale (singer), Silu Seppälä (brother), Outi Mäenpää (fellow worker), Marja Packalén (doctor), Richard Reitinger (man in the bar), Helga Viljanen (office employee), Kurt Silas (policeman), Ismo Keinänen (policeman), Klaus Heydemann (worker).

PREMIERE

Finnish: 12 Jan. 1990

BIBLIOGRAPHY

Baecque, 1990. Article plus review; analysis of a sequence from the film.

TUNTEMATON SOTILAS **[THE UNKNOWN SOLDIER].** This film, in its time, was the culmination of the Finnish cinema potential (or possibly it overreached it!); at the same time, the film was a peculiar exception, perhaps for exactly the same reasons. Surprisingly, *Edvin Laine's work as a war movie was without precedent: The theme of war had thus far been touched upon only in military farces, and in any event, it had no successors. Apparently the war had been too great a trauma, and when Väinö Linna's masterly novel *Tuntematon sotilas* was published in 1954, it sparked a significant intellectual and emotional process. Under Edvin Laine's energetic command, the film turned out to be the greatest manifesto of talent SF ever brought forth; it showed what Finnish cinema was capable of when true inspiration drove every last person taking part in the project.

The film was an "instant classic" of Finnish cinema, a realistic war movie, and a group portrait of Finland and her men during the Continuation War (1941–1944). It is also an essay about Finnish death. The actors are the country's best, and the rich dialogue of Linna's novel has attained a kind of mythic immortality among the Finnish nation. The scope of the film is simply remarkable; it moves from placid moments of stabilized warfare, when war comes to resemble ordinary, everyday peacetime, to horrifying total destruction, when human beings and nature are blindly massacred; from tranquil, laid-back scenes that have an atmosphere of easy improvisation to extreme expressions of neurosis, fear, and psychosis. There is one scene in the film that has all these elements: Thick smoke descends on the forest in a way that catches something of life's impenetrable, accidental, and cruel randomness—a glimpse of death itself at work. Contemporaries considered the film one of the greatest war movies of all time, likely a correct evaluation.

CREW

Director: Edvin Laine. Script: Juha Nevalainen, after a novel by Väinö Linna. Cinematographer: Pentti Unho, Osmo Harkimo, Olavi Tuomi, Antero Ruuhonen. Sound: Kurt Vilja, Taisto Lindegren, Yrjö Saari, Kaarlo Nissilä. Music: Ahti Sonninen. Art Director: Aarre Koivisto. Editor: Armas Vallasvuo, Osmo Harkimo. Executive Producer: *T. J. Särkkä. Producer: Suomen Filmiteollisuus.

CAST

Kosti Klemelä (Koskela), Heikki Savolainen (Hietanen), Reino Tolvanen (Rokka), Veikko Sinisalo (Lahtinen), Åke Lindman (Lehto), Pentti Siimes (Määttä), Leo Riuttu (Vanhala), Kaarlo Halttunen (Rahikainen), Matti Ranin (Kariluoto), Jussi Jurkka (Lammio), *Tauno Palo (Sarastie), Pentti Irjala (Kaarna), Vilho Siivola (Mäkilä), Martti Romppanen (Sihvonen), Tapio Hämäläinen (Salo), Olavi Ahonen (Riitaoja), Tarmo Manni (Honkajoki), Veli-Matti Kaitala (Hauhia).

PREMIERE

Finnish: 23 Dec. 1955

AWARD

Berlin 1956 (Catholic Film Organization Prize—Reginald)

TYÖMIEHEN PÄIVÄKIRJA [THE WORKER'S DIARY]. It is seldom that Finnish cinema has been in such bad shape as it was in the mid-1960s when *Risto Jarva directed *Työmiehen päiväkirja* [The worker's diary]. It was a revelation: Now Finnish cinema had discovered realism, people of flesh and blood, a true milieu and not just a backdrop for an entertainment package. We might say that this film had reached the level of the best new European cinema. Today the film is still valid: Its realism is not just monochrome naturalism but a multilevel construct, where dreams, fantasies, remembrances, and the multiple strata of reality all meet. Furthermore, the film is a thoughtful summary of the turning points in the history of independent Finland (the civil war of 1918, the traumatic war years of 1939–1944, the vicissitudes of class struggle). The powerful screen presence of two ordinary people in their "marriage across the boundaries of class" makes this oeuvre extraordinarily moving. The working-class man is played by amateur (Paul Osipow), a painter, and the officeworker by professional *Elina Salo.

CREW

Director, Editor, and Executive Producer: Risto Jarva. Script: Risto Jarva, Jaakko Pakkasvirta. Cinematographer: *Antti Peippo, Lasse Naukkarinen. Sound: Jaakko Pakkasvirta, Anssi Blomstedt, Ensio Lumes. Music: Kari Rydman. Producer: Filminor.

CAST

Elina Salo (Ritva Margareta Vehoniemi), Paul Osipow (Juhani Vehoniemi), Titta Karakorpi (Laura), Pentti Irjala (Ritva's uncle), Matti Ruohola (Erik), Heikki Hämäläinen (Matti), Irma Seikkula (uncle's wife), Pertti Lumirae (Raimo), Marja Korhonen (Ritva's boss), Kullervo Kalske (foreman).

PREMIERE

Finnish: 26 Feb. 1967

VAIVAISUKON MORSIAN [THE WOODEN PAUPER'S BRIDE]. Among *Toivo Särkkä's works, *Vaivaisukon morsian* [The wooden pauper's bride] emerges as one of his greatest achievements with the Pohjanmaa theme; it is shot through with a particular ice-cold passion. Its connection with our atavistic instincts and collective fervor—the power of religious thinking over individuals—is truly very impressive. It operates in that area Swedish *Sjöström and Danish Dreyer (both Särkkä's contemporaries) had investigated: a mythic landscape where supernatural events are just as significant as everyday ones. It is a tale of the emergence of a religious stance and spiritual pathos, the need of a legend (*Ansa Ikonen, the epoch's most popular female star, as the saint), and hidden violence. For once, the film explicitly illustrates the power Särkkä had, and even though it does not reach the true dimensions of legend, its universal recitative of tolerance leaves its mark. There is an aura of "amour fou" about the film: Its finest image shows Ansa Ikonen, with her hair flying, struggling to cling to a wooden "poor boy"—an image that merges eroticism, longing, and an absurd faith.

CREW

Director and Executive Producer: Toivo Särkkä. Script: Toivo Särkkä, after a short story and a play by Jarl Hemmer. Cinematographer: Marius Raichi. Sound: Georg Brodén. Music: Väinö Haapalainen. Art Director: Karl Fager. Editor: Armas Vallasvuo. Producer: Suomen Filmiteollisuus.

CAST

Ansa Ikonen (Anna Kristina Ringars), Eino Kaipainen (Antti), *Tauno Palo (Elias Matinpoika Berg), Aku Korhonen (carpenter), Urho Sommersalmi (Metsä-Olli), Jalmari Rinne (rural police chief), Yrjö Tuominen (clergyman), Uuno Laakso (painter), Siiri Angerkoski (Anna's mother), Veikko Linna (blacksmith), Annie Mörk (woman from Koskikylä), Mervi Järventaus (a woman of few words).

PREMIERE

Finnish: 16 Jan. 1944

VALKOINEN PEURA [THE WHITE REINDEER]. This was the first Finnish film to be acclaimed internationally. It is an account of the far North, where deep emotions, raw natural elements, and the unquestioned constraints of a unique primitive society prevail. All this has been caught by the masterly camera work of *Erik Blomberg. The focus of this work is Mirjami Kuosmanen, Blomberg's wife and the film's screenwriter. She is a strange and striking figure—now a witch, now a reindeer. She can be a dozen different women, all of a different age, all looking different, always on a point of metamorphosis. She is a real threat to the society depicted in the film, for she is a dangerous, uncontrollable element. A theme like this—the compulsion to destroy someone who is different—plus portraying a woman's position and the fragility of her identity make the film comparable to Jaques Tourneur's cult horror movie *Cat People*. Erotica must be something sinful; free love and its violent outcome are indivisible. *Valkoinen peura* is also a film about marriage, about the complex relationship between a man and a woman, about that outrageous fancy, or fact, that everyone—as in a strange dream—kills the thing he loves best.

CREW

Director, Cinematographer, and Editor: Erik Blomberg. Script: Mirjami Kuosmanen, Erik Blomberg. Sound: Evan Englund, Taisto Lindegren. Music: Einar Englund. Art Director: Osmo Osva. Executive Producer: *Aarne Tarkas. Producer: Junior-Filmi.

CAST

Mirjami Kuosmanen (Pirita), Kalervo Nissilä (Aslak), Åke Lindman (forest officer), Arvo Lehesmaa (Tsalkku-Nilla), Jouni Tapiola (reindeer-herdsman), Pentti Irjala (sorcerer), Aarne Tarkas (fiancé), Tyyne Haarla (elderly woman), Kauko Laurikainen (man in the Kota), Evald Terho (Pirita's father), Heimo Lepistö (rich man).

PREMIERE

Finnish: 25 July 1952

AWARD

Cannes 1953: Best Film Based on Folk Legend

VALKOISET RUUSUT [WHITE ROSES]. This film is one of those secretive and fragmented wartime family sagas, a story of a family that never was. But above all it is a story about love and absence of love, eternal emotions and inconsistent emotions, life and art. How did the roles of man and woman get written during the war? The dominant trait of this film's artist (in the Ophuls version he is a pianist, whereas *Hannu Leminen portrays him as a writer) is selfishness: Here we have a man in the sheer panic of Don Juanism. Right from the start the film is in code—secret signs between people, and just hints of those signs. It celebrates emotions and then doubts them; it tells about purity and then shows the inevitable end station of love, where we encounter a materialistic, tepid human being who is basically sick and tired of himself. A film like this was exceptional during the war, when emotions were a kind of vital second front while the nation was concretely engaged in war.

CREW

Director, Art Director, and Editor: Hannu Leminen. Script: Eino Seisjoki (= Hannu Leminen), *Ilmari Unho. Cinematographer: Felix Forsman. Sound: Pertti Kuusela, Kurt Vilja. Music: Väinö Haapalainen. Executive Producer: *T. J. Särkkä. Producer: Suomen Filmiteollisuus.

CAST

Helena Kara (Auli Ranta), *Tauno Palo (Arvo Helavalta), Aku Korhonen (Severi), Aino Lohikoski (Alma Ranta), Hugo Hytönen (caretaker Enne), Mervi Järventaus (Ilona Enne), Toppo Elonperä (Antti Koskela), Ester Toivonen (Irma), Ture Ara (Mauno Kallio), Arvi Tuomi (teacher), Toini Vartiainen (Auli's classmate), Liisa Nevalainen (woman at Arvo's party), Anton Soini (shopkeeper), Arvo Lehesmaa (doctor), Topo Leistelä (professor), Arvo Kuusla (journalist).

PREMIERE

Finnish: 12 Sept. 1943

VARASTETTU KUOLEMA [STOLEN DEATH]. In this film, the bitter and ominous early spring of 1918 (the setting for Runar Schildt's short story) has been changed to the year 1905, because the civil war theme was still too sensitive for the Finnish nation. While the film is suffused by a youthful experimental spirit, there is real substance beneath the surface and a close connection with prewar connotations, as is the case in all "real" historical films. The theme is movement from darkness into light. There are great expectations of national sovereignty to solve all the problems, there are dreams about freedom and love, and there is death. The film contains many of the most memorable images in Finnish cinema, particularly those somber interiors recorded by *Erik Blomberg's camera (expressing the unreality of all underground activity) and those clouds, against the bright sky, serving as a contrast to the capital's official facade. Probably the most well-known sequence of the film is the scene in which the lovers make their escape through a backyard where there are white sheets hanging out to dry. In the final scene, nature and the sea literally explode into the picture, just like freedom erupting.

CREW

Director: *Nyrki Tapiovaara. Script: Eino Mäkinen, Erik Blomberg, after a short story by Runar Schildt. Cinematographer: Olavi Gunnari, Erik Blomberg. Sound: Lauri Pulkkila. Music: George de Godzinsky. Art Director: Kille Oksanen, Ilmari Tapiovaara. Editor: Erik Blomberg, Nyrki Tapiovaara. Producer: Erik Blomberg.

CAST

Tuulikki Paananen (Manja), Ilmari Mänty (Robert Hedman), Santeri Karilo (Jonni Claesson), Annie Mörk (Matami Johansson), Bertha Lindberg (Robert's mother), Hertta Leistén (aunt), Gabriel Tossu (shoemaker), Ilmari Parikka (prison guard), Aku Peltonen (chapel guard), Aatos Kenst, Viljo Kervinen, Paavo Kuoppala, and Yrjö Salminen (Robert's friends), Kusti Laitinen (gendarme officer), Emil Kokkonen (soldier), Ida Salin (woman), Nyrki Tapiovaara (conductor), Erik Blomberg (shop assistant), Maija Nuutinen (woman).

PREMIERE

Finnish: 4 Sept. 1938

YKSITYISALUE **[PRIVATE PROPERTY].** This film, the second in *Maunu Kurkvaara's trilogy, begins with a suicide. Why has a celebrated architect become tired of life? Aging, the terror of mediocrity, the arrogance of housing developers with their obvious connection with the emptiness and selfishness of modern life, disappointments in close, personal relationships, in short, breakdown in communication—all these ingredients are manifest in the film. But they cannot provide the final answer in a situation that simply cannot be explained away. These themes are the familiar ones in modern cinema: loneliness, lack of communication, shame. In this film, they are given flesh and blood; they are "Kurkvaara's own queries about the freedom and liability of the artist." Here is an authentic and impressive "X-ray of the body of society."

CREW

Director, Script, Cinematographer, Art Director, Editor, and Executive Producer: Maunu Kurkvaara. Sound: Tuomo Kattilakoski. Music: Usko Meriläinen. Producer: Kurkvaara-Filmi.

CAST

Jarno Hiilloskorpi (Pentti Vaara), Kalervo Nissilä (Toivo Koski), Kyllikki Forssell (Mrs. Margit Koski), Sinikka Hannula (Kaisu), Pehr-olof Sirén (Mäkelä), Sointu Angervo (Soili), Kaarlo Halttunen (Carlstedt), Sasu Haapanen (builder), Esko Mannermaa (Salin), Aimo Tepponen (draftsman), Tauno Söder (Rape Solman), Nils Brandt (investigator), Mirja Lehtinen (Kipa), Sirpa Silventoinen (Pirkko).

PREMIERE

Finnish: 5 Oct. 1962

ZOMBIE JA KUMMITUSJUNA **[ZOMBIE AND THE GHOST TRAIN].** The events of this film take place "on borrowed time." Zombie is a musician, a vagabond drunkard who burns his candle at both ends. But the film is also about friendship and love; it offers a new version of the fact that the world is a different place now—not only as a cited truth and not only as a flashback; it emerges in a sentence in *Mika Kaurismäki's first film *Arvottomat* [The worthless]: "Love does not die. It just leaves us. We die." Recognition of this certainty is the starting point of the film's scale, sounds, and space. It is a light film, visually elegant, as instinctive as improvised music.

In the main role is Silu Seppälä, an amateur actor and professional musician who plays the bass guitar in the wildly popular Leningrad Cowboys rock band, and for this role he received the prize for best actor at the San Sebastian Film Festival. Part of the film takes place in Turkey. As "abroad" is often just a setting for a Finnish outsider saddled with his awkwardness, here a foreign country is a cradle of real emotion, an account of its fading ripples. Zombie cannot face life with a clear head—nothing more complicated than that. He is self-destructive and definitely "the guilty" in the Kafkaesque universe that the "normal" society proves to be. The smile that the little man destined to be destroyed brings to the world of shadows is filled with hidden meanings.

CREW

Director, Editor, and Executive Producer: Mika Kaurismäki. Script: Mika Kaurismäki, after a story by Sakke Järvenpää, Mika Kaurismäki, and Pauli Pentti. Cinematographer: Olli Varja. Sound: Antti Ortamo, Jouko Lumme. Music: Mauri Sumén. Art Director: Kari Laine. Producer: Marianna Films/Villealfa Filmproductions.

CAST

Silu Seppälä (Zombie), Marjo Leinonen (Marjo), *Matti Pellonpää (Harri), Vieno Saaristo (mother), Juhani Niemelä (father), Sakke Järvenpää, Mato Valtonen, Mauri Sumén, Jyri Närvänen, and Jarmo Haapanen (Mulefukkers), Jussi Rinne, Matti Viholainen, and Roger Nieminen (Ghost Train), Marko Rauhala (barber), Kauko Laurikainen (doctor), Heikki Sippari (policeman), Juho Rastas (old man), Ali Özgentürk (bartender), Süheyl Egriboz (hotel keeper), Nüvit Özdogru (carpet dealer), Halil Ergün (man in the bar), Hafiz Hoca (musician).

PREMIERE

Finnish: 26 July 1991

GENERAL BIBLIOGRAPHY

BOOKS ON FINNISH CINEMA

Bagh, Peter von. *Suomalaisen elokuvan kultainen kirja*. Helsinki: Otava, 1992. In Finnish, includes full filmography until 1992.

Connah, Roger. *K/K: A Couple of Finns and Some Donald Ducks. Cinema in Society*. Helsinki: VAPK-kustannus, 1991. Focus on Kaurismäki brothers.

Cowie, Peter. *Finnish Cinema*. (New ed.). Helsinki: VAPK-kustannus and the Finnish Film Archive, 1991. Includes selected filmographies; covers the whole history of Finnish film.

Hillier, Jim, ed. *Cinema in Finland*. London: British Film Institute, 1975. Still useful in spite of its limited size, especially in its coverage of the 1960s and early 1970s situation.

Suomen kansallisfilmografia (The Finnish National Filmography). Vols. 1–10. Helsinki: Finnish Film Foundation. The first seven volumes, including the cinema to 1970, exist by 1999. A mighty effort, one of the very best of its kind in the world, owing to the fact that a filmography of less than 1,000 titles makes it possible to concentrate properly on each title. Each entry includes extensive filmographical documentation, information about where the film was shot, an overview of criticism of the time, and so on. The editor of the series is Kari Uusitalo, the pioneer of Finnish film history writing.

GENERAL STUDIES ON SCANDINAVIAN CINEMA

Béranger, Jean. *Le nouveau cinéma Scandinave (de 1957 à 1968)*. Paris: Le Terrain Vague, 1968. 177 pages on Swedish cinema, 70 pages on Danish cinema, 50 pages on Finnish cinema, and 20 pages on Norwegian—and as such with more than a little too strong emphasis on Swedish cinema, considering the book is not only about the Golden Age of Swedish cinema.

Cowie, Peter. *Scandinavian Cinema. Le cinéma des pays nordiques*. Paris: 1990. Exists also in an English version. Useful introduction based on a lifelong interest in Nordic countries; Cowie has likewise published a separate monograph on each of the national cinematographies.

Lachmann, Mikael, and Hauke Lange-Fuchs. *Film in Skandinavien 1945–1993*. Berlin: Henschel, 1993. A relatively small book—and one of the most useful and knowledgeable.

Usai, Paolo Cherchi. *Schiave bianche allo specchio—le origini del cinema in Scandinavia (1896–1918)*. Pordenone: Le giornate del cinema muto, 1986. Excellent information about early Swedish and Danish cinema; zero on Finnish and Norwegian.

ARTICLES

Baecque, Antoine de. "La perfection d'un crime. La fabrique de sentiments." *Cahiers du Cinéma* 431–432 (May 1990): 58–59, 105–106. Article plus review; analysis of a sequence from the film *Tulitikkutehtaan tyttö*.

Soila, Tytti. "Five Songs of the Scarlet Flower." *Screen* 35, no. 3 (Autumn 1994): 265–274. A discussion of the question of nationality with reference to the five remakes of the Scandinavian story *The Song of the Scarlet Flower* (1918, 1934, 1938, 1956, 1971).

GENERAL INFORMATION

The Finnish Film Archive
  Suomen elokuva-arkisto
  Pursimiehenkatu 29–31
  Box 177
  FIN-00151 Helsinki, Finland
  Phone: +358–9-615 400
  Fax: +358–9-615 402 42
  Telex: 125960
  Internet: http:// www.sea.fi

The Finnish Film Foundation
  Suomen elokuvasäätiö
  Kanavakatu 12
  FIN-00160 Helsinki, Finland
  Phone: +358–9-6220 300
  Fax: +358–9-622 3060
  E-mail: ses@ses.fi
  Internet: http://www.ses.fi/

INTERNATIONAL FILM FESTIVALS

Espoo Ciné Film Festival
  Festival Office
  Box 95
  FIN-02101 Espoo, Finland
  Phone: +358–9-466 599
  Fax: +358–9-466 458

Internet: http://www.espoo.fi/cine/
Annually in August.

Helsinki Film Festival—Love & Anarchy
Festival Office
Box 889
FIN-00101 Helsinki, Finland
Phone: +358–9-6843 5230
Fax: +358–9-6843 5232
Internet: http://hiff.fi/
Annually in September.

Midnight Sun Film Festival
Festival Office
Malminkatu 36
FIN-00100 Helsinki, Finland
Phone: +358–9-685 2242
Fax: +358–9-694 5560
Internet: http://www.msfilmfestival.fi/
Annually in June.

Oulu International Children's Film Festival
Festival Office
Torikatu 8
FIN-90100 Oulu, Finland
Phone: +358–8-881 1291
Fax: +358–8-881 1290
Internet: http://www.ouka.fi/oek/ festinfo.htm
Annually in November.

Tampere International Short Film Festival
Festival Office
Box 305
FIN-33101 Tampere
Finland
Tullikamari 2nd floor
Tullikamarinaukio 2
33100 Tampere
Phone: +358–3-219 6149
Fax: +358–3-223 0121
Internet:http://www.tampere.fi/festival/film/
Annually in March.

UNIVERSITY EDUCATION

University of Art and Design
  Helsinki UIAH Department of Film and TV
  Taideteollinen korkeakoulu
  Elokuvataiteen laitos
  Hämeentie 135 C
  FIN-00560 Helsinki, Finland
  Phone: +358–9-7563 0100
  Fax: +358–9-634 303
  Internet: http//www.uiah.fi/eto/

ASSOCIATIONS

The Association of Finnish Film Directors
  Suomen elokuvaohjaajaliitto SELO ry
  c/o Olli Soinio
  Hummelsund 19
  FIN-06100 Porvoo, Finland
  Phone: +358–9-174 244

The Association of Finnish Film Workers
  Suomen Elokuva—ja Videotyöntekijäin Liitto SET ry
  Meritullinkatu 33
  FIN-00170 Helsinki, Finland
  Phone: +358–9-135 6370
  Fax: +358–9-135 6658

FILM JOURNALS

Filmihullu
  Malminkatu 36
  FIN-00100 Helsinki, Finland
  Phone: +358–9-685 1414
  Fax: +358–9-694 5560
  Internet: http://www.kaapeli.fi/~filmihul/

Lähikuva
  Box 75
  FIN-20501 Turku, Finland

INDEX

Page numbers for main entries in the Guide are set in **boldfaced** type. Translation of Swedish film titles for real U.S. distribution titles after slash. Translation of other Swedish and Finnish film titles in brackets.

About the Authors

PER OLOV QVIST is former editor of the film journal *Filmhäftet*. He received his doctorate in film from the University of Stockholm.

PETER VON BAGH is a film historian, author, and documentarist. He has worked for The Finnish Film Archive (1967–1985), is editor-in-chief of the film journal *Filmihullu* (since 1971), and artistic director of The Midnight Sun Film Festival (since 1986).

ISBN 0-313-30377-0

EAN

9 780313 303777

90000>

HARDCOVER BAR CODE